1000
QUOTABLE
POEMS

1000 QUOTABLE POEMS

*An Anthology of
Modern Verse*

COMPILED BY

THOMAS CURTIS CLARK

AND

ESTHER A. GILLESPIE

BONANZA BOOKS
New York

THIS BOOK IS DEDICATED *TO THE POETS*
TORCHBEARERS OF FAITH ACROSS THE CENTURIES

The poems included in this book were originally published as two volumes:

QUOTABLE POEMS I and QUOTABLE POEMS II

Esther A. Gillespie collaborated with Thomas Curtis Clark in compiling the first volume.

ACKNOWLEDGMENTS

Acknowledgment is here made of the generous cooperation of both contributing poets and of publishers in the bringing together of this anthology of "quotable poems."

The publishers have made every effort to trace the ownership of all copyrighted poems. To the best of their knowledge they have secured all necessary permission from authors or their authorized agents, or from both. Should there prove to be any question regarding the use of any poem, the publishers herewith express regret for such unconscious error. They will be pleased, upon notification of such error, to make proper acknowledgment in future editions of this book.

Detailed acknowledgment to poets and publishers will be found at the end of the book.

The Publishers

Copyright MCMXXXVII by Harper & Row Publishers, Inc.
All rights reserved.

This 1985 edition is published by Bonanza Books, distributed by Crown Publishers, Inc., by arrangement with Harper & Row, Publishers, Inc.

Printed and Bound in the United States of America

Library of Congress Cataloging in Publication Data
Main entry under title:

1000 quotable poems.

Originally published as 2 v. in 1928-31 under title: Quotable poems.
1. Poetry—Collections. I. Clark, Thomas Curtis, 1877–1953. II. Gillespie, Esther A. III. Title. PN6101.Q68 1985 821'.008 85-11344
ISBN: 0-517-481219

h g f e d c b a

QUOTABLE
POEMS

VOLUME ONE

Each in His Own Tongue

A fire-mist and a planet,
   A crystal and a cell,
A jellyfish and a saurian,
   And caves where the cavemen dwell;
Then a sense of law and beauty,
   And a face turned from the clod —
Some call it Evolution,
   And others call it God.

A haze on the far horizon,
   The infinite, tender sky;
The ripe, rich tint of the cornfields,
   And the wild geese sailing high —
And all over upland and lowland,
   The charm of the goldenrod —
Some of us call it Autumn,
   And others call it God.

Like tides on a crescent sea-beach,
   When the moon is new and thin,
Into our hearts high yearnings
   Come welling and surging in —
Come from the mystic ocean,
   Whose rim no foot has trod,
Some of us call it Longing,
   And others call it God.

1

A picket frozen on duty —
　　A mother starved for her brood —
Socrates drinking the hemlock,
　　And Jesus on the rood;
And millions who, humble and nameless,
　　The straight, hard pathway trod —
Some call it Consecration,
　　And others call it God.

William Herbert Carruth

What Christ Said

I said, " Let me walk in the fields."
　　He said, "No; walk in the town."
I said, " There are no flowers there."
　　He said, " No flowers, but a crown."

I said, " But the skies are black,
　　There is nothing but noise and din; "
And he wept as he sent me back;
　　" There is more," he said, " there is sin."

I said, " But the air is thick,
　　And fogs are veiling the sun."
He answered, " Yet souls are sick,
　　And souls in the dark undone."

I said, " I shall miss the light,
　　And friends will miss me, they say."
He answered, " Choose tonight
　　If I am to miss you, or they."

I pleaded for time to be given.
　　He said, " Is it hard to decide?

It will not seem hard in Heaven
  To have followed the steps of your Guide."

I cast one look at the fields,
  Then set my face to the town;
He said, "My child, do you yield?
  Will you leave the flowers for the crown?"

Then into his hand went mine;
  And into my heart came he;
And I walk in a light divine,
  The path I had feared to see.

George MacDonald

Invictus

Out of the night that covers me,
  Black as the pit from pole to pole,
I thank whatever gods may be
  For my unconquerable soul.

In the fell clutch of circumstance
  I have not winced nor cried aloud.
Under the bludgeonings of chance
  My head is bloody, but unbowed.

Beyond this place of wrath and tears
  Looms but the Horror of the shade,
And yet the menace of the years
  Finds and shall find me unafraid.

It matters not how strait the gate,
  How charged with punishment the scroll,
I am the master of my fate:
  I am the captain of my soul.

William Ernest Henley

My Prayer

Great God, I ask thee for no meaner pelf
Than that I may not disappoint myself;
That in my action I may soar as high
As I can now discern with this clear eye.
And next in value, which Thy kindness lends,
That I may greatly disappoint my friends,
Howe'er they think or hope that it may be,
They may not dream how Thou'st distinguished me.

That my weak hand may equal my firm faith,
And my life practise more than my tongue saith;
    That my low conduct may not show,
        Nor my relenting lines,
    That I Thy purpose did not know,
        Or overrated Thy designs.

Henry David Thoreau

Opportunity

Master of human destinies am I.
Fame, love, and fortune on my footsteps wait,
Cities and fields I walk; I penetrate
Deserts and seas remote, and, passing by
Hovel, and mart, and palace, soon or late
I knock unbidden, once at every gate!
If sleeping, wake — if feasting, rise before
I turn away. It is the hour of fate,
And they who follow me reach every state
Mortals desire, and conquer every foe
Save death; but those who doubt or hesitate,
Condemned to failure, penury and woe,

Seek me in vain and uselessly implore —
I answer not, and I return no more.

John James Ingalls

Opportunity

They do me wrong who say I come no more
  When once I knock and fail to find you in;
For every day I stand outside your door
  And bid you wake, and rise to fight and win.

Wail not for precious chances passed away!
  Weep not for golden ages on the wane!
Each night I burn the records of the day —
  At sunrise every soul is born again!

Dost thou behold thy lost youth all aghast?
  Dost reel from righteous retribution's blow?
Then turn from blotted archives of the past
  And find the future's pages white as snow.

Art thou a mourner? Rouse thee from thy spell;
  Art thou a sinner? Sins may be forgiven;
Each morning gives thee wings to fly from hell,
  Each night a star to guide thy feet to heaven.

Laugh like a boy at splendors that have sped,
  To vanished joys be blind and deaf and dumb;
My judgments seal the dead past with the dead,
  But never bind a moment yet to come.

Though deep in mire, wring not your hands and weep;
  I lend my arm to all who say, " I can! "
No shame-faced outcast ever sank so deep,
  But yet might rise again and be a man!

Walter Malone

Sonnet On His Blindness

When I consider how my light is spent
  Ere half my days, in this dark world and wide,
  And that one talent, which is death to hide,
Lodged with me useless, though my soul more bent
To serve therewith my Maker, and present
  My true account, lest He, returning, chide:
  " Doth God exact day labor, light denied? "
I fondly ask; but Patience, to prevent
  That murmur, soon replies, " God doth not need
  Either man's work, or His own gifts; who best
  Bear His mild yoke, they serve Him best.
    His state
Is kingly. Thousands at His bidding speed,
  And post o'er land and ocean without rest;
  They also serve who only stand and wait."

John Milton

Where Is the Real Non-Resistant?

Who can surrender to Christ, dividing his best with the
    stranger,
Giving to each what he asks, braving the uttermost danger
All for the enemy, Man? Who can surrender till death
His words and his works, his house and his lands,
His eyes and his heart and his breath?

Who can surrender to Christ? Many have yearned toward
    it daily.
Yet they surrender to passion, wildly or grimly or gaily:
Yet they surrender to pride, counting her precious and
    queenly;
Yet they surrender to knowledge, preening their feathers
    serenely.

Who can surrender to Christ? Where is the man so tran-
    scendent,
So heated with love of his kind, so filled with the spirit
    resplendent
That all of the hours of his day his song is thrilling and
    tender,
And all of his thoughts to our white cause of peace
          Surrender, surrender, surrender?
                        Vachel Lindsay

Faith

O World, thou choosest not the better part!
It is not wisdom to be only wise,
And on the inward vision close the eyes,
But it is wisdom to believe the heart.
Columbus found a world, and had no chart,
Save one that Faith deciphered in the skies;
To trust the soul's invincible surmise
Was all his science and his only art.
Our knowledge is a torch of smoky pine
That lights the pathway but one step ahead
Across a void of mystery and dread.
Bid, then, the tender light of Faith to shine
By which alone the mortal heart is led
Unto the thinking of the thought divine.
                        George Santayana

A High Way and a Low

To every man there openeth
A way, and ways, and a way,
And the high soul climbs the high way,
And the low soul gropes the low;

And in between, on the misty flats,
The rest drift to and fro.
But to every man there openeth
A high way and a low,
And every man decideth
The way his soul shall go.

John Oxenham

The World Is Too Much With Us

The world is too much with us; late and soon,
    Getting and spending, we lay waste our powers:
    Little we see in Nature that is ours;
We have given our hearts away, a sordid boon!
This sea that bares her bosom to the moon;
    The winds that will be howling at all hours,
    And are up-gathered now like sleeping flowers;
For this, for everything, we are out of tune;
It moves us not. — Great God! I'd rather be
    A Pagan suckled in a creed outworn;
So might I, standing on this pleasant lea,
    Have glimpses that would make me less forlorn;
Have sight of Proteus, rising from the sea;
    Or hear old Triton blow his wreathéd horn.

William Wordsworth

The Celestial Surgeon

If I have faltered more or less
In my great task of happiness;
If I have moved among my race
And shown no shining morning face;

If beams from happy human eyes
Have moved me not; if morning skies,
Books, and my food, and summer rain
Knocked on my sullen heart in vain: —
Lord, thy most pointed pleasure take
And stab my spirit broad awake.

Robert Louis Stevenson

Vestigia

I took a day to search for God,
And found Him not. But as I trod
    By rocky ledge, through woods untamed,
    Just where one scarlet lily flamed,
I saw His footprint in the sod.

Then suddenly, all unaware,
Far off in the deep shadows, where
    A solitary thrush
    Sang through the holy twilight hush —
I heard His voice upon the air.

And even as I marveled how
God gives us Heaven here and now,
    In stir of wind that hardly shook
    The poplar leaves beside the brook —
His hand was light upon my brow.

At last with evening as I turned
Homeward, and thought what I had learned
    And all that there was still to probe —
    I caught the glory of His robe
Where the last fires of sunset burned.

Back to the world with quickening start
I looked and longed for any part
  In making saving Beauty be . . .
  And from that kindling ecstasy
I knew God dwelt within my heart.

Bliss Carman

Be Strong!

Be strong!
We are not here to play — to dream, to drift.
We have hard work to do and loads to lift.
Shun not the struggle — face it; 'tis God's gift.

  Be strong!
Say not the days are evil. Who's to blame?
And fold the hands and acquiesce. — O shame!
Stand up, speak out, and bravely, in God's name.

Be strong!
It matters not how deep entrenched the wrong,
How hard the battle goes, the day how long;
Faint not — fight on! Tomorrow comes the song.

Maltbie D. Babcock

Blind

" Show me your God! " the doubter cries.
I point him to the smiling skies;
I show him all the woodland greens;
I show him peaceful sylvan scenes;
I show him winter snows and frost;
I show him waters tempest-tost;

I show him hills rock-ribbed and strong;
I bid him hear the thrush's song;
I show him flowers in the close —
The lily, violet and rose;
I show him rivers, babbling streams;
I show him youthful hopes and dreams;
I show him maids with eager hearts;
I show him toilers in the marts;
I show him stars, the moon, the sun;
I show him deeds of kindness done;
I show him joy, I show him care,
And still he holds his doubting air,
And faithless goes his way, for he
Is blind of soul, and cannot see!

John Kendrick Bangs

Not By Bread Alone

If thou of fortune be bereft,
And thou dost find but two loaves left
To thee — sell one, and with the dole
Buy hyacinths to feed thy soul.

But not alone does beauty bide
Where bloom and tint and fragrance hide;
The minstrel's melody may feed
Perhaps a more insistent need.

But even beauty, howe'er blent
To ear and eye, fails to content;
Only the heart, with love afire,
Can satisfy the soul's desire.

James Terry White

From God Prays

And the Lord God whispered and said to me,
" These things shall be, these things shall be,
Nor help shall come from the scarlet skies,
Till the people rise!
Till the people rise, my arm is weak;
I cannot speak till the people speak;
When men are dumb, my voice is dumb —
I cannot come till my people come."
And the Lord God's presence was white, so white,
Like a pillar of stars against the night,
" Millions on millions pray to me
Yet hearken not to hear me pray;
Nor comes there any to set me free
Of all who plead from night to day.
So God is mute and Heaven is still
While the nations kill."

.   .   .   .

" Think you I planted my image there
That men should trample it to despair?
Who fears the throe that rebellion brings? "
" Help them stand, O Christ! " I prayed,
" Thy people are feeble and sore afraid."
" My people are strong," God whispered me
" Broad as the land, great as the sea;
They will tower as tall as the tallest skies
Up to the level of my eyes,
When they dare to rise.
Yea, all my people everywhere!
Not in one land of black despair
But over the flaming earth and sea
Wherever wrong and oppression be
The shout of my people must come to me.

Not till their spirit break the curse
May I claim my own in the universe;
And this the reason of war and blood
That men may come to their angelhood.
If the people rise, if the people rise,
I will answer them from the swarming skies."

Angela Morgan

The Carpenter

I wonder what he charged for chairs at Nazareth.
And did men try to beat him down
And boast about it in the town —
" I bought it cheap for half-a-crown
From that mad Carpenter? "

And did they promise and not pay,
Put it off to another day;
O, did they break his heart that way,
My Lord, the Carpenter?

I wonder did he have bad debts,
And did he know my fears and frets?
The gospel writer here forgets
To tell about the Carpenter.

But that's just what I want to know.
Ah!   Christ in glory, here below
Men cheat and lie to one another so;
It's hard to be a carpenter.

G. A. Studdert-Kennedy

The Problem

Not from a vain or shallow thought
His awful Jove young Phidias brought;
Never from lips of cunning fell
The thrilling Delphic oracle;
Out from the heart of nature rolled
The burdens of the Bible old;
The litanies of nations came,
Like the volcano's tongue of flame,
Up from the burning core below —
The canticles of love and woe;
The hand that rounded Peter's dome,
And groined the aisles of Christian Rome,
Wrought in a sad sincerity;
Himself from God he could not free;
He builded better than he knew; —
The conscious stone to beauty grew.

. . . .

These temples grew as grows the grass;
Art might obey, but not surpass.
The passive Master lent his hand
To the vast soul that o'er him planned;
And the same power that reared the shrine
Bestrode the tribes that knelt within.
Ever the fiery Pentecost
Girds with one flame the countless host,
Trances the heart through chanting choirs,
And through the priest the mind inspires.

The word unto the prophet spoken
Was writ on tables yet unbroken;
The word by seers and sibyls told,
In groves of oak, or fanes of gold,

Still floats upon the morning wind,
Still whispers to the willing mind.
One accent of the Holy Ghost
The heedless world hath never lost.

.   .   .   .

Ralph Waldo Emerson

The Nameless Saints

What was his name?   I do not know his name.
I only know he heard God's voice and came,
    Brought all he had across the sea
    To live and work for God and me;
        Felled the ungracious oak;
        Dragged from the soil
        With horrid toil
    The thrice-gnarled roots and stubborn rock;
With plenty piled the haggard mountain-side;
And at the end, without memorial, died.
No blaring trumpets sounded out his fame,
He lived — he died — I do not know his name.

No form of bronze and no memorial stones
Show me the place where lie his mouldering bones.
    Only a cheerful city stands
    Builded by his hardened hands.
        Only ten thousand homes
        Where every day
        The cheerful play
    Of love and hope and courage comes.
These are his monuments, and these alone,
There is no form of bronze and no memorial stone.

And I?
Is there some desert or some pathless sea
Where Thou, good God of angels, wilt send me?
  Some oak for me to rend; some sod,
    Some rock for me to break,
    Some handful of His corn to take
    And scatter far afield
    Till it, in turn, shall yield
      Its hundredfold
      Of grains of gold
  To feed the waiting children of my God?
Show me the desert, Father, or the sea.
Is it Thine enterprise?   Great God, send me.
And though this body lie where ocean rolls,
Count me among all Faithful Souls.

Edward Everett Hale

He Cometh Late

The strings of camels come in single file,
  Bearing their burdens o'er the desert sands.
Swiftly the boats go plying on the Nile —
  The needs of men are met on every hand,
But still I wait
For the messenger of God who cometh late.

I see a cloud of dust rise on the plain.
  The measured tread of troops falls on my ear.
The soldier comes, the empire to maintain,
  Bringing the pomp of war, the reign of fear.
But still I wait
For the messenger of God who cometh late.

They set me watching o'er the desert drear,
  Where dwells the darkness, as the deepest night;

From many a mosque there comes the call to prayer —
  I hear no voice that calls on God for light.
But still I wait
For the messenger of God who cometh late.

Author Unknown

To Love, at Last, the Victory

There was a man who saw God face to face.
  His countenance and vestments evermore
  Glowed with a light that never shone before,
Saving from him who saw God face to face.
And men, anear him for a little space,
  Were sorely vexed at the unwonted light.
Those whom the light did blind rose angrily.
They bore his body to a mountain height
  And nailed it to a tree; then went their way;
  And he resisted not nor said them nay,
Because that he had seen God face to face.

There was a man who saw Life face to face,
  And ever as he walked from day to day,
  The deathless mystery of being lay
Plain as the path he trod in loneliness;
And each deep-hid inscription could he trace;
  How men have fought and loved and fought again;
  How in lone darkness souls cried out for pain;
How each green foot of sod from sea to sea
Was red with blood of men slain wantonly;
  How tears of pity warm as summer rain
Again and ever washed the stains away,
  Leaving to Love, at last, the victory.
Above the strife and hate and fever pain,
The squalid talk and walk of men.

He saw the vision changeless as the stars
That shone through temple gates or prison bars,
Or to the body nailed upon the tree,
Through each mean action of the life that is,
The marvel of the Life that yet shall be.

David Starr Jordan

The Choir Invisible

Oh, may I join the choir invisible
Of those immortal dead who live again
In minds made better by their presence; live
In pulses stirred to generosity,
In deeds of daring rectitude, in scorn
For miserable aims that end with self,
In thoughts sublime that pierce the night like stars,
And with their mild persistence urge men's search
To vaster issues. So to live is heaven:
To make undying music in the world,
Breathing a beauteous order that controls
With growing sway the growing life of man.
So we inherit that sweet purity
For which we struggled, failed, and agonized
With widening retrospect that bred despair.
Rebellious flesh that would not be subdued,
A vicious parent shaming still its child,
Poor anxious penitence, is quick dissolved;
Its discords, quenched by meeting harmonies,
Die in the large and charitable air.
And all our rarer, better, truer self,
That sobbed religiously in yearning song,
That watched to ease the burden of the world,
Laboriously tracing what must be,
And what may yet be better, — saw within

A worthier image for the sanctuary,
And shaped it forth before the multitude,
Divinely human, raising worship so
To higher reverence more mixed with love, —
That better self shall live till human Time
Shall fold its eyelids, and the human sky
Be gathered like a scroll within the tomb
Unread forever. This is life to come, —
Which martyred men have made more glorious
For us who strive to follow. May I reach
That purest heaven, — be to other souls
The cup of strength in some great agony,
Enkindle generous ardor, feed pure love,
Beget the smiles that have no cruelty —
Be the sweet presence of a good diffused,
And in diffusion even more intense.
So shall I join the choir invisible
Whose music is the gladness of the world.

George Eliot

They Softly Walk

They are not gone who pass
Beyond the clasp of hand,
Out from the strong embrace.
They are but come so close
We need not grope with hands,
Nor look to see, nor try
To catch the sound of feet.
They have put off their shoes
Softly to walk by day
Within our thoughts, to tread
At night our dream-led paths
Of sleep.

They are not lost who find
The sunset gate, the goal
Of all their faithful years.
Not lost are they who reach
The summit of their climb,
The peak above the clouds
And storms. They are not lost
Who find the light of sun
And stars and God.

Hugh Robert Orr

In Such an Age!

To be alive in such an age!
With every year a lightning page
Turned in the world's great wonder-book
Whereon the leaning nations look
Where men speak strong for brotherhood
For peace and universal good;
When miracles are everywhere
And every inch of common air
Throbs a tremendous prophecy
Of greater marvels yet to be.
O, Thrilling Age!
O, Willing Age!
When steel and stone and rail and rod
Welcome the utterance of God
A trump to shout his wonder through
Proclaiming all that man can do.

To be alive in such an age!
To live in it!
To give in it!
Rise, soul, from thy despairing knees,

What if thy lips have drunk the lees?
The passion of a larger claim
Will put thy puny grief to shame.
Fling forth thy sorrow to the wind
And link thy hope with humankind:
Breathe the world-thought, do the world-deed,
Think highly of thy brother's need.
Give thanks with all thy flaming heart,
Crave but to have in it a part —
Give thanks and clasp thy heritage —
To be alive in such an age!

Angela Morgan

The House by the Side of the Road

There are hermit souls that live withdrawn
   In the place of their self-content;
There are souls like stars, that dwell apart,
   In a fellowless firmament;
There are pioneer souls that blaze their paths
   Where highways never ran —
But let me live by the side of the road
   And be a friend to man.

Let me live in a house by the side of the road
   Where the race of men go by —
The men who are good and the men who are bad,
   As good and as bad as I.
I would not sit in the scorner's seat
   Nor hurl the cynic's ban —
Let me live in a house by the side of the road
   And be a friend to man.

I see from my house by the side of the road,
　　By the side of the highway of life,
The men who press with the ardor of hope,
　　The men who are faint with the strife,
But I turn not away from their smiles and tears,
　　Both parts of an infinite plan —
Let me live in a house by the side of the road
　　And be a friend to man.

I know there are brook-gladdened meadows ahead,
　　And mountains of wearisome height;
That the road passes on through the long afternoon
　　And stretches away to the night.
And still I rejoice when the travelers rejoice
　　And weep with the strangers that moan,
Nor live in my house by the side of the road
　　Like a man who dwells alone.

Let me live in my house by the side of the road,
　　Where the race of men go by —
They are good, they are bad, they are weak, they are strong,
　　Wise, foolish — so am I.
Then why should I sit in the scorner's seat,
　　Or hurl the cynic's ban?
Let me live in my house by the side of the road
　　And be a friend to man.

Sam Walter Foss

Reply

Man prayed his way up from the beast
　　And drove his will with love and pain
And each slow failing trial increased
　　His infinitesimal gain.

We cannot know if dawning came
   Upon a snow-wrapped solitude,
Or as a spirit-bearing flame
   Through a dark wood.

Perhaps on the appointed day,
   When great trees fanned the golden air,
The wild thing slept, from joyous play,
   With visions vast and fair.

While with the young at her warm breast,
   Their helplessness beneath her eyes,
Some mother-creature sudden guessed
   At human love; surmise

Of the long struggle for the right
   Against the sum of human ills,
Then turned her eyes to a far light
   Beyond the shadowed hills.

Each found, god-hid, a strange belief
   In something always past the goal
That gave them love and work and grief
   To find a soul.

They never saw the stony climb
   Beyond the foothills of the day,
Nor knew they pledged eternal time
   Unto the Way!
                              Janet Norris Bangs

Citizen of the World

No longer of him be it said,
" He hath no place to lay his head."

In every land a constant lamp
Flames by his small and mighty camp.

There is no strange and distant place
That is not gladdened by his face.

And every nation kneels to hail
The Splendor shining through its veil.

Cloistered beside the shouting street,
Silent, he calls me to his feet.

Imprisoned for his love of me
He makes my spirit greatly free.

And through my lips that uttered sin
The King of Glory enters in.

Joyce Kilmer

Chartless

I never saw a moor,
    I never saw the sea,
Yet know I how the heather looks,
    And what a wave must be.

I never spoke with God,
    Nor visited in heaven;
Yet certain am I of the spot
    As if the chart were given.

Emily Dickinson

We Break New Seas Today

Each man is Captain of his Soul,
And each man his own Crew,
But the Pilot knows the Unknown Seas,
And he will bring us through.

We break new seas today —
Our eager keels quest unaccustomed waters,
And, from the vast uncharted waste in front,
The mystic circles leap
To greet our prows with mightiest possibilities,
Bringing us — What?

   Dread shoals and shifting banks?
   And calms and storms?
   And clouds and biting gales?
   And wreck and loss?
   And valiant fighting times?
And, maybe, death! — and so, the Larger Life!

For, should the Pilot deem it best
To cut the voyage short,
He sees beyond the sky-line, and
He'll bring us into Port!

John Oxenham

Look to This Day

Look to this day!
For it is life, the very life of life.
In its brief course lie all the varieties and realities of your
    existence:
The bliss of growth;

The glory of action;
The splendor of beauty;
For yesterday is already a dream, and tomorrow is only
    a vision;
But today, well lived, makes every yesterday
A dream of happiness, and every tomorrow a vision of hope.
Look well, therefore, to this day!
Such is the salutation of the dawn!

From the Sanskrit

Lord, Take Away Pain

The cry of man's anguish went up unto God,
    " Lord, take away pain!
The shadow that darkens the world Thou hast made;
    The close-coiling chain
That strangles the heart; the burden that weighs on the
    wings that would soar —
Lord, take away pain from the world Thou hast made,
    That it love Thee the more! "

Then answered the Lord to the cry of His world:
    " Shall I take away pain,
And with it the power of the soul to endure,
    Made strong by the strain?
Shall I take away pity, that knits heart to heart,
    And sacrifice high?
Will ye lose all your heroes that lift from the fire
    White brows to the sky?
Shall I take away love, that redeems with a price,
    And smiles at its loss?
Can ye spare from your lives that would climb unto mine
    The Christ on his cross? "

Found on the wall of a Denver hospital

Prayer of Steel

Lay me on an anvil, O God!
Beat me and hammer me into a crowbar.
Let me pry loose old walls;
Let me lift and loosen old foundations.

Lay me on an anvil, O God!
Beat and hammer me into a steel spike.
Drive me into the girders that hold a skyscraper together.
Take red-hot rivets and fasten me into the central girders.
Let me be the great nail holding a skyscraper through blue
    nights into white stars.

Carl Sandburg

I Saw God Wash the World

I saw God wash the world last night
    With his sweet showers on high,
And then, when morning came, I saw
    Him hang it out to dry.

He washed each tiny blade of grass
    And every trembling tree;
He flung his showers against the hill,
    And swept the billowing sea.

The white rose is a cleaner white,
    The red rose is more red,
Since God washed every fragrant face
    And put them all to bed.

There's not a bird; there's not a bee
    That wings along the way

But is a cleaner bird and bee
  Than it was yesterday.

I saw God wash the world last night.
  Ah, would He had washed me
As clean of all my dust and dirt
  As that old white birch tree.
                              William L. Stidger

Why?

Why do we follow, like a flock of sheep,
  Tradition with a crook,
Or leave the vastness of the calling deep
  To paddle in a brook,
When on the hills of sunrise stands the Lord —
Triumphant with a lifted flaming sword?

Why, when upon our lips the great new Name
  Waits eager to be said,
When cloven tongues of Pentecostal flame
  Burn over every head,
Do we build Babel towers to the sky
From bricks and mortar, who have wings to fly?
                              Robert Norwood

Days

Daughters of Time, the hypocritic Days,
Muffled and dumb like barefoot dervishes,
And marching single in an endless file,
Bring diadems and fagots in their hands.
To each they offer gifts after his will.
Bread, kingdoms, stars, and sky that holds them all.

I, in my pleachèd garden, watched the pomp,
Forgot my morning wishes, hastily
Took a few herbs and apples, and the Day
Turned and departed silent. I, too late,
Under her solemn fillet saw the scorn.

Ralph Waldo Emerson

Prayer for Courage

Why should I long for what I know
    Can never be revealed to me?
I only pray that I may grow
    As sure and bravely as a tree.

I do not ask why tireless grief
    Remains, or why all beauty flies;
I only crave the blind relief
    Of branches groping toward the skies.

Let me bring every seed to fruit,
    Sharing, whatever comes to pass,
The strong persistence of the root,
    The patient courage of the grass.

Heartened by every source of mirth,
    I shall not mind the wounds and scars,
Feeling the solid strength of earth,
    The bright conviction of the stars.

Louis Untermeyer

Credo

Not what, but Whom, I do believe!
    That, in my darkest hour of need,

Hath comfort that no mortal creed
To mortal man may give.
Not what, but Whom!
 For Christ is more than all the creeds,
 And his full life of gentle deeds
 Shall all the creeds outlive.
Not what I do believe, but Whom!
 Who walks beside me in the gloom?
 Who shares the burden wearisome?
 Who all the dim way doth illume,
 And bids me look beyond tne tomb
 The larger life to live?
Not what I do believe, but Whom!
Not what, but Whom!

John Oxenham

Prayer

White Captain of my soul, lead on;
I follow thee, come dark or dawn.
Only vouchsafe three things I crave:
Where terror stalks, help me be brave!
Where righteous ones can scarce endure
The siren call, help me be pure!
Where vows grow dim, and men dare do
What once they scorned, help me be true!

Robert Freeman

Jesus of the Scars

If we never sought, we seek thee now;
 Thine eyes burn through the dark, our only stars;
We must have sight of thorn-pricks on thy brow,
 We must have thee, O Jesus of the Scars.

The heavens frighten us; they are too calm;
  In all the universe we have no place.
Our wounds are hurting us; where is the balm?
  Lord Jesus, by thy Scars we claim thy grace.

If when the doors are shut, thou drawest near,
  Only reveal those hands, that side of thine;
We know today what wounds are, have no fear,
  Show us thy Scars, we know the countersign.

The other gods were strong; but thou wast weak;
  They rode, but thou didst stumble to a throne;
But to our wounds God's wounds alone can speak,
  And not a god has wounds, but thou alone.

Edward Shillito

The Man With the Hoe

*Written after seeing Millet's world-famous painting of a
brutalized toiler.*

God made man in his own image,
in the image of God made He him. — *Genesis.*

Bowed by the weight of centuries he leans
Upon his hoe and gazes on the ground,
The emptiness of ages in his face,
And on his back the burden of the world.
Who made him dead to rapture and despair,
A thing that grieves not and that never hopes,
Stolid and stunned, a brother to the ox?
Who loosened and let down this brutal jaw?
Whose was the hand that slanted back this brow?
Whose breath blew out the light within this brain?

Is this the Thing the Lord God made and gave
To have dominion over sea and land;
To trace the stars and search the heavens for power;
To feel the passion of Eternity?
Is this the dream He dreamed who shaped the suns
And markt their ways upon the ancient deep?
Down all the caverns of Hell to their last gulf
There is no shape more terrible than this —
More tongued with censure of the world's blind greed —
More filled with signs and portents for the soul —
More packt with danger to the universe.

What gulfs between him and the seraphim!
Slave of the wheel of labor, what to him
Are Plato and the swing of Pleiades?
What the long reaches of the peaks of song,
The rift of dawn, the reddening of the rose?
Through this dread shape the suffering ages look;
Time's tragedy is in that aching stoop;
Through this dread shape humanity betrayed,
Plundered, profaned and disinherited,
Cries protest to the Judges of the World,
A protest that is also prophecy.

O masters, lords and rulers in all lands,
Is this the handiwork you give to God,
This monstrous thing distorted and soul-quencht?
How will you ever straighten up this shape;
Touch it again with immortality;
Give back the upward looking and the light;
Rebuild in it the music and the dream;
Make right the immemorial infamies,
Perfidious wrongs, immedicable woes?

O masters, lords and rulers in all lands,
How will the future reckon with this Man?

How answer his brute question in that hour
When whirlwinds of rebellion shake all shores?
How will it be with kingdoms and with kings —
With those who shaped him to the thing he is —
When this dumb Terror shall rise to judge the world,
After the silence of the centuries?

Edwin Markham

Ich Dien

     I serve.
With unaggressive mien I fit into
   The niche designed for me, nor murmuring raise
   That in the dull, eventless hours of praise
No fair emoluments to me accrue.

     I serve.
I serve the will of God.   In my estate
   I train my soul contented to abide;
   Meseems 'tis nobler thus, than if I tried
With futile efforts to o'erride my fate.

     I serve.
Perchance the greater heroes scorn my part;
   Seen from their loftier altitude it may
   Appear ignoble.   Be it so, I say,
Their smiles derisive shall not vex my heart.

     I serve;
From my appointed path nor sway nor swerve.
   What tho' the Eternal Wisdom did accord
   Mean use for me?   His love is my reward
If in mine own allotted sphere, I serve.

Susie M. Best

Awareness

God — let me be aware.
Let me not stumble blindly down the ways,
Just getting somehow safely through the days,
Not even groping for another hand,
Not even wondering why it all was planned,
Eyes to the ground unseeking for the light,
Soul never aching for a wild-winged flight,
Please, keep me eager just to do my share.
God — let me be aware.

God — let me be aware.
Stab my soul fiercely with others' pain,
Let me walk seeing horror and stain.
Let my hands, groping, find other hands.
Give me the heart that divines, understands.
Give me the courage, wounded, to fight.
Flood me with knowledge, drench me in light.
Please, keep me eager just to do my share.
God — let me be aware.

Miriam Teichner

Submission

A crystal mirror, I;
     Fate flung me — how prosaic — in the dust;
Now, shattered, here I lie.
Dear God, O help me try
     To be a rare mosaic — in the dust!

Jessie E. Williams

The Disciple

I could not leave thee, Christ! For when I tried
To leave thee for alluring ways aside
From thine own way, thy power withheld me, kept
My feet from wandering too far, inept
And aimless, down a dwindling path that led
Through mazed confusion to the house of dread.

I could not leave thee, Christ! For when I yearned
With passionate intensity and burned
With fiery torment to assuage my thirst
For freedom by a turbid stream that burst
In gushing torrents from a naked hill —
Thou ledst me back to waters deep and still.

I could not leave thee, Christ! For when I sought
To fling aside thy counsel, when I thought
That in my crazy freedom I should find
Some way of life for body, soul and mind
Better than thou didst teach, I heard thee say,
" Come back to me, for thou hast lost thy way."

I would not leave thee, Christ! For I am lame
From wandering, and the consuming flame
Of passion has gone out and left my soul
A smouldering ember, and the criss-crossed scroll
Of life ends as it started with the line,
" I cannot leave thee, Christ! For I am thine."

Dwight Bradley

Live Christ

Live Christ! — and though the way may be
In this world's sight adversity,
He who doth heed thy every need
Shall give thy soul prosperity.

Live Christ! — and though the road may be
The narrow street of poverty,
He had not where to lay his head,
Yet lived in largest liberty.

Live Christ! — and though the road may be
The straight way of humility,
He who first trod that way of God
Will clothe thee with his dignity.

Live Christ! — and though thy life may be
In much a valedictory,
The heavy cross brings seeming loss,
But wins the crown of victory.

Live Christ! — and all thy life shall be
A High Way of Delivery —
A Royal Road of goodly deeds,
Gold-paved with sweetest charity.

Live Christ! — and all thy life shall be
A sweet uplifting ministry,
A sowing of the fair white seeds
That fruit through all eternity.

John Oxenham

Our Daily Bread

Back of the loaf is the snowy flour,
  And back of the flour the mill;
And back of the mill is the wheat, and the shower,
  And the sun, and the Father's will.

Maltbie D. Babcock

The Touch of Human Hands

The touch of human hands —
That is the boon we ask;
For groping, day by day,
Along the stony way,
We need the comrade heart
That understands,
And the warmth, the living warmth
Of human hands.

The touch of human hands;
Not vain, unthinking words,
Nor that cold charity
Which shuns our misery;
We seek a loyal friend
Who understands,
And the warmth, the pulsing warmth
Of human hands.

The touch of human hands —
Such care as was in him
Who walked in Galilee
Beside the silver sea;

We need a patient guide
Who understands,
And the warmth, the loving warmth
Of human hands.

Thomas Curtis Clark

The Night Has a Thousand Eyes

The night has a thousand eyes,
    And the day but one;
Yet the light of the bright world dies
    With the dying sun.

The mind has a thousand eyes,
    And the heart but one;
Yet the light of a whole life dies
    When love is done.

Francis William Bourdillon

My Pilot

My bark is wafted to the strand
    By breath divine,
And on the helm there rests a hand
    Other than mine.

One who has known in storms to sail
    I have on board;
Above the raging of the gale
    I hear my Lord.

He holds me with the billows' might —
    I shall not fall:

If sharp, 'tis short; if long, 'tis light;
   He tempers all.

Safe to the land — safe to the land,
   The end is this;
And then with him go hand in hand
   Far into bliss.

                Washington Gladden

The Journey

I go not where I will but must;
   This planet ship on which I ride
   Is drawn by a resistless tide;
I touch no pilot wheel but trust

That One who holds the chart of stars,
   Whose fathom-lines touch lowest deeps
   Whose eye the boundless spaces sweeps,
Will guide the ship through cosmic bars.

My soul goes not a chosen way;
   A current underruns my life
   That moves alike in peace or strife,
And turns not for my yea or nay.

Not on the bridge, but at the mast,
   I sail o'er this far-streaming sea;
   I will arrive: enough for me
My Captain's smile and words at last.

                John T. McFarland

The Mystery

He came and took me by the hand
   Up to a red rose tree,
He kept his meaning to himself,
   But gave a rose to me.

I did not pray him to lay bare
  The mystery to me;
Enough the rose was heaven to smell,
  And his own face to see.

Ralph Hodgson

Outwitted

He drew a circle that shut me out —
Heretic, rebel, a thing to flout.
But Love and I had the wit to win:
We drew a circle that took him in!

Edwin Markham

Approaches

When thou turn'st away from ill,
Christ is this side of thy hill.

When thou turn'st toward good,
Christ is walking in thy wood.

When thy heart says, " Father, pardon! "
Then the Lord is in thy garden.

When stern Duty wakes to watch
Then his hand is on the latch.

But when Hope thy song doth rouse,
Then the Lord is in the house.

When to love is all thy wit,
Christ doth at thy table sit.

When God's will is thy heart's pole,
Then Christ is thy very soul.

George MacDonald

The Song of a Heathen

If Jesus Christ is a man —
    And only a man — I say
That of all mankind I cleave to him
    And to him will I cleave alway.

If Jesus Christ is a god —
    And the only God — I swear
I will follow him through heaven and hell,
    The earth, the sea, and the air!

Richard Watson Gilder

Seekers

Friends and loves we have none, nor wealth nor blest abode,
But the hope of the City of God at the other end of the road.

Not for us are content, and quiet, and peace of mind,
For we go seeking a city that we shall never find.

There is no solace on earth for us — for such as we —
Who search for a hidden city that we shall never see.

Only the road and the dawn, the sun, the wind, and the rain,
And the watch fire under stars, and sleep, and the road again.

We seek the City of God, and the haunt where beauty dwells,
And we find the sunny mart and the sound of burial bells.

Never the golden city, where radiant people meet,
But the dolorous town where mourners are going about the
    street.

We travel the dusty road till the light of the day is dim,
And sunset shows us spires away on the wide world's rim.

We travel from dawn to dusk, till the day is past and by,
Seeking the Holy City beyond the rim of the sky.

Friends and loves we have none, nor wealth nor blest abode,
But the hope of the City of God at the other end of the road.
                                        John Masefield

Recessional

God of our fathers, known of old,
    Lord of our far-flung battle-line,
Beneath whose awful Hand we hold
    Dominion over palm and pine —
Lord God of Hosts, be with us yet,
Lest we forget — lest we forget!

The tumult and the shouting dies;
    The Captains and the Kings depart:
Still stands Thine ancient sacrifice,
    An humble and a contrite heart.
Lord God of Hosts, be with us yet,
Lest we forget — lest we forget!

Far-called, our navies melt away;
    On dune and headland sinks the fire:
Lo, all our pomp of yesterday
    Is one with Nineveh and Tyre!

Judge of the Nations, spare us yet,
Lest we forget — lest we forget!

If, drunk with sight of power, we loose
    Wild tongues that have not Thee in awe,
Such boasting as the Gentiles use,
    Or lesser breeds without the Law —
Lord God of Hosts, be with us yet,
Lest we forget — lest we forget!

For heathen heart that puts her trust
    In reeking tube and iron shard,
All valiant dust that builds on dust,
    And guarding calls not Thee to guard,
For frantic boast and foolish word —
Thy mercy on Thy people, Lord!

                            Rudyard Kipling

I Am the Last

Stricken to earth, the sword snapped in his hand,
    Shield cast away, down-beaten to the knee,
He sees the foes he made above him stand —
    Now he has only Me.

The towers are fallen; at his feet they lie
    Wrecks of the hopes that now he will not see,
Naked unto the blast, Death drawing nigh —
    Now he has only Me.

But he has Me. The last illusions fade,
    The trumpet sounds no more, and man, set free
From tyranny of dreams his pride has made,
    At last has only Me.

For many loves he now has only one,
　　His many gods before the tempest flee,
His light is dying, and his day is done,
　　But he at last has Me.

Edward Shillito

The Quest

I asked for bread!
　　Life led me to a plain,
　　And put a plough at hand,
　　And bade me toil until my bread I earned.

I asked for drink!
　　Life led me to a sand
　　As dry as tearless grief —
　　Forced me to find the springs of sympathy.

I asked for joy!
　　Life led me to a street,
　　And had me hear the cries
　　Of wayward souls who waited to be freed.

I asked for words!
　　Life led me to a wood,
　　Set me in solitude
　　Where speech is still and wisdom comes by prayer.

I asked for love!
　　Life led me to a hill,
　　And bound me to a cross
　　To bear and lift and to be hanged upon.

Chester B. Emerson

Brothers of the Faith

In Christ there is no East nor West,
  In him no South nor North;
But one great fellowship of love
  Throughout the whole wide earth.

In him shall true hearts everywhere
  Their high communion find;
His service is the golden cord
  Close-binding all mankind.

Join hands then, brothers of the faith,
  Whate'er your race may be;
Who serves my Father as a son
  Is surely kin to me.

In Christ now meet both East and West,
  In him meet South and North;
All Christly souls are one in him
  Throughout the whole wide earth.

John Oxenham

From Abt Vogler

Builder and maker Thou, of houses not made with hands!
What, have fear of change from Thee who art ever the same?
Doubt that Thy power can fill the heart that Thy power
  expands?
There shall never be one lost good! What was, shall live
  as before;
The evil is null, is nought, is silence implying sound;

What was good, shall be good, with, for evil, so much good
    more;
On the earth the broken arc; in the heaven, the perfect
    round.

All we have willed or hoped or dreamed of good, shall exist;
Not its semblance, but itself; no beauty, nor good, nor
    power
Whose voice has gone forth, but each survives for the
    melodist
When eternity affirms the conception of an hour.
The high that proved too high, the heroic for earth too hard,
The passion that left the ground to lose itself in the sky,
Are music sent up to God by the lover and the bard;
Enough that He heard it once: we shall hear it by and by.

Robert Browning

These Are the Gifts I Ask

These are the gifts I ask
Of Thee, Spirit serene:
Strength for the daily task,
Courage to face the road,
Good cheer to help me bear the traveler's load,
And, for the hours of rest that come between,
An inward joy of all things heard and seen.

These are the sins I fain
Would have Thee take away:
Malice and cold disdain,
Hot anger, sullen hate,
Scorn of the lowly, envy of the great,
And discontent that casts a shadow gray
On all the brightness of the common day.

Henry van Dyke

Up-Hill

Does the road wind up-hill all the way?
  Yes, to the very end.
Will the day's journey take the whole long day?
  From morn to night, my friend.

But is there for the night a resting place?
  A roof when the slow dark hours begin.
May not the darkness hide it from my face?
  You cannot miss that inn.

Shall I meet other wayfarers at night?
  Those who have gone before.
Then must I knock, or call when just in sight?
  They will not keep you standing at that door.

Shall I find comfort, travel-sore and weak?
  Of labor you shall find the sum.
Will there be beds for me and all who seek?
  Yea, beds for all who come.
                                Christina Rossetti

Lost and Found

I missed him when the sun began to bend;
I found him not when I had lost his rim;
With many tears I went in search of him,
Climbing high mountains which did still ascend,
And gave me echoes when I called my friend;
Through cities vast and charnel-houses grim,
And high cathedrals where the light was dim,

Through books and arts and works without an end,
But found him not — the friend whom I had lost.
And yet I found him — as I found the lark,
A sound in fields I heard but could not mark;
I found him nearest when I missed Him most;
I found him in my heart, a life in frost,
A light I knew not till my soul was dark.

George MacDonald

My Faith

This body is my house — it is not I:
Herein I sojourn till, in some far sky,
I lease a fairer dwelling, built to last
Till all the carpentry of time is past.
When from my high place viewing this lone star,
What shall I care where these poor timbers are?

What though the crumbling walls turn dust and loam —
I shall have left them for a larger home!
What though the rafters break, the stanchions rot,
When earth hath dwindled to a glimmering spot!
When thou, clay cottage, fallest, I'll immerse
My long-cramped spirit in the universe.

Through uncomputed silences of space
I shall yearn upward to the leaning Face.
The ancient heavens will roll aside for me,
As Moses monarch's the dividing sea.
This body is my house — it is not I;
Triumphant in this faith I live, and die.

Frederick Lawrence Knowles

Earth Is Enough

We men of earth have here the stuff
Of Paradise — we have enough!
We need no other stones to build
The stairs into the Unfulfilled —
No other ivory for the doors —
No other marble for the floors —
No other cedar for the beam
And dome of man's immortal dream.
Here on the paths of every-day —
Here on the common human way —
Is all the busy gods would take
To build a Heaven, to mold and make
New Edens. Ours the task sublime
To build eternity in time!

Edwin Markham

Who Knows a Mountain?

Who knows a mountain?
One who has gone
To worship its beauty
In the dawn;
One who has slept
On its breast at night;
One who has measured
His strength to its height;

One who has followed
Its longest trail,
And laughed in the face
Of its fiercest gale;

One who has scaled its peaks,
And has trod
Its cloud-swept summits
Alone with God.

Ethel Romig Fuller

Youth and Death

Death is but life's escape: a rung
On which life climbs from where it clung
To a new height of youth. Forever
Death clogs our feet in vain endeavor
To hold us — trying still to keep
Life fast in habit, ease or sleep,
In sluggard blood and ageing brain . . .
Forever life breaks free again,
Outwitting death by death. We perish
To wake us from the graves we cherish.
We lose — that youth may gain — our breath,
And God remains alive by death.

E. Merrill Root

From The God-Maker, Man

As the skull of man grows broader,
    So do his creeds;
And the gods they are shaped in his image,
    And mirror his needs;
And he clothes them with thunders and beauty,
    He clothes them with music and fire,
Seeing not, as he bows by their altars,
    That he worships his own desire;
And mixed with his trust there is terror,
    And mixed with his madness is ruth,

And every man grovels in error
  Yet every man glimpses a truth.

For all the creeds are false, and all the creeds are true;
  And low at the shrines where my brothers bow, there will
    I bow too;
For no form of a god, no fashion
  Man has made in his desperate passion
But is worthy some worship of mine;
  Not too hot with a gross belief,
Nor yet too cold with pride,
  I will bow down where my brothers bow,
      Humble, but open-eyed.

Don Marquis

From Fragments

Let me go where'er I will
I hear a sky-born music still;
It sounds from all things old,
It sounds from all things young,
From all that's fair, from all that's foul,
Peals out a cheerful song.

It is not only in the rose,
It is not only in the bird,
Not only where the rainbow glows,
Nor in the song of women heard,
But in the darkest, meanest things
There alway, alway, something sings.

'Tis not in the high stars alone,
Not in the cups of budding flowers,
Nor in the redbreast's mellow tone,

Nor in the bow that smiles in showers,
But in the mud and scum of things
There alway, alway, something sings.

Ralph Waldo Emerson

Break Down the Walls

Break down the old dividing walls
Of sect, and rivalry, and schism,
And heal the body of Thy Christ
With anoint of Thy chrism.

Let the strong wind of Thy sweet grace
Sweep through Thy cumbered house, and chase
The miasms from the Holy Place!

Let Thy white beam of light beat in,
And from each darkest corner win
The shadows that have sheltered sin!

Cleanse it of shibboleths and strife,
End all the discords that were rife,
Heal the old wounds and give new life!

Break down the hedges that have grown
So thickly all about Thy throne,
And clear the paths, that every soul
That seeks Thee — of himself alone
May find, and be made whole! —

One church, one all-harmonious voice,
One passion for Thy high Employs,
One heart of gold without alloys,
One striving for the higher joys,

One Christ, one Cross, one only Lord,
One living of the Holy Word.

John Oxenham

The Anvil — God's Word

Last eve I passed beside a blacksmith's door,
　And heard the anvil ring the vesper chime;
Then looking in, I saw upon the floor
　Old hammers, worn with beating years of time.

" How many anvils have you had," said I,
　" To wear and batter all these hammers so? "
" Just one," said he, and then, with twinkling eye,
　" The anvil wears the hammers out, you know."

And so, thought I, the anvil of God's Word,
　For ages skeptic blows have beat upon;
Yet, though the noise of falling blows was heard,
　The anvil is unharmed — the hammers gone.

Author Unknown

In Thy Presence

Lord, what a change within us one short hour
Spent in Thy presence will prevail to make!
What heavy burdens from our bosoms take,
What parched grounds refresh as with a shower!
We kneel, and all around us seems to lower;
We rise, and all, the distant and the near,
Stands forth in sunny outline brave and clear;
We kneel, how weak; we rise, how full of power!
Why, therefore, should we do ourselves this wrong,
Or others, that we are not always strong,

That we are ever overborne with care,
That we should ever weak or heartless be,
Anxious or troubled, when with us is prayer,
And joy and strength and courage are with Thee!

Archbishop Trench

A Warrior's Prayer

Long since, in sore distress, I heard one pray,
    " Lord, who prevailest, with resistless might,
Ever from war and strife keep me away,
    My battles fight! "

I know not if I play the Pharisee,
    And if my brother after all be right;
But mine shall be the warrior's plea to Thee —
    Strength for the fight.

I do not ask that Thou shalt front the fray,
    And drive the warring foeman from my sight;
I only ask, O Lord, by night, by day,
    Strength for the fight.

When foes upon me press, let me not quail,
    Nor think to turn me into coward flight,
I only ask, to make my arms prevail,
    Strength for the fight!

Paul Lawrence Dunbar

Comrade Jesus

Thanks to Saint Matthew, who had been
At mass-meetings in Palestine,
We know whose side was spoken for
When Comrade Jesus had the floor.

" Where sore they toiled and hard they lie,
Among the great unwashed dwell I; —
The tramp, the convict, I am he;
Cold-shoulder him, cold-shoulder me."

By Dives' door, with thoughtful eye,
He did tomorrow prophesy:
" The kingdom's gate is low and small;
The rich can scarce wedge through at all."

" A dangerous man," said Caiaphas;
" An ignorant demagogue, alas!
Friend of low women, it is he
Slanders the upright Pharisee."

For law and order, it was plain,
For Holy Church, he must be slain.
The troops were there to awe the crowd,
And violence was not allowed.

Their clumsy force with force to foil
His strong, clean hands he would not soil.
He saw their childishness quite plain
Between the lightnings of his pain.

Between the twilights of his end,
He made his fellow-felon friend;
With swollen tongue and blinding eyes,
Invited him to Paradise.

Ah, let no local him refuse!
Comrade Jesus hath paid his dues.
Whatever other be debarred,
Comrade Jesus hath his red card.

Sarah N. Cleghorn

Symbol

My faith is all a doubtful thing,
　Wove on a doubtful loom, —
Until there comes, each showery spring,
　A cherry tree in bloom;
And Christ who died upon a tree
　That death had stricken bare,
Comes beautifully back to me,
　In blossoms, everywhere.

David Morton

From Intimations of Immortality

Our birth is but a sleep and a forgetting;
The Soul that rises with us, our life's Star,
　　Hath had elsewhere its setting
　　And cometh from afar;
　　Not in entire forgetfulness,
　　And not in utter nakedness,
But trailing clouds of glory do we come
　　From God, who is our home:
Heaven lies about us in our infancy!
Shades of the prison-house begin to close
　　Upon the growing Boy,
But he beholds the light, and whence it flows,
　　He sees it in his joy;
The Youth, who daily farther from the east
　　Must travel, still is Nature's priest,
　　And by the vision splendid
　　Is on his way attended;
At length the Man perceives it die away,
And fade into the light of common day.

William Wordsworth

Soliloquy from " Hamlet "

To be, or not to be; that is the question;
Whether 'tis nobler in the mind to suffer
The slings and arrows of outrageous fortune,
Or to take arms against a sea of troubles,
And by opposing end them. To die: to sleep:
No more; and by a sleep to say we end
The heart-ache and the thousand natural shocks
That flesh is heir to; 'tis a consummation
Devoutly to be wished. To die; to sleep;
To sleep: perchance to dream: aye, there's the rub;
For in that sleep of death what dreams may come,
When we have shuffled off this mortal coil,
Must give us pause: there's the respect
That makes calamity of so long life;
For who would bear the whips and scorns of time,
The oppressor's wrong, the proud man's contumely,
The pangs of despis'd love, the law's delay,
The insolence of office, and the spurns
That patient merit of the unworthy takes,
When he himself might his quietus make
With a bare bodkin? Who would fardels bear,
To grunt and sweat under a weary life,
But that the dread of something after death —
The undiscover'd country from whose bourn
No traveler returns — puzzles the will
And makes us rather bear those ills we have
Than fly to others that we know not of?
Thus conscience does make cowards of us all,
And thus the native hue of resolution
Is sicklied o'er with the pale cast of thought,
And enterprises of great pith and moment
With this regard their currents turn awry,
And lose the name of action.

William Shakespeare

We Would See Jesus

We would see Jesus! We would look upon
The light in that divinely human face,
Where lofty majesty and tender grace
    In blended beauty shone.

We would see Jesus, and would hear again
The voice that charmed the thousands by the sea,
Spoke peace to sinners, set the captives free,
    And eased the sufferers' pain.

We would see Jesus, yet not him alone —
But see ourselves as in our Maker's plan;
And in the beauty of the Son of Man
    See man upon his throne.

We would see Jesus, and let him impart
The truth he came among us to reveal,
Till in the gracious message we should feel
    The beating of God's heart.

W. J. Suckow

Sanctuary

Let us put by some hour of every day
For holy things! — whether it be when dawn
Peers through the window pane, or when the noon
Flames, like a burnished topaz, in the vault,
Or when the thrush pours in the ear of eve
Its plaintive monody; some little hour
Wherein to hold rapt converse with the soul,
From sordidness and self a sanctuary,
Swept by the winnowing of unseen wings,
And touched by the White Light Ineffable!

Clinton Scollard

Simon the Cyrenian Speaks

He never spoke a word to me,
 And yet he called my name,
He never gave a sign to me,
 And yet I knew and came.

At first I said, "I will not bear
 His cross upon my back;
He only seeks to place it there
 Because my skin is black."

But he was dying for a dream,
 And he was very weak,
And in his eyes there shone a gleam
 Men journey far to seek.

It was himself my pity bought;
 I did for Christ alone
What all of Rome could not have wrought
 With bruise of lash or stone.

Countee Cullen

My Garden

A garden is a lovesome thing, God wot!
Rose plot,
 Fringed pool,
Fern'd grot —
 The veriest school
 Of peace; and yet the fool
Contends that God is not —
Not God! in gardens! when the eve is cool?
 Nay, but I have a sign;
 'Tis very sure God walks in mine.

Thomas Edward Brown

Invocation

Truth, be more precious to me than the eyes
Of happy love; burn hotter in my throat
Than passion, and possess me like my pride;
More sweet than freedom, more desired than joy,
More sacred than the pleasing of a friend.

Max Eastman

The Zest of Life

Let me but live my life from year to year,
　With forward face and unreluctant soul.
　Not hastening to, nor turning from the goal;
Not mourning for the things that disappear
In the dim past, nor holding back in fear
　From what the future veils; but with a whole
　And happy heart, that pays its toll
To youth and age, and travels on with cheer.
So let the way wind up the hill or down,
　Through rough or smooth, the journey will be joy;
　Still seeking what I sought but when a boy,
New friendship, high adventure, and a crown,
　I shall grow old, but never lose life's zest,
　Because the road's last turn will be the best.

Henry van Dyke

Give Us Great Dreams

Give us great dreams, O God, while Thou art giving,
　And keep the end; it is enough if we
Live by the hope, nor falter in the living,
　That lures us on from dust to dignity.

Give us the courage of the soul's high vision,
Though its fulfillment here we never see;
The heart to make and keep the brave decision,
And faith to leave the ultimate with Thee.

Marie LeNart

Sundown

When the wounded in hospital came to die, said a British
officer, their last request in many cases was for the prayer,
" Now I lay me down to sleep."

When my sun of life is low,
When the dewy shadows creep,
Say for me before I go
" Now I lay me down to sleep."

I am at the journey's end,
I have sown and I must reap;
There are no more ways to mend —
Now I lay me down to sleep.

Nothing more to doubt or dare,
Nothing more to give or keep;
Say for me the children's prayer,
" Now I lay me down to sleep."

Who has learned along the way —
Primrose path or stony steep —
More of wisdom than to say,
" Now I lay me down to sleep "?

What have you more wise to tell
When the shadows round me creep?
All is over, all is well. . . .
Now I lay me down to sleep.

Bert Leston Taylor

Earth's Common Things

Seek not afar for beauty. Lo! it glows
  In dew-wet grasses all about thy feet;
  In birds, in sunshine, childish faces sweet,
In stars and mountain summits topped with snows.

Go not abroad for happiness. For see,
  It is a flower that blossoms at thy door!
  Bring love and justice home, and then no more
Thou'lt wonder in what dwelling joy may be.

Dream not of noble service elsewhere wrought;
  The simple duty that awaits thy hand
  Is God's voice uttering a divine command,
Life's common deeds build all that saints have thought

In wonder-workings, or some bush aflame,
  Men look for God and fancy Him concealed;
  But in earth's common things He stands revealed
While grass and flowers and stars spell out His name.

                              Minot J. Savage

A Prayer for Inspiration

The prayers I make will then be sweet indeed,
  If Thou the spirit give by which I pray;
  My unassisted heart is barren clay,
Which of its native self can nothing feed;
Of good and pious works Thou art the seed
  Which quickens where Thou say'st it may;
  Unless Thou show us then Thine own true way.
No man can find it!   Father, Thou must lead!
Do Thou, then, breathe those thoughts into my mind

By which such virtue may in me be bred
That in Thy holy footsteps I may tread;
The fetters of my tongue do Thou unbind,
That I may have the power to sing of Thee
And sound Thy praises everlastingly.

Michelangelo Buonarotti, translation
by William Wordsworth

Haste Not!   Rest Not!

Without haste! without rest!
Bind the motto to thy breast;
Bear it with thee as a spell;
Storm or sunshine, guard it well!
Haste not!   Let no thoughtless deed
Mar for aye the spirit's speed!
Ponder well, and know the right,
Onward then, with all thy might!
Haste not! years can ne'er atone
For one reckless action done.
Rest not!   Life is sweeping by,
Go and dare, before you die;
Something mighty and sublime
Leave behind to conquer time!
Haste not! rest not! calmly wait;
Meekly bear the storms of fate!
Duty be thy polar guide —
Do the right whate'er betide!

J. W. von Goethe

Purpose

We know the paths wherein our feet should press;
Across our hearts are written Thy decrees;
Yet now, O Lord, be merciful to bless
With more than these.

Grant us the will to fashion as we feel,
Grant us the strength to labor as we know,
Grant us the purpose, ribb'd and edged with steel,
  To strike the blow.

Knowledge we ask not — knowledge Thou hast lent;
But, Lord, the will — there lies our bitter need;
Give us to build above the deep intent
  The deed, the deed.

                              John Drinkwater

Courage

I love the man who dares to face defeat
  And risks a conflict with heroic heart;
  I love the man who bravely does his part
Where Right and Wrong in bloody battle meet.

When bugles blown by cowards sound retreat,
  I love the man who grasps his sword again
  And sets himself to lead his fellow-men
Far forward through the battle's din and heat.

For he who joins the issue of life's field
  Must fully know the hazard of the fray,
    And dare to venture ere he hope to win;
  Must choose the risk and then refuse to yield
    Until the sunset lights shall close the day
    And God's great city lets the victor in.

                              Ozora S. Davis

From Rabbi Ben Ezra

Grow old along with me!
The best is yet to be,
The last of life, for which the first was made:
Our times are in His hand
Who saith " A whole I planned,
Youth shows but half; trust God: see all nor be afraid! "

. . . .

Poor vaunt of life indeed,
Were man born but to feed
On joy, to solely seek and find and feast:
Such feasting ended, then
As sure an end to men;
Irks care the crop-full bird?   Frets doubt the maw-crammed
     beast?

Rejoice we are allied
To That which doth provide
And not partake, effect and not receive!
A spark disturbs our clod;
Nearer we hold of God
Who gives, than of His tribes that take, I must believe.

Then, welcome each rebuff
That turns earth's smoothness rough,
Each sting that bids nor sit nor stand but go!
Be our joys three-parts pain!
Strive, and hold cheap the strain;
Learn, nor account the pang; dare, never grudge the throe!

Let us not always say
" Spite of this flesh today
I strove, made head, gained ground upon the whole! "

As the bird wings and sings,
Let us cry " All good things
Are ours, nor soul helps flesh more, now, than flesh helps
soul! "

Therefore I summon age
To grant youth's heritage,
Life's struggle having so far reached its turn:
Thence shall I pass, approved
A man, for aye removed
From the undeveloped brute; a god though in the germ.

Thoughts hardly to be packed
Into a narrow act,
Fancies that broke through language and escaped;
All I could never be,
All, men ignored in me,
This, I was worth to God, whose wheel the pitcher shaped.

Aye, note that Potter's wheel,
That metaphor! and feel
Why time spins fast, why passive lies our clay —
Thou, to whom fools propound,
When the wine makes its round,
" Since life fleets, all is change; the Past gone, seize today! "

Fool! All that is, at all,
Lasts ever, past recall;
Earth changes, but thy soul and God stand sure:
What entered into thee,
That was, is, and shall be:
Time's wheel runs back or stops: Potter and clay endure.

He fixed thee mid this dance
Of plastic circumstance,
This Present, thou, forsooth, wouldst fain arrest:

Machinery just meant
To give thy soul its bent,
Try thee and turn thee forth, sufficiently impressed.

.   .   .   .   .   .

So, take and use Thy work:
Amend what flaws may lurk,
What strain o' the stuff, what warpings past the aim!
My times be in Thy hand!
Perfect the cup as planned!
Let age approve of youth, and death complete the same!

Robert Browning

From Pippa Passes

All service ranks the same with God:
If now, as formerly He trod
Paradise, His presence fills
Our earth, each only as God wills
Can work — God's puppets, best and worst,
Are we; there is no last nor first.

Say not " a small event! " Why " small " ?
Costs it more pain than this, ye call
A " great event," should come to pass,
Than that? Untwine me from the mass
Of deeds which make up life, one deed
Power shall fall short in or exceed!

Robert Browning

" Follow Me "

Will not our hearts within us burn
On the darkening road,

If a White Presence we can discern —
    Despite an ancient load?

Whither goest thou, pilgrim Friend?
    Lone Figure far ahead,
Wilt thou not tarry until the end —
    And break our bread?

Follow we must amid sun or shade,
    Our faith to complete,
Journeying where no path is made —
    Save by His feet!

                            Joseph Fort Newton

Vision

We by no shining Galilean lake
Have toiled, but long and little fruitfully
In waves of a more old and bitter sea
Our nets we cast; large winds, that sleep and wake
Around the feet of dawn and sunset, make
Our spiritual inhuman company,
And formless shadows of water rise and flee
All night around us till the morning break.

Thus our lives wear — shall it be ever thus?
Some idle day, when least we look for grace,
Shall we see stand upon the shore indeed
The visible Master, and the Lord of us,
And leave our nets, nor question of his creed,
Following the Christ within a young man's face?

                            Edward Dowden

Polonius' Advice to Laertes

There, — my blessing with you!
And these few precepts in thy memory
See thou character. — Give thy thoughts no tongue,
Nor any unproportion'd thought his act.
Be thou familiar, but by no means vulgar.
The friends thou hast, and their adoption tried,
Grapple them to thy soul with hoops of steel;
But do not dull thy palm with entertainment
Of each new-hatched, unfledged comrade.   Beware
Of entrance to a quarrel; but being in,
Bear't that the opposed may beware of thee.
Give every man thine ear, but few thy voice:
Take each man's censure, but reserve thy judgment.
Costly thy habit as thy purse can buy,
But not expressed in fancy; rich, not gaudy:
For the apparel oft proclaims the man.
Neither a borrower nor a lender be,
For loan oft loses both itself and friend,
And borrowing dulls the edge of husbandry.
This above all: to thine own self be true,
And it must follow, as the night the day,
Thou canst not then be false to any man.

William Shakespeare

From " Hamlet "

To a Waterfowl

Whither, 'midst falling dew,
    While glow the heavens with the last steps of day,
Far, through their rosy depths, dost thou pursue
    Thy solitary way?

Vainly the fowler's eye
  Might mark thy distant flight to do thee wrong,
As, darkly painted on the crimson sky,
  Thy figure floats along.

Seek'st thou the plashy brink
  Of weedy lake, or marge of river wide,
Or where the rocking billows rise and sink
  On the chafed ocean's side?

There is a Power whose care
  Teaches thy way along that pathless coast —
The desert and illimitable air —
  Lone wandering, but not lost.

All day thy wings have fanned,
  At that far height, the cold, thin atmosphere,
Yet stoop not weary, to the welcome land,
  Though the dark night is near.

And soon that toil shall end;
  Soon shalt thou find a summer home, and rest,
And scream among thy fellows; reeds shall bend,
  Soon, o'er thy sheltered nest.

Thou'rt gone! the abyss of heaven
  Hath swallowed up thy form; yet on my heart
Deeply hath sunk the lesson thou hast given,
  And shall not soon depart.

He who, from zone to zone,
  Guides through the boundless sky thy certain flight,
In the long way that I must tread alone,
  Will lead my steps aright.

                    William Cullen Bryant

Hour by Hour

God broke our years to hours and days, that
        Hour by hour
        And day by day,
We might be able all along
To keep quite strong.
Should all the weight of life
Be laid across our shoulders, and the future, rife
With woe and struggle, meet us face to face
        At just one place,
        We could not go;
Our feet would stop; and so
God lays a little on us every day.
And never, I believe, on all the way,
Will burdens bear so deep
Or pathways lie so steep
But we can go, if by God's power,
We only bear the burden by the hour.

George Klingle

Man-Making

We are all blind until we see
    That in the human plan
Nothing is worth the making if
    It does not make the man.

Why build these cities glorious
    If man unbuilded goes?
In vain we build the work, unless
    The builder also grows.

Edwin Markham

Creeds

How pitiful are little folk —
    They seem so very small;
They look at stars, and think they are
    Denominational.

Willard Wattles

The Singing Saviors

" Dead men tell no tales! " they chuckled,
As the singing saviors died,
A few serene, the many shackled,
Scourged, tortured, crucified.

Dead men tell no tales. . . . Is Shelley
Dust blown dumbly over the ground?
Are Keats and Burns silenced wholly?
Do Milton's stiff lips give no sound?

Is Shakespeare voiceless, Dante tongueless?
And, in this black, protesting year,
Is the dead Jesus wordless, songless?
Listen. . . . They are all that you can hear!

Clement Wood

Anchored to the Infinite

The builder who first bridged Niagara's gorge,
Before he swung his cable, shore to shore,
Sent out across the gulf his venturing kite
Bearing a slender cord for unseen hands

To grasp upon a further cliff and draw
A greater cord, and then a greater yet;
Till at last across the chasm swung
The cable — then the mighty bridge in air!

So we may send our little timid thought
Across the void, out to God's reaching hands
Send out our love and faith to thread the deep,
Thought after thought until the little cord
Has greatened to a chain no chance can break,
And — we are anchored to the Infinite!

Edwin Markham

Service

There are strange ways of serving God;
You sweep a room or turn a sod,
And suddenly, to your surprise,
You hear the whirr of seraphim,
And find you're under God's own eyes
And building palaces for Him.

Herman Hagedorn

Song

What trees were in Gethsemane,
   What flowers were there to scent,
When Christ for you, and Christ for me,
   Into his garden went?

The fragrant cedar tree was there,
   The lily pale and slim;
They saw his grief, they heard his prayer,
   And wept their dews for him.

And that is why the cedars green
And why the lilies white
Do whisper of the Master's love
In gardens, late at night.

Charles G. Blanden

Barter

A book you may buy for a shilling
  Where quaint little shops tempt the throng,
And love, though your guineas are useless,
  Perhaps may be had for a song.

You may, should the volume displease you,
  Exchange it or sell it again;
But love that you buy with your singing
  Can only be bartered for pain.

Earle V. Eastwood

If Hearts Are Dust

If hearts are dust, hearts' loves remain,
And somewhere, far beyond the plane
Of earthly thought, beyond the sea
That bounds this life, they will meet thee,
And hold thee face to face again;
And when is done life's restless reign,
If I hereafter but regain
Heart's love, why should I troubled be
  If hearts are dust?

By love's indissoluble chain
I know the grave does not retain

Heart's love; the very faith in me
Is pledge of an eternity,
Where I shall find heart's love again,
   If hearts are dust.

James Terry White

Via Lucis

If ever I dig out
   Into the upper air —
Through dogma, creed and doubt —
   I'll surely find Him there.

But ever as I mount,
   I hear some wise one say:
" Your striving does not count;
   Truth walks the priestly way."

Charles G. Blanden

Barnacles

My soul is sailing through the sea,
But the Past is heavy and hindereth me,
The Past hath crusted and cumbrous shells
That hold the flesh of cold sea smells about my soul.
The huge waves wash, the high waves roll,
Each barnacle clingeth and worketh dole
   And hindereth me from sailing!

Old Past, let go and drop i' the sea
Till fathomless waters cover thee!
For I am living and thou art dead;

Thou drawest back, I strive ahead the day to find.
Thy shells unbind!   Night comes behind;
I needs must hurry with the wind
   And trim me best for sailing.

Sidney Lanier

Thy Blessing, Lord, on All Vacation Days!

Thy blessing, Lord, on all vacation days!
For weary ones who seek the quiet ways,
Fare forth beyond the thunder of the street,
The marvel of Emmaus Road repeat;
Thy comradeship so graciously bestow
Their hearts shall burn within them as they go.

Grant those who turn for healing to the sea
May find the faith that once by Galilee
Flamed brighter than the glowing fire of coals.
And when thou hast refreshed their hungry souls,
Speak the old words again, beside the deep,
Bid all who love thee, Master, feed thy sheep!

Be thou with those who bide where mountains rise,
Where yearning earth draws nearest to the skies!
Give them the peace, the courage that they ask:
New strength to face the waiting valley task,
New light to lead through shrouding valley haze!
Thy blessing, Lord, on all vacation days!

Molly Anderson Haley

Quatrain

Here is the Truth in a little creed,
Enough for all the roads we go:
In Love is all the law we need,
In Christ is all the God we know.

Edwin Markham

He Whom a Dream Hath Possessed

He whom a dream hath possessed knoweth no more of
doubting,
For mist and the blowing of winds, and the mouthing of
words he scorns;
Not the sinuous speech of schools he hears, but a knightly
shouting,
And never comes darkness down, yet he greeteth a million
morns.

He whom a dream hath possessed knoweth no more of
roaming;
All roads and the flowing of waves and the speediest flight
he knows,
But wherever his feet are set, his soul is forever homing,
And going, he comes, and coming he heareth a call, and goes.

He whom a dream hath possessed knoweth no more of
sorrow,
At death and dropping of leaves and the fading of suns
he smiles,
For a dreamer remembers no past, and scorns the desire
of tomorrow,
And a-dream in a sea of doom, sets surely the ultimate isles.

He whom a dream hath possessed treads the impalpable
    marches,
From the dust of a day's long road he leaps to a laughing
    star,
And the ruins of worlds that fall he views from eternal
    arches,
And rides God's battlefield in a flashing and golden car.

Shaemus O'Sheel

Our Christ

I know not how that Bethlehem's Babe
    Could in the God-head be;
I only know the Manger Child
    Has brought God's life to me.

I know not how that Calvary's cross
    A world from sin could free:
I only know its matchless love
    Has brought God's love to me.

I know not how that Joseph's tomb
    Could solve death's mystery:
I only know a living Christ,
    Our immortality.

Harry Webb Farrington

God

God is beauty,
God is love,
God is understanding,
God is quietness and rest,

God is peace. God is the song of ecstasy, that bursts in the
    springtime;
God is the blue of a calm day in summer.
God is the faith that comes where there is no reason for
    faith.
God is the voice of a bell, the peal of a trumpet.
God is timeless, spaceless.
God is all heights and all depths.
God is law and the maker of law,
God is beyond all and in all.
God is simplicity, enveloped by us in complexity.
God is perfection among imperfections.
God is a perfect poem,
God is God.   *Catherine Cate Coblentz*

A Prayer for Christian Unity

O Master of the Galilean Way,
Forgive us for the vows we fail to keep:
Forgive us that we so neglect thy sheep,
So idly waste this shining harvest day!
Forgive us for the stumblingblocks we lay
Along the paths by which men seek thee!
Sweep
From our small minds the strife that holds thee cheap!
Break thou the bread of life with us, we pray!

What matter if we cannot understand
The mystery of Love that is Divine,
Nor pierce the veil! Dear Lord, our faith increase
To know that, since our hands may reach thy hand,
Our lives are made all-powerful, through thine,
To heal a wounded world and bring it peace!
                                    Molly Anderson Haley

Windows of the Soul

Let there be many windows in your soul,
That all the glory of the universe
May beautify it. Not the narrow pane
Of one poor creed can catch the radiant rays
That shine from countless sources. Tear away
The blinds of superstition. Let the light
Pour through fair windows, broad as truth itself,
And high as heaven. . . . Tune your ear
To all the wordless music of the stars,
And to the voice of Nature; and your heart
Shall turn to truth and goodness as the plant
Turns to the sun. A thousand unseen hands
Reach down to help you to their peace-crowned heights;
And all the forces of the firmament
Shall fortify your strength. Be not afraid
To thrust aside half-truths and grasp the whole.

Ella Wheeler Wilcox

From " Progress "

For A' That and A' That

Is there for honest poverty
That hangs his head, and a' that?
The coward slave, we pass him by;
We dare be poor for a' that!
For a' that, and a' that,
Our toils obscure, and a' that;
The rank is but the guinea stamp —
The man's the gowd for a' that!

What tho' on hamely fare we dine,
Wear hodden gray, and a' that?

Gie fools their silks, and knaves their wine —
A man's a man for a' that!
For a' that, and a' that,
Their tinsel show, and a' that;
The honest man, though e'er sae poor,
Is king o' men, for a' that!

Ye see yon birkie ca'd a lord,
Wha struts, an' stares, an' a' that —
Tho' hundreds worship at his word,
He's but a coof for a' that;
For a' that, and a' that,
His riband, star, and a' that;
The man of independent mind,
He looks an' laughs at a' that.

A prince can mak a belted knight,
A marquis, duke, and a' that;
But an honest man's aboon his might —
Gude faith, he mauna fa' that!
For a' that, and a' that,
Their dignities, and a' that;
The pith o' sense, and pride o' worth,
Are higher rank than a' that.

Then let us pray that come it may, —
As come it will for a' that, —
That sense and worth, o'er a' the earth,
May bear the gree, and a' that.
For a' that, and a' that,
It's comin' yet, for a' that —
That man to man, the warld o'er,
Shall brithers be for a' that.

Robert Burns

Years Are Coming

Years are coming, years are going, creeds may change and
   pass away,
But the light of love is growing stronger, surer, day by day.
Be ye as the light of morning, like the beauteous dawn un-
   fold,
With your radiant lives adorning all the world in hues of
   gold.
Selfish claims will soon no longer raise their harsh discordant
   sounds,
For the law of love will conquer, bursting hatred's narrow
   bounds.
Human love will spread a glory filling men with gladsome
   mirth,
Songs of joy proclaim the story of a fair, transfigured earth.
                                             Author Unknown

Paul

He found life a pattern
Woven by the Law
And men colorless threads in the fabric;
Save one,
Whose face shone
While jagged stones carved the last darkness,
And Another,
Whose light and voice
Illumined a desert road.
Thereafter,
Frail but unafraid,
He journeyed into the dawn —
Tearing the pattern to shreds
To free souls
From the tyranny of the dark.   *Earl B. Marlatt*

The Teacher

He sent men out to preach the living Word,
　Aflame with all the ardor of his fire;
They spoke the Truth, wherever truth was heard
　But back to him they brought their hearts'-desire;
They turned to him through all the lengthening days
　With each perplexity of life or creed.
His deep reward, not that they spoke his praise,
　But that they brought to him their human need.
　　　　　　　　　　Hildegarde Hoyt Swift

God's Dreams

Dreams are they — but they are God's dreams!
Shall we decry them and scorn them?
That men shall love one another,
That white shall call black man brother,
That greed shall pass from the market-place,
That lust shall yield to love for the race,
That man shall meet with God face to face —
Dreams are they all,
　But shall we despise them —
　God's dreams!

Dreams are they — to become man's dreams!
Can we say nay as they claim us?
That men shall cease from their hating,
That war shall soon be abating,
That the glory of kings and lords shall pale,
That the pride of dominion and power shall fail,
That the love of humanity shall prevail —
Dreams are they all,
　But shall we despise them —
　God's dreams!　　　　*Thomas Curtis Clark*

Mercy

The quality of mercy is not strained;
It droppeth as the gentle rain from heaven
Upon the place beneath: it is twice blest, —
It blesseth him that gives and him that takes:
'Tis mightiest in the mightiest; it becomes
The thronèd monarch better than his crown:
His sceptre shows the force of temporal power,
The attribute to awe and majesty,
Wherein doth sit the dread and fear of kings;
But mercy is above this sceptred sway, —
It is enthronèd in the hearts of kings,
It is an attribute to God himself;
And earthly power doth then show likest God's,
When mercy seasons justice.

William Shakespeare

From " The Merchant of Venice "

My Creed

I would be true, for there are those who trust me;
    I would be pure, for there are those who care;
I would be strong, for there is much to suffer;
    I would be brave, for there is much to dare.

I would be friend of all — the foe, the friendless;
    I would be giving and forget the gift;
I would be humble, for I know my weakness;
    I would look up — and laugh — and love — and lift.

Howard Arnold Walter

Just For Today

Lord, for tomorrow and its needs
  I do not pray:
Keep me, my God, from stain of sin
  Just for today.

Let me both diligently work
  And duly pray,
Let me be kind in word and deed
  Just for today.

Let me be slow to do my will,
  Prompt to obey,
Help me to mortify my flesh
  Just for today.

Let me no wrong or idle word
  Unthinking say:
Set Thou a seal upon my lips
  Just for today.

Let me in season, Lord, be grave,
  Let me be gay,
Let me be faithful to Thy grace,
  Just for today.

And if today my tide of life
  Should ebb away,
Give me Thy sacraments divine,
  Sweet Lord, today.

So for tomorrow and its needs
  I do not pray
But keep me, guide me, love me, Lord,
  Just for today.

Samuel Wilberforce

Closing the Doors

I have closed the door on Doubt,
I will go by what light I can find,
And hold up my hands and reach them out
To the glimmer of God in the dark, and call —
I am Thine, though I grope and stumble and fall,
I serve, and Thy service is kind.

I have closed the door on Fear.
He has lived with me far too long.
If he were to break forth and reappear,
I should lift up my eyes and look at the sky,
And sing aloud, and run lightly by;
He will never follow a song.

I have closed the door on Gloom.
His house has too narrow a view;
I must seek for my soul a wider room
With windows to open and let in the sun,
And radiant lamps when the day is done,
And the breeze of the world blowing through.

Irene P. McKeehan

His Name

I have lifted my eyes to the strength of the hills
  At the dawn of the day;
Felt the quickening stir of power that thrills,
  Seen the night drift away;
Caught the first flush of dawn. Who is this, then, that fills
  With His spirit my clay?

He that slumbereth not while I slumber, nor sleeps
   While, protected, I sleep;
Who creates, shall sustain — who gave life shall renew —
   Who hath promised, shall keep:

My shade from the sun and my shelter from the storm,
   In the dark a clear flame,
It is He — ever Friend and Preserver, O Soul!
   The Lord is His name!

Charles Poole Cleaves

His Cross

He burned no fiery cross
   To frighten men at night;
He bore his burning pain
   In sharpest noonday light;
He wore no hiding mask
   Below his crown of thorn;
He healed the flesh of men
   Whose flesh by men was torn.

He offered love to all
   And took with soul unbowed
Jeering, abuse, and blows,
   The spittle of the crowd.
How strange it is that men
   Should lift his banner high
When they go out to kill
   As he went out to die!

Marguerite Wilkinson

The Common Things

I have a cup of common clay,
And from its depths I drink each day
The water of a living dream
Drawn from a bright and nameless stream.

I have a cloak of common stuff;
A faded thing, and coarse and rough;
But we have weathered night and storm
And kept a heart serene and warm.

And with my staff of common wood,
A happy pilgrim, I have stood
Beside the temple all day long
And bought contentment with a song.

I go upon a common way,
And every night and every day
Is full of common peace, and pain,
And dew and stars, and dust and rain.

And when I die a common death,
And close my eyes and yield my breath,
Let me lie down in common earth,
Where all green growing things have birth.

Barbara Young

Out of the Vast

There's a part of the sun in the apple,
  There's a part of the moon in a rose;
There's a part of the flaming Pleiades
  In every leaf that grows.

Out of the vast comes nearness;
    For the God whose love we sing
Lends a little of His heaven
    To every living thing.

August Wright Bamberger

Into the Sunset

    Let me die, working.
Still tackling plans unfinished, tasks undone!
Clean to its end, swift may my race be run.
No laggard steps, no faltering, no shirking;
    Let me die, working!

    Let me die, thinking.
Let me fare forth still with an open mind,
Fresh secrets to unfold, new truths to find,
My soul undimmed, alert, no question blinking;
    Let me die, thinking!

    Let me die, laughing.
No sighing o'er past sins; they are forgiven.
Spilled on this earth are all the joys of heaven;
    Let me die, laughing!

S. Hall Young

The Surgeon's Hands

His face? I know not whether it be fair,
Or lined and grayed to mark the slipping years.
His eyes? I do not glimpse the pity there,
Or try to probe their depths for hopes or fears
Only upon his wondrous hands I gaze,
And search my memory through so fittingly

To voice their loveliness. In still amaze
I bow before their quiet dignity.
They make the crooked straight and heal old sores;
The blind to see, the war-torn clean and whole.
Throughout the suffering world they touch the doors
That open wide to life. The bitter bowl
Of pain they sweeten till the weary rest,
As though the hands of Christ had served and blest.

Ida Norton Munson

Three Gates

If you are tempted to reveal
A tale to you someone has told
About another, make it pass,
Before you speak, three gates of gold.
These narrow gates: First, " Is it true? "
Then, " Is it needful? " In your mind
Give truthful answer. And the next
Is last and narrowest, " Is it kind? "
And if to reach your lips at last
It passes through these gateways three,
Then you may tell the tale, nor fear
What the result of speech may be.

From the Arabian

Myself

I have to live with myself, and so
I want to be fit for myself to know;
Always to look myself straight in the eye.
I don't want to stand, with the setting sun
And hate myself for the things I've done.

I want to go out with my head erect;
I want to deserve all men's respect;
But here in the struggle for fame and pelf
I want to be able to like myself.
I don't want to look at myself and know
That I'm bluster and bluff and empty-show.
I never can fool myself, and so
Whatever happens I want to be
Self-respecting and conscience-free.

Author Unknown

The Book

Softly I closed the book as in a dream
And let its echoes linger to redeem
Silence with music, darkness with its gleam.

That day I worked no more. I could not bring
My hands to toil, my thoughts to trafficking.
A new light shone on every common thing.

Celestial glories flamed before my gaze.
That day I worked no more. But, to God's praise,
I shall work better all my other days.

Winfred Ernest Garrison

The Inevitable

I like the man who faces what he must
  With step triumphant and a heart of cheer;
  Who fights the daily battle without fear;
Sees his hopes fail, yet keeps unfaltering trust
That God is God; that somehow, true and just

His plans work out for mortals; not a tear
  Is shed when fortune, which the world holds dear,
Falls from his grasp; better, with love, a crust
Than living in dishonor; envies not,
  Nor loses faith in man; but does his best
Nor ever mourns over his humbler lot,
  But with a smile and words of hope, gives zest
To every toiler; he alone is great
Who by a life heroic conquers fate.

Sarah K. Bolton

Hymn for a Household

Lord Christ, beneath thy starry dome
We light this flickering lamp of home,
And where bewildering shadows throng
Uplift our prayer and evensong.
Dost thou, with heaven in thy ken
Seek still a dwelling-place with men,
Wandering the world in ceaseless quest?
O Man of Nazareth, be our guest!

Lord Christ, the bird his nest has found,
The fox is sheltered in his ground,
But dost thou still this dark earth tread
And have no place to lay thy head?
Shepherd of mortals, here behold
A little flock, a wayside fold
That wait thy presence to be blest —
O Man of Nazareth, be our guest!

Daniel Henderson

The Stream of Faith

From heart to heart, from creed to creed,
  The hidden river runs;
It quickens all the ages down,
  It binds the sires to sons —
The stream of Faith, whose source is God,
  Whose sound, the sound of prayer,
Whose meadows are the holy lives
    Upspringing everywhere.

And still it moves, a broadening flood;
  And fresher, fuller, grows.
A sense as if the sea were near
  Towards which the river flows.
O Thou who art the secret Source
  That rises in each soul,
Thou art the Ocean, too — thy charm,
  That ever-deepening roll!

William Channing Gannett

Child

The young child, Christ, is straight and wise
And asks questions of the old men, questions
Found under running water for all children,
And found under shadows thrown on still waters
By tall trees looking downward, old and gnarled,
Found to the eyes of children alone, untold,
Singing a low song in the loneliness.
And the young child, Christ, goes on asking
And the old men answer nothing and only know love
For the young child, Christ, straight and wise.

Carl Sandburg

Abou Ben Adhem

Abou Ben Adhem — may his tribe increase —
Awoke one night from a deep dream of peace,
And saw within the moonlight in his room,
Making it rich and like a lily in bloom,
An angel writing in a book of gold.
Exceeding peace had made Ben Adhem bold,
And to the presence in the room he said:
" What writest thou? " The vision raised its head,
And with a look made all of sweet accord,
Answered: " The names of those who love the Lord."
" And is mine one? " said Abou. " Nay, not so,"
Replied the angel. Abou spoke more low,
But cheerly still; and said: " I pray thee, then,
Write me as one that loves his fellow-men."
The angel wrote, and vanished. The next night
It came again with a great wakening light,
And shewed the names whom love of God had blessed,
And lo! Ben Adhem's name led all the rest.

Leigh Hunt

I Shall Not Pass Again This Way

The bread that bringeth strength I want to give,
The water pure that bids the thirsty live:
I want to help the fainting day by day;
I'm sure I shall not pass again this way.

I want to give the oil of joy for tears,
The faith to conquer crowding doubts and fears.
Beauty for ashes may I give alway:
I'm sure I shall not pass again this way.

I want to give good measure running o'er,
And into angry hearts I want to pour
The answer soft that turneth wrath away;
I'm sure I shall not pass again this way.

I want to give to others hope and faith,
I want to do all that the Master saith;
I want to live aright from day to day;
I'm sure I shall not pass again this way.

Author Unknown

A Virile Christ

Give us a virile Christ for these rough days!
You painters, sculptors, show the warrior bold;
And you who turn mere words to gleaming gold,
Too long your lips have sounded in the praise
Of patience and humility. Our ways
Have parted from the quietude of old;
We need a man of strength with us to hold
The very breach of Death without amaze.
Did he not scourge from temple courts the thieves?
And make the arch-fiend's self again to fall?
And blast the fig-tree that was only leaves?
And still the raging tumult of the seas?
Did he not bear the greatest pain of all,
Silent, upon the cross on Calvary?

Rex Boundy

Ultima Veritas

In the bitter waves of woe,
    Beaten and tossed about
By the sullen winds that blow
    From the desolate shores of doubt —

When the anchors that faith had cast
  Are dragging in the gale,
I am quietly holding fast
  To the things that cannot fail:

I know that right is right;
  That it is not good to lie;
That love is better than spite,
  And a neighbor than a spy;

I know that passion needs
  The leash of a sober mind;
I know that generous deeds
  Some sure reward will find;

That the rulers must obey;
  That the givers shall increase;
That Duty lights the way
  For the beautiful feet of Peace; —

In the darkest night of the year,
  When the stars have all gone out,
That courage is better than fear,
  That faith is truer than doubt;

And fierce though the fiends may fight,
  And long though the angels hide,
I know that Truth and Right
  Have the universe on their side;

And that somewhere, beyond the stars,
  Is a Love that is better than fate;
When the night unlocks her bars
  I shall see Him, and I will wait.

Washington Gladden

There Is No Unbelief

There is no unbelief;
Whoever plants a seed beneath the sod
And waits to see it push away the clod —
    He trusts in God.

There is no unbelief;
Whoever says beneath the sky,
" Be patient, heart; light breaketh by and by,"
    Trusts the Most High.

There is no unbelief;
Whoever sees 'neath winter's field of snow,
The silent harvest of the future grow —
    God's power must know.

There is no unbelief;
Whoever lies down on his couch to sleep,
Content to lock each sense in slumber deep,
    Knows God will keep.

There is no unbelief;
Whoever says " tomorrow," " the unknown,"
" The future," trusts that power alone
    He dares disown.

There is no unbelief;
The heart that looks on when the eyelids close,
And dares to live when life has only woes,
    God's comfort knows.

There is no unbelief;
For this by day and night unconsciously
The heart lives by the faith the lips deny.
    God knoweth why.

Elizabeth York Case

The Real Christ

Behold him now where he comes!
  Not the Christ of our subtle creeds,
But the lord of our hearts, of our homes,
  Of our hopes, our prayers, our needs;
The brother of want and blame,
  The lover of women and men,
With a love that puts to shame
  All passions of mortal ken. . . .

Ah, no! thou life of the heart,
  Never shalt thou depart!
Not till the leaven of God
  Shall lighten each human clod;
Not till the world shall climb
  To thy height serene, sublime,
Shall the Christ who enters our door
  Pass to return no more.
                    Richard Watson Gilder

Waiting

Serene, I fold my hands and wait,
  Nor care for wind, or tide, or sea;
I rave no more 'gainst Time or Fate,
  For, lo! my own shall come to me.

I stay my haste, I make delays,
  For what avails this eager pace?
I stand amid the eternal ways,
  And what is mine shall know my face.

Asleep, awake, by night or day,
   The friends I seek are seeking me;
No wind can drive my bark astray,
   Nor change the tide of destiny.

What matter if I stand alone?
   I wait with joy the coming years;
My heart shall reap where it hath sown,
   And garner up its fruit of tears.

The waters know their own and draw
   The brook that springs in yonder heights;
So flows the good with equal law
   Unto the soul of pure delights.

The stars come nightly to the sky;
   The tidal wave unto the sea;
Nor time, nor space, nor deep, nor high,
   Can keep my own away from me.

               John Burroughs

St. Francis

Would I might wake St. Francis in you all,
Brother of birds and trees, God's Troubadour,
Blinded with weeping for the sad and poor;
Our wealth undone, all strict Franciscan men,
Come, let us chant the canticle again
Of mother earth and the enduring sun.
God make each soul the lonely leper's slave;
God make us saints, and brave.

               Vachel Lindsay

From Our Master

We may not climb the heavenly steeps
  To bring the Lord Christ down;
In vain we search the lowest deeps,
  For him no depths can drown.

But warm, sweet, tender, even yet
  A present help is he;
And faith has still its Olivet
  And love its Galilee.

The healing of his seamless dress
  Is by our beds of pain;
We touch him in life's throng and press,
  And we are whole again.

Through him the first fond prayers are said
  Our lips of childhood frame;
The last low whispers of the dead
  Are burdened with his name.

Our Lord and Master of us all!
  Whate'er our name or sign,
We own thy sway, we hear thy call
  We test our lives by thine.

              John Greenleaf Whittier

The Faith of Christ's Freemen

Our faith is not in dead saints' bones,
  In altars of vain sacrifice;
Nor is it in the stately stones
  That rise in beauty toward the skies.

Our faith is in the Christ who walks
   With men today, in street and mart;
The constant Friend who thinks and talks
   With those who seek him with the heart.

We would not spurn the ancient lore,
   The prophet's word or psalmist's prayer;
But lo! our Leader goes before,
   Tomorrow's battles to prepare.

His Gospel calls for living men,
   With singing blood and minds alert;
Strong men, who fall to rise again,
   Who strive and bleed, with courage girt.

We serve no God whose work is done,
   Who rests within His firmament:
Our God, His labors but begun,
   Toils evermore, with power unspent.

God was and is and e'er shall be;
   Christ lived and loved — and loves us still;
And man goes forward, proud and free,
   God's present purpose to fulfill.
                   Thomas Curtis Clark

Jesus the Carpenter

If I could hold within my hand
   The hammer Jesus swung,
Not all the gold in all the land,
Nor jewels countless as the sand,
   All in the balance flung,
Could weigh the value of that thing
Round which his fingers once did cling.

If I could have the table Christ
    Once made in Nazareth,
Not all the pearls in all the sea,
Nor crowns of kings or kings to be
    As long as men have breath,
Could buy that thing of wood he made —
The Lord of Lords who learned a trade.

Yea, but his hammer still is shown
    By honest hands that toil,
And round his table men sit down;
And all are equals, with a crown
    Nor gold nor pearls can soil;
The shop of Nazareth was bare —
But brotherhood was builded there.

Charles M. Sheldon

Steadfast

It fortifies my soul to know
That though I perish, truth is so;
That, wheresoe'er I stray and range,
Whate'er I do, Thou dost not change.
I steadier step when I recall
That, if I slip, Thou dost not fall.

Arthur Hugh Clough

The Dream

Ah, great it is to believe the dream
As we stand in youth by the starry stream;
But a greater thing is to fight life through,
And say at the end, " The dream is true! "

Edwin Markham

From The Eternal Goodness

I know not what the Future hath
    Of marvel or surprise,
Assured alone that life and death
    His mercy underlies.

And if my heart and flesh are weak
    To bear an untried pain,
Thy bruised reed He will not break,
    But strengthen and sustain.

.   .   .   .

And so beside the Silent Sea
    I wait the muffled oar;
No harm from Him can come to me
    On ocean or on shore.

I know not where His islands lift
    Their fronded palms in air;
I only know I cannot drift
    Beyond His love and care.

O brothers! if my faith is vain,
    If hopes like these betray,
Pray for me that my feet may gain
    The sure and safer way.

And Thou, O Lord! by whom are seen
    Thy creatures as they be,
Forgive me if too close I lean
    My human heart on Thee!

John Greenleaf Whittier

Extracts from " In Memoriam "

Thou wilt not leave us in the dust:
Thou madest man, he knows not why,
He thinks he was not made to die;
And Thou hast made him: Thou art just.

. . . .

Our little sytems have their day;
They have their day and cease to be:
They are but broken lights of Thee,
And Thou, O Lord, art more than they.

. . . . . .

We have but faith: we cannot know;
For knowledge is of things we see;
And yet we trust it comes from Thee,
A beam in darkness, let it grow.

. . . . . .

I held it truth, with him who sings
To one clear harp with divers tones,
That men may rise on stepping-stones
Of their dead selves to higher things.

. . . . . .

Oh yet we trust that somehow good
Will be the final goal of ill,
To pangs of nature, sins of will,
Defects of doubt, and taints of blood;

That nothing walks with aimless feet;
That not one life shall be destroyed,
Or cast as rubbish to the void,
When God hath made the pile complete.

Behold, we know not anything;
I can but trust that good shall fall
At last — far off — at last, to all,
And every winter change to spring.

So runs my dream: but what am I?
An infant crying in the night:
An infant crying for the light:
And with no language but a cry.

The wish, that of the living whole
No life may fail beyond the grave,
Derives it not from what we have
The likest God within the soul?

Are God and Nature then at strife,
That Nature lends such evil dreams?
So careful of the type she seems,
So careless of the single life;

That I, considering everywhere
Her secret meaning in her deeds,
And finding that of fifty seeds
She often brings but one to bear,

I falter where I firmly trod,
And falling with my weight of cares
Upon the great world's altar-stairs
That slope through darkness up to God.

I stretch lame hands of faith, and grope
And gather dust and chaff, and call
To what I feel is Lord of all,
And faintly trust the larger hope.

.   .   .   .

Perplext in faith, but pure in deeds,
At last he beat his music out.
There lives more faith in honest doubt,
Believe me, than in half the creeds.

Alfred Tennyson

Acceptance

I cannot think nor reason,
    I only know he came
With hands and feet of healing
    And wild heart all aflame.

With eyes that dimmed and softened
    At all the things he saw,
And in his pillared singing
    I read the marching law.

I only know he loves me,
    Enfolds and understands —
And oh, his heart that holds me,
    And oh, his certain hands!   *Willard Wattles*

Love and Law

True Love is founded in rocks of Remembrance
    In stones of Forbearance and mortar of Pain.
The workman lays wearily granite on granite,
    And bleeds for his castle 'mid sunshine and rain.

Love is not velvet, not all of it velvet,
    Not all of it banners, not gold-leaf alone.
'Tis stern as the ages and old as Religion,
    With Patience its watchword, and Law for its throne.

Vachel Lindsay

The All-Loving

So the All-Great were the All-Loving too —
So, through the thunder comes a human voice
Saying, " O heart I made, a heart beats here!
Face, my hands fashioned, see it in myself.
Thou hast no power nor may'st conceive of mine,
But love I gave thee, with myself to love,
And thou must love me who have died for thee! "
Robert Browning

The Goal

All roads that lead to God are good;
   What matters it, your faith, or mine;
   Both center at the goal divine
Of love's eternal brotherhood.

A thousand creeds have come and gone;
   But what is that to you or me?
   Creeds are but branches of a tree,
The root of love lives on and on.

Though branch by branch proves withered wood,
   The root is warm with precious wine;
   Then keep your faith, and leave me mine;
All roads that lead to God are good.
Ella Wheeler Wilcox

The Unchanging

Let nothing distress thee, nothing affright thee;
All things are passing, God never changeth.
Henry Wadsworth Longfellow

Our Calvary

The tree
That fell last year
Knows now just why it fell;
Why came that hell
Of axe and saw, and leaping, clear blue flame.
To the world's uses it was set
In pit, or ship, or polished cabinet,
Or other needs of man.
The spirit of the tree
Knows now the plan
Of that, its agony.

So we,
Fall'n in the mire,
Shall some day surely know
Why life held blow
On blow, and sacrificial fire and knife;
Seeing one stand the firmer for our rout,
Or some brave, laughing ship of youth sail out
The braver for our pain.
So — knowing, seeing — we
Shall smile again
At this, our Calvary.

Constance Holm

From The New Spoon River

The urge of the seed: the germ.
The urge of the germ: the stalk.
The urge of the stalk: leaves.
The urge of leaves: the blossom.

The urge of the blossom: to scatter pollen.
The urge of the pollen: the imagined dream of life
The urge of life: longing for tomorrow.
The urge of tomorrow: Pain.
The urge of Pain: God.

Edgar Lee Masters

Spinning

Like a blind spinner in the sun,
    I tread my days;
I know that all the threads will run
    Appointed ways;
I know each day will bring its task,
And being blind, no more I ask.

I do not know the use or name
    Of that I spin,
I only know that someone came,
    And laid within
My hand the thread, and said, " Since you
Are blind, but one thing you can do."

Sometimes the threads so rough and fast
    And tangled fly,
I know wild storms are sweeping past
    And fear that I
Shall fall; but dare not try to find
A safer place, since I am blind.

I know not why, but I am sure
    That time and place,
In some great fabric to endure
    Past time and race
My threads will have; so from the first,
Though blind, I never felt accurst.

I think, perhaps, this trust has sprung
        From one short word
Said over me when I was young —
        So young, I heard
It, knowing not that God's name signed
My brow, and sealed me His, though blind.

But whether this be seal or sign,
        Within, without,
It matters not.   The bond Divine
        I never doubt.
I know He set me here, and still
And glad, and blind, I wait His will;

But listen, listen, day by day,
        To hear their tread
Who bear the finished web away,
        And cut the thread,
And bring God's message in the sun,
" Thou poor blind spinner, work is done."
                    Helen Hunt Jackson

Faith

If I lay waste and wither up with doubt
The blessed fields of heaven where once my Faith
Possessed itself serenely safe from death;
If I deny things past finding out;
Or if I orphan my own soul from One
That seemed a Father, and make void the place
Within me where He dwelt in Power and Grace,
What do I gain by what I have undone?
                    William Dean Howells

Good Company

Today I have grown taller from walking with the trees,
These seven sister-poplars who go softly in a line;
And I think my heart is whiter for its parley with a star
That trembled out at nightfall and hung above the pine.
The call-note of a redbird from the cedars in the dusk
Woke his happy mate within me to an answer free and fine;
And a sudden angel beckoned from a column of blue
    smoke —
*Lord, who am I that they should stoop — these holy folk
    of thine?*
                                        Karle Wilson Baker

Spirit's House

From naked stones of agony
I will build a house for me;
As a mason all alone
I will raise it, stone by stone,
And every stone where I have bled
Will show a sign of dusky red.
I have not gone the way in vain,
For I have good of all my pain;
My spirit's quiet house will be
Built of naked stones I trod
On roads where I lost sight of God.

                            Sara Teasdale

The Kingdom of Heaven

Said the Lord God, " Build a house,
    Cleave its treasure from the earth,

With the jarring powers of hell
   Strive with formless might and mirth,
Tribes and warmen build it well."

Then the raw red sons of men
   Brake the soil, and lopped the wood,
But a little and they shrill,
   " Lord, we cannot view thy good,"
And the wild men clamor still.

Said the Lord God, " Build a house,
   Smoke and iron, spark and steam,
Speak and vote and buy and sell;
   Let a new world throb and stream,
Seers and makers, build it well."

Strove the cunning men and strong,
   But a little and they cry,
" Lord, mayhap we are but clay,
   And we cannot know the why,"
And the wise men doubt today.

Yet though worn and deaf and blind,
   Force and savage, king and seer
Labour still, they know not why;
   At the dim foundation here,
Knead and plough and think and ply.

Till at last, mayhap, hereon,
   Fuse of passion and accord,
Love its crown and peace its stay,
   Rise the city of the Lord
That we darkly build today.

Gilbert K. Chesterton

From The Higher Catechism

And what is faith? The anchored trust that at the core
  of things
Health, goodness, animating strength flow from exhaustless
  springs;
That no star rolls unguided down the rings of endless maze,
That no feet tread an aimless path through wastes of empty
  days;
That trusts the everlasting voice, the glad, calm voice that
  saith
That Order grows from Chaos, and that life is born from
  death;
That from the wreck of rending stars behind the storm and
  scathe,
There dwells a heart of central calm; — and this, and this
  is faith.

Sam Walter Foss

The Larger Prayer

At first I prayed for Light:
  Could I but see the way,
How gladly, swiftly would I walk
  To everlasting day.

And next I prayed for Strength:
  That I might tread the road
With firm, unfaltering feet and win
  The heaven's serene abode.

And then I asked for Faith:
  Could I but trust my God,
I'd live enfolded in His peace,
  Though foes were all abroad.

But now I pray for Love:
Deep love to God and man,
A living love that will not fail,
However dark his plan.

And Light and Strength and Faith
Are opening everywhere;
God only waited for me, till
I prayed the larger prayer.

Mrs. E. D. Cheney

The Chambered Nautilus

This is the ship of pearl, which poets feign
Sails the unshadow'd main —
The venturous bark that flings
On the sweet summer wind its purple wings,
In gulfs enchanted, where the siren sings,
And coral reefs lie bare,
Where the cold sea-maids rise to sun their streaming hair.

Its webs of living gauze no more unfurl;
Wrecked is the ship of pearl!
And every chamber'd cell,
Where its dim dreaming life was wont to dwell,
As the frail tenant shaped his growing shell,
Before thee lies revealed —
Its iris'd ceiling rent, its sunless crypt unsealed!

Year after year beheld the silent toil
That spread his lustrous coil;
Still, as the spiral grew,
He left the past year's dwelling for the new,
Stole with soft step the shining archway through,
Built up its idle door,
Stretch'd in his last-found home, and knew the old no more.

Thanks for the heavenly message brought by thee,
Child of the wandering sea,
  Cast from her lap forlorn!
  From thy dead lips a clearer note is born
  Than ever Triton blew from wreathèd horn!
While on mine ear it rings,
Through the deep caves of thought I hear a voice that
    sings, —

Build thee more stately mansions, oh, my soul,
As the swift seasons roll!
  Leave thy low-vaulted past!
  Let each new temple, nobler than the last,
  Shut thee from heaven with a dome more vast,
Till thou at length art free,
Leaving thine outgrown shell by life's unresting sea!
Oliver Wendell Holmes

The Happiest Heart

Who drives the horses of the sun
  Shall lord it but a day;
Better the lowly deed were done,
  And kept the humble way.

The rust shall find the sword of fame,
  The dust will hide the crown;
Ay, none shall nail so high his name
  Time will not tear it down.

The happiest heart that ever beat
  Was in some common breast
That found the common daylight sweet,
  And left to Heaven the rest.
John Vance Cheney

Indirection

Fair are the flowers and the children, but their subtle sug-
gestion is fairer;
Rare is the roseburst of dawn, but the secret that clasps it
is rarer;
Sweet the exultance of song, but the strain that precedes it
is sweeter;
And never was poem yet writ, but the meaning mastered
the meter.

Never a daisy that grows, but a mystery guideth the growing;
Never a river that flows, but a majesty scepters the flowing;
Never a Shakespeare that soared, but a stronger than he did
enfold him,
Nor ever a prophet foretells, but a mightier seer hath fore-
told him.

Back of the canvas that throbs the painter is hinted and
hidden;
Into the statue that breathes the soul of the sculpture is
bidden;
Under the joy that is felt lift the infinite issues of feeling;
Crowning the glory revealed is the glory that crowns the
revealing.

Great are the symbols of being, but that which is symboled
is greater;
Vast the create and beheld, but vaster the inward creator;
Back of the sound broods the silence, back of the gift
stands the giving;
Back of the hand that receives thrill the sensitive nerves of
receiving.

Space is nothing to spirit, the deed is outdone by the doing;
The heart of the wooer is warm, but warmer the heart of
    the wooing;
And up from the pits where these shiver, and up from the
    heights where those shine,
Twin voices and shadows swim starward, and the essence of
    life is divine.

Richard Realf

When I Awake I Am Still With Thee

Still, still with Thee, when purple morning breaketh,
    When the bird waketh and the shadows flee;
Fairer than morning, lovelier than the daylight,
    Dawns the sweet consciousness, I am with Thee!

Alone with Thee, amid the mystic shadows,
    The solemn hush of nature newly born;
Alone with Thee, in breathless adoration,
    In the calm dew and freshness of the morn.

Still, still with Thee, as to each new-born morning
    A fresh and solemn splendor still is given,
So doth this blessed consciousness awakening,
    Breathe, each day, nearness unto Thee and heaven.

When sinks the soul, subdued by toil, to slumber,
    Its closing eye looks up to Thee in prayer;
Sweet the repose beneath Thy wings o'ershading,
    But sweeter still to wake and find Thee there.

So shall it be at last, in that bright morning
    When the soul waketh and life's shadows flee;
Oh, in that hour fairer than daylight dawning,
    Shall rise the glorious thought, I am with Thee!

Harriet Beecher Stowe

Via, et Veritas, et Vita

"You never attained to Him? " " If to attain
  Be to abide, then that may be."
"Endless the way, followed with how much pain! "
  " The way was He."

Alice Meynell

Rain Song

It isn't raining rain to me,
  It's raining daffodils;
In every dimpling drop I see
  Wildflowers on the hills.
A cloud of gray engulfs the day
  And overwhelms the town;
It isn't raining rain to me,
  It's raining roses down.

It isn't raining rain to me,
  But fields of clover bloom,
Where any buccaneering bee
  May find a bed and room.
A health, then, to the happy,
  A fig to him who frets;
It isn't raining rain to me,
  It's raining violets.

Robert Loveman

A Poet Lived in Galilee

A Poet lived in Galilee,
  Whose mother dearly knew him,
And his beauty like a cooling tree
  Drew many people to him.

He had sweet-hearted things to say,
    And he was angry only
When people were unkind. That day
    He'd stand there straight and lonely,

And tell them what they ought to do:
" Love other folks," he pleaded,
" As you love me and I love you; "
    Yet almost no one heeded.

A Poet lived in Galilee.
They stared at him and slew him.
What would they do to you and me
    If we could say we knew him?

                              Witter Bynner

Guilty

I never cut my neighbor's throat;
    My neighbor's gold I never stole;
I never spoiled his house and land;
    But God have mercy on my soul!

For I am haunted night and day
    By all the deeds I have not done;
O unattempted loveliness!
    O costly valor never won!

                        Marguerite Wilkinson

My World

God gave my world to me,
And I rebelliously
    Cried out, " How small!
    And is this all? "
His words were sad, yet mild:
" All that you love, my child."

Myself that moment died,
And born anew I cried:
" Love, take control
And lead my soul
To serve my small estate; "
And lo, my world is great!

C. R. Piety

The Way

Who seeks for heaven alone to save his soul,
May keep the path, but will not reach the goal;
While he who walks in love may wander far,
But God will bring him where the Blessed are.

Henry van Dyke

Revelation

All things burn with the fire of God —
Violets bursting from the sod;
The hill-top, tip-toe cherry tree,
Shouting with silver ecstasy;
Wild birds blowing down the wind;
Blue-brook music far and thinned;
Many-hued roses; rains that beat
On spreading fields of yellow wheat;
Sun-flame, moon-flame, flame of star;
Opal-walled heaven where bright clouds are;
Dreams, and pain, and love's desire. . . .
All things burn with God's white fire.

Verne Bright

God Give Us Men!

God give us men! A time like this demands
Strong minds, great hearts, true faith and ready hands;
Men whom the lust of office does not kill;
Men whom the spoils of office cannot buy;
Men who possess opinions and a will;
Men who have honor; men who will not lie;
Men who can stand before a demagogue
And damn his treacherous flatteries without winking!
Tall men, sun-crowned, who live above the fog
In public duty, and in private thinking;
For while the rabble, with their thumb-worn creeds
Their large professions and their little deeds,
Mingle in selfish strife, lo! Freedom weeps,
Wrong rules the land and waiting Justice sleeps.

Josiah Gilbert Holland

" I Am the Way "

Thou art the Way.
Hadst thou been nothing but the goal,
    I cannot say
If thou hadst ever met my soul.

    I cannot see —
I, child of process — if there lies
    An end for me,
Full of repose, full of replies.

    I'll not reproach
The road that winds, my feet that err,
    Access, Approach
Art thou, Time, Way, Wayfarer.

Alice Meynell

In His Good Time

I go to prove my soul,
I see my way as birds their trackless way,
I shall arrive. — What time, what circuit first,
I ask not: but unless God send His hail
Of blinding fireballs, sleet, or stifling snow,
In some time, His Good time, I shall arrive;
He guides me and the bird.   In His good time.

Robert Browning

Pippa's Song

The year's at the spring,
The day's at the morn;
Morning's at seven:
The hillside's dew pearled;
The lark's on the wing;
The snail's on the thorn;
God's in His heaven —
All's right with the world!

Robert Browning

From " Pippa Passes "

The Heart of the Eternal

There's a wideness in God's mercy,
  Like the wideness of the sea;
There's a kindness in His justice,
  Which is more than liberty.

For the love of God is broader
  Than the measures of man's mind;

And the heart of the Eternal
Is most wonderfully kind.

If our love were but more simple,
We should take Him at His word,
And our lives would be all sunshine
In the sweetness of our Lord.

Frederick W. Faber

Gradatim

Heaven is not gained at a single bound;
But we build the ladder by which we rise
From the lowly earth to the vaulted skies,
And we mount to its summit round by round.

I count this thing to be grandly true,
That a noble deed is a step toward God —
Lifting the soul from the common sod
To a purer air and a broader view.

We rise by the things that are 'neath our feet;
By what we have mastered of good and gain;
By the pride deposed and the passion slain;
And the vanquished ills that we hourly meet.

We hope, we aspire, we resolve, we trust,
When the morning calls us to life and light,
But our hearts grow weary, and, ere the night,
Our lives are trailing the sordid dust.

We hope, we resolve, we aspire, we pray,
And we think that we mount the air on wings
Beyond the recall of sensual things,
While our feet still cling to the heavy clay.

Wings for the angels, but feet for men!
    We may borrow the wings to find the way —
    We may hope, and resolve, and aspire, and pray,
But our feet must rise, or we fall again.

Only in dreams is a ladder thrown
    From the weary earth to the sapphire walls;
    But the dream departs, and the vision falls,
And the sleeper wakes on his pillow of stone.

Heaven is not reached at a single bound:
    But we build the ladder by which we rise
    From the lowly earth to the vaulted skies, ·
And we mount to its summit round by round.

                                        J. G. Holland

From The Vision of Sir Launfal

" Lo, it is I, be not afraid!
In many climes, without avail,
Thou hast spent thy life for the Holy Grail;
Behold, it is here — this cup which thou
Didst fill at the streamlet for me but now;
This crust is my body broken for thee,
The water his blood that died on the tree;
The holy supper is kept, indeed,
In whatso we share with another's need;
Not what we give, but what we share,
For the gift without the giver is bare;
Who gives himself with his alms feeds three —
Himself, his hungering neighbor, and Me."

                                James Russell Lowell

Loveliest of Trees

Loveliest of trees, the cherry now
Is hung with bloom along the bough,
And stands about the woodland ride
Wearing white for Eastertide.

Now, of my threescore years and ten,
Twenty will not come again,
And take from seventy springs a score,
It only leaves me fifty more.

And since to look at things in bloom
Fifty springs are little room,
About the woodlands I will go
To see the cherry hung with snow.

A. E. Housman

Tomorrow and Tomorrow

Tomorrow, and tomorrow, and tomorrow,
Creeps on this petty pace from day to day
To the last syllable of recorded time;
And all our yesterdays have lighted fools
The way to dusty death. Out, out, brief candle!
Life's but a walking shadow, a poor player
That struts and frets his hour upon the stage
And then is heard no more. It is a tale
Told by an idiot, full of sound and fury,
Signifying nothing.

William Shakespeare

From " Macbeth "

Our Little Life

Our revels now are ended. These our actors,
As I foretold you, were all spirits, and
Are melted into air, into thin air;
 And, like the baseless fabric of this vision,
The cloud-capp'd towers, the gorgeous palaces,
The solemn temples, the great globe itself,
Yea, all which it inherit, shall dissolve,
And, like this insubstantial pageant faded,
Leave not a rack behind. We are such stuff
As dreams are made of, and our little life
Is rounded with a sleep.

William Shakespeare

From " The Tempest "

The True Need

I do not wish to see my sins more plain,
But this: to know Thy life, without a stain.

I would not see the vileness of my heart,
But this would know: how pure and true Thou art.

I would forget my paltry life, so small,
 And know Thy greatness, Thou, my All in All.

Oh! teach me not how deep my spirit's night,
But flood me with Thy beams, Thou Perfect Light!

Thomas Curtis Clark

Others

Lord, help me live from day to day
  In such a self-forgetful way
Than even when I kneel to pray
  My prayers will be for OTHERS.

Help me in all the work I do
  To ever be sincere and true
And know that all I do for YOU
  Must needs be done for OTHERS.

Let Self be crucified and slain
  And buried deep, and all in vain
May efforts be to rise again
  Unless to live for OTHERS.

And when my work on earth is done
  And my new work in heaven begun
May I forget the crown I've won
  While thinking still of OTHERS.

Others, Lord, yes, others
  Let this my motto be;
Help me to live for Others
  That I may live like Thee.

Charles D. Meigs

Self-Dependence

Weary of myself, and sick of asking
What I am and what I ought to be,
At the vessel's prow I stand, which bears me
Forwards, forwards, o'er the starlit sea.

And a look of passionate desire
O'er the sea and to the stars I send;
" Ye, who from my childhood up have claimed me,
Calm me, ah, compose me to the end!

" Ah, once more," I cried, " ye stars, ye waters,
On my heart your mighty charm renew;
Still, still let me, as I gaze upon you,
Feel my soul becoming vast like you! "

From the intense, clear, star sown vault of heaven,
Over the lit sea's unquiet way,
In the rustling night air came the answer —
" Woulds't thou be as these are? Live as they.

" Unaffrighted by the silence round them,
Undistracted by the sights they see,
These demand not that the things without them
Yield them love, amusement, sympathy.

" And with joy the stars perform their shining,
And the sea its long moon-silvered roll;
For self-poised they live, nor pine with noting
All the fever of some differing soul.

" Bounded by themselves, and unregardful
In what state God's other works may be,
In their own tasks all their powers pouring,
These attain the mighty life you see."

O, air born voice! long since, severely clear,
A cry like thine in mine own heart I hear —
" Resolve to be thyself; and know that he
Who finds himself loses his misery! "

Matthew Arnold

When Night Comes

When night comes, list thy deeds; make plain the way
'Twixt heaven and thee; block it not with delays;
But perfect all before thou sleep'st: then say:
There's one sun more strung on my Bead of days.
What's good score up for joy; the bad, well scanned,
Wash off with tears, and get thy Master's hand.

Henry Vaughan

The Pilgrim Way

But once I pass this way,
And then — and then, the silent Door
  Swings on its hinges —
  Opens . . . Closes —
  And no more
  I pass this way.
  So while I may
  With all my might,
  I will assay
  Sweet comfort and delight
To all I meet upon the Pilgrim Way,
For no man travels twice
  The Great Highway
That climbs through darkness up to light,
  Through night
  To day.   *John Oxenham*

The Unknown God

The Unknown God — alas! His feet
  Go ways we know not of.

Nay, here where morn is fresh and sweet,
 He walks the fields we love.

Yet often have I seen His face
 And felt Him touch my brow —
Within a blossom's kiss and grace,
 When I bent down the bough.
     Charles G. Blanden

The Luminous Hands of God

Out of the base, insensate clod
The luminous, strong Hands of God
Have shaped us; and all sin can do
Cannot prevent the shining through
And on our lives of that pure light
Which God's effulgent Hand keeps bright.
     Eleanor Kenly Bacon

Life

Life is like a wayside bloom
 The butterfly disdains,
But where the probing honey-bee
 Finds nectar for her pains.
     Wayne Gard

Boundaries

Man cannot look round the roadway's curve
 Or beyond a mountain see,
And yet he dares to fashion creeds
 And bound eternity.
     Catherine Cate Coblentz

Thy Sea Is Great, Our Boats Are Small

O Maker of the Mighty Deep,
    Whereon our vessels fare,
Above our life's adventure keep
    Thy faithful watch and care.
In Thee we trust, whate'er befall;
Thy sea is great, our boats are small.

We know not where the secret tides
    Will help us or delay,
Nor where the lurking tempest hides,
    Nor where the fogs are gray.
We trust in Thee, whate'er befall;
Thy sea is great, our boats are small.

When outward bound we boldly sail
    And leave the friendly shore,
Let not our hearts of courage fail
    Until the voyage is o'er.
We trust in Thee, whate'er befall;
Thy sea is great, our boats are small.

When homeward bound, we gladly turn,
    Oh! bring us safely there,
Where harbor-lights of friendship burn
    And peace is in the air.
We trust in Thee, whate'er befall;
Thy sea is great, our boats are small.

Beyond the circle of the sea,
    When voyaging is past,
We seek our final port in Thee;
    Oh! bring us home at last.

In Thee we trust, whate'er befall;
Thy sea is great, our boats are small.
                                    Henry van Dyke

Knowledge

Whoso has felt the Spirit of the Highest
    Cannot confound nor doubt Him nor deny:
Yea, with one voice, O, world, though thou deniest,
    Stand thou on that side, for on this am I.

Rather the earth shall doubt when her retrieving
    Pours in the rain and rushes from the sod.
Rather than he for whom the great conceiving
    Stirs in his soul to quicken into God.

Ay, though thou then shouldst strike from him his glory,
    Blind and tormented, maddened and alone,
Even on the cross would he maintain his story,
    Yes, and in hell would whisper, I have known.
                                    Frederick W. H. Myers
From " St. Paul "

The House of Pain

Unto the Prison House of Pain none willingly repair —
    The bravest who an entrance gain
Reluctant linger there; —
For Pleasure, passing by that door, stays not to cheer the
        sight,
And Sympathy but muffles sound and banishes the light.

Yet in the Prison House of Pain things full of beauty blow —
    Like Christmas roses, which attain
Perfection with the snow —
Love, entering, in his mild warmth the darkest shadows
        melt,
And often, where the hush is deep, the waft of wings is felt.

Ah, me! the Prison House of Pain! — what lessons there are
  bought! —
Lessons of a sublimer strain
Than any elsewhere taught;
Amid its loneliness and bloom, grave meanings grow more
  clear,
For to no earthly dwelling-place seems God so strangely near!

Florence Earle Coates

The Doors in the Temple

Three doors are in the temple
  Where men go up to pray,
And they that wait at the outer gate
  May enter by either way.

There are some that pray by asking;
  They lie on the Master's breast,
And, shunning the strife of the lower life,
  They utter their cry for rest.

There are some that pray by seeking;
  They doubt where their reason fails,
But their minds' despair is the ancient prayer
  To touch the print of the nails.

Father, give each his answer —
  Each in his kindred way.
Adapt thy light to his form of night,
  And grant him his needed day.

George Matheson

From The Marshes of Glynn

As the marsh-hen secretly builds on the watery sod,
Behold I will build me a nest on the greatness of God:

I will fly in the greatness of God as the marsh-hen flies
In the freedom that fills all space 'twixt the marsh and the
    skies:
By so many roots as the marsh-grass sends in the sod
I will heartily lay me a-hold on the greatness of God:
Oh, like to the greatness of God is the greatness within
The range of the marshes, the liberal marshes of Glynn.

Sidney Lanier

Unrest

A fierce unrest seethes at the core
    Of all existing things:
It was the eager wish to soar
    That gave the gods their wings.

From what flat wastes of cosmic slime,
    And stung by what quick fire,
Sunward the restless races climb! —
    Men risen out of mire!

There throbs through all the worlds that are
    This heart-beat hot and strong,
And shaken systems, star by star,
    Awake and glow in song.

But for the urge of this unrest
    These joyous spheres are mute;
But for the rebel in his breast
    Had man remained a brute.

When baffled lips demanded speech,
    Speech trembled into birth —
(One day the lyric word shall reach
    From earth to laughing earth.) —

When man's dim eyes demanded light,
   The light he sought was born —
His wish, a Titan, scaled the height
   And flung him back the morn!

From deed to dream, from dream to deed,
   From daring hope to hope,
The restless wish, the instant need,
   Still lashed him up the slope!

   .   .   .   .   .   .

I sing no governed firmament,
   Cold, ordered, regular —
I sing the stinging discontent
   That leaps from star to star!

Don Marquis

God Is Not Dumb

God is not dumb, that He should speak no more!
If thou hast wanderings in the wilderness
And findest not Sinai — 'tis thy soul is poor!
There towers the mountain of the Voice no less,
Which whoso seeks shall find — but he who bends
Intent on manna still and mortal ends,
 Sees it not — neither hears its thundered lore.

James Russell Lowell

Prayer

Be not afraid to pray, to pray is right.
Pray, if thou canst with hope, but ever pray,
Though hope be weak, — or sick with long delay.
Pray in the darkness, if there be no light.

Far is the time, remote from human sight,
When war and discord on the earth shall cease;
Yet every prayer for universal peace
Avails the blessed time to expedite.
Whate'er is good to wish, ask that of heaven,
Though it be what thou canst not hope to see;
Pray to be perfect, though material leaven
Forbid the spirit so on earth to be;
But if for any wish thou canst not pray,
Then pray to God to cast that wish away.

Hartley Coleridge

Work

Let me but do my work from day to day,
   In field or forest, at the desk or loom,
In roaring market-place or tranquil room;
Let me but find it in my heart to say,
When vagrant wishes beckon me astray,
   " This is my work; my blessing, not my doom;
Of all who live, I am the one by whom
   This work can best be done in the right way."

Then shall I see it not too great, nor small,
   To suit my spirit and to prove my powers;
Then shall I cheerful greet the laboring hours,
And cheerful turn, when the long shadows fall
At eventide, to play and love and rest,
Because I know for me my work is best.

Henry van Dyke

The Common Problem

The common problem — yours, mine, everyone's —
Is not to fancy what were fair in life
Provided it could be; but, finding first
What may be, then find how to make it fair
Up to our means — a very different thing!
My business is not to remake myself
But *make* the absolute *best* of what God made.

Robert Browning

Prayer

More things are wrought by prayer
Than this world dreams of. Wherefore, let thy voice
Rise like a fountain for me night and day.
For what are men better than sheep or goats
That nourish a blind life within the brain,
If, knowing God, they lift not hands of prayer
Both for themselves and those who call them friend?
For so the whole round earth is every way
Bound by gold chains about the feet of God.

Alfred Tennyson

From " Idylls of the King "

Love

As far as human need exists,
    Or echoes call,
Love, limitless, divine, persists
    About us all.

Its pulsing waters never tell
  Of bounding shore;
They surge and roll and rise and swell
  Forevermore.

Charles Russell Wakeley

A Mightier Church

A mightier church shall come, whose covenant word
Shall be the deeds of love. Not "credo" then —
"Amo" shall be the password through the gates.
Man shall not ask his brother any more,
"Believest thou?" but "Lovest thou?" and all,
And all shall answer at God's altar, "Lord, I love."
For Hope may anchor, Faith may steer, but Love,
Great Love alone, is captain of the soul.

Henry B. Carpenter

Life

Forenoon, and afternoon, and night! Forenoon,
And afternoon, and night! Forenoon, and — what!
The empty song repeats itself. No more,
Yea, that is Life; make this forenoon sublime,
This afternoon a psalm, this night a prayer,
And Time is conquered, and thy crown is won.

Edward Rowland Sill

Host and Guest

  I may not claim
Entrance to Thy high feast, so sin-marred I;
  And yet, for all my shame,
Some scattered crumbs I crave before I die.

" Lo! at Thy door I knock, and I will be
In Thine own house Thy guest, and sup with Thee."

How shall I spread
A table Thou canst condescend to share?
How shall my coarse-made bread
And tasteless wine for Thee prove fitting fare?
" Lo! My own flesh and blood, to salve Thy need,
I bring — and these are meat and drink indeed."

No robe is mine
Wherein I may, when once is set the board,
Close at Thy side recline,
With Thy fair splendor matched in due accord.
" Lo! I bestow on Thee, for ample dress
The glorious garment of My righteousness."

Henry W. Clark

The Bohemian Hymn

In many forms we try
To utter God's infinity,
But the boundless hath no form,
And the Universal Friend
Doth as far transcend
An angel as a worm.

The great Idea baffles wit,
Language falters under it,
It leaves the learned in the lurch;
No art, nor power, nor toil can find
The measure of the eternal Mind,
Nor hymn, nor prayer, nor church.

Ralph Waldo Emerson

Immanence

Enthroned above the world although He sit,
Still is the world in Him and He in it;
  The selfsame power in yonder sunset glows
That kindled in the words of Holy Writ.

Richard Hovey

Transcendence

Though one with all that sense or soul can see,
Not imprisoned in His own creation, He,
  His life is more than stars or winds or angels —
The sun doth not contain Him nor the sea.

Richard Hovey

Dust

I heard them in their sadness say
  " The earth rebukes the thought of God;
We are but embers wrapped in clay,
  A little nobler than the sod."

But I have touched the lips of clay,
  Mother, thy rudest sod to me
Is thrilled with fire of hidden day,
  And haunted by all mystery.

George William Russell (A.E.)

God's Garden

The years are flowers and bloom within
  Eternity's wide garden:

The rose for joy, the thorn for sin,
   The gardener, God, to pardon
All wilding growths, to prune, reclaim,
And make them rose-like in His name.
                              Richard Burton

Silence

I need not shout my faith.   Thrice eloquent
   Are quiet trees and the green listening sod;
Hushed are the stars, whose power is never spent;
   The hills are mute: yet how they speak of God!
                              Charles Hanson Towne

Prospice

Fear death? — to feel the fog in my throat,
   The mist in my face,
When the snows begin, and the blasts denote
   I am nearing the place,
The power of the night, the press of the storm,
   The post of the foe;
Where he stands, the Arch Fear in a visible form,
   Yet the strong man must go:
For the journey is done and the summit attained,
   And the barriers fall,
Though a battle's to fight ere the guerdon be gained,
   The reward of it all.
I was ever a fighter, so — one fight more,
   The best and the last!
I would hate that death bandaged my eyes, and forbore,
   And bade me creep past.
No! let me taste the whole of it, fare like my peers
   The heroes of old.

Bear the brunt, in a minute pay glad life's arrears
  Of pain, darkness and cold.
For sudden the worst turns to the best to the brave,
  The black minute's at end,
And the elements' rage, the fiend-voices that rave
  Shall dwindle, shall blend,
Shall change, shall become first a peace out of pain,
  Then a light, then thy breast,
O thou soul of my soul!   I shall clasp thee again,
  And with God be the rest!

Robert Browning

Faith

O never star
Was lost; here
We all aspire to heaven and there is heaven
Above us.
If I stoop
Into a dark tremendous sea of cloud,
It is but for a time; I press God's lamp
Close to my breast; its splendor soon or late
Will pierce the gloom.   I shall emerge some day.

Robert Browning

Betrayal

Still, as of old,
Man by himself is priced.
For thirty pieces Judas sold
Himself, not Christ.

Author Unknown

Alpha and Omega

Yea, through life, death, through sorrow and through sin-
    ning,
Christ shall suffice me, for he hath sufficed;
Christ is the end, for Christ was the beginning,
Christ the beginning, for the end is Christ.

F. W. H. Myers

From " St. Paul "

Men Told Me, Lord

Men told me, Lord, it was a vale of tears
Where Thou hadst placed me; wickedness and woe
My twain companions whereso I might go;
That I through ten and three score weary years
Should stumble on, beset by pains and fears,
Fierce conflict round me, passions hot within,
Enjoyment brief and fatal, but in sin.
When all was ended then I should demand
Full compensation from Thine austere hand:
For 'tis Thy pleasure, all temptation past,
To be not just but generous at last.

Lord, here am I, my three score years and ten
Are counted to the full; I've fought Thy fight,
Crossed Thy dark valleys, scaled Thy rocks' harsh height,
Borne all the burdens Thou dost lay on men
With hand unsparing, three score years and ten.
Before Thee now I make my claim, O Lord!
What shall I pay Thee as a meet reward?

I ask for nothing! Let the balance fall!
All that I am or know, or may confess

But swells the weight of my indebtedness;
Burdens and sorrows stand transfigured all;
Thy hand's rude buffet turns to a caress,
For Love, with all the rest, Thou gavest me here,
And Love is heaven's very atmosphere.
Lo, I have dwelt with Thee, Lord! Let me die:
I could no more through all eternity!

David Starr Jordan

Home at Last

To an open house in the evening,
Home shall men come,
To an older place than Eden,
And a taller town than Rome.
To the end of the way of the wandering star,
To the things that cannot be and that are,
To the place where God was homeless,
And all men are at home.

Gilbert K. Chesterton

God Is at the Organ

God is at the organ;
    I can hear
A mighty music echoing,
    Far and near.

God is at the organ
    And the keys
Are storm-strewn billows,
    Moorlands, trees.

God is at the organ,
  I can hear
A mighty music, echoing
  Far and near.

Egbert Sandford

From The Fire-Bringer

I stood within the heart of God;
  It seemed a place that I had known:
(I was blood-sister to the clod,
  Blood-brother to the stone.)

I found my love and labor there,
  My house, my raiment, meat and wine,
My ancient rage, my old despair —
  Yea, all things that were mine.

I saw the spring and summer pass,
  The trees grow bare, and winter come;
All was the same as once it was
  Upon my hills at home.

Then suddenly in my own heart
  I felt God walk and gaze about;
He spoke; His words seemed held apart
  With gladness and with doubt.

" Here is my meat and wine," He said,
  " My love, my toil, my ancient care;
Here is my cloak, my book, my bed,
  And here my old despair."

" Here are my seasons: winter, spring,
  Summer the same, and autumn spills
The fruits I look for; everything
  As on my heavenly hills."

William Vaughn Moody

Duty

When Duty comes a-knocking at your gate,
Welcome him in; for if you bid him wait,
He will depart only to come once more
And bring seven other duties to your door.

Edwin Markham

I Know a Name

I know a soul that is steeped in sin,
  That no man's art can cure;
But I know a Name, a Name, a Name,
  That can make that soul all pure.

I know a life that is lost to God,
  Bound down by things of earth;
But I know a Name, a Name, a Name,
  That can bring that soul new birth.

I know of lands that are sunk in shame,
  Of hearts that faint and tire;
But I know a Name, a Name, a Name,
  That can set those lands on fire.
Its sound is a brand, its letters flame,
I know a Name, a Name, a Name,
  That will set those lands on fire.

Author Unknown

Creed and Deed

What care I for caste or creed?
It is the deed, it is the deed;
What for class or what for clan?
It is the man, it is the man;
Heirs of love, and joy, and woe,
Who is high, and who is low?
Mountain, valley, sky, and sea,
Are for all humanity.

What care I for robe or stole?
It is the soul, it is the soul;
What for crown, or what for crest?
It is the heart within the breast;
It is the faith, it is the hope,
It is the struggle up the slope,
It is the brain and eye to see,
One God and one humanity.

Robert Loveman

Sculptors of Life

Chisel in hand stood a sculptor boy
  With his marble block before him,
And his eye lit up with a gleam of joy
  When his life dream passed before him.

He carved it well on the shapeless stone
  With many a sharp incision;
That angel dream he made his own,
  His own that angel vision.

Sculptors of life are we as we stand
   With our souls uncarved before us,
Waiting the time when at God's command
   Our life dream shall pass o'er us.

If we carve it well on the shapeless stone,
   With many a sharp incision,
That angel dream we make our own,
   Our own that angel vision.

George W. Doane

What is the Church?

The Church is man when his awed soul goes out
In reverence to a mystery that swathes him all about.
When any living man in awe gropes Godward in his search,
Then in that hour, that living man becomes the living
   Church,
Then though in wilderness or in waste, his soul is swept
   along
Down naves of prayer, through aisles of praise, up altar-stairs
   of song,
And when man fronts the mystery with spirit bowed in
   prayer,
There is the universal Church — the Church of God is there.

Sam Walter Foss

One Ship Drives East

One ship drives east and another west,
   While the selfsame breezes blow;
'Tis the set of the sail and not the gale
   That bids them where to go.

Like the winds of the air are the ways of fate,
 As we journey along through life;
'Tis the set of the soul that decides the goal,
 And not the storm or the strife.

Ella Wheeler Wilcox

Enough

The grass creeps everywhere,
But only here and there
 A rose looks up;
The gods are kind indeed:
The draught we mostly need
 Is in our cup.

Charles G. Blanden

City Priest

So he droned on, of parish work and claims;
Of weddings, funerals, the constant call
Upon his time and strength; and through it all
Came mention of rich men with powerful names,
Who were his friends. He spoke of sport and games
To lure the young from the low dancing-hall,
And while he talked I watched the lift and fall
Of well-kept hands, gesturing of his aims.
I did not follow all the things he said.
Those smooth hands vanished from my sight. Instead,
A picture built itself before my sight
Of a rough work-bench, where with saw and blade
A young Lad labored at his Father's trade.
I cannot think that Jesus' hands were white!

Anne Higginson Spicer

Creativity

This poem is recognized as one of the oldest Chinese folk-poems which has come down to the present time. It may be roughly dated 2500 B.C.

When the sun rises, I go to work;
When the sun goes down, I take my rest;
I dig the well from which I drink;
I farm the soil that yields my food.
I share creation; kings do no more.

Translation by Y. S. Han

Testimony

My garden bears testimony to divinity;
I sow the seed, itself a mystery;
Invoke the graces of the sun;
Implore the ministry
Of the rain; and yet, when this is done,
It is God
Who thrusts up
Through the imprisoning clod
Miracles of emerald leaf and radiant bloom,
Fashioned of fabrics from a heavenly loom.
Surely none but God can,
Within a seed's pin-point of space,
Pack a blue-print of the cosmos' swaying grace;
Or, from a dry brown root release
The phlox in all its still white peace.
He hangs the rose upon the thorn,
And lifts the lily's samite cup
Brimmed with the dewy nectar of the morn.

It is God alone, knowing infinity,
May be so prodigal of beauty
That he gives to the errant winds the poppy
And the rose, or yields to winter's devastating hold
Autumn's arabesques of flame and gold.

Eva Moad Turner

But When Ye Pray

But when ye pray, say *our* — not *mine* or *thine;*
  Our debts, *our* debtors, and *our* daily bread!
Before the thronged cathedral's gracious shrine,
  Or in thy closet's solitude instead,
Whoe'er thou art, where'er thou liftest prayer,
  However humble or how great thou be,
Say *our,* thy brother man including there,
  And more and more it may be thou shalt see
Upon life's loom how thread to thread is bound;
  None for himself, but man and fellow-man,
Or near or far, meet on one common ground,
  Sons of one Father since the world began.
    So shall God's Kingdom come in might and power
    When all can pray, not mine, or thine, but *our.*

Frances Crosby Hamlet

For An Hour

I may not keep the heights I gain
  In those rare hours of ecstasy
When, scorning ease, despising pain,
  Forgetting self, and winning free
  From all that most entangles me,
I leave the low miasmic plain
  Of sloth and doubt and greed to be

Companion of the heavenly train
Who tread the loftier ways; who keep
    A tryst with stars, nor shrink nor cower
In craven fear or sluggish sleep,
    Nor seek the ease of blossomed bower.
    My earth-bound soul lacks breath and power
To hold a path so nobly steep,
    Yet God be praised that for an hour
I gained the heights I could not keep.
                    Winfred Ernest Garrison

The Bible

We search the world for truth. We cull
The good, the true, the beautiful,
From graven stone and written scroll,
And all old flower-fields of the soul;
And, weary seekers of the best,
We come back laden from our quest,
To find that all the sages said
Is in the Book our mothers read.
                    John Greenleaf Whittier

Sympathy

Ask God to give thee skill
    In comfort's art,
That thou may'st consecrated be
    And set apart
Unto a life of sympathy,
For heavy is the weight of ill
    In every heart;
And comforters are needed much
        Of Christlike touch.   *A. E. Hamilton*

Gather Us In

Gather us in: we worship only Thee;
In varied names we stretch a common hand;
In diverse forms a common soul we see;
In many ships we seek one spirit-land;
Gather us in!

George Matheson

Prayer for the Churches

O God, within whose sight
All men have equal right
   To worship Thee,
Break every bar that holds
Thy flock in diverse folds;
Thy will from none withholds
   Full liberty.

Lord, set Thy churches free
From foolish rivalry!
   Lord, make all free!
Let all past bitterness
Now and forever cease,
And all our souls possess
   True charity.

John Oxenham

Man and God

Whoso draws near to God one step through doubtings dim
God will advance a mile in blazing light to him.

Author Unknown

The Country Faith

Here in the country's heart
    Where the grass is green
Life is the same sweet life
    As it e'er hath been.

Trust in a God still lives,
    And the bell at morn
Floats with a thought of God
    O'er the rising corn.

God comes down in the rain,
    And the crop grows tall —
This is the country faith,
    And the best of all!

Norman Gale

A B C's In Green

The trees are God's great alphabet:
With them He writes in shining green
Across the world His thoughts serene.

He scribbles poems against the sky
With a gay, leafy lettering,
For us and for our bettering.

The wind pulls softly at His page,
And every star and bird
Repeats in dutiful delight His word,
And every blade of grass
Flutters to class.

Like a slow child that does not heed,
I stand at summer's knees,
And from the primer of the wood
I spell that life and love are good,
I learn to read.

Leonora Speyer

The Book of Books

Within this ample volume lies
The mystery of mysteries.
Happiest they of human race
To whom their God has given grace
To read, to fear, to hope, to pray,
To lift the latch, to force the way;
But better had they ne'er been born
That read to doubt or read to scorn.

Sir Walter Scott

Cling to Faith

Cleave ever to the sunnier side of doubt,
And cling to faith beyond the forms of faith;
She reels not at the storm of warring words;
She brightens at the clash of " Yes " and " No ";
She sees the best that glimmers through the worst;
She feels the sun is hid but for the night;
She spies the summer through the winter bud;
She tastes the fruit before the blossom falls;
She hears the lark within the songless egg;
She finds the fountain where they wailed " Mirage! "

Alfred Tennyson

The Stimulus of Friendship

Because of your firm faith, I kept the track
Whose sharp set stones my strength had almost spent —
I could not meet your eyes, if I turned back,
　　　So on I went.

Because of your strong love, I held my path
When battered, worn and bleeding in the fight —
How could I meet your true eyes, blazing wrath?
　　　So I kept right.

Author Unknown

Live Each Day

Wouldst thou fashion for thyself a seemly life?
Then do not fret over what is past and gone;
　And spite of all thou may'st have left behind
Live each day as if thy life were just begun.

J. W. von Goethe

From Divina Commedia

Oft have I seen at some cathedral door
A laborer, pausing in the dust and heat,
Lay down his burden, and with reverent feet
Enter, and cross himself, and on the floor
Kneel to repeat his paternoster o'er;
Far off the noises of the world retreat;
The loud vociferations of the street
Become an undistinguishable roar.
So, as I enter here from day to day,
And leave my burden at this minster gate,

Kneeling in prayer, and not ashamed to pray,
The tumult of the time disconsolate
To inarticulate murmurs dies away,
While the eternal ages watch and wait.
                    Henry Wadsworth Longfellow

From Life

Our share of night to bear,
    Our share of morning,
Our blank in bliss to fill,
    Our blank in scorning.

Here a star, and there a star,
    Some lost their way.
Here a mist, and there a mist,
    Afterwards — day!
                    Emily Dickinson

If Still They Live

If still they live, whom touch nor sight
    Nor any subtlest sense can prove,
Though dwelling past our day and night,
    At farthest star's remove —

Oh, not because these skies they change
    For upper deeps of sky unknown,
Shall that which made them ours grow strange,
    For spirit holds its own;

Whether it pace this earth around,
    Or cross, with printless, buoyant feet,
The unreverberant Profound
    That hath no name nor mete!   *Edith M. Thomas*

Despised and Rejected

Homeless!
The Living Bread
Hungered
While all beside were fed.
To their warm holes the foxes ran,
Birds flew to nest when the west was red,
But the Son of Man
Had not where to lay His head.

Open Door
Henceforth for all
Hungers,
Hearth and Banquet Hall
For hurt and loneliness is He
Thrust from Nazareth to roam
Vagabond of Galilee,
Who is every outcast's Home.

Katharine Lee Bates

Test

Not those elate upon the mountain height
Of his transfiguration, who declare
Their will to rear crude tabernacles there,
Are worthy liegemen in the Master's sight.
True ministers of grace are those who dare
Descend with him into the irksome night
Below, where blind souls whimper for the light,
And tortured bodies wait their healing care.

Not weary sleepers in Gethsemane,
Who wake to flee from sin's pursuing host,

Then go a-fishing back to Galilee —
But those who labor though the cause seem lost,
To spread abroad the flames of Pentecost,
Shall find in Christ — peace, after victory.

Helen Pursell Roads

In the Way of Peace

Jesus, whose love rekindles dying fires
    Flickering to ashes in our aching hearts,
Be Thou the goal of all our best desires,
    The dawn from which our longing ne'er departs.

When night's grim loneliness throbs like a wound,
    And day's bright sunshine stabs us like a sword,
Us, with thy peace, like traveler's cloak, around,
    Enfold as we go forward, O our Lord.

Through the sharp thorns that lie along our way
    Make thou a path for tired and bleeding feet;
And bring us to the wonder of that day
    When Love and Memory in Thee shall meet.

Lauchlan MacLean Watt

Fishers

Tangled in nets
Of our wild philosophy,
Caught in the backlash
Of ideas ill-cast,
Heaving the lead
Into unplumbed infinity,
Baffled, we stand

Beside the shore at last.
Snagged barbs, snarled lines,
Torn sails!   What fishers we!
Teach us thy skill
O Man of Galilee.

Albert Reginald Gold

The Master Blacksmith

He beats us out upon the anvil of the days
And tempers us in strange and secret ways.
He heats us in the passions and the joys
And happiness of life — such fire employs;
Then cools us in the sorrow and the pain —
Heats us, and cools — then cools us once again;
Till, if the iron be good, He makes us men,
Or if the iron be poor, He scraps us then
Perchance to try again another day
To temper in some surer, sterner way.

Arnold Andrews

A Prayer

Dear God, the light is come, our outgrown creeds
Drop from us as a garment, and our sight
Grows clear to see ourselves and Thee aright;
We trust our love to meet our utmost needs,
And know Thy hand sustains us. The foul breeds
Of nameless doubts and fears that thronged the night
Like phantoms disappear in Truth's clear light;
Self only, now our upward way impedes:
For Thou hast given new bottles for Truth's wine: —
Hast given a larger faith to help us live

A larger life; new knowledge that will give
A lamp to lead us on to the divine:
And though our feet may falter in the way,
Yet shall our eyes behold Love's Perfect Day!

Author Unknown

What If

What if we carved truth in the graveyards?
Would the dead arise
And push up the stones defaming their bones,
And in pained surprise
Demand we explain why their peace was undone
. . . But the dead may sleep — our conventions hold
That naught but good of their lives be told.

What if we wrote truth in the press?
Would the public read
If we should sometime delete all the crime?
Would headlines recede
If life, sound, unspoiled, were the news broadcast?
As a people do we a press maintain
For national good or for personal gain?

What if we preached truth in the pulpit?
Would the theme be fresh?
Would the world crowd in as it flocked to him
Who was God made flesh?
Would they know the truth, that it makes them free?
. . . Would the church be aggrieved as on that day
When Christ years ago pointed out the way?

What if we chose truth as our lodestar?
Could we find the way?
Is the truth for you just what I must do?

Could we spend our day
In blazing the road for timorous feet,
Through loneliness, scorn and personal loss?
There was One who did — he died on the cross.

Gertrude B. Gunderson

Building

Upon the wreckage of thy yesterday
Design thy structure of tomorrow. Lay
Strong corner-stones of purpose, and prepare
Great blocks of wisdom cut from past despair.
Shape mighty pillars of resolve, to set
Deep in the tear-wet mortar of regret.
Believe in God — in thine own self believe,
All thou hast hoped for thou shalt yet achieve.

Ella Wheeler Wilcox

True Brotherhood

God, what a world, if men in street and mart
Felt that same kinship of the human heart
Which makes them, in the face of fire and flood,
Rise to the meaning of True Brotherhood.

Ella Wheeler Wilcox

The Search

No one could tell me where my soul might be;
I searched for God, and He eluded me;
I sought my brother out, and found all three.

Ernest Crosby

The Bible of the Race

Slowly the Bible of the race is writ,
And not on paper leaves, or leaves of stone.
Each age, each kindred, adds a verse to it,
Texts of despair or hope, of joy or moan.
While rolls the sea, while mists the mountain shroud,
While thunder's surges burst on cliffs of cloud,
Still at the prophet's feet the nations sit.

James Russell Lowell

Duty

I slept, and dreamed that life was Beauty;
I woke, and found that life was Duty.
Was thy dream then a shadowy lie?
Toil on, poor heart, unceasingly;
And thou shalt find thy dream to be
A truth and noonday light to thee.

Ellen Sturgis Hooper

Live and Help Live

" Live and let live! " was the call of the Old —
The call of the world when the world was cold —
The call of men when they pulled apart —
The call of the race with a chill on the heart.
But " Live and help live! " is the cry of the New —
The cry of the world with the Dream shining through —
The cry of the Brother World rising to birth —
The cry of the Christ for a Comrade-like earth.

Edwin Markham

The Soul of Jesus Is Restless

The soul of Jesus is restless today;
Christ is tramping through the spirit-world,
Compassion in his heart for the fainting millions;
He trudges through China, through Poland,
Through Russia, Austria, Germany, Armenia;
Patiently he pleads with the Church,
Tenderly he woos her.
The wounds of his body are bleeding afresh for the sorrows
    of his shepherdless people.
We besiege him with selfish petitions,
We weary him with our petty ambitions,
From the needy we bury him in piles of carven stone,
We obscure him in the smoke of stuffy incense,
We drown his voice with the snarls and shrieks of our dis-
    gruntled bickerings,
We build temples to him with hands that are bloody,
We deny him in the needs and sorrows of the exploited " least
    of his brethren."
The soul of Jesus is restless today,
But eternally undismayed.

Cyprus R. Mitchell

The Whole Duty of Man

To love our God with all our strength and will;
To covet nothing, to devise no ill
Against our neighbors; to procure or do
Nothing to others which we would not do
Our very selves; not to revenge our wrong;
To be content with little; not to long
For wealth and greatness; to despise or jeer
No man, and, if we be despised, to bear;

To feed the hungry; to hold fast our crown;
To take from others naught; to give our own —
These are his precepts, and alas, in these
What is so hard but faith can do with ease?

Henry Vaughan

Love's Vigil

Love will outwatch the stars, and light the skies
When the last star falls, and the silent dark devours;
God's warrior, he will watch the allotted hours,
And conquer with the look of his sad eyes:
He shakes the kingdom of darkness with his sighs,
His quiet sighs, while all the Infernal Powers
Tremble and pale upon their central towers,
Lest, haply, his bright universe arise.

All will be well if we have strength to wait
Till his lost Pleiad, white and silver-shod,
Regains her place to make the perfect Seven;
Then all the worlds will know that Love is Fate —
That somehow he is greater even than Heaven —
That in the Cosmic Council he is God.

Edwin Markham

Forgive

Forgive, O Lord, our severing ways,
The rival altars that we raise,
The wrangling tongues that mar thy praise!

Thy grace impart! In time to be
Shall one great temple rise to Thee —
Thy Church our broad humanity.

White flowers of love its walls shall climb,
Soft bells of peace shall ring its chime,
Its days shall all be holy time.

A sweeter song shall then be heard,
Confessing, in a world's accord,
The inward Christ, the living Word.

That song shall swell from shore to shore.
One hope, one faith, one love restore
The seamless robe that Jesus wore.

John Greenleaf Whittier

Gardens

Go make thy garden fair as thou canst,
   Thou workest never alone;
Perhaps he whose plot is next to thine
   May see it and mend his own.

Author Unknown

Revelation

I made a pilgrimage to find the God:
I listened for His voice at holy tombs,
Searched for the print of His immortal feet
In dust of broken altars: yet turned back
With empty heart. But on the homeward road
A great light came upon me, and I heard
The God's voice singing in a nestling lark;
Felt His sweet wonder in a swaying rose;
Received His blessing from a wayside well;
Looked on His beauty in a lover's face;
Saw His bright hand send signals from the suns.

Edwin Markham

Faith to Each Other

Taught by no priest, but by our beating hearts:
Faith to each other; the fidelity
Of men whose pulse leaps with kindred fire,
Who in the flash of eyes, the clasp of hands,
Nay, in the silent bodily presence, feel
The mystic stirrings of a common life
That makes the many one.

Author Unknown

The Universal Language

The wise men ask, " What language did Christ speak? "
They cavil, argue, search, and little prove,
O Sages, leave your Syriac and your Greek!
Christ spoke the universal language — LOVE.

Ella Wheeler Wilcox

The Poet's Simple Faith

You say, " Where goest Thou? " I cannot tell,
And still go on. But if the way be straight
I cannot go amiss: before me lies
Dawn and the day: the night behind me: that
Suffices me: I break the bounds: I see,
And nothing more; believe and nothing less.
My future is not one of my concerns.

Victor Hugo
Trans. by Edward Dowden

We Live by Faith

We live by faith; but faith is not the slave
Of text and legend. Reason's voice and God's;
Nature's and Duty's, never are at odds.
What asks our Father of His children, save
Justice, mercy and humility,
A reasonable service of good deeds,
Pure living, tenderness to human needs,
Reverence and trust, and prayer for light to see
The Master's footprints in our daily ways.

John Greenleaf Whittier

I am the Door

A traveler once, when skies were rose and gold
With Syrian sunset, paused beside the fold
Where an Arabian shepherd housed his flock,
Only a circling wall of rough, grey rock —
No door, no gate, but just an opening wide
Enough for snowy, huddling sheep to come inside.
" So," questioned he, " then no wild beasts you dread? "
" Ah, yes, the wolf is near," the shepherd said.
" But " — strange and sweet the words Divine of yore
Fell on his startled ear: " *I am the door!*
When skies are sown with stars, and I may trace
The velvet shadows in this narrow space,
I lay me down. No silly sheep may go
Without the fold but I, the shepherd, know.
Nor need my cherished flock close-sheltered, warm,
Fear ravening wolf, save o'er my prostrate form."
O word of Christ — illumined evermore
For us his timid sheep — " I am the *door!* "

Author Unknown

A Voice

The Father too, does He not see and hear?
And seems He far who dwells so very near?
Fear not, my child, there is no need to fear.

The days may darken and the tempest lower;
Their power is nothing to the Father's power;
Lift up thy heart and watch with me this hour.

The Shepherd loves and seeks the straying sheep;
Them that are His He must forever keep;
Oh dry thine eyes, there is no need to weep.

Though night falls round Him and cold rains are blown,
And bleak the hills, He searches still alone,
And search He must until He find His own.
Samuel Valentine Cole

Jesus Christ — And We

Christ has no hands but our hands
    To do his work today;
He has no feet but our feet
    To lead men in his way;
He has no tongue but our tongues
    To tell men how he died;
He has no help but our help
    To bring them to his side.

We are the only Bible
    The careless world will read;
We are the sinner's gospel,
    We are the scoffer's creed;

We are the Lord's last message
  Given in deed and word —
What if the line is crooked?
  What if the type is blurred?

What if our hands are busy
  With other work than his?
What if our feet are walking
  Where sin's allurement is?
What if our tongues are speaking
  Of things his lips would spurn?
How can we hope to help him
  Unless from him we learn?

Annie Johnson Flint

A Prayer for Love

God, give me love! I do not only pray
  That perfect love may be bestowed on me;
  But let me feel the lovability
Of every soul I meet along the way.
Though it be hidden from the light of day
  And every eye but Love's, Oh! I would see
  My brother in the monarch and the bee —
In every spirit clothed in mortal clay!

Give me the gift of loving! I will claim
  No other blessing from the Lord of Birth,
For he who loves needs no high-sounding name,
  Nor power nor treasure to proclaim his worth;
His soul has lit at Life's immortal flame
  A lamp that may illumine all the earth.

Elsa Barker

For Us

If we have not learned that God's in man,
   And man in God again,
That to love thy God is to love thy brother,
And to serve thy Lord is to serve each other —
   Then Christ was born in vain!

If we have not learned that one man's life
   In all men lives again;
That each man's battle, fought alone,
Is won or lost for everyone —
   Then Christ hath lived in vain!

If we have not learned that death's no break
   In life's unceasing chain,
That the work in one life well begun
In others is finished, by others is done —
   Then Christ hath died in vain!

If we have not learned of immortal life,
   And a future free from pain,
The Kingdom of God in the heart of man,
And the living world on heaven's plan —
   Then Christ arose in vain!

Charlotte Perkins Gilman

A Hymn of Unity

We come, we come, we come
   O'er mountain, plain and sea,
Whose feet have trod the ways of God,
   We come to thee,
With one accord
   To sing one faith for life and death,
One hope, one Lord.

But not alone we come,
　The valiant ones we boast,
The saints who pray for us today,
　A glorious host;
With one accord
　We cry with these from bended knees
To thee our Lord.

From clamorous strife we come,
　From fearing rivalries,
To sue thy grace for all our ways,
　Thy healing peace;
With one accord
　From many lands we raise our hands
To thee our Lord.

One brotherhood we come,
　Our glory in one Name,
One cross our sign, one love divine
　Our hearts to inflame;
With one accord
　We sing one faith in life and death,
One hope, one Lord.

Robert Freeman

The Bible

When I am tired, the Bible is my bed;
Or in the dark, the Bible is my light;
When I am hungry, it is vital bread;
Or fearful, it is armor for the fight.
When I am sick, 'tis healing medicine;
Or lonely, thronging friends I find therein.

If I would work, the Bible is my tool;
Or play, it is a harp of happy sound.

If I am ignorant, it is my school;
If I am sinking, it is solid ground.
If I am cold, the Bible is my fire;
And wings, if boldly I aspire.

Should I be lost, the Bible is my guide;
Or naked, it is raiment, rich and warm.
Am I imprisoned, it is ranges wide;
Or tempest-tossed, a shelter from the storm.
Would I adventure, 'tis a gallant sea;
Or would I rest, it is a flowery lea.

Does gloom oppress?   The Bible is a sun.
Or ugliness?   It is a garden fair.

Author Unknown

God's Dream

" The man's a dreamer! "   Good!   That places him
   In close relationship with God.   For down
   In the most wretched quarter of town
God stands and dreams *His* dream; amid the grim,
Ensanguined battle wreckage; in the dim,
   Cold twilights where old superstitions frown;
   And where the mutterings of race hatred drown
The sacred cadences of Love's fond hymn.

Today I met him on an uptown street
Calling for dreamers, — pleading in the heat
   Of holy passion for more dream-swept hearts
   To hold in all the world's discordant parts
The Torch of Brotherhood, that its Love-gleam
Might speed the progress of His gracious Dream!

William Norris Burr

A Prayer

I would, dear Jesus, I could break
The hedge that creeds and hearsay make,
And, like the first disciples, be
In person led and taught by thee.

I read thy words, so strong and sweet;
I seek the footprints of thy feet;
But men so mystify the trace
I long to see thee face to face.

Wouldst thou not let me at thy side
In thee, in thee, so sure confide?
Like John, upon thy breast recline
And feel thy heart make mine divine.

John D. Long

The Quest

For years I sought the Many in the One,
   I thought to find lost waves and broken rays,
The rainbow's faded colors in the sun,
   The dawns and twilights of forgotten days.

But now I seek the One in every form,
   Scorning no vision that a dewdrop holds,
The gentle Light that shines behind the storm,
   The Dream that many a twilight hour enfolds.

Eva Gore-Booth

By One Great Heart

By one great Heart the Universe is stirred;
  By its strong pulse stars climb the darkening blue;
  It throbs in each fresh sunset's changing hue,
And thrills through low sweet song of every bird;

By It, the plunging blood reds all men's veins;
  Joy feels that heart against his rapturous own,
  And on It Sorrow breathes her sharpest groan:
It bounds through gladness and the deepest pains.

Passionless beating through all Time and Space,
  Relentless, calm, majestic in Its march,
  Alike, though Nature shake heaven's endless arch,
Or man's heart break, because of some dead face!

'Tis felt in sunshine, greening the soft sod,
  In children's smiling, as in mothers' tears:
  And, for strange comfort, through the aching years,
Men's hungry souls have named the great Heart, God!
                                    Margaret Deland

A Prayer

God of the Granite and the Rose!
  Soul of the Sparrow and the Bee!
The mighty tide of Being flows
  Through countless channels, Lord, from Thee.
It leaps to life in grass and flower,
  Through every grade of being runs,
Till from Creation's radiant tower
  Thy glory flames in stars and suns.

God of the Granite and the Rose!
   Soul of the Sparrow and the Bee!
The mighty tide of Being flows
   Through all Thy creatures back to Thee.
Thus round and round the circle runs,
   A mighty sea without a shore,
While men and women, stars and suns,
   Unite to praise Thee evermore.

Lizzie Doten

Flower in the Cranned Wall

Flower in the crannied wall,
I pluck you out of the crannies,
I hold you here, root and all, in my hand,
Little flower — but if I could understand
What you are, root and all, and all in all,
I should know what God and man is.

Alfred Tennyson

Preparedness

For all your days prepare,
   And meet them ever alike:
When you are the anvil, bear —
   When you are the hammer, strike.

Edwin Markham

Jesus

Jesus, whose lot with us was cast,
Who saw it out, from first to last:
Patient and fearless, tender, true,
Carpenter, vagabond, felon, Jew:

Whose humorous eye took in each phase
Of full, rich life this world displays,
Yet evermore kept fast in view
The far-off goal it leads us to:
Who, as your hour neared, did not fail —
The world's fate trembling in the scale —
With your half-hearted band to dine,
And chat across the bread and wine:
Then went out firm to face the end,
Alone, without a single friend:
Who felt, as your last words confessed,
Wrung from a proud unflinching breast
By hours of dull ignoble pain,
Your whole life's fight was fought in vain:
Would I could win and keep and feel
That heart of love, that spirit of steel.

Author Unknown

The Testing

When, in the dim beginning of the years,
God mixed in man the raptures and the tears,
And scattered through his brain the starry stuff,
He said, " Behold! Yet this is not enough,
For I must test his spirit to make sure
That he can dare the vision and endure.

" I will withdraw My face,
Veil Me in shadow for a certain space,
And leave behind only a broken clue,
A crevice where the glory glimmers through,
Some whisper from the sky,
Some footprint in the road to track Me by.

" I will leave man to make the fateful guess,
Will leave him torn between the no and yes,

Leave him unresting till he rests in Me,
Drawn upward by the choice that makes him free —
Leave him in tragic loneliness to choose,
With all in life to win or all to lose."

Edwin Markham

A Hymn for the New Age

O Master of the modern day,
    Our hearts are kindled as we know
Thou walkest still along life's way
    As in the ages long ago!
And by the magic of Thy will
New worlds Thou art creating still.

We thank Thee that the truth moves on
    With wireless wave and healing ray;
That yester's noon was but the dawn
    Of brighter glories in our day.
And now by faith, in holy dream
We glimpse tomorrow's grander gleam.

We thank Thee that thou rulest still
    This goodly orb on which we dwell —
That Thou dost still reveal Thy will
    To those who would the dark dispel —
That upward o'er the peaks of time
Thy plan unfolds in form sublime.

Help us to keep Thee as our guest
    While speeding o'er the highways grand,
Or cleave the air at Thy behest
    To give some soul a helping hand!
Thy tireless Spirit leads the way
To heal the woes that throng our day!

Enlarge our minds to grasp Thy thought,
  Enlarge our hearts to work Thy plan,
Assured Thy purpose faileth not
  To put Thy spirit into man!
God of the present age and hour,
Thrill us anew with holy power!

William Steward Gordon

Thy Neighbor

Who is thy neighbor? He whom thou
  Hast power to aid or bless;
Whose aching heart or burning brow
  Thy soothing hand may press.

Thy neighbor? 'Tis the fainting poor
  Whose eye with want is dim;
Oh, enter thou his humble door
  With aid and peace for him.

Thy neighbor? He who drinks the cup
  When sorrow drowns the brim;
With words of high sustaining hope
  Go thou and comfort him.

Thy neighbor? 'Tis the weary slave,
  Fettered in mind and limb;
He hath no hope this side the grave;
  Go thou and ransom him.

Thy neighbor? Pass no mourner by;
  Perhaps thou canst redeem
A breaking heart from misery;
  Go share thy lot with him.

Author Unknown

" For God So Loved the World "

" For God so loved the world " — nor you, nor me,
    Nor any favored few;
Nor any numbers, if but numbers be
    The world within our view.

Who loves the rose may find each petal fair,
    And count them one by one,
Yet is the total life and beauty there
    A something not undone.

Who builds a house builds more than wood on wood,
    Builds more than room with room;
Nor day by day can tell the total mood,
    The hearth's consummate bloom.

No wind-blown sand hill of dissevered souls,
    No riven mine, or thine,
This world that with the cosmic rhythm rolls,
    This unity divine.

Nor any fragmentary love enfolds
    One sprout of life unfurled;
But all with all in one communion holds,
    For God so loved — the world.

                                    Robert Whitaker

Prayer

I asked for bread; God gave a stone instead.
Yet, while I pillowed there my weary head,
The angels made a ladder of my dreams,
Which upward to celestial mountains led.

And when I woke beneath the morning's beams,
Around my resting place fresh manna lay;
And, praising God, I went upon my way.
    For I was fed.

God answers prayer; sometimes, when hearts are weak,
He gives the very gifts believers seek.
But often faith must learn a deeper rest,
And trust God's silence when He does not speak;
For He whose name is Love will send the best.
Stars may burn out, nor mountain walls endure,
But God is true, His promises are sure
    For those who seek.

Author Unknown

The Christ of Common Folks

I love the name of Christ the Lord, the Man of Galilee,
Because he came to live and toil among the likes of me.
Let others sing the praises of a mighty King of kings;
I love the Christ of common folks, the Lord of common
    things.

The beggars and the feeble ones, the poor and sick and blind,
The wayward and the tempted ones, were those he loved to
    find;
He lived with them to help them like a brother and a friend,
Or like some wandering workman finding things to mend.

I know my Lord is still my kind of folks to this good day;
I know because he never fails to hear me when I pray.
He loves the people that he finds in narrow dingy streets,
And brings a word of comfort to the weary one he meets.

My job is just a poor man's job, my home is just a shack,
But on my humble residence he has never turned his back.
Let others sing their praises to a mighty King of kings;
I love the Christ of common folks, the Lord of common
    things.

George T. Liddell

Seeking

Where the sun shines in the street
There are very many feet
Seeking God, all unaware
That their hastening is a prayer.
Perhaps these feet would deem it odd
(Who think they are on business bent)
If someone went
And told them, " You are seeking God."

Mary Carolyn Davies

Specula

When He appoints thee, go thou forth —
    It matters not
If south or north,
    Bleak waste or sunny plot.
Nor think, if haply He thou seek'st be late,
    He does thee wrong.
To stile or gate
    Lean thou thy head, and long!
It may be that to spy thee He is mounting
    Upon a tower,
Or in thy counting
    Thou hast mista'en the hour.

But, if He comes not, neither do thou go
   Till Vesper chime,
Belike thou then shalt know
   He hath been with thee all the time.
          Thomas Edward Brown

Quit You Like Men

Quit you like men, be strong;
  There's a burden to bear,
  There's a grief to share,
  There's a heart that breaks 'neath a load of care —
But fare ye forth with a song.

Quit you like men, be strong;
  There's a battle to fight,
  There's a wrong to right,
  There's a God who blesses the good with might —
So fare ye forth with a song.

Quit you like men, be strong;
  There's a work to do,
  There's a world to make new,
  There's a call for men who are brave and true —
On! on with the song!

Quit you like men, be strong;
  There's a year of grace,
  There's a God to face,
  There's another heat in the great world race —
Speed! speed with a song!
          William Herbert Hudnut

I Have a Rendezvous With Life

I have a rendezvous with Life,
In days I hope will come,
Ere youth has sped, and strength of mind,
Ere voices sweet grow dumb.
I have a rendezvous with Life,
When Spring's first heralds hum.
Sure some would cry it's better far
To crown their days with sleep
Than face the road, the wind and rain,
To heed the calling deep.
Though wet nor blow nor space I fear,
Yet fear I deeply, too,
Lest Death should meet and claim me ere
I keep Life's rendezvous.

Countee Cullen

How Did He Live?

So he died for his faith. That is fine.
    More than most of us do.
But stay. Can you add to that line
    That he lived for it, too?

It is easy to die. Men have died
    For a wish or a whim —
From bravado or passion or pride.
    Was it harder for him?

But to live; every day to live out
    All the truth that he dreamt,
While his friends met his conduct with doubt,
    And the world with contempt.

Was it thus that he plodded ahead,
    Never turning aside?
Then we'll talk of the life that he led.
    Never mind how he died.
                              Ernest Crosby

" Thy Will be Done "

" Thy will be done." Why always bow the head
In anguish when these sacred words are said?
More light than darkness falleth from above;
The will of God shows clearest through His love.

Why should we kneel in fear, as God were foe,
    When unto Him we pray, " Thy will be done " ?
Why learn to " bend and kiss the rod " in woe?
    On just and unjust shines His blessed sun.

" Thy will be done." Is there no other way
Than crying out of sorrow, thus to pray?
God's daily gifts outweigh the heaviest loss;
The crown is ours as surely as the cross.

If aught we know, we know that joy reigns there;
Then let us, as we pray the Christ-taught prayer,
Lift up our hearts in joy at blessings given:
Thy will be done on earth, *as it is done in Heaven.*
                              Louise Peabody Sargent

The Builder

Smoothing a cypress beam
    With a scarred hand,
I saw a carpenter
    In a far land.

Down past the flat roofs
   Poured the white sun;
But still he bent his back,
   The patient one.

And I paused surprised
   In that queer place
To find an old man
   With a haunting face.

"Who art thou, carpenter,
   Of the bowed head;
And what buildest thou?"
   "Heaven," he said.

Willard Wattles

Quiet Work

One lesson, Nature, let me learn from thee,
One lesson which in every wind is blown,
One lesson of two duties kept at one
Though the loud world proclaim their enmity —
Of toil unsevered from tranquillity;
Of labor, that in lasting fruit outgrows
Far noisier schemes, accomplished in repose,
Too great for haste, too high for rivalry.

Yes, while on earth a thousand discords ring,
Man's fitful uproar mingling with his toil,
Still do thy sleepless ministers move on,
Their glorious tasks in silence perfecting;
Still working, blaming still our vain turmoil;
Laborers that shall not fail, when man is gone

Matthew Arnold

The Light of God is Falling

The light of God is falling
  Upon life's common way;
The Master's voice still calling,
  " Come, walk with me today."
No duty can seem lowly
  To him who lives with thee,
And all of life grows holy,
  O Christ of Galilee.

Who shares his life's pure pleasures,
  And walks the honest road,
Who trades with heaping measures,
  And lifts his brother's load,
Who turns the wrong down bluntly,
  And lends the right a hand;
He dwells in God's own country,
  He tills the Holy Land.

Where human lives are thronging
  In toil and pain and sin,
While cloistered hearts are longing
  To bring the Kingdom in,
O Christ, the Elder Brother
  Of proud and beaten men,
When they have found each other,
  Thy Kingdom will come then.

Thy ransomed host in glory,
  All souls that sin and pray,
Turn toward the cross that bore thee;
  " Behold the man! " they say:

And while thy Church is pleading
For all who would do good,
We hear thy true voice leading
Our song of brotherhood.

Louis F. Benson

Wanderers

Our feet have wandered from thy path,
    Thou lowly Christ of Galilee,
Sweet prophet of the helping hand,
    Meek Lord of love and sympathy.

Thy faith was but to walk with God
    With humble heart and open mind,
But we have builded shrines of stone
    In which to worship — spirit-blind!

We lift our heads in loveless prayers,
    We glory in our well-wrought creed,
Though righteousness alone avails,
    Though mercy is the only need.

Break down, O Christ, our heartless faiths,
    And give to us that spirit fine
Which feels in thee a Comrade strong,
    In every soul a friend of thine.

Thomas Curtis Clark

Evening Prayer

If I have wounded any soul today,
If I have caused one foot to go astray,
If I have walked in my own willful way —
    Good Lord, forgive!

If I have uttered idle words or vain,
If I have turned aside from want or pain,
Lest I myself should suffer through the strain —
    Good Lord, forgive!

If I have craved for joys that are not mine,
If I have let my wayward heart repine,
Dwelling on things of earth, not things divine —
    Good Lord, forgive!

If I have been perverse, or hard, or cold,
If I have longed for shelter in Thy fold
When Thou hast given me some part to hold —
    Good Lord, forgive!

Forgive the sins I have confessed to Thee,
Forgive the secret sins I do not see,
That which I know not, Father, teach Thou me —
    Help me to live.

                              C. Maud Battersby

Real Presence

Not on an altar shall mine eyes behold Thee;
    Though Thou art sacrifice, Thou too art Priest;
Bend, that the feeble arms of Love enfold Thee,
    So Faith shall bloom, increased.

Not on a Cross, with passion buds around Thee,
    Thorn-crowned and lonely, in Thy suffering;
Nay, but as watching Mary met and found Thee,
    Dawn-robed, the Risen King.

Not in the past, but in the present glorious,
Not in the future, that I cannot span,
Living and breathing, over death victorious,
My God . . . my Brother-Man.

Ivan Adair

Lo, I Am With You Always

Wide fields of corn along the valleys spread;
The rain and dews mature the swelling vine;
I see the Lord in multiplying bread;
I see him turning water into wine;
I see him working all the works divine
He wrought when Salemward his steps were led;
The selfsame miracles around him shine;
He feeds the famished; he revives the dead;
He pours the flood of light on darkened eyes;
He chases tears, diseases, fiends away;
His throne is raised upon these orient skies;
His footstool is the pave whereon we pray.
Ah, tell me not of Christ in Paradise,
For he is all around us here today.

John Charles Earle

A Creed

In fellowship of living things,
In kindred claims of Man and Beast,
In common courtesy that brings
Help from the greater to the least,
In love that all life shall receive,
Lord, I believe.

In peace, earth's passion far above,
     In pity, measured not nor priced,
In all souls luminous with love,
     Alike in Buddha and in Christ,
In any rights that wrongs retrieve,
     Lord, I believe.

In truth that falsehood cannot span,
     In the majestic march of Laws,
That weed and flower and worm and man
     Result from one Supernal Cause,
In doubts that dare and faiths that cleave,
     Lord, I believe.

Ellen Glasgow

On the Twenty-third Psalm

In " pastures green " ?   Not always; sometimes He
Who knoweth best, in kindness leadeth me
In weary ways, where heavy shadows be.

And by " still waters " ?   No, not always so;
Ofttimes the heavy tempests round me blow,
And o'er my soul the waves and billows go.

But when the storm beats loudest, and I cry
Aloud for help, the Master standeth by,
And whispers to my soul, " Lo, it is I."

So, where He leads me, I can safely go,
And in the blest hereafter I shall know,
Why, in His wisdom, He hath led me so.

Author Unknown

Tomorrow's News

There will be news tomorrow:
    News of sorrow
May be; hard and sharp and cutting:
    Shutting
  Off a breath of sweetness,
    Life's completeness
    Shattering further;
  Clashing hard on one another
Hope and faith: but God will choose
    The wisest news.
If I tonight
  Were given to write,
By my own will, the words to shape
Tomorrow's course, sleep would escape
    Me, and the wings
Of my light heart would be bound. God ordereth things;
    And I but pray:
    Shape Thou my destiny,
    And use me to Thy will.
    Or let me lie quite still
    Within Thy hand. The news
    Will be as God shall choose.

George Klingle

Our Dim Eyes Seek a Beacon

Our dim eyes seek a beacon,
And our weary feet a guide,
And our hearts of all life's mystery
Seek a meaning and a key;

But a cross shines on our pathway,
On it hangs the Crucified,
And he answers all our longings
With the whisper, " Follow Me."

Life is a duty — dare it;
Life is a burden — bear it;
Life is a thorn-crown — wear it;
Though it break thy heart in twain,
Though the burden bear thee down,
Close thy lips and stand the pain,
First the Cross, and then the Crown.

Author Unknown

God Meets Me in the Mountains

God meets me in the mountains when I climb alone and high,
  Above the wrangling sinners and the jangling devotees,
Up where the tapered spruce will guide my glances to the sky
  And canyon walls will mutely preach their mighty homilies
In hush so dense that I can sense — is it my pulses drum-
    ming?
  Or God's light footfall, coming through the silvery aspen
    trees?

Some way I seem to lose him in the jostle of the street,
  But on a twisty deer trail, as I trudge along alone,
A mystic presence in the forest often stays my feet —
  No vision borrowed from a saint, but awesomely my own.
I feel it smite my spirit white, the prophet's taintless passion,
  As ancient as the fashion of the pine tree's rugged cone.

For me no school could give it life, as none can deal it death.
  Up through the pines' red pillars and across the snow and
    shale.

Where science and theology alike are but a breath,
  I follow marks that make the wisest book an idle tale.
Why should I squint at faded print to glimpse his timeworn
    traces?
  God walks the lonely places yet, where men first found his
    trail.

Where pines reach up the mountains and the mountains up
    the blue,
  And, tense with some expectancy, the lifting ledges frown,
The high desire of the hills is my desire too,
  For there my spirit laughs to fling its worldly duffle down
And, shaking free exultantly, calls to its great companion!
  God meets me in the canyon when I miss him in the town.
                           Badger Clark

Life's Illusion

He toiled and saved his earnings every day,
  But starved his mind, and grasped at common things;
His prisoned soul ne'er struggled out of clay,
  His better nature never found its wings.

He hoped to sit with Happiness at last,
  Mansioned, sufficient, when he would be old;
But he was just a graveyard! and the past
  Left naught for him but a rude pile of gold.
                    Alexander Louis Fraser

Our Christ

In Christ I feel the heart of God
  Throbbing from heaven through earth;
Life stirs again within the clod,
  Renewed in beauteous birth;

The soul springs up, a flower of prayer,
Breathing His breath out on the air.

In Christ I touch the hand of God,
    From His pure Height reached down,
By blessed ways before untrod,
    To lift us to our crown;
Victory that only perfect is
Through loving sacrifice, like His.

Holding His hand, my steadied feet
    May walk the air, the seas;
On life and death His smile falls sweet,
    Lights up all mysteries;
Stranger nor exile can I be
In new worlds where He leadeth me.

Lucy Larcom

Gethsemane

There is a way which man hath trod
For lo, these thronging, countless years;
It is the way of life, of God;
It is the way of night, of tears;
Its winding we may not foresee;
It is the way — Gethsemane.

It is the way whereby we know
Life's larger meanings and its claims,
The fellowship of human woe,
Our partnership with others' pains.
It is the way which seems to be
Life's only way — Gethsemane.

Charles Russell Wakeley

The Passion Flower

Thou lowly, meek and lovely flower,
But yesterday, at evening's hour,
As trudged I upward with my load,
I saw thee blooming by the road,
And stayed my steps to wonder there
That beauty so supremely fair
Should waste its loveliness on me —
Even as the Flower of Calvary!

Charles G. Blanden

The Welcome

God spreads a carpet soft and green
    O'er which we pass;
A thick-piled mat of jeweled sheen —
    And that is Grass.

Delightful music woos the ear;
    The grass is stirred
Down to the heart of every spear —
    Ah, that's a Bird.

Clouds roll before a blue immense
    That stretches high
And lends the soul exalted sense —
    That scroll's a Sky.

Green rollers flaunt their sparkling crests;
    Their jubilee
Extols brave Captains and their quests —
    And that is Sea.

New-leaping grass, the feathery flute,
  The sapphire ring,
The sea's full-voiced, profound salute —
  Ah, that is Spring!

                              Arthur Powell

Judean Hills Are Holy

Judean hills are holy,
  Judean fields are fair,
For one can find the footprints
  Of Jesus everywhere.

One finds them in the twilight
  Beneath the singing sky,
Where shepherds watch in wonder
  White planets wheeling by.

His trails are on the hillsides
  And down the dales and deeps;
He walks the high horizons
  Where vesper silence sleeps.

He haunts the lowly highways
  Where human hopes have trod
The Via Dolorosa
  Up to the heart of God.

He looms, a lonely figure,
  Along the fringe of night,
As lonely as a cedar
  Against the lonely light.

Judean hills are holy,
Judean hills are fair,
For one can find the footprints
Of Jesus everywhere.

William L. Stidger

Bread and Roses

(In a parade of the strikers of Lawrence, Mass., some young girls carried a banner inscribed, " We want Bread, and Roses too! ")

As we come marching, marching, in the beauty of the day,
A million darkened kitchens, a thousand mill-lofts gray
Are touched with all the radiance that a sudden sun dis-
closes,
For the people hear us singing, " Bread and Roses, Bread
and Roses."

As we come marching, marching, we battle, too, for men —
For they are women's children and we mother them again.
Our lives shall not be sweated from birth until life closes —
Hearts starve as well as bodies: Give us Bread, but give us
Roses!

As we come marching, marching, unnumbered women dead
Go crying through our singing their ancient song of Bread;
Small art and love and beauty their drudging spirits knew —
Yet, it is bread we fight for — but we fight for Roses, too.

As we come marching, marching, we bring the Greater
Days —
The rising of the women means the rising of the race —

No more the drudge and idler — ten that toil where one re-
  poses —
But a sharing of life's glories: Bread and Roses, Bread and
  Roses!

James Oppenheim

Crusaders

They have taken the tomb of our Comrade Christ —
  Infidel hordes that believe not in Man;
Stable and stall for his birth sufficed,
  But his tomb is built on a kingly plan.
They have hedged him round with pomp and parade,
  They have buried him deep under steel and stone —
But we come leading the great Crusade
  To give our Comrade back to his own.

Elizabeth Waddell

Reminder

Each star that rises and doth fade,
Each bird that sings its song and sleeps,
Each spark of spirit fire that leaps
Within me — of One Flame are made!

John Galsworthy

If He Should Come

If Jesus should tramp the streets tonight,
  Storm-beaten and hungry for bread,
Seeking a room and a candle light
  And a clean though humble bed,

Who would welcome the Workman in,
  Though he came with panting breath,
His hands all bruised and his garments thin —
  This Workman from Nazareth?

Would rich folk hurry to bind his bruise
  And shelter his stricken form?
Would they take God in with his muddy shoes
  Out of the pitiless storm?
Are they not too busy wreathing their flowers
  Or heaping their golden store —
Too busy chasing the bubble hours
  For the poor man's God at the door?

And if he should come where churchmen bow,
  Forgetting the greater sin,
Would he pause with a light on his wounded brow,
  Would he turn and enter in?
And what would he think of their creeds so dim,
  Of their weak, uplifted hands,
Of their selfish prayers going up to him
  Out of a thousand lands?

Edwin Markham

Immanence

And canst thou find God in the crystal sphere
Which hangs from every grass blade in the dawn?
And dost thou find the Infinite more near
When breath of summer bows the waving corn?
And has the formless deep of night no soul?
Is it mere chaos — or a God-filled whole?
Is silence nothing more than sign of death,
Or dull restraint of life's activity?

Canst thou not feel o'er all the Spirit's breath —
That sure disproof of our mortality?
And does the cosmic vast appal thy sense,
Or canst thou smile to see God's immanence?

F. Barrie Flint

The Modern Saint

He looks not holy; simple in his belief;
His creed for mystic visions do not scan;
His face has lines cut there by others' grief,
And in his eyes is love of fellow-man.

Not self nor self-salvation is his care;
He yearns to make the world a sunnier clime
To live in; and his mission everywhere
Is strangely like the Christ's in olden time.

No medieval mystery, no crowned
Dim figure, halo-ringed, uncanny bright,
A Modern Saint!   A man who treads earth's ground
And ministers to men with all his might.

Richard Burton

The Unseen World

The spirits of the dead are with us still;
    Part of our being, instinct to our life,
    Familiars light and dark; all space is rife
With influences that mould our plastic will,
Unseen yet felt, unknown yet guessed at, till
    Death plucks away the mask of flesh, or strife
    Of soul wears out the body as a knife
Frets through its sheath then feels a naked thrill.

For nature wars within us with a sense
   Mysterious, conjoined, yet not of her,
Subduing yet subdued; but when the tense
   Bond of their union slackens, then the whirr
Of the soul's wings is heard, our essence soars
Transfigured, lighted from the eternal shores.

                   Craven Langstroth Betts

The Debt

Because the years are few, I must be glad;
Because the silence is so near, I sing;
'Twere ill to quit an inn where I have had
Such bounteous fare, nor pay my reckoning.
I would not, from some gleaming parapet
Of Sirius or Vega, bend my gaze
On a remembered sparkle and regret
That from it thanklessly I went my ways
Up through the starry colonnades, nor found
Violets in any Paradise more blue
Than those that blossomed on my own waste ground,
Nor vespers sweeter than the robins knew.

Though Earth be but an outpost of delight,
Heaven's wild frontier by tragedy beset,
Only a Shakespeare may her gifts requite,
Only a happy Raphael pay his debt.
Yet I — to whom even as to those are given
Cascading foam, emblazoned butterflies,
The moon's pearl chariot through the massed clouds driven,
And the divinity of loving eyes —
Would make my peace now with mine hostess Earth,
Give and take pardon for all brief annoy,
And toss her, far beneath my lodging's worth,
Poor that I am, a coin of golden joy.

                   Katharine Lee Bates

Alone God Sufficeth

Let nothing disturb thee,
Nothing affright thee;
All things are passing;
God never changeth;
Patient endurance
Attaineth to all things;
Who God possesseth
In nothing is wanting;
Alone God sufficeth.

Henry Wadsworth Longfellow

Translations from " Saint Teresa "

Evolution

Out of the dusk a shadow,
    Then, a spark;
Out of the cloud a silence,
    Then, a lark;
Out of the heart a rapture,
    Then a pain;
Out of the dead, cold ashes,
    Life again.

John Bannister Tabb

POEMS

FOR THE GREAT DAYS

OF THE YEAR

The New Year

I am the New Year, and I come to you pure and unstained,
Fresh from the hand of God.
Each day, a precious pearl to you is given
That you must string upon the silver thread of Life.
Once strung can never be unthreaded but stays
An undying record of your faith and skill.
Each golden, minute link you then must weld into the chain
    of hours
That is no stronger than its weakest link.
Into your hands is given all the wealth and power
To make your life just what you will.
I give to you, free and unstinted, twelve glorious months
Of soothing rain and sunshine golden;
The days for work and rest, the nights for peaceful slumber.
All that I have I give with love unspoken.
All that I ask — *you keep the faith unbroken!*

J. D. Templeton

The Old Year

What is the Old Year? 'Tis a book
On which we backward sadly look,
Not willing quite to see it close,
For leaves of violet and rose
Within its heart are thickly strewn,
Marking love's dawn and golden noon;

207

And turned-down pages, noting days
Dimly recalled through Memory's haze;
And tear-stained pages, too, that tell
Of starless nights and mournful knell
Of bells tolling through trouble's air
The De Profundis of despair —
The laugh, the tear, the shine, the shade,
All 'twixt the covers gently laid;
No uncut leaves; no page unscanned;
Close it and lay it in God's hand.

Clarence Urmy

A New Leaf

He came to my desk with quivering lip —
  The lesson was done.
" Dear Teacher, I want a new leaf," he said,
  " I have spoiled this one."
I took the old leaf, stained and blotted,
And gave him a new one all unspotted,
  And into his sad eyes smiled,
  " Do better, now, my child."

I went to the throne with a quivering soul —
  The old year was done.
" Dear Father, hast Thou a new leaf for me?
  I have spoiled this one."
He took the old leaf, stained and blotted,
And gave me a new one all unspotted,
  And into my sad heart smiled,
  " Do better, now, my child."

Kathleen Wheeler

For the New Year

Are you sheltered, curled up and content by your world's
     warm fire?
  Then I say that your soul is in danger,
The sons of the Light, they are down with God in the mire,
  God in the manger.

So rouse from your perilous ease; to your sword and your
     shield!
  Your ease is the ease of the cattle!
Hark, hark, where the bugles are calling: out to some field —
  Out to some battle.   *Edwin Markham*

To Age

Welcome, old friend!   These many years
    Have we lived door by door;
The Fates have laid aside their shears
    Perhaps for some few more.

    .   .   .   .

Rather what lies before my feet
    My notice shall engage:
He who hath braved Youth's dizzy heat
    Dreads not the frost of age.
                    Walter Savage Landor

The New Year

A Flower unblown: a Book unread:
A Tree with fruit unharvested:
A Path untrod: a House whose rooms
Lack yet the heart's divine perfumes:
This is the Year that for you waits
Beyond Tomorrow's mystic gates.
                    Horatio Nelson Powers

A Way to a Happy New Year

To leave the old with a burst of song,
To recall the right and forgive the wrong;
To forget the thing that binds you fast
To the vain regrets of the year that's past;
To have the strength to let go your hold
Of the not worth while of the days grown old,
To dare go forth with a purpose true,
To the unknown task of the year that's new;
To help your brother along the road
To do his work and lift his load;
To add your gift to the world's good cheer,
Is to have and to give a Happy New Year.

Robert Brewster Beattie

A New Start

I will start anew this morning with a higher, fairer creed;
I will cease to stand complaining of my ruthless neighbor's
    greed;
I will cease to sit repining while my duty's call is clear;
I will waste no moment whining, and my heart shall know
    no fear.

I will look sometimes about me for the things that merit
    praise;
I will search for hidden beauties that elude the grumbler's
    gaze.
I will try to find contentment in the paths that I must tread;
I will cease to have resentment when another moves ahead.

I will not be swayed by envy when my rival's strength is
    shown;
I will not deny his merit, but I'll strive to prove my own;

I will try to see the beauty spread before me, rain or shine;
I will cease to preach your duty, and be more concerned with
    mine.   *Author Unknown*

Ring Out, Wild Bells

Ring out, wild bells, to the wild sky,
The flying cloud, the frosty light:
The year is dying in the night;
Ring out, wild bells, and let him die.

Ring out the old, ring in the new,
Ring, happy bells, across the snow:
The year is going, let him go;
Ring out the false, ring in the true.

Ring out the grief that saps the mind,
For those that here we see no more;
Ring out the feud of rich and poor,
Ring in redress to all mankind.

.   .   .   .

Ring out false pride in place and blood,
The civic slander and the spite;
Ring in the love of truth and right,
Ring in the common love of good.

Ring out old shapes of foul disease;
Ring out the narrowing lust of gold;
Ring out the thousand wars of old,
Ring in the thousand years of peace.

Ring in the valiant man and free,
The larger heart, the kindlier hand;
Ring out the darkness of the land,
Ring in the Christ that is to be.

                                      Alfred Tennyson

The Message of the New Year

I asked the New Year for some message sweet,
Some rule of life with which to guide my feet;
I asked, and paused: he answered soft and low,
    " God's will to know."

" Will knowledge then suffice, New Year? " I cried;
And, ere the question into silence died,
The answer came, " Nay, but remember, too,
    God's will to do."

Once more I asked, " Is there no more to tell? "
And once again the answer sweetly fell,
" Yes! this thing, all other things above:
    God's will to love."

Author Unknown

Gratitude

For sunlit hours and visions clear,
For all remembered faces dear,
For comrades of a single day,
Who sent us stronger on our way,
For friends who shared the year's long road,
And bore with us the common load,
For hours that levied heavy tolls,
But brought us nearer to our goals,
For insights won through toil and tears,
We thank the Keeper of our years.

Clyde McGee

Song

What have the years left us?
  What will they bring?
Life — life's not bereft us:
  Still we can sing.

Time, drop shades around us;
  Death, call us hame;
Say not that you found us
  Sorry we came.

Charles G. Blanden

January

We pause beside this door:
Thy year, O God, how shall we enter in?
The footsteps of a Child
Sound close beside us.   Listen, he will speak!
His birthday bells have hardly rung a week,
Yet has he trod the world's press undefiled.
" Enter through me," he saith, " nor wander more;
For lo!   I am the Door."

Lucy Larcom

The New Year

Standing with folded wings of mystery,
The New Year waits to greet us — you and me.

Her arms are full of gifts; her feet are shod
All fitly for rough roads or velvet sod;
Her eyes are steady with belief in God.

Her voice falls sweetly as a vesper bell
Where trust and hope all lesser notes dispel;
Scarce knowing why, we feel that all is well.

She smiles a little as she turns away,
Breathing a promise for each coming day;
And we — we pause a little while to pray!

Lillian Gard

Live in the Present

Forget the past and live the present hour;
Now is the time to work, the time to fill
The soul with noblest thoughts, the time to will
Heroic deeds, to use whatever dower
Heaven has bestowed, to test our utmost power.

Now is the time to love, and better still,
To serve our loved ones, over passing ill
To rise triumphant; thus the perfect flower
Of life shall come to fruitage; wealth amass
For grandest giving ere the time be gone.

Be glad today, tomorrow may bring tears;
Be brave today, the darkest night will pass,
And golden rays will usher in the dawn;
Who conquers now shall rule the coming years.

Sarah K Bolton

LINCOLN'S BIRTHDAY

The Martyr Chief

Nature, they say, doth dote,
And cannot make a man
Save on some worn-out plan,
Repeating as by rote:
For him her Old-World moulds aside she threw,
And, choosing sweet clay from the breast
Of the unexhausted West,
With stuff untainted shaped a hero new,
Wise, steadfast in the strength of God, and true.

.   .   .   .

His was no lonely mountain-peak of mind,
Thrusting to thin air o'er our cloudy bars,
A seamark now, now lost in vapors blind,
Broad prairie rather, genial, level-lined,
Fruitful and friendly for all human kind.

.   .   .   .

Great captains, with their guns and drums,
Disturb our judgment for the hour,
But at last silence comes:
These are all gone, and, standing like a tower,
Our children shall behold his fame,
The kindly-earnest, brave, foreseeing man,
Sagacious, patient, dreading praise, not blame,
New birth of our new soil, the first American.

James Russell Lowell

From Lincoln, The Man of the People

The color of the ground was in him, the red earth,
The smack and tang of elemental things:
The rectitude and patience of the cliff,
The good-will of the rain that loves all leaves,
The friendly welcome of the wayside well,
The courage of the bird that dares the sea,
The gladness of the wind that shakes the corn,
The pity of the snow that hides all scars,
The secrecy of streams that make their way
Under the mountain to the rifted rock,
The tolerance and equity of light
That gives as freely to the shrinking flower
As to the great oak flaring to the wind —
To the grave's low hill as to the Matterhorn
That shoulders out the sky.

. . . .

So came the Captain with the mighty heart;
And when the judgment thunders split the house,
Wrenching the rafters from their ancient rest,
He held the ridgepole up, and spiked again
The rafters of the Home. He held his place —
Held the long purpose like a growing tree —
Held on through blame and faltered not at praise —
Towering in calm rough-hewn sublimity.
And when he fell in whirlwind, he went down
As when a lordly cedar, green with boughs,
Goes down with a great shout upon the hills,
And leaves a lonesome place against the sky.

Edwin Markham

He Leads Us Still

Dare we despair? Through all the nights and days
Of lagging war he kept his courage true.
Shall doubt befog our eyes? A darker haze
But proved the faith of him who ever knew

That right must conquer. May we cherish hate
For our poor griefs, when never word nor deed
Of rancor, malice, spite of low or great,
In his large soul one poison-drop could breed?

He leads us still! O'er chasms yet unspanned
Our pathway lies; the work is but begun;
But we shall do our part and leave our land
The mightier for noble battles won.
Here truth must triumph, honor must prevail:
The nation Lincoln died for cannot fail!

Arthur Guiterman

On a Bust of Lincoln

This was a man of mighty mould
    Who walked erewhile our earthly ways,
Fashioned as leaders were of old
    In the heroic days!

Mark how austere the rugged height
    Of brow — a will not wrought to bend!
Yet in the eyes behold the light
    That made the foe a friend!

Sagacious he beyond the test
    Of quibbling schools that praise or ban;
Supreme in all the broadest, best,
    We hail American.

When bronze is but as ash to flame,
    And marble but as wind-blown chaff,
Still shall the luster of his name
    Stand as his cenotaph!

Clinton Scollard

Lincoln

Hurt was the nation with a mighty wound,
And all her ways were filled with clam'rous sound.
Wailed loud the South with unremitting grief,
And wept the North that could not find relief.
Then madness joined its harshest tone to strife;
A minor note swelled in the song of life
Till, stirring with the love that filled his breast,
But still unflinching at the right's behest
Grave Lincoln came, strong-handed, from afar —
The mighty Homer of the lyre of war!
'Twas he who bade the raging tempest cease,
Wrenched from his harp the harmony of peace,
Muted the strings that made the discord, Wrong,
And gave his spirit up in thund'rous song.
O mighty Master of the mighty lyre,
Earth heard and trembled at thy strains of fire:
Earth learned of thee what Heav'n already knew,
And wrote thee down among her treasured few!

Paul Lawrence Dunbar

The Eyes of Lincoln

Sad eyes, that were patient and tender,
Sad eyes, that were steadfast and true,
And warm with the unchanging splendor
Of courage no ills could subdue!

Eyes dark with the dread of the morrow,
And woe for the day that was gone,
The sleepless companions of sorrow,
The watchers that witnessed the dawn.

Eyes tired from the clamor and goading,
And dim from the stress of the years,
And hollowed by pain and foreboding,
And strain by repression of tears.

Sad eyes that were wearied and blighted,
By visions of sieges and wars,
Now watch o'er a country united
From the luminous slopes of the stars.

Walt Mason

Lincoln's Gettysburg Address

(November 19, 1863)

Fourscore and seven years ago our fathers brought forth
    upon this continent a new nation,
Conceived in liberty, and dedicated to the proposition that
    all men are created equal.

Now we are engaged in a great civil war, testing whether
    that nation, or any nation, so conceived and so dedi-
    cated, can long endure.
We are met on a great battlefield of that war.
We have come to dedicate a portion of that field as a final
    resting place for those who here gave their lives that
    that nation might live.
It is altogether fitting and proper that we should do this.

But in a larger sense we cannot dedicate, we cannot con-
    secrate, we cannot hallow this ground.
The brave men, living and dead, who struggled here, have
    consecrated it far above our poor power to add or
    detract.

The world will little note nor long remember what we say
   here,
But it can never forget what they did here.

It is for us, the living, rather, to be dedicated here to the
   unfinished work which they who fought here have thus
   far so nobly advanced.
It is rather for us to be here dedicated to the great task
   remaining before us;
That from these honored dead we take increased devotion to
   that cause for which they gave the last full measure of
   devotion;
That we here highly resolve that these dead shall not have
   died in vain;
That this nation, under God, shall have a new birth of free-
   dom;
And that government of the people, by the people, and for the
   people,
Shall not perish from the earth.

O Captain!   My Captain!

O Captain! my Captain! our fearful trip is done;
The ship has weather'd every rack, the prize we sought is
   won;
The port is near, the bells I hear, the people all exulting,
While follow eyes the steady keel, the vessel grim and
   daring:

> But O heart! heart! heart!
>   O the bleeding drops of red,
> Where on the deck my Captain lies,
>   Fallen cold and dead.

O Captain! my Captain! rise up and hear the bells;
Rise up — for you the flag is flung — for you the bugle
trills;
For you bouquets and ribbon'd wreaths — for you the
shores a-crowding;
For you they call, the swaying mass, their eager faces
turning:

Here Captain! dear father!
This arm beneath your head;
It is some dream that on the deck
You've fallen cold and dead.

My Captain does not answer, his lips are pale and still;
My father does not feel my arm, he has no pulse or will;
The ship is anchor'd safe and sound, its voyage closed and
done;
From fearful trip the victor ship comes in with object won:

Exult, O shores, and ring, O bells!
But I, with mournful tread,
Walk the deck my Captain lies,
Fallen cold and dead.

Walt Whitman

The Master

(In Memory of Lincoln)

We need him now — his rugged faith that held
Fast to the rock of Truth through all the days
Of moil and strife, the sleepless nights; upheld
By very God was he — that God who stays

All hero-souls who will but trust in Him,
And trusting, labor as if God were not.
His eyes beheld the stars, clouds could not dim
Their glory; but his task was not forgot:

To keep his people one; to hold them true
To that fair dream their fathers willed to them —
Freedom for all; to spur them; to renew
Their hopes in bitter days; strife to condemn.
Such was his task, and well his work was done —
Who willed us greater tasks, when set his sun.

Thomas Curtis Clark

WASHINGTON'S BIRTHDAY

Washington

Soldier and statesman, rarest unison;
High-poised example of great duties done
Simply as breathing, a world's honors worn
As life's indifferent gifts to all men born;
Dumb for himself, unless it were to God,
But for his barefoot soldier eloquent,
Tramping the snow to coral where they trod,
Held by his awe in hollow-eyed content;
Modest, yet firm as Nature's self; unblamed
Save by the men his nobler temper shamed;
Not honored then or now because he wooed
The popular voice, but that he still withstood;
Broad-minded, higher-souled, there is but one
Who was all this and ours and all men's — Washington.

James Russell Lowell

Washington

Oh, hero of our younger race!
  Great builder of a temple new!
Ruler, who sought no lordly place!
  Warrior who sheathed the sword he drew!

Lover of men, who saw afar
  A world unmarred by want or war,
Who knew the path, and yet forbore
  To tread, till all men should implore;
Who saw the light, and led the way
  Where the gray world might greet the day;

Father and leader, prophet sure,
  Whose will in vast works shall endure,
How shall we praise him on this day of days,
  Great son of fame who has no need of praise?

How shall we praise him? Open wide the doors
  Of the fair temple whose broad base he laid.
Through its white halls a shadowy cavalcade
  Of heroes moves o'er unresounding floors —
Men whose brawned arms upraised these colors high
  And reared the towers that vanish in the sky, —
The strong who, having wrought, can never, never die.

Harriet Monroe

Inscription at Mt. Vernon

Washington, the brave, the wise, the good,
Supreme in war, in council, and in peace.
Valiant without ambition, discreet without fear, confident
  without assumption.

In disaster calm; in success moderate; in all, himself.
The hero, the patriot, the Christian.
The father of nations, the friend of mankind,
Who, when he had won all, renounced all, and sought in the
  bosom of his family and of nature, retirement, and in
  the hope of religion, immortality.

Washington

Long are the years since he fell asleep
  Where the Potomac flows gently by,
There where Mt. Vernon's green stretches sweep
  Under the blue Virginia sky.
Warrior and statesman and patriot true,
  Well had he wielded both sword and pen.
Truly, they said as they laid him to rest,
  " First in the hearts of his countrymen."
Long are the years — and the land he loved
  Stands among nations, grown strong and great;
True to his vision of long ago,
  Proud of the hand that so shaped her fate.
Time but adds splendor to fame so fair,
  Years but test greatness — and now as then
Sleeps he in peace on Mt. Vernon's hill,
  " First in the hearts of his countrymen."

B. Y. Williams

LENT AND EASTER

A Ballad of Trees and the Master

Into the woods my Master went,
Clean forspent, forspent.
Into the woods my Master came,
Forspent with love and shame.
But the olives they were not blind to him,
The thorn-tree had a mind to him
When into the woods he came.

Out of the woods my Master went,
And he was well content.
Out of the woods my Master came,
Content with death and shame.
When Death and Shame would woo him last,
From under the trees they drew him last:
'Twas on a tree they slew him — last
When out of the woods he came.

Sidney Lanier

Judas

They called him King; and I would have no King:
  Let all be equal, ay, let none be best.
  Why should the weakling John be ever pressed
Against his bosom, Peter urged to fling
His clumsy zeal about, while I must bring,
  Forsooth, the bag behind, and feed the rest,
  Never be praised or flattered or caressed,
Although so watchful in my stewarding?

They called him Son of God. In rage I saw
  This vain idolatry. Was I not wise,
  Not honest, not in truth administering
The holy precepts of our sacred law? —
  Oh, God! Those pleading, tender, earnest eyes!
  Oh, God! Oh, God! why did I do this thing?

Gamaliel Bradford

Gethsemane

  Breathes there a man who claimeth not
    One lonely spot,
      His own Gethsemane,
  Whither with his inmost pain
  He fain
    Would weary plod,
  Find the surcease that is known
  In wind a-moan
    And sobbing sea,
  Cry his sorrow hid of men,
  And then —
    Touch hands with God.   *Edmund Leamy*

Gethsemane

All those who journey, soon or late,
Must pass within the garden's gate;
Must kneel alone in darkness there,
And battle with some fierce despair.
God pity those who cannot say:
" Not mine but thine "; who only pray:
" Let this cup pass," and cannot see
The purpose in Gethsemane.

Ella Wheeler Wilcox

Atonement

Atonement? Lord, who doth atone today?
   Uplifted on the Cross, canst thou not see
Atonement died somewhere along the way
   Between the Tomb and dark Gethsemane?

Thine be the hyssop and the bitter draught,
   Thine be the anguish and the ridicule:
They were not all at Calvary who laughed —
   The knave, the soldier, Pharisee and fool!

They were not all at Calvary who bid
   Their tawdry baubles for thy seamless robe,
Or, while the very sun its radiance hid,
   The spear upraised, thy tortured flesh to probe.

And yet, dear Lord, a few keep watch with thee,
   A few thy truth with earnest hearts still seek,
Like those who slumbered through thine agony —
   The spirit willing, though the flesh be weak.

And so, with traitor, thief and Magdalene,
   In thine immortal prayer include us too,
And by the sacrifice that maketh clean
   Forgive us — we know not what we do!
Marie LeNart

Men Follow Simon

They spat in his face and hewed him a cross
On that dark day.
The cross was heavy; Simon bore it
Golgotha way.
   O Master, the cross is heavy!

They ripped his hands with driven nails
And flayed him with whips.
They pressed the sponge of vinegar
To his parched lips.
    O Master, thy dear blood drips!

Men follow Simon, three and three,
And one and one
Down through valleys and up long hills
Into the sun.
    O Master, Master — into the sun!
                Raymond Kresensky

His Hands

The hands of Christ
  Seem very frail,
For they were broken
  By a nail.

But only they reach
  Heaven at last
Whom these frail, broken
  Hands hold fast.
           John Richard Moreland

The Dying Thief

" Even on the cross a man will make a prayer."
  Ay, but when eyes grow faint with instant death
And the voice fails, to have beside you there
  In range of darkening eye and thickening breath,

Grace superabundant, grace that more outstrips
  Desire than even desire outruns our due —
  To meet the pitiful half ironic plea
Just uttered ere the lips
  Relax in silence — giving rendezvous
  This very day in Paradise with Me!

Did ever paladin adventuring out
  To face the great uncharted enterprise,
Choose for companion in the crucial bout
  A sorrier squire with whom to agonize?
    Yet in that earthquake — darkened after
    Of dereliction, when the seventh sword
    So pierced the Dolorous Mother's heart that she
Was fallen dumb in swoon,
    Thou midst the railers didst salute thy Lord —
    Thou hadst the heart to cry, *Remember me!*
                              J. S. Phillimore

Indifference

When Jesus came to Golgotha they hanged him on a tree,
They drave great nails through hands and feet, and made a
  Calvary;
They crowned him with a crown of thorns, red were his
  wounds and deep,
For those were crude and cruel days, and human flesh was
  cheap.

When Jesus came to Birmingham, they simply passed him
  by,
They never hurt a hair of him, they only let him die;
For men had grown more tender, and they would not give
  him pain,
They only just passed down the street, and left him in the
  rain.

Still Jesus cried, " Forgive them for they know not what
  they do,"
And still it rained the winter rain that drenched him through
  and through;
The crowds went home and left the streets without a soul to
  see,
And Jesus crouched against a wall and cried for Calvary.

G. A. Studdert-Kennedy

Calvary

If he could doubt on his triumphal cross,
How much more I, in the defeat and loss
Of seeing all my selfish dreams fulfilled,
Of having lived the very life I willed,
Of being all that I desired to be?
My God, my God!   Why hast Thou forsaken me?

William Dean Howells

Good Friday

You drove the nails in his white, white feet;
  I pierced each tender hand:
And we laughed as we lifted the cross on high —
  Too wise to understand.

You gave him the gall and vinegar;
  I thrust the lance in his side;
Yet they say it was years and years ago
  That the Saviour was crucified.

Edgar Daniel Kramer

There is a Man on the Cross

Whenever there is silence around me
By day or by night —
I am startled by a cry.
It came down from the cross —
The first time I heard it.
I went out and searched —
And found a man in the throes of crucifixion,
And I said, " I will take you down,"
And I tried to take the nails out of his feet.
But he said, " Let them be
For I cannot be taken down
Until every man, every woman, and every child
Come together to take me down."
And I said, " But I cannot hear you cry.
What can I do? "
And he said, " Go about the world —
Tell everyone that you meet —
There is a man on the cross."

Elizabeth Cheney

I See His Blood Upon the Rose

I see his blood upon the rose
   And in the stars the glory of his eyes,
His Body gleams amid eternal snows,
   His tears fall from the skies.

I see his face in every flower;
   The thunder and the singing of the birds
Are but his voice — and carven by his power
   Rocks are his written words.

All pathways by his feet are worn,
  His strong heart stirs the ever-beating sea,
His crown of thorns is twined with every thorn,
  His cross is every tree.

Joseph Mary Plunkett

The Thief on the Cross

Three crosses rose on Calvary against the iron sky,
Each with its living burden, each with its human cry,
And all the ages watched there, and there were you and I.

One bore the God incarnate, reviled by man's disdain,
Who through the woe he suffered for our eternal gain,
With joy of infinite loving assuaged his infinite pain.

On one the thief repentant conquered his cruel doom,
Who called at last on Christ and saw his glory through the
    gloom.
For him after the torment souls of the blest made room.

And one the unrepentant bore, who his harsh fate defied.
To him, the child of darkness, all mercy was denied;
Nailed by his brothers on the cross, he cursed his God and
    died.

Ah, Christ, who met in Paradise him who had eyes to see,
Didst thou not greet the other in hell's black agony?
And if he knew thy face, Lord, what did he say to thee?

Harriet Monroe

Good Friday

Peter and James and John,
The sad tale runneth on —
All slept and thee forgot;
One said he knew thee not.

Peter and James and John,
The sad tale runneth on —
I am that one, the three;
Thus have I done to thee.

Under a garden wall
I lay at evenfall;
I waked. Thou calledst me;
I had not watched with thee.

Peter and James and John,
The sad tale runneth on —
By the priest's fagot hot
I said I knew thee not.

The little maid spake out:
"With him thou wentest about."
"This Man I never met — "
I hear the cock crow yet.

                    Lizette Woodworth Reese

Calvary

Friendless and faint, with martyred steps and slow,
Faint for the flesh, but for the spirit free,
Stung by the mob that came to see the show,
The Master toiled along to Calvary;
We gibed him, as he went, with houndish glee,
Till his dim eyes for us did overflow;
We cursed his vengeless hands thrice wretchedly —
And this was nineteen hundred years ago.

But after nineteen hundred years the shame
Still clings, and we have not made good the loss
That outraged faith has entered in his name.

Ah, when shall come love's courage to be strong!
Tell me, O Lord — tell me, O Lord, how long
Are we to keep Christ writhing on the cross!

Edwin Arlington Robinson

For Me

Under an Eastern sky,
Amid a rabble cry,
A man went forth to die,
　　For me!

Thorn-crowned his blessed head,
Blood-stained his every tread,
Cross-laden on he sped,
　　For me!

Pierced glow his hands and feet,
Three hours o'er him did beat
Fierce rays of noon-tide heat,
　　For me!

Thus wert thou made all mine,
Lord make me wholly thine,
Give grace and strength divine,
　　To me!

In thought and word and deed,
Thy will to do; oh! lead my feet
E'en though they bleed,
　　To thee!

Author Unknown

Waking Thought

Waking I look to Jesus on the Rood
   And thank him that the ghostly night is gone;
Until my soul had seen the Holy Cross
   I never knew the dawn.

All colors were as darkness save the hues
   That even our dull bodily eyes can see,
But now is God grown fair beyond the East
   Upon His blessed tree.
                    Marguerite Wilkinson

Good Friday

I for thy sake was pierced with heavy sorrow,
   And bore the cross,
Yet heeded not the sharpness of the arrow,
   Nor shame and loss.

So faint not thou, whate'er the burden be,
But bear it bravely, even to Calvary.
                    Girolamo Savonarola

In the Garden

My sins, my sins, my Savior!
   Their guilt I never knew
Till with thee in the desert
   I near thy passion drew;
Till with thee in the garden
   I heard thy pleading prayer,
And saw the sweat-drops bloody
   That told thy sorrow there.
                    J. B. S. Monsell

Recognition

When Christ went up to Calvary,
   His crown upon his head,
Each tree unto its fellow-tree
   In awful silence said:
" Behold the Gardener is he
   Of Eden and Gethsemane! "

John B. Tabb

The Stranger

I saw him where the rose was red
Pressing the cruel thorns between
His hands until his pale palms bled,
As he walked through my garden-space
And on his face
Such sorrow as I had not seen.

" Sad Stranger, who are you that walk
Where loveliness has birth?
Why are your palms all torn and dark? "
He broke another rose blood-red
And turned and said:
" Yourself stripped of your mask of mirth."

John Richard Moreland

Immunity

Think you to escape
What mortal man can never be without?
What saint upon earth has ever lived apart from cross and
   care?

Why, even Jesus Christ, our Lord, was not even for one hour
    free from his passion's pain.
Christ says, " He needs must suffer,
Rising from the dead,
And enter thus upon his glory."
And how do *you* ask for another road
Than this — the Royal Pathway of the Holy Cross.
                                Thomas à Kempis

Crucifixion

" Lord, must I bear the whole of it, or none? "
" Even as I was crucified, My son."

" Will it suffice if I the thorn-crown wear? "
" To take the scourge, My shoulders were made bare."

" My hands, O Lord, must I be pierced in both? "
" Twain gave I to the hammer, nothing loth."

" But surely, Lord, my feet need not be nailed? "
" Had Mine not been, then love had not prevailed."

" What need I more, O Lord, to fill my part? "
" Only the spear-point in a broken heart."
                              Frederick George Scott

The Ninth Hour

After the shameful trial in the hall,
    The mocking and the scourging, and the pain
    Of Peter's words; to Herod, and again
To Pilate's judgment-seat, the royal pall,
To cross itself, the vinegar and gall;

The thieves close by, discipleship proved vain,
The scoffing crowd, his mother's tears like rain,
There came one moment, bitterest of all.
Yet in that cry, when flesh and spirit failed,
Last effort of the awful way he trod,
Which shook the earth, nor left the temple veiled,
In that exceeding great and bitter cry
Was conquest. The centurion standing by
Said, Truly this man was the Son of God.

Caroline Hazard

Christ's Giving

The spirit of self-sacrifice
Stays not to count the price.

Christ did not of his mere abundance cast
Into the empty treasury of man's store:
The First and Last
Gave until even he could give no more;
His very living,
Such was Christ's giving.

Anna E. Hamilton

If Easter be not True

If Easter be not true,
Then all the lilies low must lie;
The Flanders poppies fade and die;
The spring must lose her fairest bloom
For Christ were still within the tomb —
If Easter be not true.

If Easter be not true.
Then faith must mount on broken wing;
Then hope no more immortal spring;
Then hope must lose her mighty urge;
Life prove a phantom, death a dirge —
    If Easter be not true.

If Easter be not true.
'Twere foolishness the cross to bear;
He died in vain who suffered there;
What matter though we laugh or cry,
Be good or evil, live or die,
    If Easter be not true?

If Easter be not true —
But it is true, and Christ is risen!
And mortal spirit from its prison
Of sin and death with him may rise!
Worthwhile the struggle, sure the prize,
    Since Easter, aye, is true!

Henry H. Barstow

My Risen Lord

My risen Lord, I feel thy strong protection;
I see thee stand among the graves today;
I am the Way, the Life, the Resurrection,
    I hear thee say,
And all the burdens I have carried sadly
Grow light as blossoms on an April day;
My cross becomes a staff, I journey gladly
    This Easter day.

Author Unknown

The Strife is O'er

The strife is o'er, the battle done;
The victory of life is won;
The song of triumph has begun.
    Alleluia!

The powers of death have done their worst,
But Christ their legions hath dispersed;
Let shouts of holy joy outburst.
    Alleluia!

The three sad days are quickly sped;
He rises glorious from the dead;
All glory to our risen Head!
    Alleluia!

He closed the yawning gates of hell;
The bars from heaven's high portals fell
Let hymns of praise his triumph tell!
    Alleluia!

Lord! by the stripes which wounded thee,
From death's dread sting thy servants free,
That we may live and sing to thee!
    Alleluia!

Author Unknown
Translated by Francis Potts

There Was a Garden

A cross — One staggering beneath the weight.
(Golgotha shivered, but knew not why)
A mob — goading with spears of scarlet hate
This One condemned to die.

" Now in the place where he was crucified
There was a garden." Her olive trees
Leaned over the wall and shuddering sighed
To the sobbing breeze.

The lilies stirred from sleep and wept at the sound
Of the tumult cleaving the day;
And the grasses said: *We stand on holy ground —
It was God who passed this way.*

Men mocked him. Their frenzy billowed and grew
To ghastly impact on Calvary's sod.
Only the garden bowed her heart and knew
He was the Son of God.

Marie Barton

Easter Sacraments

There is a Soul Gethsemane
　Where I must kneel,
A prayer which I must pray
　Till I can feel
That, though the anguish redden on my brow,
　And Calvary's begun,
From him I'll take the sacrament of Love —
　" Thy will, not mine, be done."

There is a Resurrection Life
　That I must share,
A tomb that I must leave;
　And though I bear
The wounds which I have won upon my cross,
　Transfigured, they will shine —
A sacramental pledge of Love with Faith,
　To make his rising mine.

Henry Park Schauffler

For Palm Sunday

Ride on, ride on in majesty!
Hark! all the tribes " Hosanna " cry:
O Saviour meek, pursue Thy road,
With palms and scattered garments strewed.

Ride on, ride on in majesty!
In lowly pomp ride on to die!
O Christ, Thy triumphs now begin
O'er captive death and conquered sin.

Ride on, ride on in majesty!
In lowly pomp ride on to die!
Bow Thy meek head to mortal pain!
Then take, O God, Thy power, and reign!

Henry Milman

Rest Remaineth

Easter day breaks!
Christ rises! Mercy every way is infinite —
Earth breaks up; time drops away;
In flows heaven with its new day
Of endless life —
What is left for us save in growth
Of soul to rise up . . .
From the gift looking to the giver,
And from the cistern to the river,
And from the finite to infinity,
And from man's dust to God's divinity.

Robert Browning

Calvary and Easter

A song of sunshine through the rain,
   Of spring across the snow;
A balm to heal the hurts of pain,
   A peace surpassing woe.
Lift up your heads, ye sorrowing ones,
   And be ye glad of heart,
For Calvary and Easter Day
   Were just three days apart!

With shudder of despair and loss
   The world's deep heart is wrung,
As, lifted high upon his cross,
   The Lord of Glory hung —
When rocks were rent, and ghostly forms
   Stole forth in street and mart;
But Calvary and Easter Day,
Earth's blackest day, and whitest day,
   Were just three days apart.

Author Unknown

Resurrection

Waken, O world, if you would glimpse the wonder
   Of God's great primal plan.
Open, O ears, if you would hear the thunder
   Hurled from the heights to man.
How long shall Christ's high message be rejected?
   Two thousand years have passed since it was told.
Must One again be born and resurrected
   Ere man shall grasp again the secret ages old?

What, then, the miracle of Easter Day?
  What meant the riven tomb, the hidden Might
That conquered death and rolled away the stone
  And brought the Master back to mortal sight?
This! That throughout the worlds, One Life, unbroken —
  Rushes and flames in an unending vow.
Death *cannot* be, and never has been, spoken —
  God and immortal life are *here* and *now!*

Angela Morgan

Easter Carol

O Earth! throughout thy borders
  Re-don thy fairest dress;
And everywhere, O Nature!
  Throb with new happiness;
Once more to new creation
  Awake, and death gainsay,
For death is swallowed up of life,
  And Christ is risen today!

Let peals of jubilation
  Ring out in all the lands;
With hearts of deep elation
  Let sea with sea clasp hands;
Let one supreme Te Deum
  Roll round the World's highway,
For death is swallowed up of life,
  And Christ is risen today!

George Newell Lovejoy

Easter Music

Blow, golden trumpets, sweet and clear,
Blow soft upon the perfumed air;

Bid the sad earth to join our song,
" *To Christ does victory belong!* "

Oh, let the winds your message bear
To every heart of grief and care;
Sound through the world the joyful lay,
" *Our Christ hath conquered Death today!* "

On cloudy wings let glad words fly
Through the soft blue of echoing sky:
Ring out, O trumpets, sweet and clear,
" *Through Death immortal Life is here!* "
                                        Margaret Wade Deland

An Easter Wish

May the glad dawn
    Of Easter morn
    Bring joy to thee.

May the calm eve
    Of Easter leave
    A peace divine with thee.

May Easter night
    On thine heart write,
    O Christ, I live for thee!
                        Author Unknown

What Does Easter Mean to You?

What does Easter mean to you?
Stately church with cushioned pew,
Where, Lenten season gone at last
And days of self-denial past,

Richly-clad, devoted throngs
Of worshipers unite in songs
Of praise in lily-scented air?
Is this what makes your Easter fair?

Does it mean the end of winter's reign,
Bright skies and welcome warmth again,
Singing of birds, budding of trees,
Sweet spring odors on the breeze
From daffodil and crocus bed
And balsam branches overhead?
Sad is the world and cold and gray,
If this is all of Easter Day.

But if this blessed season brings
A firmer faith in holy things;
Assurance of a living Lord;
A strengthening of the tender chord
Of love that binds us to the life to come
Where loved ones 'wait us in the heavenly home,
No pain or loss can e'er efface the bliss,
Dear friend, of Easter when it means all this.

May Ricker Conrad

Easter

Sing, soul of mine, this day of days.
   The Lord is risen.
Toward the sunrising set thy face.
   The Lord is risen.
Behold he giveth strength and grace;
For darkness, light; for mourning, praise;
For sin, his holiness; for conflict, peace.

Arise, O soul, this Easter Day!
Forget the tomb of yesterday,
For thou from bondage art set free;
Thou sharest in his victory
And life eternal is for thee,
Because the Lord is risen.

Author Unknown

An Easter Prayer

Lord, now that spring is in the world,
   And every tulip is a cup
Filled with the wine of thy great love,
   Lift thou me up.

Raise thou my heart as flowers arise
   To greet the glory of thy day,
With soul as clean as lilies are,
   And white as they.

Let me not fear the darkness now,
   Since Life and Light break through thy tomb;
Teach me that doubts no more oppress,
   No more consume.

Show me that thou art April, Lord,
   And thou the flowers and the grass;
Then, when awake the soft spring winds,
   I'll hear thee pass!

Charles Hanson Towne

For Easter

Oh, let me know
The power of the resurrection;
Oh, let me show
Thy risen life in calm and clear reflection;

Oh, let me give
Out of the gifts thou freely gavest;
Oh, let me live
With life abundantly because thou livest.

Frances Ridley Havergal

Easter

Say not that death is king, that night is lord,
That loveliness is passing, beauty dies;
Nor tell me hope's a vain, deceptive dream
Fate lends to life, a pleasing, luring gleam
To light awhile the earth's despondent skies,
Till death brings swift and sure its dread reward.
Say not that youth deceives, but age is true,
That roses quickly pass, while cypress bides,
That happiness is foolish, grief is wise,
That stubborn dust shall choke our human cries.
Death tells new worlds, and life immortal hides
Beyond the veil, which shall all wrongs undo.
This was the tale God breathed to me at dawn
When flooding sunrise told the night was gone.

Thomas Curtis Clark

The Birth of the Flowers

God spoke! and from the arid scene
Sprang rich and verdant bowers,
Till all the earth was soft with green —
He smiled, and there were flowers.

Mary M. Fenollosa

Hope

He died!

And with him perished all that men hold dear;
Hope lay beside him in the sepulcher,
Love grew corse cold, and all things beautiful beside
      Died when he died.

He rose!

And with him hope arose, and life and light.
Men said, "Not Christ but Death died yesternight."
And joy and truth and all things virtuous
      Rose when he rose.

Author Unknown

Resurrection

In this brown seed, so dry and hard,
I see a flower in my door yard.
You, chrysalis in winding sheet,
Are butterfly all dainty sweet.
All life is warmed by spring's sweet breath,
And Christ our Lord has conquered death.

Agnes W. Storer

The Sacrament

" This is my body, which is given for you;
    Do this," he said, " and break, rememb'ring me."
O Lamb of God, our Paschal off'ring true,
    To us the Bread of Life each moment be.

" This is my blood, for sins' remission shed " ;
　He spake, and passed the cup of blessing round;
So let us drink, and, on life's fullness fed,
　With heavenly joy each quickening pulse shall bound.

Some will betray thee — " Master, is it I? "
　Leaning upon thy love, we ask in fear —
Ourselves mistrusting, earnestly we cry
　To thee, the Strong, for strength, when sin is near.

But round us fall the evening shadows dim;
　A saddened awe pervades our darkening sense;
In solemn choir we sing the parting hymn,
　And hear thy voice, " Arise, let us go hence."
　　　　　　　　　　　　Charles L. Ford

Sursum Corda

After the comfortable words come these:
　" Lift up your hearts."
Before the altar he, we on our knees —
　Lift up your hearts.
And powerless though we be then to obey,
The high command goes with us through the day:
　Lift up your hearts.

From pondering earth's long mysterious woe,
　Lift up your hearts.
With sacrifices filled to overflow;
　Lift up your hearts.
Shame expiates the lifting up of sense —
The lifting up of mind is life's expense —
　Lift up your hearts.

No goodlier; no more vital words may be —
  Lift up your hearts.
In mirth, in loneliness, in agony.
  Lift up your hearts.
Nay, show no sign in look, in voice, in word;
Answer, We lift them up unto the Lord!
  Lift up your hearts.

Annie Lake Townsend

Golgotha

Our crosses are hewn from different trees,
But we all must have our Calvaries;
We may climb the height from a different side,
But we each go up to be crucified;
As we scale the steep, another may share
The dreadful load that our shoulders bear,
But the costliest sorrow is all our own —
For on the summit we bleed alone.

Frederick Lawrence Knowles

The Bread of Life

Break thou the Bread of Life,
  Dear Lord, to me;
As thou didst break the loaves
  Beside the sea.
Beyond the sacred page
  I seek thee, Lord.
My spirit pants for thee,
  O Living Word!

Bless thou the truth, dear Lord,
  To me — to me —
As thou didst bless the bread
  By Galilee;
Then shall all bondage cease,
  All fetters fall,
And I shall find my peace
  My all-in-all.

Mary A. Lathbury

This is My Body

He was the Word that spake it,
  He took the bread and brake it;
And what that Word did make it,
  I do believe and take it.

John Donne

L'Envoi

O love triumphant over guilt and sin,
My Soul is soiled, but thou shalt enter in;
My feet must stumble if I walk alone,
Lonely my heart, till beating by thine own,
My will is weakness till it rest in thine,
Cut off, I wither, thirsting for the Vine,
My deeds are dry leaves on a sapless tree,
My life is lifeless till it live in thee!

Frederick Lawrence Knowles

MOTHER'S DAY

Mother O' Mine

If I were hanged on the highest hill,
  Mother o' mine, O mother o' mine!
I know whose love would follow me still,
  Mother o' mine, O mother o' mine!
If I were drowned in the deepest sea,
  Mother o' mine, O mother o' mine!
i know whose tears would come down to me,
  Mother o' mine, O mother o' mine!
If I were damned by body and soul,
I know whose prayers would make me whole,
  Mother o' mine, O mother o' mine!

Rudyard Kipling

Mother's Love

Her love is like an island
  In life's ocean, vast and wide,
A peaceful, quiet shelter
  From the wind, and rain, and tide.

'Tis bound on the north by Hope,
  By Patience on the west,
By tender Counsel on the south,
  And on the east by Rest.

Above it like a beacon light
  Shine faith, and truth, and prayer;
And through the changing scenes of life,
  I find a haven there.

Author Unknown

The Mother of the House

Strength and dignity are her clothing;
   And she laugheth at the time to come.
She openeth her mouth to wisdom;
   And the law of kindness is in her tongue.
She looketh well to the ways of her household,
   And eateth not the bread of idleness;
Her children rise up and call her blessed,
   Her husband, also, and he praiseth her, saying:
" Many daughters have done virtuously,
   But thou excelleth them all."

Proverbs 31:25–29

Dear Old Mothers

I love old mothers — mothers with white hair
   And kindly eyes, and lips grown soft and sweet
With murmured blessings over sleeping babes.
   There is something in their quiet grace
That speaks the calm of Sabbath afternoons;
   A knowledge in their deep, unfaltering eyes
That far outreaches all philosophy.

Time, with caressing touch about them weaves
   The silver-threaded fairy-shawl of age,
While all the echoes of forgotten songs
   Seem joined to lend sweetness to their speech.

Old mothers! as they pass with slow-timed step,
   Their trembling hands cling gently to youth's strength.
Sweet mothers! — as they pass, one sees again
   Old garden-walks, old roses, and old loves.

Charles S. Ross

The Watcher — Mother

She always leaned to watch for us,
  Anxious if we were late,
In winter by the window,
  In summer by the gate;

And though we mocked her tenderly,
  Who had such foolish care,
The long way home would seem more safe
  Because she waited there.

Her thoughts were all so full of us —
  She never could forget!
And so I think that where she is
  She must be watching yet,

Waiting till we come home to her,
  Anxious if we are late —
Watching from heaven's window,
  Leaning from heaven's gate.
                              Margaret Widdemer

Our Mothers

O magical word, may it never die from the lips that love to
    speak it,
Nor melt away from the trusting hearts that even would
    break to keep it.
Was there ever a name that lived like thine! Will there ever
    be another?
The angels have reared in heaven a shrine to the holy name
    of Mother.
                              Author Unknown

A Message

If there is any way, dear Lord
  In which my heart may send her word
    Of my continued love,
And of my joy in her relief
  From pain — a joy not even grief
    And loneliness may rise above,

Reveal it to me . . . for I long
  To keep intact the tie so strong
    Between us, from my birth,
That when we meet (as meet we must)
  There shall be naught but perfect trust,
    Such as we always knew on earth!

Anna Nelson Reed

To Mother — in Heaven

Now there shall be a new song and a new star,
  A new voice in the wind to whisper me;
And I shall stand within this harbor bar
  And watch a new light tossing down the sea.

My childish terror of the Lord shall cease;
  And my dread fear of blind and horrid fate;
And from my sin I shall have sure release
  Because in heaven She is my advocate.

Bennett Weaver

MEMORIAL DAY

Concord Hymn

By the rude bridge that arched the flood,
   Their flag to April's breeze unfurled,
Here once the embattled farmers stood,
   And fired the shot heard round the world.

The foe long since in silence slept;
   Alike the conqueror silent sleeps;
And Time the ruined bridge has swept
   Down the dark stream which seaward creeps.

On this green bank, by this soft stream,
   We set today a votive stone,
That memory may their deed redeem,
   When, like our sires, our sons are gone.

Spirit, that made those spirits dare
   To die, and leave their children free,
Bid Time and Nature gently spare
   The shaft we raise to them and thee.

Ralph Waldo Emerson

The New Memorial Day

" Under the roses the blue;
   Under the lilies the gray."

Oh, the roses we plucked for the blue,
   And the lilies we twined for the gray,
We have bound in a wreath,
And in silence beneath
   Slumber our heroes today.

Over the new-turned sod
   The sons of our fathers stand,
And the fierce old fight
Slips out of sight
   In the clasp of a brother's hand.

For the old blood left a stain
   That the new has washed away,
And the sons of those
That have faced as foes
   Are marching together today.

Oh, the blood that our fathers gave!
   Oh, the tide of our mothers' tears!
And the flow of red,
And the tears they shed,
   Embittered a sea of years.

But the roses we plucked for the blue,
   And the lilies we twined for the gray
We have bound in a wreath,
And in glory beneath
   Slumber our heroes today.

Albert Bigelow Paine

Decoration Day Prayer

Lord of our fathers, hear our prayer
    For those who paid the price;
Our stalwart youth, so brave and fair,
    Who made the sacrifice.

They slumber in the cypress' shade,
    They, who so nobly died;
Facing destruction unafraid,
    All for a nation's pride.

We honor them and weep to think
    Of youthful hearts so still.
O Lord, that youth like this should drink
    So soon from Lethe's rill!

The price of peace is far too high
    In youthful limb and life.
To You, O gracious God, we cry
    Through clouds of hate and strife.

We pray that in the hearts of man
    The flame of hate may die;
That clouds of war no more shall span
    Our nation's peaceful sky.

Lord of our fathers, hear our prayer
    For youth now free and gay;
We pray that You may ever spare
    Them from the awful fray.

                Arthur Roszelle Bemis, Jr.

Memorial Day

A day of tender memory,
　A day of sacred hours,
Of little bands of marching men,
　Of drums and flags and flowers.

A day when a great nation halts
　Its mighty, throbbing pace,
It pays its meed of gratitude
　And love with willing grace.

A day when battles are retold,
　And eulogies are said,
When dirges sound, and chaplains read
　The office for the dead.

A day when fairest, sweetest blooms
　Are laid upon each grave,
And wreaths are hung on monuments,
　And banners, half-mast, wave.

A day to keep from year to year
　In memory of the dead;
Let music sound, and flowers be laid
　Upon each resting-bed.

Emma A. Lent

" Gone West "

In the language of the trenches, " Gone West " means killed.

Out to the world's dim boundary line,
Where the sky burns red — blood red, like wine,
And the fairest of all the stars doth shine —
  Gone West.

Out where beauty, in death still bright,
Casts her glove in the teeth of the night,
And, dying, still promises light, more light —
  His rest.

Night may conquer, but hark how the morn
Calls to the stars on the new moon's horn,
Till, like a warrior king, comes dawn —
  'Tis best.

G. A. Studdert-Kennedy

Little Green Tents

Little green tents where the soldiers sleep,
And the sunbeams play, and the women weep,
Are covered with flowers today;
And between the tents walk the weary few,
Who were young and stalwart in sixty-two
When they went to the war away.

The little green tents are built of sod,
And they are not long, and they are not broad,
But the soldiers have lots of room;
And the sod is a part of the land they saved,
When the flag of the enemy darkly waved,
The symbol of dole and doom.

The little green tent is a thing divine;
The little green tent is a country's shrine,
Where patriots kneel and pray.
And the brave men left, so old, so few,
Were young and stalwart in sixty-two,
When they went to the war away.

Walt Mason

Memorial Day

To all the heart-wounds touched afresh this day
  As on the Soldier's resting place we lay
Thy flowers, Christ, in tender memory,
  Give healing thou,
      This eventide.

And for the sorrowing ones who yet remain,
  To whom the heart-break and the bitter pain
Come like the memory of an old song's sad refrain,
  Have pity thou,
      This eventide.

For all the losses of the lonely years —
  For all the weight of shed and unshed tears,
For all forebodings, and all coming fears,
  Give quietness,
      This eventide.

By all the flower of youth in battle slain,
  By all the woman's heritage of pain;
The prayer that it may not have been in vain.
  We leave with thee,
      This eventide.

Emerette H. Dunning

INDEPENDENCE DAY

America the Beautiful

O beautiful for spacious skies,
　For amber waves of grain,
For purple mountain majesties
　Above the fruited plain!
　　America! America!
　God shed his grace on thee
And crown thy good with brotherhood
　From sea to shining sea!

O beautiful for pilgrim feet,
　Whose stern, impassioned stress
A thoroughfare for freedom beat
　Across the wilderness!
　　America! America!
　God mend thine every flaw,
Confirm thy soul in self-control,
　Thy liberty in law!

O beautiful for heroes proved
　In liberating strife,
Who more than self their country loved,
　And mercy more than life!
　　America! America!
　May God thy gold refine
Till all success be nobleness
　And every gain divine!

O beautiful for patriot dream
  That sees beyond the years
Thine alabaster cities gleam
  Undimmed by human tears!
    America! America!
God shed His grace on thee
And crown thy good with brotherhood
  From sea to shining sea!

Katharine Lee Bates

From The Ship of State

Thou, too, sail on, O ship of State!
Sail on, O Union, strong and great!
Humanity with all its fears,
With all its hopes of future years,
Is hanging breathless on thy fate!
We know what Master laid thy keel,
What workmen wrought thy ribs of steel,
Who made each mast, and sail, and rope,
What anvils rang, what hammers beat,
In what a forge and what a heat
Were shaped the anchors of thy hope!
Fear not each sudden sound and shock,
'Tis of the wave and not the rock;
'Tis but the flapping of the sail,
And not a rent made by the gale!
In spite of rock and tempest's roar,
In spite of false lights on the shore,
Sail on, nor fear to breast the sea!
Our hearts, our hopes, are all with thee,
Our hearts, our hopes, our prayers, our tears,
Our faith, triumphant o'er our fears,
Are all with thee, — are all with thee!

Henry Wadsworth Longfellow

Stanzas from The Present Crisis

When a deed is done for Freedom, through the broad earth's
    aching breast
Runs a thrill of joy prophetic, trembling on from east to
    west,
And the slave, where'er he cowers, feels the soul within him
    climb
To the awful verge of manhood, as the energy sublime
Of a century bursts full-blossomed on the thorny stem of
    Time.

Careless seems the great Avenger: history's pages but record
One death-grapple in the darkness 'twixt old systems and the
    Word;
Truth forever on the scaffold, Wrong forever on the
    throne, —
Yet that scaffold sways the future, and, behind the dim
    unknown,
Standeth God within the shadow, keeping watch above his
    own.

Once to every man and nation comes the moment to decide;
In the strife of Truth with Falsehood, for the good or evil
    side,
Some great cause, God's new Messiah, offering each the bloom
    or blight,
Parts the goats upon the left hand and the sheep upon the
    right,
And the choice goes by forever 'twixt that darkness and that
    light.

For humanity sweeps onward: where today the martyr
    stands,
On the morrow crouches Judas with the silver in his hands;

Far in front the cross stands ready and the crackling fagots
    burn,
While the hooting mob of yesterday in silent awe return
To glean up the scattered ashes into History's golden
    urn.

New occasions teach new duties; Time makes ancient good
    uncouth;
They must upward still, and onward, who would keep abreast
    of Truth;
Lo, before us gleam her camp-fires! we ourselves must Pil-
    grims be,
Launch our Mayflower, and steer boldly through the des-
    perate winter sea,
Nor attempt the Future's portal with the Past's blood-rusted
    key.

James Russell Lowell

Battle Hymn of the Republic

Mine eyes have seen the glory of the coming of the Lord;
He is trampling out the vintage where the grapes of wrath
    are stored;
He hath loosed the fateful lightning of his terrible swift
    sword;
        His truth is marching on.

CHORUS

    Glory! Glory Hallelujah!
    Glory! Glory Hallelujah!
    Glory! Glory Hallelujah!
    His truth is marching on.

I have seen him in the watch-fires of a hundred circling
    camps;
They have builded him an altar in the evening dews and
    damps;
I can read his righteous sentence by the dim and flaring
    lamps;
    His day is marching on. — Cho.

I have read a fiery gospel writ in burnished rows of steel:
" As ye deal with my contemners, so with you my grace shall
    deal."
Let the hero born of woman crush the serpent with his heel,
    Since God is marching on. — Cho.

He has sounded forth the trumpet that shall never call
    retreat;
He is sifting out the hearts of men before his judgment
    seat;
Oh, be swift, my soul, to answer him; be jubilant my feet;
    Our God is marching on. — Cho.

In the beauty of the lilies Christ was born across the sea,
With a glory in his bosom that transfigures you and me;
As he died to make men holy, let us die to make men free,
    While God is marching on. — Cho.
                   Julia Ward Howe

Your Flag and My Flag

Your flag and my flag,
    And how it flies today,
In your land and my land,
    And half a world away!

Rose-red and blood-red,
　The stripes forever gleam;
Snow-white and soul-white —
　The good forefather's dream;
Sky-blue and true-blue,
　With stars to gleam aright —
The gloried guidon of the day;
　A shelter through the night.

Your flag and my flag!
　To every star and stripe
The drums beat as hearts beat
　And fifers shrilly pipe!
Your flag and my flag —
　A blessing in the sky;
Your hope and my hope —
　It never hid a lie!
Home land and far land
　And half the world around,
Old Glory hears our glad salute
　And ripples to the sound.

Your flag and my flag!
　And, Oh! how much it holds —
Your land and my land —
　Secure within its folds!
Your heart and my heart
　Beat quicker at the sight.
Sun-kissed and wind-tossed —
　Red and blue and white.
The one flag — the great flag —
　The flag for me and you
Glorified all else beside,
　The red and white and blue.

Wilbur D. Nesbit

My America

More famed than Rome, as splendid as old Greece,
And saintlier than Hebrew prophet's dream;
A shrine of beauty, Italy-inspired;
A nobler France, by truth and freedom fired;
As hale as England, treasuring the gleam
Of knightly Arthur; though a land of peace,
As brave as Sparta — till all hellish wars shall cease.

In thoughts, as wise as is her prairie sea;
In deeds, as splendid as her mountain piles;
As noble as her mighty river tides.
Let her be true, a land where right abides;
Let her be clean, as sweet as summer isles;
And let her sound the note of liberty
For all the earth, till every man and child be free!

Thomas Curtis Clark

Love of Country

Breathes there a man with soul so dead
Who never to himself hath said:
" This is my own, my native land " ?
Whose heart hath ne'er within him burned
As home his footsteps he hath turned,
    From wandering on a foreign strand?
If such there breathe, go mark him well;
For him no minstrel raptures swell;
High though his titles, proud his name,
Boundless his wealth as wish can claim,
Despite those titles, power and pelf,
The wretch concentered all in self,

Living, shall forfeit fair renown,
And, doubly dying, shall go down
To the vile dust from whence he sprung,
Unwept, unhonored, and unsung.

Sir Walter Scott

Patriotism

He serves his country best
Who lives pure life and doeth righteous deed,
And walks straight paths however others stray,
And leaves his sons, as uttermost bequest,
A stainless record which all men may read;
This is the better way.

No drop but serves the slowly lifting tide;
No dew but has an errand to some flower;
No smallest star but sheds some helpful ray,
And man by man, each helping all the rest,
Make the firm bulwark of the country's power;
There is no better way.

Susan Coolidge

LABOR DAY

Aristocrats of Labor

They claim no guard of heraldry,
They scorn the knightly rod;
Their coats of arms are noble deeds,
Their peerage is from God!

W. Stewart

The Gospel of Labor

This is the Gospel of Labor —
  Ring it, ye bells of the kirk —
The Lord of love came down from above
  To live with the men who work.
This is the rose that he planted
  Here in the thorn-cursed soil —
Heaven is blessed with perfect rest;
  But the blessing of earth is toil.

Henry van Dyke

The Thinker

Back of the beating hammer
  By which the steel is wrought,
Back of the workshop's clamor
  The seeker may find the thought,
The thought that is ever master
  Of iron and steam and steel,
That rises above disaster
  And tramples it under heel.

The drudge may fret and tinker
  Or labor with lusty blows,
But back of him stands the thinker,
  The clear-eyed man who knows;
For into each plow or saber,
  Each piece and part and whole,
Must go the brains of labor,
  Which gives the work a soul.

Back of the motor's humming,
   Back of the bells that sing,
Back of the hammer's drumming,
   Back of the cranes that swing,
There is the eye which scans them,
   Watching through stress and strain,
There is the mind which plans them —
   Back of the brawn, the brain.

Might of the roaring boiler,
   Force of the engine's thrust,
Strength of the sweating toiler,
   Greatly in these we trust,
But back of them stands the schemer,
   The thinker who drives things through,
Back of the job — the dreamer
   Who's making the dream come true.

                              Berton Braley

The Day and the Work

To each man is given a day and his work for the day;
And once, and no more, he is given to travel this way.
And woe if he flies from the task, whatever the odds;
For the task is appointed to him on the scroll of the gods.

There is waiting a work where only your hands can avail;
And so, if you falter, a chord in the music will fail.
We may laugh to this sky, we may lie for an hour in the sun;
But we dare not go hence till the labor appointed is done.

To each man is given a marble to carve for the wall;
A stone that is needed to heighten the beauty of all;
And only his soul has the magic to give it a grace;
And only his hands have the cunning to put it in place.

We are given one hour to parley and struggle with Fate,
Our wild hearts filled with the dream, our brains with the
 high debate.
It is given to look on life once, and once only to die:
One testing, and then at a sign we go out of the sky.

Yes, the task that is given to each man, no other can do;
So your work is awaiting: it has waited through ages for you.
Edwin Markham

Song of Christian Workingmen

Our Master toiled, a carpenter
 Of busy Galilee;
He knew the weight of ardent tasks
 And ofttimes, wearily,
He sought, apart, in earnest prayer
For strength, beneath his load of care.

He took a manly share of work,
 No thoughtless shirker he.
From dawn to dusk, before his bench,
 He labored faithfully.
He felt just pride in work well done
And found rest sweet, at setting sun.

His Father worked, and he rejoiced
 That honest toil was his —
To whom was given grace to know
 Divinest mysteries:
And shall not we find toiling good
Who serve in labor's brotherhood?
Thomas Curtis Clark

The Master's Man

My Master was a worker
　With daily work to do,
And he who would be like him
　Must be a worker, too;
Then welcome honest labor
　And honest labor's fare,
For where there is a worker
　The Master's man is there.

My Master was a comrade,
　A trusty friend and true,
And he who would be like him
　Must be a comrade too;
In happy hours of singing,
　In silent hours of care,
Where goes a loyal comrade,
　The Master's man is there.

My Master was a helper,
　The woes of life he knew,
And he who would be like him
　Must be a helper too;
The burden will grow lighter,
　If each will take a share,
And where there is a helper
　The Master's man is there.

Then, brothers, brave and manly,
　Together let us be,
For he, who is our Master,
　The Man of men was he;

The men who would be like him
Are wanted everywhere,
And where they love each other
The Master's men are there.

William G. Tarrant

Work

Work thou for pleasure.
    Paint or sing or carve
The thing thou lovest,
    Though the body starve.
Who works for glory
    Misses oft the goal,
Who works for money
    Coins his very soul.
Work for the work's sake,
    Then, and it might be
That these things shall
    Be added unto thee.

Kenyon Cox

Labor

We have fed you all for a thousand years,
    And you hail us still unfed,
Though there's never a dollar of all your wealth
    But marks the workers' dead.
We have yielded our best to give you rest,
    And you lie on crimson wool;
For if blood be the price of all your wealth
    Good God, we ha' paid in full!

There's never a mine blown skyward now
    But we're buried alive for you;
There's never a wreck drifts shoreward now
    But we are its ghastly crew:

Go reckon our dead by the forges red,
    And the factories where we spin.
If blood be the price of your cursèd wealth
    Good God, we ha' paid it in!

We have fed you all for a thousand years,
    For that was our doom, you know,
From the days when you chained us in your fields
    To the strike of a week ago.
You ha' eaten our lives and our babes and wives,
    And we're told it's your legal share;
But, if blood be the price of your lawful wealth,
    Good God, we ha' bought it fair.

Author Unknown

COLUMBUS DAY

Columbus

Behind him lay the gray Azores,
    Behind, the gates of Hercules;
Before him not the ghost of shores,
    Before him only shoreless seas.
The good mate said, " Now we must **pray,**
    For lo! the very stars are gone,
Speak, admiral, what shall I say? "
    " Why, say ' Sail on! Sail on and on! ' "

" My men grow mutinous day by day;
    My men grow ghastly, wan and weak."
The stout mate thought of home; a spray
    Of salt wave washed his swarthy cheek.

" What shall I say, brave admiral, say,
   If we sight naught but seas at dawn? "
" Why, we shall say at break of day,
   ' Sail on! Sail on! Sail on and on! ' "

They sailed and sailed as winds might blow,
   Until at last the blanched mate said:
" Why, now not even God would know,
   Should I and all my men fall dead.
These very winds forget their way,
   For God from these dead seas is gone,
Now, speak, brave admiral, speak and say."
   He said, " Sail on! Sail on and on! "

They sailed. They sailed. Then spoke the mate:
   " This mad sea shows its teeth tonight.
He curls his lip, he lies in wait
   With lifted teeth as if to bite!
Brave admiral, say but one good word.
   What shall we do when hope is gone? "
The words leaped as a leaping sword,
   " Sail on! Sail on! Sail on and on! "

Then pale and worn he kept his deck,
   And peered through darkness. Ah, that night,
Of all dark nights! And then a speck —
   A light! A light! A light! A light!
It grew, a starlit flag, unfurled!
   It grew to be Time's burst of dawn.
He gained a world, he gave the world
   Its grandest lesson, " On and on."

Joaquin Miller

The Prayer of Columbus

One effort more, my altar this bleak sand;
That Thou, O God, my life hast lighted,
With ray of light, steady, ineffable, vouchsafed of Thee,
Light rare untellable, lighting the very light,
Beyond all signs, descriptions, languages;
For that, O God, be it my latest word, here on my knees,
Old, poor, and paralyzed, I thank Thee.

My terminus near,
The clouds already closing in upon me,
The voyage balk'd, the course disputed, lost,
I yield my ships to Thee.
My hands, my limbs grow nerveless,
My brain feels rack'd, bewildered,
Let the old timbers part, I will not part,
I will cling fast to Thee, O God, though the waves buffet me,
Thee, Thee at least I know.

Walt Whitman

Columbus the World-Giver

Who doubts has met defeat ere blows can fall;
Who doubts must die with no palm in his hand;
Who doubts shall never be of that high band
Which clearly answer — Present! to Death's call.
For Faith is life, and, though a funeral pall
Veil our fair Hope, and on our promised land
A mist malignant hang, if Faith but stand
Among our ruins, we shall conquer all.
O faithful soul, that knew no doubting low;
O Faith incarnate, lit by Hope's strong flame,

And led by Faith's own cross to dare all ill
And find our world! — but more than this we owe
To thy true heart; thy pure and glorious name
Is one clear trumpet call to Faith and Will.

Maurice Francis Egan

ARMISTICE DAY

This Is War

War
I abhor,
And yet how sweet
The sound along the marching street
Of drum and fife; and I forget
Wet eyes of widows, and forget
Broken old mothers, and the whole
Dark butchery without a soul.

Without a soul — save this bright drink
Of heady music, sweet as hell;
And even my peace-abiding feet
Go marching with the marching street,
For yonder goes the fife,
And what care I for human life!

The tears fill my astonished eyes
And my full heart is like to break,
And yet 'tis all embannered lies,
A dream those little drummers make.

Oh, it is wickedness to clothe
Yon hideous, grinning thing that stalks

Hidden in music, like a queen
That in a garden of glory walks,
Till good men love the thing they loathe.

Art, thou hast many infamies,
But not an infamy like this —
Oh, snap the fife and still the drum,
And show the monster as she is.

Richard Le Gallienne

The Jewish Conscript

They have dressed me up in a soldier's dress,
    With a rifle in my hand,
And have sent me bravely forth to shoot
    My own in a foreign land.

Oh, many shall die for the fields of their homes,
    And many in conquest wild,
But I shall die for the fatherland
    That murdered my little child.

How many hundreds of years ago —
    The nations wax and cease! —
Did the God of our fathers doom us to bear
    The flaming message of peace!

We are the mock and the sport of time!
    Yet why should I complain! —
For the Jew that they hung on the bloody cross,
    He also died in vain.

Florence Kiper Frank

Apparitions

Who goes there, in the night,
　　Across the storm-swept plain?
We are the ghosts of a valiant war —
　　A million murdered men!

Who goes there, at the dawn,
　　Across the sun-swept plain?
We are the hosts of those who swear:
　　It shall not be again!
　　　　　　　　　　Thomas Curtis Clark

The Victory Which Is Peace

When navies are forgotten
　　And fleets are useless things,
When the dove shall warm her bosom
　　Beneath the eagle's wings;

When the memory of battles
　　At last is strange and old,
When nations have one banner
　　And creeds have found one fold;

When the Hand that sprinkles midnight
　　With its dust of powdered suns
Has hushed this tiny tumult
　　Of sects, and swords, and guns,

Then hate's last note of discord
　　In all God's world shall cease
In the conquest which is service,
　　In the victory which is peace.
　　　　　　　　　Frederick Lawrence Knowles

Peace

O brother, lift a cry, a long world-cry
   Sounding from sky to sky —
The cry of one great word,
   Peace, peace, the world-will clamoring to be heard —
A cry to break the ancient battle-ban,
To end it in the sacred name of Man!

Edwin Markham

When War Shall Be No More

Were half the power that fills the world with terror,
   Were half the wealth bestowed on camps and courts,
Given to redeem the human mind from error,
   There were no need of arsenals and forts.

The warrior's name would be a name abhorrèd!
   And every nation, that should lift again
Its hand against a brother, on its forehead
   Would wear forevermore the curse of Cain!

Down the dark future, through long generations,
   The echoing sounds grow fainter and then cease;
And like a bell, with solemn, sweet vibrations,
   I hear once more the voice of Christ say, " Peace! "

Peace! and no longer from its brazen portals
   The blast of war's great organ shakes the skies!
But beautiful as the songs of the immortals,
   The holy melodies of Love arise.

Henry Wadsworth Longfellow

The Dead

Blow out, you bugles, over the rich Dead!
  There's none of these so lonely and poor of old,
  But, dying, has made us rarer gifts than gold.
These laid the world away; poured out the red
Sweet wine of youth; gave up the years to be
  Of work and joy, and that unhoped serene
  That men call age; and those who would have been
Their sons, they gave, their immortality.
Blow, bugles, blow! They brought us, for our dearth,
  Holiness, lacked so long, and Love and Pain.
Honor has come back, as a king, to earth,
  And paid his subjects with a royal wage;
And Nobleness walks in our ways again;
  And we have come into our heritage.

Rupert Brooke

He Shall Speak Peace

Hatred and greed and pride shall die,
Cannon and swords shall prostrate lie;
Warring shall end, the world shall cry —
    For He shall speak peace.

Rivers shall nevermore run red,
Terror shall hide his bloody head,
Life shall no more for lust be shed —
    For He shall speak peace.

They shall not strive in earth again,
Honor will come to dwell with men;
Children will bide in safety then —
    For He shall speak peace.

Desolate plains, now bleak and cold,
Burst forth again in green and gold;
Birds of the trenches sing, as of old —
    For He shall speak peace.

Thomas Curtis Clark

Victory

Ye that have faith to look with fearless eyes
    Beyond the tragedy of a world at strife,
And know that out of death and night shall rise
    The dawn of ampler life:
Rejoice, whatever anguish rend the heart,
    That God has given you the priceless dower
To live in these great times and have your part
    In Freedom's crowning hour,
That ye may tell your sons who see the light
    High in the heavens — their heritage to take —
" I saw the powers of darkness take their flight;
    I saw the morning break."

Owen Seaman

The Man He Killed

" Had he and I but met
    By some old ancient inn,
We should have sat us down to wet
    Right many a nipperkin.

" But ranged as infantry,
    And staring face to face,
I shot at him as he at me,
    And killed him in his place.

" I shot him dead because —
    Because he was my foe,
Just so: my foe of course he was;
    That's clear enough; although

" He thought he'd 'list, perhaps,
    Offhand like — just as I —
Was out of work — had sold his traps —
    No other reason why.

" Yes; quaint and curious war is!
    You shoot a fellow down
You'd treat if met where any bar is,
    Or help to half a crown."

Thomas Hardy

Brotherhood

The crest and crowning of all good,
Life's final star is Brotherhood;
For it will bring again to Earth
Her long-lost Poesy and Mirth,
Will send new light on every face,
A kingly power upon the race,
And till it comes, we men are slaves,
And travel downward to the dust of graves.

Come, clear the way then, clear the way:
Blind creeds and kings have had their day.
Break the dead branches from the path:
Our hope is in the aftermath —
Our hope is in heroic men,
Star-led to build the world again.
To this Event the ages ran:
Make way for Brotherhood — make way for Man.

Edwin Markham

Peace

Not with the high-voiced fife,
  Nor with the deep-voiced drum,
To mark the end of strife
  The perfect Peace shall come.

Nor pomp nor pageant grand
  Shall bring War's blest surcease,
But silent, from God's hand
  Shall come the perfect Peace!

Clinton Scollard

The Universal Republic

Upon the skyline i' the dark
The Sun that now is but a spark;
  But soon will be unfurled
The glorious banner of us all,
The flag that rises ne'er to fall,
  Republic of the World!

Victor Hugo

The Morning Breaks

Beyond the war-clouds and the reddened ways,
I see the Promise of the Coming Days!
I see His Sun arise, new charged with grace
Earth's tears to dry and all her woes efface!
Christ lives! Christ loves! Christ rules!
No more shall Might,
Though leagued with all the Forces of the Night,

Ride over Right. No more shall Wrong
The world's gross agonies prolong.
Who waits His Time shall surely see
The triumph of His Constancy; —
When without let, or bar, or stay,
The coming of His Perfect Day
Shall sweep the Powers of Night away; —
And Faith, replumed for nobler flight,
And Hope, aglow with radiance bright,
And Love, in loveliness bedight,
Shall greet the morning light!

John Oxenham

The World-Man

Make room for the World-man!
  Prepare ye the way!
And hasten the coming
  Of Love's Triumph-day.

Make room for the World-man!
  No power can withhold
The dream of the ages
  By prophets foretold.

O hearts of the millions,
  List, list for the Voice!
The deserts shall blossom,
  The nations rejoice.

O hearts of the nations,
  List, list to the call,
And welcome the World-man,
  Great brother of all.

Where, where shall we seek him?
    My vision is true!
O hearts of the millions,
    He liveth in You!

Henry Victor Morgan

Peace Must Come as a Troubadour

They have pictured Peace at the wheel and loom
While swallows chirp in the nested eaves;
They have shown you fields with their tawny sheaves
And meadow vales where the daisies bloom.
But War rides out to the trumpet shout,
In scarlet and gold and silver and blue.
His strong old song throbs hard in you,
And you swing to your saddle with never a doubt.

They have pictured Peace in mauve and gray,
The pale old man in cowl and gown,
Walled in from the quiet old-world town,
Chanting the twilight hours away.
But down in the pushing, lusting crowd,
Down in the weary, sweating throng,
The faint, slow notes of Evensong
Are lost, for the horns of War are loud.

So Peace must come as a troubadour,
Singing to thatch and turret and spire,
Of smoking feast and of ruddy fire,
Of sleeping babes for the rich and poor.
But the song of Peace must soar and rise
To high adventure and pain and death,
For Youth will wager his dying breath
For a cause that wings to the very skies.

Marie Drennan

THANKSGIVING DAY

Prayer to the Giver

Lord, I am glad for the great gift of living —
   Glad for Thy days of sun and of rain;
Grateful for joy, with an endless thanksgiving,
   Grateful for laughter — and grateful for pain.

Lord, I am glad for the young April's wonder,
   Glad for the fulness of long summer days;
And now when the spring and my heart are asunder,
   Lord, I give thanks for the dark autumn ways.

Sun, bloom, and blossom, O Lord, I remember,
   The dream of the spring and its joy I recall;
But now in the silence and pain of November,
   Lord, I give thanks to Thee, Giver of all!

Charles Hanson Towne

We Thank Thee, Lord

We thank Thee, Lord,
For all Thy Golden Silences —
Silence of moorlands rolling to the skies,
Heath-purpled, bracken-clad, aflame with gorse;
Silence of deep woods' mystic cloistered calm;
Silence of wide seas basking in the sun;
Silence of white peaks soaring to the blue;
Silence of dawnings, when, their matins sung,
The little birds do fall asleep again;

For the deep silence of the golden noons;
Silence of gloamings and the setting sun;
Silence of moonlit nights and patterned glades;
Silence of stars, magnificently still,
Yet ever chanting their Creator's skill;
Deep unto deep, within us sound sweet chords
Of praise beyond the reach of human words;
In our souls' silence, feeling only Thee —
  We thank Thee, thank Thee,
  Thank Thee, Lord!

John Oxenham

Thanksliving

Were thanks with every gift expressed,
 Each day would be Thanksgiving;
Were gratitude its very best,
 Each life would be thanksliving.

Chauncey R. Piety

Harvest

Though the long seasons seem to separate
 Sower and reaper or deeds dreamed and done,
Yet when a man reaches the Ivory Gate
 Labor and life and seed and corn are one.

Because thou art the doer and the deed,
 Because thou art the thinker and the thought,
Because thou art the helper and the need,
 And the cold doubt that brings all things to naught;

Therefore in every gracious form and shape
 The world's dear open secret thou shalt find,
From the one beauty there is no escape
 Nor from the sunshine of the eternal mind.

The patient laborer, with guesses dim,
   Follows this wisdom to its secret goal,
He knows all deeds and dreams exist in him,
   And all men's God in every human soul.
                              Eva Gore-Booth

A Thankful Heart

Lord, Thou hast given me a cell
   Wherein to dwell,
A little house whose humble roof
   Is weatherproof. . . .
Low is my porch as is my fate,
   Both void of state,
And yet the threshold of my door
   Is worn by the poor
Who hither come and freely get
   Good words or meat.
'Tis Thou that crown'st my glittering hearth
   With guileless mirth.
All these and better Thou dost send
   Me to this end,
That I should render for my part
   A thankful heart.   *Robert Herrick*

Thank God!

Thank God for life!
E'en though it bring much bitterness and strife,
   And all our fairest hopes be wrecked and lost,
E'en though there be more ill than good in life,
   We cling to life and reckon not the cost.
      Thank God for life!

Thank God for love!
For though sometimes grief follows in its wake,
  Still we forget love's sorrow in love's joy,
And cherish tears with smiles for love's dear sake;
  Only in heaven is bliss without alloy.
      Thank God for love!

Thank God for pain!
No tear hath ever yet been shed in vain,
  And in the end each sorrowing heart shall find
No curse, but blessings in the hand of pain;
  Even when he smiteth, then is God's most kind.
      Thank God for pain!

Thank God for death!
Who touches anguished lips and stills their breath
  And giveth peace unto each troubled breast;
Grief flies before thy touch, O blessed death;
  God's sweetest gift; thy name in heaven is Rest.
      Thank God for death!

Author Unknown

We Thank Thee

Not for our lands, our wide-flung prairie wealth,
  Our mighty rivers born of friendly spring.
Our inland seas, our mountains proud and high,
  Forests and orchards richly blossoming;
Not for these, Lord, our deepest thanks are said
  As, humbly glad, we hail this day serene;
Not for these most, dear Father of our lives,
  But for the love that in all things is seen.

We thank Thee not for prestige born of war,
  For dauntless navies built for battle stress;
Nor would we boast of armies massed for strife;
  These all are vain, O Lord of kindliness.
What need have we of swords and bayonets,
  Of mighty cannon belching poisoned flame!
O, woo us from the pagan love of these
  Lest we again defile Thy sacred name.

We thank Thee, Lord, on this recurring day,
  For liberty to worship as we will;
We thank Thee for the hero souls of old
  Who dared wild seas their mission to fulfill.
O, gird our hearts with stalwart faith in good,
  Give us new trust in Thy providing hand,
And may a spirit born of brotherhood
  Inspire our hearts and bless our native land.
                    Thomas Curtis Clark

Psalm

They have burned to Thee many tapers in many temples:
I burn to Thee the taper of my heart.
They have sought Thee at many altars, they have carried
    lights to find Thee:
I find Thee in the white fire of my heart.
                    Jessie E. Sampter

CHRISTMAS DAY

The Time Draws Near

The time draws near the birth of Christ:
   The moon is hid; the night is still;
   The Christmas bells from hill to hill
Answer each other in the mist.

Four voices of four hamlets round,
   From far and near, on mead and moor,
   Swell out and fail, as if a door
Were shut between me and the sound:

Each voice four changes on the wind,
   That now dilate, and now decrease,
   Peace and good will, good will and peace,
Peace and good will, to all mankind.

                     Alfred Tennyson

Christmas Everywhere

Everywhere, everywhere, Christmas tonight!
Christmas in lands of the fir-tree and pine,
Christmas in lands of the palm-tree and vine,
Christmas where snow peaks stand solemn and white,
Christmas where cornfields stand sunny and bright.
Christmas where children are hopeful and gay,
Christmas where old men are patient and gray,
Christmas where peace, like a dove in his flight,
Broods o'er brave men in the thick of the fight;
Everywhere, everywhere, Christmas tonight!

For the Christ-child who comes is the Master of all;
No palace too great, no cottage too small.
                                        Phillips Brooks

Unto Us a Son Is Given

Given, not lent,
And not withdrawn — once sent,
This Infant of mankind, this One,
Is still the little welcome Son.

New every year,
New born and newly dear,
He comes with tidings and a song,
The ages long, the ages long;

Even as the cold
Keen winter grows not old,
As childhood is so fresh, foreseen,
And spring in the familiar green.

Sudden as sweet
Come the expected feet.
All joy is young, and new all art,
And He, too, Whom we have by heart.
                                        Alice Meynell

Three Gifts

Gold and frankincense and myrrh,
    Lord, they brought to Thee;
And myrrh was death, and incense prayer,
    And gold was victory.

But first is last as last was first;
The myrrh they gave Thee in Thy thirst
    Upon the tree.
And through the solemn centuries
    The prayers of saints have risen
From hearth and chancel, crypt and tomb,
    From pyre and from prison.
Now never was the mystic power
    Of the gold fulfilled;
Yet draweth on the mighty hour
    By the Father willed
When every knee shall bow to Him
    Who on the cross was lift,
And every tongue acclaim Him king;
    This is the golden gift.

Edward Judson Hanna

The Shepherd Speaks

Out of the midnight sky a great dawn broke,
And a voice singing flooded us with song.
In David's city was he born, it sang,
A Saviour, Christ the Lord. Then while I sat
Shivering with the thrill of that great cry,
A mighty choir a thousand-fold more sweet
Suddenly sang, Glory to God, and Peace —
Peace on the earth; my heart, almost unnerved
By that swift loveliness, would hardly beat.
Speechless we waited till the accustomed night
Gave us no promise more of sweet surprise;
Then scrambling to our feet, without a word
We started through the fields to find the Child.

John Erskine

The Three Wise Men

The First

I came from Tigris' sandy plain
　　Where I beheld the wondrous star,
With my slow-creeping camel train
　　I nightly followed it afar.

The Second

I came from Persia's table-land
　　That lies beyond the Syrian dawn;
A candle in an angel's hand
　　It seemed, before the stars had gone.

The Third

And I, 'mid mountains heav'nward piled,
　　I saw the star that led them west;
I, too, with them would seek the Child.
　　I, too, would make the Holy Quest.

The Three

We asked in great Jerusalem,
　　But none could tell us of his birth,
And then to little Bethlehem
　　We came — the least of all the earth.

There came we to our journey's goal;
　　No farther had we need to roam;
There was a home for every soul
　　Where Christ himself could find no home.

John Finley

A Christmas Prayer

We open here our treasures and our gifts;
And some of it is gold,
And some is frankincense,
And some is myrrh;
For some has come from plenty,
Some from joy,
And some from deepest sorrow of the soul.
But Thou, O God, dost know the gift is love,
Our pledge of peace, our promise of good will.
Accept the gift and all the life we bring.

Herbert H. Hines

God With Us

There were three lights that night:
The star above the darkness, crystal fair,
The foremost angel's garment flaming white,
    The baby's circled hair.

Three sounds upon the hill:
A sudden song; low drawn, a woman's sigh;
And, when the midnight deepened gray and chill,
    A little, little cry.

Three woes: a witless lamb
Lost from the scattered flock; its mother grieving;
The long, deep slumber of the townfolk — blind
    And deaf and unbelieving.

Three wonders: dark-browed kings
Riding from far; young shepherds' lifted faces;
The silver beauty raining from the star
    On Bethlehem's dark places.

There were Faith, Hope and Love:
Faith that had known, Hope that had waited well,
Love that had wrought; and in their trembling midst,
     Immanuel!
           Nancy Byrd Turner

Star of the East

Star of the East, that long ago
    Brought wise men on their way
Where, angels singing to and fro,
    The Child of Bethlehem lay —
Above that Syrian hill afar
Thou shinest out tonight, O Star!

Star of the East, the night were drear
    But for the tender grace
That with thy glory comes to cheer
    Earth's loneliest, darkest place;
For by that charity we see
Where there is hope for all and me.

Star of the East! show us the way
    In wisdom undefiled
To seek that manger out and lay
    Our gifts before the child —
To bring our hearts and offer them
Unto our King in Bethlehem!
           Eugene Field

The Christmas Symbol

Only a manger, cold and bare,
  Only a maiden mild,
Only some shepherds kneeling there,
  Watching a little Child;
And yet that maiden's arms enfold
  The King of Heaven above;
And in the Christ-Child we behold
  The Lord of Life and Love.

Only an altar high and fair,
  Only a white-robed priest,
Only Christ's children kneeling there
  Keeping the Christmas feast;
And yet beneath the outward sign
  The inward Grace is given, —
His Presence, who is Lord Divine
  And King of earth and heaven.

Author Unknown

The Kings of the East

The Kings of the East are riding
  Tonight to Bethlehem.
The sunset glows dividing,
The Kings of the East are riding;
A star their journey guiding,
  Gleaming with gold and gem
The Kings of the East are riding
  Tonight to Bethlehem.

There beams above the manger
The child-face of a star;
Amid the stars a stranger,
It beams above a manger;
What means this ether-ranger
To pause where poor folk are
There beams above a manger
The child-face of a star.

Katharine Lee Bates

How Far to Bethlehem

" How far is it to Bethlehem town? "
Just over Jerusalem hills adown,
Past lovely Rachel's white-domed tomb —
Sweet shrine of motherhood's young doom.

It isn't far to Bethlehem town —
Just over the dusty roads adown,
Past Wise Men's well, still offering
Cool draughts from welcome wayside spring;
Past shepherds with their flutes of reed
That charm the woolly sheep they lead;
Past boys with kites on hilltops flying,
And soon you're there where Bethlehem's lying.
Sunned white and sweet on olived slopes,
Gold-lighted still with Judah's hopes.

And so we find the Shepherd's field
And plain that gave rich Boaz yield;
And look where Herod's villa stood.
We thrill that earthly parenthood
Could foster Christ who was all-good;

And thrill that Bethlehem town today
Looks down on Christian homes that pray.

It isn't far to Bethlehem town!
It's anywhere that Christ comes down
And finds in people's friendly face
A welcome and abiding place.
The road to Bethlehem runs right through
The homes of folks like me and you.

Madeleine Sweeny Miller

The Way to Bethlehem

Long was the way to Bethlehem
  To those who sought of old,
By burning sands and bitter springs
  And nights of haunting cold,
Bearing their nard and frankincense,
  Their precious gems and gold.

Hard was the way to Bethlehem,
  So far it seemed, so far,
By flowerless vales and arid slopes
  And barren heights that bar,
With ne'er an omen for a guide
  Until they saw the star.

But then the way to Bethlehem,
  It was no longer lone;
Joy was their comrade, those who trod
  O'er bruising shard and stone,
Until they found for king a Child,
  A manger for his throne.

Upon the way to Bethlehem,
    Till time shall bring release,
However dim and rough the path
    May not our footsteps cease,
Since at the end for us awaits
    The guerdon of his peace!

Clinton Scollard

The Christmas Tree

If Christ could ever be born again,
    Who would his Mother be?
" I," said Sorrow; and " I," said Pain;
    And " I," said Poverty.

But how, were Christ so made again,
    Could one be born of Three?
" Are not the griefs of earth a strain
    Of the Blessed Trinity? "

And who, on his birth-night, again
    His worshipers would be?
" Love," said Sorrow; and " Pity," said Pain;
    And " Peace," said Poverty.

And who the seers, from what strange lands,
    Would come to look at him?
" The simple and wise, with serving hands,
    And little ones light of limb."

And what would the kings of earth do then?
    " Put simple and wise to flight;
While loud in the darkened homes of men
    Little ones cried for light."

What use, what use, if once again
  The world rejects the Sign?
" Christ will still be a Lover of men,
  And his heart may be yours and mine.

" For this is the Tree whose blessed yield
  Bears seed in darkest ground;
And a wound by those bright leaves is healed,
  Wherever a wound is found."

Edward Shillito

Christmas Bells

I heard the bells on Christmas Day
Their old familiar carols play,
And wild and sweet the words repeat
Of peace on earth, good will to men!

I thought how, as the day had come,
The belfries of all Christendom
Had rolled along the unbroken song
Of peace on earth, good will to men!

And in despair I bowed my head;
" There is no peace on earth," I said;
" For hate is strong, and mocks the song
Of peace on earth, good will to men."

Then pealed the bells more loud and deep:
" God is not dead, nor doth he sleep!
The wrong shall fail, the right prevail,
With peace on earth, good will to men! "

Till, ringing, singing on its way,
The world revolved from night to day,
A voice, a chime, a chant sublime,
Of peace on earth, good will to men!

Henry Wadsworth Longfellow

That Holy Thing

They all were looking for a king
 To slay their foes and lift them high;
Thou cam'st, a little baby thing
 That made a woman cry.

O Son of Man, to right my lot
 Naught but thy presence can avail;
Yet on the road thy wheels are not,
 Nor on the sea thy sail!

My how or why thou wilt not heed,
 But come down thine own secret stair,
That thou mayst answer all my need —
 Yea, every bygone prayer.

George MacDonald

Peace on Earth

Shepherds there were who in the fields by night
Kept watch, not wisting that a chorus bright
Of angels would to them the news convey —
The dawning of the world's most potent day.

Countless the nights of darkness and of fear
The world has watched through, but the message clear
Of prophets, martyrs, saints, and poets brought
The healing word for which it blindly sought.

Visions from God — through men must come the word,
Till the whole earth to action deeply stirred
From war and dread and hatred wins release,
And hails once more as King the Prince of Peace.

Helen Wieand Cole

Gifts

Three kings there were from Orient who came,
Led by a star with strange, compelling flame,
    A Prince's sign;
And shepherds, too, followed its beckoning light,
Till in a manger, lo, ineffable sight,
    Godhood benign!
That blessed the givers of the royal gold,
But smiled upon the lambkin from the fold.

We, too, may bring our frankincense and myrrh,
And pay our tribute there, as though we were
    Of kingly birth;
But 'tis not gifts like these that He doth prize
So much as those which come in lowlier wise
    From the poor of earth,
Who having naught of gold or treasure-trove
Bring that of which they have the chiefest, *love*.

Helen Wieand Cole

The Voice of Christmas

I cannot put the Presence by, of him, the Crucified,
Who moves men's spirits with his love as doth the moon the
    tide;
Again I see the Life he lived, the godlike Death he died.

Again I see upon the cross that great Soul-battle fought,
Into the texture of the world the tale of which is wrought
Until it hath become the woof of human deed and thought —

And, joining with the cadenced bells that all the morning
    fill,
His cry of agony doth yet my inmost being thrill,
Like some fresh grief from yesterday that tears the heart-
    strings still.

I cannot put his presence by, I meet him everywhere;
I meet him in the country town, the busy market-square;
The Mansion and the Tenement attest his presence there.

Upon the funneled ships at sea he sets his shining feet;
The Distant Ends of Empire not in vain his Name repeat, —
And, like the presence of a rose, he makes the whole world
    sweet.

He comes to break the barriers down raised up by barren
    creeds;
About the globe from zone to zone, like sunlight he proceeds;
He comes to give the World's starved heart the perfect love
    it needs —

The Christ whose friends have played him false, whom Dog-
    mas have belied,
Still speaking to the hearts of men — though shamed and
    crucified,
The Master of the centuries who will not be denied!

                                            Harry Kemp

Star of My Heart

Star of my heart, I follow from afar.
Sweet Love on high, lead on where shepherds are,
Where Time is not, and only dreamers are.
Star from of old, the Magi-Kings are dead
And a foolish Saxon seeks the manger-bed.
O lead me to Jehovah's child
Across this dreamland lone and wild,
Then I will speak this prayer unsaid,
And kiss his little haloed head —
" My star and I, we love thee, little child."

Except the Christ be born again tonight
In dreams of all men, saints and sons of shame,
The world will never see his kingdom bright.
Stars of all hearts, lead onward through the night
Past death-black deserts, doubts without a name,
Past hills of pain and mountains of new sin
To that far sky where mystic births begin,
Where dreaming ears the angel-song shall win.
Our Christmas shall be rare at dawning there,
And each shall find his brother fair,
Like a little child within:
All hearts of the earth shall find new birth
And wake, no more to sin.

Vachel Lindsay

POEMS ON

IMMORTALITY

IMMORTALITY

Crossing The Bar

Sunset and evening star,
  And one clear call for me!
And may there be no moaning of the bar,
  When I put out to sea,

But such a tide as moving seems asleep,
  Too full for sound and foam,
When that which drew from out the boundless deep
  Turns again home.

Twilight and evening bell,
  And after that the dark!
And may there be no sadness of farewell,
  When I embark;

For though from out our bourne of Time and Place
  The flood may bear me far,
I hope to see my Pilot face to face
  When I have crossed the bar.

Alfred Tennyson

I Am the Reaper

I am the Reaper.
All things with heedful hook
Silent I gather.
Pale roses touched with the spring,

Tall corn in summer,
Fruits rich with autumn, and frail winter blossoms —
Reaping, still reaping —
All things with heedful hook
Timely I gather.

I am the Sower.
All the unbodied life
Runs through my seed-sheet.
Atom with atom wed,
Each quickening the other,
Fall through my hands, ever changing, still changeless.
Ceaselessly sowing,
Life, incorruptible life,
Flows from my seed-sheet.

Maker and breaker,
I am the ebb and the flood,
Here and Hereafter,
Aped through the tangle and coil
Of infinite nature,
Viewless and soundless I fashion all being.
Taker and giver,
I am the womb and the grave,
The Now and the Ever.

William Ernest Henley

Death

I am the key that parts the gates of Fame;
I am the cloak that covers cowering Shame;
I am the final goal of every race;
I am the storm-tossed spirit's resting-place.

The messenger of sure and swift relief,
Welcomed with wailings and reproachful grief,
The friend of those that have no friend but me,
I break all chains, and set all captives free.

I am the cloud that, when earth's day is done,
An instant veils an unextinguished sun;
I am the brooding hush that follows strife,
The waking from a dream that man calls — life.

Florence Earle Coates

Margaritae Sorori

(So Be My Passing)

A late lark twitters from the quiet skies:
And from the west,
Where the sun, his day's work ended,
Lingers as in content,
There falls on the old, gray city
An influence luminous and serene,
A shining peace.

The smoke ascends
In a rose-and-golden haze. The spires
Shine and are changed. In the valley
Shadows rise. The lark sings on. The sun,
Closing his benediction,
Sinks, and the darkening air
Thrills with a sense of the triumphing night —
Night with her train of stars
And her great gift of sleep.

So be my passing!
My task accomplished and the long day done,
My wages taken, and in my heart

Some late lark singing,
Let me be gathered to the quiet west,
The sundown splendid and serene,
Death.

William Ernest Henley

From Compensation

And after he has come to hide
Our lambs upon the other side,
We know our Shepherd and our Guide.

And thus, by ways not understood,
Out of each dark vicissitude,
God brings us compensating good.

For Faith is perfected by fears,
And souls renew their youth with years,
And Love looks into heaven through tears.

Phœbe Cary

Sorrow

Count each affliction, whether light or grave,
God's messenger sent down to thee; do thou
With courtesy receive him; rise and bow;
And, ere his shadow pass thy threshold, crave
Permission first his heavenly feet to lave;
Then lay before him all thou hast; allow
No cloud of passion to usurp thy brow,
Or mar thy hospitality; no wave
Of mortal tumult to obliterate
The soul's marmoreal calmness: Grief should be,
Like joy, majestic, equable, sedate;

Confirming, cleansing, raising, making free;
Strong to consume small troubles; to commend
Great thoughts, grave thoughts, thoughts lasting to the end.
Aubrey De Vere

Prayer For One Dead

How can I cease to pray for thee?   Somewhere
In God's wide universe thou art today.
Can He not reach thee with His tender care?
Can He not hear me when for thee I pray?
Somewhere thou livest and hast need of Him,
Somewhere thy soul sees higher heights to climb,
And somewhere, too, there may be valleys dim
Which thou must pass to reach the heights sublime.
Then all the more because thou canst not hear
Poor human words of blessing, will I pray,
O true, brave heart, God bless thee, wheresoe'er
In God's wide universe thou art today!
Julia C. R. Dorr

The Last Invocation

At the last, tenderly,
From the walls of the powerful fortress'd house,
From the clasp of the knitted locks — from the keep of the
    well-closed doors,
Let me be wafted.
Let me glide noiselessly forth;
With the key of softness unlock the locks — with a whisper
Set ope the doors, O soul!
Tenderly — be not impatient,
(Strong is your hold, O mortal flesh!
Strong is your hold, O love.)
Walt Whitman

Father, to Thee

Father, to Thee we look in all our sorrow,
　　Thou art the fountain whence our healing flows;
Dark though the night, joy cometh with the morrow;
　　Safely they rest who in Thy love repose.

When fond hopes fail and skies are dark before us,
　　When the vain cares that vex our life increase —
Comes with its calm the thought that Thou art o'er us,
　　And we grow quiet, folded in Thy peace.

Naught shall affright us on thy goodness leaning,
　　Low in the heart Faith singeth still her song;
Chastened by pain, we learn life's deepest meaning,
　　And in our weakness Thou dost make us strong.

Patient, O heart, though heavy be thy sorrows!
　　Be not cast down, disquieted in vain;
Yet shalt thou praise Him when these darkened furrows,
　　Where now He plougheth, wave with golden grain.
Frederick L. Hosmer

In My Father's House

No, not cold beneath the grasses,
　　Not close-walled within the tomb;
Rather, in our Father's mansion,
　　Living, in another room.

Living, like the man who loves me,
　　Like my child with cheeks abloom,
Out of sight, at desk or schoolbook,
　　Busy, in another room.

Nearer than my son whom fortune
   Beckons where the strange lands loom;
Just behind the hanging curtain,
   Serving, in another room.

Shall I doubt my Father's mercy?
   Shall I think of death as doom,
Or the stepping o'er the threshold
   To a bigger, brighter room?

Shall I blame my Father's wisdom?
   Shall I sit enswathed in gloom,
When I know my loves are happy,
   Waiting in another room?

                    Robert Freeman

Envoy

Oh, seek me not within a tomb —
   Thou shalt not find me in the clay!
I pierce a little wall of gloom
   To mingle with the day!

I brothered with the things that pass,
   Poor giddy joy and puckered grief;
I go to brother with the grass
   And with the sunning leaf.

Nor death can sheathe me in a shroud;
   A joy-sword whetted keen with pain,
I join the armies of the cloud,
   The lightning and the rain.

Oh, subtle in the sap athrill,
   Athletic in the glad uplift,
A portion of the cosmic will,
   I pierced the planet-drift.

My God and I shall interknit
  As rain and ocean, breath and air;
And oh, the luring thought of it
    Is prayer!

John G. Neihardt

Death

Death is a dialogue between
  The spirit and the dust.
"Dissolve," says Death; the spirit, "Sir,
  I have another trust."
Death doubts it, argues from the ground.
  The spirit turns away,
Just laying off, for evidence,
  An overcoat of clay.

Emily Dickinson

Vespers

I know the night is near at hand:
  The mists lie low on hill and bay,
The autumn sheaves are dewless, dry;
  But I have had the day.

Yes, I have had, dear Lord, the day;
  When at Thy call I have the night,
Brief be the twilight as I pass
  From light to dark, from dark to light.

S. Weir Mitchell

The Inn By the Road

Ne'er was the sky so deep a hue
But that the sun came breaking through;
There never was a night so dark
But wakened to the singing lark;
Nor was there ever a lane so long
It had no turn for the weary throng;
Nor heart so sad that sometime after
There came no sound of lilting laughter:
And Death's not the end — 'neath the cold black sod —
'Tis the Inn by the Road on our way to God.

C. E. Warner

Who Goeth Hence

When death shall come to summon us at last,
    Some will remember children and the sound
Of little footsteps hallowing the past,
    As driven snowflakes hallow oft the ground.
Some will remember sunlight on a fence;
    And some the breath of blossoms in the rain;
Some will glimpse stars. And all the going hence
    Of these will be a wishing to remain.

But some will think of one who said, " And I,
    If I be lifted up will draw to me
All men." And when these latter come to die,
    With faces lifted to eternity
They shall go forth with calm, untroubled eyes,
    Like children hasting to a glad surprise.

Helen Frazee Bower

The Victors

They have triumphed who have died;
　　They have passed the porches wide,
　　Leading from the House of Night
　　To the splendid lawns of light.
　　They have gone on that far road
　　Leading to their new abode,
　　And from curtained casements we
　　Watch their going wistfully.

.　　.　　.　　.　　.

They have won, for they have read
　　The bright secrets of the dead;
　　And they gain the deep unknown,
　　Hearing Life's strange undertone.
　　In the race across the days
　　They are victors; theirs the praise,
　　Theirs the glory and the pride —
　　They have triumphed, having died!

Charles Hanson Towne

The Sea of Faith

Passage, immediate passage!   The blood burns in my veins!
Away, O soul!   Hoist instantly the anchor!
Cut the hawsers — haul out — shake out every sail!
Have we not stood here like trees in the ground long enough?
Have we not grovell'd here long enough, eating and drinking
　　like mere brutes?
Have we not darkened and daz'd ourselves with books long
　　enough?

Sail forth — steer for the deep water only,
Reckless, O soul, exploring, I with thee and thou with me,

For we are bound whither mariner has not yet dared to go,
And we will risk the ship, ourselves and all.

O my brave soul!
O farther, farther sail!
O daring joy, but safe! Are they not all the seas of God?
O farther, farther sail!

Walt Whitman

From " Passage to India "

Something Beyond

Something beyond! Though now, with joy unfounded,
    The life-task falleth from thy weary hand,
Be brave, be patient! in the fair Beyond
    Thou'lt understand.

Something beyond! Ah, if it were not so,
    Darker would be thy face, O brief today!
Earthward we'd bow beneath life's smiting woe,
    Powerless to pray.

Something beyond! The immortal morning stands
    Above the night, clear shines her prescient brow;
The pendulous star in her transfigured hands
    Lights up the Now.

Mary Clemmer

Peace! Be Still

Peace! Be still!
In this night of sorrow bow,
O my heart! Contend not thou!
What befalls thee is God's will —
Peace! Be still!

Peace!　Be still!
All thy murmuring words are vain —
God will make the riddle plain.
Wait His word and bear His will —
Peace!　Be still!

Hold thou still!
Though the good Physician's knife
Seems to touch thy very life,
Death alone He means to kill, —
Hold thou still!

Shepherd mine!
From Thy fullness give me still
Faith to do and bear Thy will,
Till the morning light shall shine,
Shepherd mine!

Author Unknown

Nearer Home

One sweetly solemn thought
　Comes to me o'er and o'er;
I'm nearer my home today
　Than I ever have been before;

Nearer my Father's house,
　Where the many mansions be;
Nearer the great white throne,
　Nearer the crystal sea.

Nearer the bound of life,
　Where we lay our burdens down;
Nearer leaving the cross,
　Nearer gaining the crown!

But the waves of that silent sea
   Roll dark before my sight
That brightly the other side
   Break on a shore of light.

Oh, if my mortal feet
   Have almost gained the brink;
If it be I am nearer home
   Even today than I think,—

Father, perfect my trust!
   Let my spirit feel, in death,
That her feet are firmly set
   On the Rock of a living faith!

Phœbe Cary

A Grave

A grave seems only six feet deep
   And three feet wide,
Viewed with the calculative eye
   Of one outside.

But when fast-bound in the chill loam
   For that strange sleep,
Who knows how wide its realm may be?
   Its depth, how deep?

John Richard Moreland

" Be Quiet: Fear Not "

Thou layest Thy hand on the fluttering heart
 And sayest, " Be still! "
The shadow and silence are only a part
 Of Thy sweet will.
Thy Presence is with me, and where Thou art
 I fear no ill.

Frances Ridley Havergal

Immortality

It must be so, Plato, thou reasonest well! —
Else whence this pleasing hope, this fond desire,
This longing after immortality?
Or whence this secret dread, and inward horror
Of falling into naught? Why shrinks the soul
Back on herself, and startles at destruction?
'Tis the divinity that stirs within us,
'Tis heaven itself that points out an hereafter,
And intimates eternity to man.

Joseph Addison

From " Cato "

At the Goal

Who would wish back the saints upon our rough
Wearisome road?
Wish back a breathless soul
Just at the goal?
My soul, praise God
For all dear souls which have enough.

Christina Rossetti

Christus Consolator

Beside the dead I knelt for prayer,
  And felt a presence as I prayed.
Lo, it was Jesus standing there;
  He smiled: " Be not afraid! "

" Lord, thou hast conquered death, we know;
  Restore again to life," I said,
" This one who died an hour ago."
  He smiled: " She is not dead."

" Asleep then, as thyself didst say;
  Yet thou canst lift the lids that keep
Her prisoned eyes from ours away; "
  He smiled: " She doth not sleep."

" Nay, then, though haply she do wake,
  And look upon some fairer dawn,
Restore her to our hearts that ache; "
  He smiled: " She is not gone."

" Alas; too well we know our loss,
  Nor hope again our joy to touch
Until the stream of death we cross."
  He smiled: " There is no such."

" Yet our beloved seem so far,
  The while we yearn to feel them near,
Albeit with thee we trust they are."
  He smiled: " And I am here."

" Dear Lord, how shall we know that they
  Still walk unseen with us and thee,
Nor sleep, nor wander far away? "
  He smiled: " Abide in Me."

Rossiter W. Raymond

Azrael

The angels in high places
    Who minister to us,
Reflect God's smile — their faces
    Are luminous;
Save one, whose face is hidden,
    (The Prophet saith),
The unwelcome, the unbidden,
    Azrael, Angel of Death.
And yet, that veilèd face, I know
    Is lit with pitying eyes,
Like those faint stars, the first to glow,
    Through cloudy winter skies.

That they may never tire,
    Angels, by God's decree,
Bear wings of snow and fire, —
    Passion and purity;
Save one, all unavailing,
    (The Prophet saith),
His wings are gray and trailing,
    Azrael, Angel of Death.
And yet the souls that Azrael brings
    Across the dark and cold,
Look up beneath those folded wings,
    And find them lined with gold.

Robert Gilbert Welsh

Requiem

Under the wide and starry sky
Dig the grave and let me lie,

Glad did I live and gladly die,
And I lay me down with a will.

This be the verse you grave for me:
" *Here he lies where he longed to be;*
Home is the sailor, home from the sea,
And the hunter home from the hill."
                              Robert Louis Stevenson

Good-Night

" Good-night, sleep well! " we say to those we love,
And watch dear faces glimmer on the stair,
And hear faint footfalls in the rooms above
                Sound on the quiet air,
Yet feel no fear, though lonely they must go
The road of slumber's strange oblivion:
                Dark always wears to dawn,
Sleep is so gentle, and so well we know,
                Wherever they have gone,
They will be safe until the morning light,
                Good-night, good-night!

Good-night, sleep well, belovèds, when the last
Slow dusk has fallen, and your steps no more
Make music on the empty upper floor,
                And day is fully past.
We who so lightly let you go alone,
Evening by evening, from our trustful sight
Into the mystery of sleep's unknown —
                We need not fear, tonight,
Death is so gentle — dark will break to dawn . . .
Love will be safe until the morning light.
                Sleep well, good-night!
                              Nancy Byrd Turner

The Rainbow

Not in the time of pleasure
  Hope doth set her bow;
But in the sky of sorrow,
  Over the vale of woe.

Through gloom and shadow look we
  On beyond the years!
The soul would have no rainbow
  Had the eyes no tears.

John Vance Cheney

In the Hour of Death

In the hour of death, after this life's whim,
When the heart beats low, and the eyes grow dim,
And pain has exhausted every limb —
The lover of the Lord shall trust in Him.

When the will has forgotten the lifelong aim,
And the mind can only disgrace its fame,
And man is uncertain of his own name —
The power of the Lord shall fill this frame.

When the last sigh is heaved, and the last tear shed,
And the coffin is waiting beside the bed,
And the widow and child forsake the dead —
The angel of the Lord shall lift this head.

For even the purest delight may pall,
And power must fail, and the pride must fall,
And the love of the dearest friends grow small —
But the glory of the Lord is all in all.

Author Unknown

Christ and the Mourners

Down on the shadowed stream of time and tears
   Voice of new grief and grief of ancient years —
Sad as when first from loving lips 'twas sighed —
   " Hadst Thou been here, my brother had not died."

Comfort us, Lord, who heards't poor Martha's plaint,
   Heal the sore heart, uplift the spirit faint —
O Thou, the Peace that cometh after strife!
   O Thou, the Resurrection and the Life!

Katherine E. Conway

Epilogue

At the midnight in the silence of the sleep-time,
   When you set your fancies free,
Will they pass to where — by death, fools think, im-
      prisoned —
Low he lies who once so loved you, whom you loved so,
            — Pity me?

Oh to love so, be so loved, yet so mistaken!
   What had I on earth to do
With the slothful, with the mawkish, the unmanly?
Like the aimless, helpless, hopeless did I drivel
            — Being — who?

One who never turned his back but marched breast forward,
   Never doubted clouds would break,
Never dreamed, though right were worsted, wrong would
      triumph,
Held we fall to rise, are baffled to fight better,
            Sleep to wake.

No, at noon-day in the bustle of man's work-time
   Greet the unseen with a cheer!
Bid him forward, breast and back as either should be,
" Strive and thrive! " cry, " Speed — fight on, fare ever
      There as here! "
                                    Robert Browning

The Ways of Death

The ways of Death are soothing and serene,
   And all the words of Death are grave and sweet,
   From camp and church, the fireside and the street,
She signs to come, and strife and song have been.

The summer night descending cool and green
   And dark, on daytime's dust and stress and heat,
The ways of death are soothing and serene,
   And all the words of Death are grave and sweet.

O glad and sorrowful, with triumphant mien
   And hopeful faces look upon and greet
   This last of all your lover's and to meet
Her kiss, the Comforter's, your spirit lean —
The ways of Death are soothing and serene.
                              William Ernest Henley

After Sunset

If light of life outlive the set of sun
   That men call death and end of all things, then
   How should not that which life held best for men
And proved most precious, though it seem undone
By force of death and woeful victory won,
   Be first and surest of revival, when
   Death shall bow down to life arisen again?

So shall the soul seen be the self-same one
That looked and spake with even such lips and eyes
As love shall doubt not then to recognize,
   And all bright thoughts and smiles of all time past
Revive, transfigured, but in spirit and sense
None other than we knew, for evidence
That love's last mortal word was not his last.

Algernon Charles Swinburne

A Shining Hope

God grant that all who watch today
   Beside their sepulchers of loss,
May find the great stone rolled away, —
   May see at last, with vision clear,
   The shining angel standing near,
And through the dimly-lighted soul
Again may joy's evangel roll
   The glory of the Cross.   *Julia H. Thayer*

Peaceful Death

Thee, holiest minister of Heaven — thee, envoy, usherer,
   guide at last of all,
Rich, florid, loosener of the stricture-knot called life,
Sweet, peaceful, welcome Death.

Walt Whitman

Paradisi Gloria

There is a city, builded by no hand,
   And unapproachable by sea or shore,
And unassailable by any band
   Of storming soldiery for evermore.

There we no longer shall divide our time
   By acts or pleasures — doing petty things
Of work or warfare, merchandise or rhyme;
   But we shall sit beside the silver springs

That flow from God's own footstool, and behold
   Sages and martyrs, and those blessed few
Who loved us once and were beloved of old,
   To dwell with them and walk with them anew,

In alternations of sublime repose,
   Musical motion, the perpetual play
Of every faculty that heaven bestows
   Through the bright, busy, and eternal day.
                  Thomas William Parsons

Heaven

   No night is there!
Though here the night comes dank and chill
And shadows every corner fill,
The deathless morning comes at last
When all of time for me is past,
   No night is there!

   No pain is there!
Though here pains wrench this mortal frame
And men are sick and weak and lame,
In that fair land awaiting me
I shall from ills and pains be free,
   No pain is there!

No tears are there!
Though here we miss the loved ones dear
And lonely are and often fear,
In heaven, our home, we'll meet them all
And answer once again their call,
        No tears are there!

        Our Christ is there!
He'll come and take us to himself,
And give to us for this world's pelf
A mansion made by his dear hand
And with us dwell in that fair land,
        Yes, Christ is there!

Clarence A. Vincent

Good-Night

Good-night!   Good-night!
Far from us day takes its flight,
But ever God's eternal love
Remains to guard us, as above
The stars watch with celestial light.
    Good-night!   Good-night!

Till tomorrow!   Till tomorrow!
Ah, we know not what may follow.
Close our eyes tonight we may,
Shall we see another day?
Mayhap in vain we say tomorrow,
    Till tomorrow!

Victor Hugo

Paradise

I cannot think of Paradise a place
Where men go idly to and fro,
With harps of gold and robes that shame the snow;
With great wide wings that brightly interlace
Whene'er they sing before the Master's face —
Within a realm where neither pain nor woe,
Nor care is found; where tempests never blow;
Where souls with hopes and dreams may run no race.
Such paradise were but a hell to me;
Devoid of all progression, I should rot,
Or shout for revolution, wide and far.
Better some simple task, a spirit free
To act along the line of self forgot —
Or help God make a blossom or a star.

Charles G. Blanden

SUBJECT INDEX

INDEX OF AUTHORS

343

A6

INDEX OF TITLES

INDEX OF FIRST LINES

ACKNOWLEDGMENTS

To both publishers and poets sincere thanks and appreciation are given for their generous coöperation in permitting the use of the copyright poems from the volumes enumerated below:

To D. Appleton & Company for *To a Waterfowl* from the " Poetical Works of William Cullen Bryant."

To Brandt & Brandt, agents for Berton Braley, for the use of *The Thinker*.

To The Century Company for *Vespers* by Dr. S. Wier Mitchell.

To the W. B. Conkey Company for the poems by Ella Wheeler Wilcox.

To the Thomas Y. Crowell Company for *The Inevitable* and *Live in the Present* from the " Poems of Sarah K. Bolton."

To Dodd, Mead & Company for *Resurrection, God Prays,* and *In Such an Age!* by Angela Morgan; for *The Kingdom of Heaven* and *Home at Last* by Gilbert K. Chesterton; for *The Dead* by Rupert Brooke; and for *A Warrior's Prayer* and *Lincoln* by Paul Lawrence Dunbar.

To Doubleday, Doran & Company for *Citizen of the World* by Joyce Kilmer; for *Good Friday* by Lizette Woodworth Reese; for *Indifference* by G. A. Studdert-Kennedy; for *Recessional* from " The Five Nations " and *Mother O' Mine* from " The Light That Failed " by Rudyard Kipling; and for the poems by John Oxenham.

To E. P. Dutton & Company for *The Debt* and *The Kings of the East* from " The Retinue and Other Poems " by Katharine Lee Bates; for *Acceptance, The Builder,* and *Creeds* from " Lanterns in Gethsemane " by Willard Wattles, and for *Approaches, Lost and Found, That Holy Thing,* and *What Christ Said* by George MacDonald.

To the Evangelical Publishers, Toronto, for *Jesus Christ — And We* by Annie Johnson Flint.

To Funk & Wagnalls Company for *Indirection* by Richard Realf from his " Poems."

To Harcourt, Brace & Company for *Prayer for Courage* from " Challenge " by Louis Untermeyer, and for *The Watcher — Mother* from " Cross Currents " by Margaret Widdemer.

To Harper & Brothers for *After Sunset* from the " Poetical Works of Algernon Charles Swinburne "; for *I Have a Rendezvous with Life* and *Simon the Cyrenian Speaks* by Countee Cullen; and for *By One Great Heart* and *Easter Music* by Margaret Wade Deland.

To the Harr Wagner Publishing Company for *Columbus* by Joaquin Miller from his " Autobiography and Favorite Poems."

To Henry Holt & Company for *Prayer of Steel* and *Child* by Carl Sandburg.

To Houghton Mifflin Company for poems by Alfred Tennyson, Robert Browning, Ralph Waldo Emerson, Henry Wadsworth Longfellow, John Burroughs, John Greenleaf Whittier, Oliver Wendell Holmes, Julia Ward Howe, James Russell Lowell, Edith M. Thomas, Florence Earle Coates, Harriet Beecher Stowe, Phœbe Cary, Richard Watson Gilder, William Vaughn Moody, John Drinkwater, and Edward Rowland Sill.

To the Marshall Jones Company for *A Voice* by Samuel Valentine Cole.

To the Mitchell Kennerly Company for *The Jewish Conscript* by Florence Kiper Frank; for *The Voice of Christmas* by Harry Kemp; and for *He Whom a Dream Hath Possessed* by Shaemus O'Sheel.

To Alfred A. Knopf, Inc., for *A Poet Lived in Galilee* from " Grenstone Poems " by Witter Bynner.

To Little, Brown & Company for poems by Emily Dickinson; for *Spinning* by Helen Hunt Jackson, and for *Patriotism* by Susan Coolidge.

To Longmans, Green & Company for *The Quest* and *Harvest* by Eva Gore-Booth.

To Lothrop, Lee & Shepard for *The Larger Prayer* by Ednah D. Cheney and for *The House by the Side of the Road* from " Dreams in Homespun " and *The Higher Catechism* from " Songs of the Average Man " by Sam Walter Foss.

To The Macmillan Company for *The Thief on the Cross* from " You and I " and *Washington* from " The Difference and Other Poems " by Harriet Monroe; for *Waking Thought* from " Citadels " by Marguerite Wilkinson; for the poems by Vachel Lindsay; for *The Mystery* by Ralph Hodgson; for *Spirit's House* by Sara Teasdale; for the poems by Matthew Arnold; for *Dust* by George W. Russell (A.E.) ; and for *Envoy* by John G. Nehardt.

To the Meigs Publishing Company for *Others* by Charles D. Meigs.

To the John Murphy Company for *The Heart of the Eternal* by Frederick W. Faber.

To G. P. Putnam's Sons for *Symbol* by David Morton.

To the Reilly & Lee Company for *Your Flag and My Flag* from " The Paths of Long Ago " by Wilbur D. Nesbit.

To Charles Scribner's Sons for poems by Robert Louis Stevenson, Maltbie D. Babcock, Henry van Dyke, Alice Meynell, Eugene Field, John Galsworthy, William Ernest Henley, Edwin Arlington Robinson, J. G. Holland, and Sidney Lanier.

To James T. White & Company for *If Hearts Are Dust* and *Not By Bread Alone* by James Terry White; and for poems by Thomas Curtis Clark.

To the Yale University Press for *Good Company* from " Blue Smoke " by Karle Wilson Baker.

Personal acknowledgment is also made to the following poets and individual owners of copyrights for the poems enumerated:

To Mrs. W. H. Carruth for *Each in His Own Tongue* by W. H. Carruth; to Elsa Barker for *A Prayer for Love;* to Louis F. Benson for *The Light of God is Falling;* to Susie M. Best for *Ich Dien;* to Gamaliel Bradford for *Judas;* to Bliss Carman for *Vestigia;* to Badger Clark for *God Meets Me in the Mountains;* to Sarah N. Cleghorn for *Comrade Jesus;* to Mrs. Samuel Valentine Cole (Helen Wieand Cole) for *A Voice* by Dr. Samuel Valentine Cole and two poems by herself; to the Rev. Chester B. Emerson for *The Quest;* to John Erskine for *The Shepherd Speaks;* to the Rev. Harry Webb Farrington for *Our Christ* (Harvard Prize poem from Rough and Brown); to John H. Finley for *The Three Wise Men;* to Wayne Gard for *Life;* to Robert W. Freeman for *A Hymn of Unity;* to Charlotte P. Gilman for *For Us;* to Arthur Guiterman for *He Leads Us Still* from " A Ballad-maker's Pack "; to Caroline Hazard for *The Ninth Hour* from " A Scallop Shell of Quiet "; to Daniel Henderson for *Hymn for a Household;* to A. E. Housman for *Loveliest of Trees* from " A Shropshire Lad "; to John Oxenham for the several poems used; to the Rev. William Herbert Hudnut for *Quit You Like Men;* to David Starr Jordan for *To Love, at Last, the Victory,* and *Men Told Me, Lord;* to Rudyard Kipling for *Recessional* from " The Five Nations " and *Mother O' Mine* from " The Light That Failed "; to George Klingle for *Hour by Hour* and *Tomorrow's News;* to Richard Le Gallienne for *This Is War;* to Marie LeNart for *Atonement* and *Give Us Great Dreams;* to Arthur L. Livermore for the use of *Immanence* and *Transcendence* by Richard Hovey; to Louis Loveman for *Creed and Deed* and the *Rain Song* by Robert Loveman; to the Rev. Clyde McGee for *Gratitude;* to Edwin Markham for the several poems used with his special permission; to Earl B. Marlatt for *Paul;* to John Masefield for *The Seekers* from " The Story of a Round-House "; to Walt Mason for *The Eyes of Lincoln* and *Little Green Tents;* to Edgar Lee Masters for an extract from *The New Spoon River;* to Mrs. Madeleine Sweeny Miller for *How Far to Bethlehem?;* to the Rev. Robert Norwood for *Why?;* to Shaemus O'Sheel for *He Whom a Dream Hath Possessed;* to Albert Bigelow Paine for *The New Memorial Day;* to Clinton Scollard for poems used; to Charles M. Sheldon for *Jesus the Carpenter;* to Charles Hanson Towne for poems used; to Nancy Byrd Turner for *Good-Night* and *God With Us;* and to Clement Wood for *The Singing Saviors.*

QUOTABLE
POEMS

VOLUME TWO

They Went Forth to Battle but They Always Fell

They went forth to battle but they always fell.
Something they saw above the sullen shields.
Nobly they fought and bravely, but not well,
And sank heart-wounded by a subtle spell.
They knew not fear that to the foeman yields,
They were not weak, as one who vainly wields
A faltering weapon; yet the old tales tell
How on the hard-fought field they always fell.

It was a secret music that they heard,
The murmurous voice of pity and of peace,
And that which pierced the heart was but a word,
Though the white breast was red-lipped where the sword
Pressed a fierce cruel kiss and did not cease
Till its hot thirst was surfeited. Ah these
By an unwarlike troubling doubt were stirred,
And died for hearing what no foeman heard.

They went forth to battle but they always fell.
Their might was not the might of lifted spears.
Over the battle-clamor came a spell
Of troubling music, and they fought not well.
Their wreaths are willows and their tribute, tears.
Their names are old sad stories in men's ears.
Yet they will scatter the red hordes of Hell,
Who went to battle forth and always fell.

Shaemas O'Sheel

Opportunity

In an old city by the storied shores,
Where the bright summit of Olympus soars,
A cryptic statue mounted toward the light —
Heel-winged, tip-toed, and poised for instant flight.
" O statue, tell your name," a traveler cried;
And solemnly the marble lips replied:
" Men call me Opportunity. I lift
My wingèd feet from earth to show how swift
My flight, how short my stay —
How Fate is ever waiting on the way."

" But why that tossing ringlet on your brow? "
" That men may seize me any moment: *Now*,
Now is my other name; today my date;
O traveler, tomorrow is too late!"

Edwin Markham

Prayer

God, though this life is but a wraith,
    Although we know not what we use;
Although we grope with little faith,
    God, give me the heart to fight— and lose.

Ever insurgent let me be,
    Make me more daring than devout;
From sleek contentment keep me free
    And fill me with a buoyant doubt.

Open my eyes to visions girt
    With beauty, and with wonder lit, —

But let me always see the dirt,
   And all that spawn and die in it.

Open my ears to music, let
   Me thrill with Spring's first flutes and drums
But never let me dare forget
   The bitter ballads of the slums.

From compromise and things half-done,
   Keep me, with stern and stubborn pride;
But when at last the fight is won,
   God, keep me still unsatisfied.

Louis Untermeyer

For Those Who Fail

" All honor to him who shall win the prize,"
   The world has cried for a thousand years;
But to him who tries and who fails and dies,
   I give great honor and glory and tears.

O great is the hero who wins a name,
   But greater many and many a time
Some pale-faced fellow who dies in shame,
   And lets God finish the thought sublime.

And great is the man with a sword undrawn,
   And good is the man who refrains from wine;
But the man who fails and yet fights on,
   Lo, he is the twin-born brother of mine!

Joaquin Miller

In Flanders Fields

In Flanders fields the poppies blow
Between the crosses, row on row,
That mark our place; and in the sky
The larks, still bravely singing, fly
Scarce heard amid the guns below.

We are the Dead. Short days ago
We lived, felt dawn, saw sunset glow,
Loved and were loved, and now we lie
        In Flanders fields.

Take up our quarrel with the foe;
To you from failing hands we throw
The torch; be yours to hold it high.
If ye break faith with us who die
We shall not sleep, though poppies grow
        In Flanders fields.

John McCrae

Sealed Orders

We bear sealed orders o'er Life's weltered sea,
    Our haven dim and far;
We can but man the helm right cheerily,
    Steer by the brightest star,

And hope that when at last the Great Command
    Is read, we then may hear
Our anchor song, and see the longed-for land
    Lie, known and very near.

Richard Burton

From Song of the Open Road

Afoot and lighthearted I take to the open road,
Healthy, free, the world before me,
The long brown path before me leading me wherever I
  choose.

Henceforth I ask not good fortune, I myself *am* good for-
  tune,
Henceforth I whimper no more, postpone no more, need
  nothing;
Done with indoor complaints, libraries, querulous criticisms,
Strong and content I travel the open road.

Walt Whitman

Joses, the Brother of Jesus

Joses, the brother of Jesus, plodded from day to day
With never a vision within him to glorify his clay;
Joses, the brother of Jesus, was one with the heavy clod,
But Christ was the soul of rapture, and soared, like a lark,
  with God.
Joses, the brother of Jesus, was only a worker in wood,
And he never could see the glory that Jesus, his brother,
  could.
"Why stays he not in the workshop?" he often used to
  complain,
"Sawing the Lebanon cedar, imparting to woods their stain?
Why must he go thus roaming, forsaking my father's
  trade,
While hammers are busily sounding, and there is gain to be
  made?"

Thus ran the mind of Joses, apt with plummet and rule,
And deeming whoever surpassed him either a knave or a
    fool —
For he never walked with the prophets in God's great garden
    of bliss —
And of all mistakes of the ages, the saddest, methinks, was
    this
To have such a brother as Jesus, to speak with him day by
    day,
But never to catch the vision which glorified his clay.

Harry Kemp

The Judgment

When before the cloud-white throne
We are kneeling to be known
In self's utter nakedness,
Mercy shall be arbitress.

Love shall quench the very shame
That is our tormenting flame;
Love, the one theology,
Set the souls in prison free —

Free as sunbeams forth to fare
Into outer darkness, where
It shall be our doom to make
Glory from each earth-mistake.

Not archangels God elects
For celestial architects;
On the stones of hell, the guilt
Of the world, is Zion built.

Katharine Lee Bates

Mountain Air

Tell me of Progress if you will,
But give me sunshine on a hill —
The grey rocks spiring to the blue,
The scent of larches, pinks and dew,
And summer sighing in the trees,
And snowy breath on every breeze.
Take towns and all that you find there,
And leave me sun and mountain air!

John Galsworthy

From Tintern Abbey

For I have learned
To look on Nature, not as in the hour
Of thoughtless youth; but hearing oftentimes
The still, sad music of humanity,
Nor harsh nor grating, though of ample power
To chasten and subdue.   And I have felt
A presence that disturbs me with the joy
Of elevated thoughts; a sense sublime,
Of something far more deeply interfused,
Whose dwelling is the light of setting suns,
And the round ocean and the living air,
And the blue sky, and in the mind of man;
A motion and a spirit, that impels
All thinking things, all objects of all thought,
And rolls through all things.   Therefore am I still
A lover of the meadows and the woods,
And mountains; and of all that we behold
From this green earth; of all the mighty world
Of eye and ear — both what they half create,

And what perceive; well pleased to recognize
In nature and the language of the sense,
The anchor of my purest thoughts, the nurse,
The guide, the guardian of my heart, and soul
Of all my moral being.

William Wordsworth

The Ideal City

O you whom God hath called and set apart
To build a city after His own heart,
Be this your task — to fill the city's veins
With the red blood of friendship; plant her plains
With seeds of peace: above her portals wreathe
Greeting and welcome: let the air we breathe
Be musical with accents of good will
That leap from lip to lip with joyous thrill;
So may the stranger find upon the streets
A kindly look in every face he meets;
So may the spirit of the city tell
All her souls within her gates that all is well;
In all her homes let gentleness be found,
In every neighborhood let grace abound,
In every store and shop and forge and mill
Where men of toil their daily tasks fulfill,
Where guiding brain and workmen's skill are wise
To shape the product of our industries,
Where treasured stores the hands of toil sustain,
Let friendship speed the work and share the gain,
And thus, through all the city's teeming life,
Let helpfulness have room with generous strife
To serve.

Washington Gladden

Calvary

I walked alone to my Calvary,
And no man carried the cross for me:
Carried the cross? Nay, no man knew
The fearful load I bent unto;
But each as we met upon the way
Spake me fair of the journey I walked that day.

I came alone to my Calvary,
And high was the hill and bleak to see;
But lo, as I scaled the flinty side,
A thousand went up to be crucified —
A thousand kept the way with me,
But never a cross my eyes could see.

Author Unknown

Good Deeds

How far that little candle throws his beams!
So shines a good deed in a naughty world.
Heaven doth with us as we with torches do;
Not light them for themselves; for if our virtues
Did not go forth of us, 'twere all alike
As if we had them not.

William Shakespeare

Abraham Lincoln Walks at Midnight
(In Springfield, Illinois)

It is portentous, and a thing of state
That here at midnight, in our little town
A mourning figure walks, and will not rest,
Near the old court-house pacing up and down,

From " Collected Poems " by Vachel Lindsay. By permission of The Macmillan Company, publishers.

Or by his homestead, or in shadowed yards
He lingers where his children used to play,
Or through the market, on the well-worn stones
He stalks until the dawn-stars burn away.

A bronzed, lank man!   His suit of ancient black,
A famous high top-hat and plain worn shawl
Make him the quaint great figure that men love,
The prairie-lawyer, master of us all.

He cannot sleep upon his hillside now.
He is among us: — as in times before!
And we who toss and lie awake for long
Breathe deep, and start, to see him pass the door.

His head is bowed.   He thinks on men and kings.
Yea, when the sick world cries, how can he sleep?
Too many peasants fight, they know not why,
Too many homesteads in black terror weep.

The sins of all the war-lords burn his heart.
He sees the dreadnoughts scouring every main.
He carries on his shawl-wrapped shoulders now
The bitterness, the folly and the pain.

He cannot rest until a spirit-dawn
Shall come; — the shining hope of Europe free:
The league of sober folk, the Workers' Earth,
Bringing long peace to Cornland, Alp and Sea.

It breaks his heart that kings must murder still.
That all his hours of travail here for men
Seem yet in vain.   And who will bring white peace
That he may sleep upon his hill again?

Vachel Lindsay

Where Is God?

"Oh, where is the sea?" the fishes cried,
    As they swam the crystal clearness through;
"We've heard from of old of the ocean's tide,
    And we long to look on the water's blue.
The wise ones speak of the infinite sea.
    Oh, who can tell us if such there be?"

The lark flew up in the morning bright,
    And sang and balanced on sunny wings;
And this was its song: "I see the light,
    I look o'er a world of beautiful things;
But, flying and singing everywhere,
    In vain I have searched to find the air."

Minot J. Savage

Deathless

I know I am deathless;
I know this orbit of mine cannot be swept by the carpenter's
    compass;
I know I shall not pass like a child's carlaque cut with a
    burnt stick at night.

Walt Whitman

From "Leaves of Grass"

We Are the Music-Makers

We are the music-makers,
    And we are the dreamers of dreams,
Wandering by lone sea-breakers,
    And sitting by desolate streams —

World-losers and world-forsakers,
  On whom the pale moon gleams;
Yet we are the movers and shakers
  Of the world forever, it seems.

With wonderful deathless ditties
  We build up the world's great cities,
And out of a fabulous story
  We fashion an empire's glory:
One man with a dream, at pleasure,
  Shall go forth and conquer a crown;
And three with a new song's measure
  Can trample a kingdom down.

We, in the ages lying
  In the buried past of the earth,
Built Nineveh with our sighing,
  And Babel itself in our mirth;
And o'erthrew them with prophesying
  To the old of the new world's worth;
For each age is a dream that is dying,
  Or one that is coming to birth.

Arthur O'Shaughnessy

In the Woods

Oh, when I am safe in my sylvan home
I tread on the pride of Greece and Rome.
But when I am stretched beneath the pines,
When the evening star so lonely shines,
I laugh at the love and the pride of man,
At the sophist's schools and the learned clan;
For what are they all in their high conceit
When man in the bush with God can meet?

Ralph Waldo Emerson

From " Good-bye, Proud World "

" In No Strange Land "

O WORLD invisible, we view thee,
O world intangible, we touch thee,
O world unknowable, we know thee,
Inapprehensible, we clutch thee!

Does the fish soar to find the ocean,
The eagle plunge to find the air —
That we ask of the stars in motion
If they have rumor of thee there?

Not where the wheeling systems darken,
And our benumbed conceiving soars! —
The drift of pinions, would we hearken,
Beats at our own clay-shuttered doors.

The angels keep their ancient places; —
Turn but a stone, and start a wing!
'Tis ye, 'tis your estrangèd faces,
That miss the many-splendored thing.

But (when so sad thou canst not sadder)
Cry; — and upon thy so sore loss
Shall shine the traffic of Jacob's ladder
Pitched betwixt Heaven and Charing Cross.

Yea, in the night, my Soul, my daughter,
Cry, — clinging Heaven by the hems;
And lo, Christ walking on the water
Not of Genesareth, but Thames!

Francis Thompson

Io Victis

I sing the hymn of the conquered, who fall in the Battle of
    Life —
The hymn of the wounded, the beaten, who died overwhelmed
    in the strife;
Not the jubilant song of the victors, for whom the resound-
    ing acclaim
Of nations was lifted in chorus, whose brows wear the chaplet
    of fame,
But the hymn of the low and the humble, the weary, the
    broken in heart,
Who strove and who failed, acting bravely a silent and des-
    perate part;
Whose youth bore no flower in its branches, whose hopes
    burned in ashes away,
From whose hands slipped the prize they had grasped at,
    who stood at the dying of day
With the wreck of their life all around them, unpitied, un-
    heeded, alone,
With Death swooping down o'er their failure, and all but
    their faith overthrown,
While the voice of the world shouts its chorus — its pæan for
    those who have won;
While the trumpet is sounding triumphant, and high to the
    breeze and the sun
Glad banners are waving, hands clapping, and hurrying feet
Thronging after the laurel crowned victors, I stand on the
    field of defeat,
In the shadow, with those who are fallen, and wounded, and
    dying, and there
Chant a requiem low, place my hand on their pain-knotted
    brows, breathe a prayer,
Hold the hand that is helpless, and whisper, " They only the
    victory win,

Who have fought the good fight, and have vanquished the
    demon that tempts us within;
Who have held to their faith unseduced by the prize that the
    world holds on high;
Who have dared for a high cause to suffer, resist, fight — if
    need be, to die."
Speak, History!   Who are Life's victors?   Unroll thy long
    annals and say,
Are they those whom the world called the victors, who won
    the success of a day?
The martyrs, or Nero?   The Spartans, who fell at Ther-
    mopylæ's tryst,
Or the Persians and Xerxes?   His judges or Socrates, Pilate
    or Christ?

William Wetmore Story

The Kings Are Passing Deathward

The kings are passing deathward in the dark
    Of days that had been splendid where they went;
Their crowns are captive and their courts are stark
    Of purples that are ruinous, now, and rent.
For all that they have seen disastrous things:
    The shattered pomp, the split and shaken throne,
They cannot quite forget the way of Kings:
    Gravely they pass, majestic and alone.

With thunder on their brows, their faces set
    Toward the eternal night of restless shapes,
They walk in awful splendor, regal yet,
    Wearing their crimes like rich and kingly capes . . .
Curse them or taunt, they will not hear or see;
The Kings are passing deathward: let them be.

David Morton

Failures

They bear no laurels on their sunless brows,
Nor aught within their pale hands as they go;
They look as men accustomed to the slow
And level onward course 'neath drooping boughs.
Who may these be no trumpet doth arouse,
These of the dark processionals of woe,
Unpraised, unblamed, but whom sad Acheron's flow
Monotonously lulls to leaden drowse?
These are the Failures. Clutched by Circumstance,
They were — say not, too weak! — too ready prey
To their own fear whose fixèd Gorgon glance
Made them as stone for aught of great essay; —
Or else they nodded when their Master-Chance
Wound his one signal, and went on his way.

Arthur W. Upson

Life Owes Me Nothing

Life owes me nothing. Let the years
Bring clouds or azure, joy or tears,
   Already a full cup I've quaffed;
   Already wept and loved and laughed,
And seen, in ever endless ways,
New beauties overwhelm the days.

Life owes me naught. No pain that waits
Can steal the wealth from memory's gates;
   No aftermath of anguish slow
   Can quench the soul-fire's early glow.
I breathe, exulting, each new breath,
Embracing Life, ignoring Death.

Life owes me nothing. One clear morn
Is boon enough for being born;
   And be it ninety years or ten,
   No need for me to question when.
While Life is mine, I'll find it good,
And greet each hour with gratitude.

Author Unknown

If This Were Enough

God, if this were enough,
That I see things bare to the buff
And up to the buttocks in mire;
That I ask not hope nor hire,
Not in the husk,
Nor dawn beyond the dusk,
Nor life beyond death:
God, if this were faith?

Having felt Thy wind in my face
Spit sorrow and disgrace,
Having seen Thine evil doom
In Golgotha and Khartoum,
And the brutes, the work of Thine hands,
Fill with injustice lands
And stain with blood the sea:
If still in my veins the glee
Of the black night and the sun
And the lost battle, run:
If, an adept,
The iniquitous lists I still accept
With joy, and joy to endure and be withstood,
And still to battle and perish for a dream of good:
God, if that were enough?

If to feel, in the ink of the slough,
And the sink of the mire,
Veins of glory and fire
Run through and transpierce and transpire,
And a secret purpose of glory in every part,
And the answering glory of battle fill my heart;
To thrill with the joy of girded men
To go on forever and fail and go on again,
And be mauled to the earth and arise,
And contend for the shade of a word and a thing not seen
    with the eyes;
With the half of a broken hope for a pillow at night
That somehow the right is the right
And the smooth shall bloom from the rough:
Lord, if that were enough?

Robert Louis Stevenson

A Morning Prayer

Let me today do something that will take
    A little sadness from the world's vast store,
And may I be so favored as to make
    Of joy's too scanty sum a little more.

Let me not hurt, by any selfish deed
    Or thoughtless word, the heart of foe or friend.
Nor would I pass unseeing worthy need,
    Or sin by silence when I should defend.

However meager be my worldly wealth,
    Let me give something that shall aid my kind —
A word of courage, or a thought of health
    Dropped as I pass for troubled hearts to find.

Let me tonight look back across the span
  'Twixt dawn and dark, and to my conscience say —
Because of some good act to beast or man —
  " The world is better that I lived today."
                              Ella Wheeler Wilcox

From Thanatopsis

So live that when thy summons comes to join
The innumerable caravan that moves
To that mysterious realm, where each shall take
His chamber in the silent halls of death,
Thou go not, like the quarry-slave at night,
Scourged to his dungeon, but, sustained and soothed
By an unfaltering trust, approach thy grave
Like one who wraps the drapery of his couch
About him, and lies down to pleasant dreams.
                              William Cullen Bryant

Count That Day Lost

If you sit down at set of sun
And count the acts that you have done,
    And, counting find
One self-denying deed, one word
That eased the heart of him who heard;
    One glance most kind,
That fell like sunshine where it went —
Then you may count that day well spent.

But if, through all the livelong day,
You've cheered no heart, by yea or nay —
    If, through it all
You've nothing done that you can trace

That brought the sunshine to one face —
  No act most small
That helped some soul and nothing cost —
Then count that day as worse than lost.

George Eliot

The Question Whither

When we have thrown off this old suit
  So much in need of mending,
To sink among the naked mute,
  Is that, think you, our ending?
We follow many, more we lead,
  And you who sadly turf us,
Believe not that all living seed
  Must flower above the surface.

Sensation is a gracious gift
  But were it cramped to station,
The prayer to have it cast adrift
  Would spout from all sensation.
Enough if we have winked to sun,
  Have sped the plough a season,
There is a soul for labor done,
  Endureth fixed as reason.

Then let our trust be firm in Good,
  Though we be of the fasting;
Our questions are a mortal brood,
  Our work is everlasting.
We Children of Beneficence
  Are in its being sharers;
And Whither vainer sounds than Whence
  For word with such wayfarers.

George Meredith

To Whom Shall the World Henceforth Belong?

To whom shall the world henceforth belong,
And who shall go up and possess it?

To the Great-Hearts — the Strong
Who will suffer no wrong,
And where they find evil redress it.

To the men of Bold Light
Whose souls seized of Right,
Found a work to be done and have done it.

To the Valiant who fought
For a soul-lifting thought,
Saw the fight to be won and have won it.

To the Men of Great Mind
Set on lifting their kind,
Who, regardless of danger, will do it.

To the Men of Good-will,
Who would cure all Life's ill,
And whose passion for peace will ensue it.

To the Men who will bear
Their full share of Life's care,
And will rest not till wrongs be all righted.

To the Stalwarts who toil
'Mid the seas of turmoil,
Till the haven of safety be sighted.

To the Men of Good Fame
Who everything claim —
This world and the next — in their Master's great name —

To these shall the world henceforth belong,
And they shall go up and possess it;
Overmuch, o'erlong, has the world suffered wrong,
We are here by God's help to redress it.

John Oxenham

Man

What a piece of work is a man! how noble in reason! how
infinite in faculty! in form and moving how express and
admirable! in action how like an angel! in apprehension
how like a god! the beauty of the world! the paragon of
animals!

William Shakespeare
From " Hamlet, Prince of Denmark "

Bring Me Men

Bring me men to match my mountains,
    Bring me men to match my plains —
Men with empires in their purpose
    And new eras in their brains.
Bring me men to match my prairies,
    Men to match my inland seas,
Men whose thought shall prove a highway
    Up to ampler destinies,
Pioneers to clear thought's marshlands
    And to cleanse old error's pen;
Bring me men to match my mountains —
    Bring me men!

Bring me men to match my forests,
    Strong to fight the storm and blast,
Branching toward the skyey future,
    Rooted in the fertile past.

Bring me men to match my valleys,
    Tolerant of sun and snow,
Men within whose fruitful purpose
    Time's consummate blooms shall grow,
Men to tame the tigerish instincts
    Of the lair and cave and den,
Cleanse the dragon slime of nature —
    Bring me men!

Bring me men to match my rivers,
    Continent cleavers, flowing free,
Drawn by the eternal madness
    To be mingled with the sea;
Men of oceanic impulse,
    Men whose moral currents sweep
Towards the wide-infolding ocean
    Of an undiscovered deep;
Men who feel the strong pulsation
    Of the central sea and then
Time their currents to its earth throb —
    Bring me men!

                              Sam Walter Foss
    From " The Coming American "

Joy and Sorrow

Sullen skies today,
    Sunny skies tomorrow;
November steals from May,
    And May from her doth borrow;
Griefs — Joys — in Time's strange dance
Interchangeably advance;
The sweetest joys that come to us
    Come sweeter for past sorrow.

                              Aubrey De Vere

Thy Kingdom Come!

Across the bitter centuries I hear the wail of men:
" Oh, would that Jesus Lord, the Christ, would come to us
    again."
We decorate our altars with ceremonious pride,
With all the outward shows of pomp His worship is
    supplied,
Great churches raise their mighty spires to pierce the sun-
    lit skies,
While in the shadow of the cross we utter blasphemies.

We know we do not do His will who lessoned us to pray,
" Our Father grant within our lives Thy Kingdom rule
    today."
The prayer He taught us, once a week we mouth with half-
    shut eye,
While in the charnel-house of words immortal meanings
    die.
Above our brothers' frailties we cry " Unclean!   Unclean! "
And with the hands that served her shame still stone the
    Magdalene.

We know within our factories that wan-cheeked women
    reel
Among the deft and droning belts that spin from wheel to
    wheel.
We know that unsexed childhood droops in dull-eyed
    drudgery —
The little children that He blessed in far-off Galilee —
Yet surely, Lord, our hearts would grow more merciful to
    them,
If Thou couldst come again to us as once in Bethlehem.

Willard Wattles

The Face of a Friend

Blessed is the man that beholdeth the face of a friend in a
 far country,
The darkness of his heart is melted in the dawning of day
 within him,
It is like the sound of sweet music heard long ago and half
 forgotten;
It is like the coming back of birds to a wood where the
 winter is ended.

Henry van Dyke

Consummation

Not poppies — plant not poppies on my grave!
 I want no anodyne to make me sleep;
I want that All-Bestowing Power, who gave
Immortal love to life, and which we crave —
 The promise of a larger life, to keep.

What that may be I know not — no one knows;
 But since love's graces I have striven to gain,
Plant o'er my soon-forgotten dust, a rose —
That flower which in love's garden ever blows —
 That thus a fragrant memory may remain.

For my fond hope has been, that I might leave
 A Flowering — even in the wayside grass —
A Touch of Bloom, life's grayness to relieve —
A Beauty, they who follow may perceive,
 That hints the scent of roses — as they pass.

James Terry White

To My Countrymen

(A Voice for Peace)

Heirs of great yesterdays, be proud with me
Of your most envied treasure of the Past;
Not wide domain; not doubtful wealth amassed;
Not ganglia cities — rival worlds to be: —
But great souls, servitors of Liberty,
Who kept the state to star-set Honor fast,
Not for ourselves alone but that, at last,
No nation should to Baal bow the knee.

Are we content to be inheritors?
Can you not hear the pleading of the sod
That canopies our heroes? Hasten, then!
Help the sad earth unlearn the vogue of war.
Be just and earn the eternal praise of men;
Be generous and win the smile of God.

Robert Underwood Johnson

Sunrise

Day!
Faster and more fast,
O'er night's brim, day boils at last:
Boils, pure gold, o'er the cloud-cap's brim
Where spurting and suppressed it lay,
For not a froth-flake touched the rim
Of yonder gap in the solid gray
Of the eastern cloud, an hour away;
But forth one wavelet, then another, curled,
Till the whole sunrise, not to be suppressed,
Rose, reddened, and its seething breast
Flickered in bounds, grew gold, then overflowed the world.

Robert Browning

From Elegy Written in a Country Churchyard

The curfew tolls the knell of parting day,
　The lowing herd winds slowly o'er the lea,
The ploughman homeward plods his weary way,
　And leaves the world to darkness and to me.

Now fades the glimmering landscape on the sight,
　And all the air a solemn stillness holds,
Save where the beetle wheels his droning flight,
　And drowsy tinklings lull the distant folds;

Save that, from yonder ivy-mantled tower,
　The moping owl does to the moon complain
Of such as, wandering near her secret bower,
　Molest her ancient, solitary reign.

Beneath those rugged elms, that yew-tree's shade,
　Where heaves the turf in many a mould'ring heap,
Each in his narrow cell forever laid,
　The rude forefathers of the hamlet sleep.

The breezy call of incense-breathing morn,
　The swallow twittering from the straw-built shed,
The cock's shrill clarion, or the echoing horn,
　No more shall rouse them from their lowly bed.

For them no more the blazing hearth shall burn,
　Or busy housewife ply her evening care;
No children run to lisp their sire's return,
　Or climb his knees the envied kiss to share.

Oft did the harvest to their sickle yield,
　Their furrow oft the stubborn glebe has broke;
How jocund did they drive their team afield!
　How bowed the woods beneath their sturdy stroke!

Let not ambition mock their useful toil,
　　Their homely joys, and destiny obscure;
Nor grandeur hear with a disdainful smile
　　The short and simple annals of the poor.

The boast of heraldry, the pomp of power,
　　And all that beauty, all that wealth e'er gave,
Await alike the inevitable hour:
　　The paths of glory lead but to the grave.

Nor you, ye proud, impute to these the fault,
　　If memory o'er their tomb no trophies raise
Where through the long-drawn aisle and fretted vault
　　The pealing anthem swells the note of praise.

Can storied urn or animated bust
　　Back to its mansion call the fleeting breath?
Can Honor's voice provoke the silent dust
　　Or Flattery soothe the dull cold ear of Death?

Perhaps in this neglected spot is laid
　　Some heart once pregnant with celestial fire;
Hands that the rod of empire might have swayed,
　　Or wak'd to ecstasy the living lyre;

But Knowledge to their eyes her ample page,
　　Rich with the spoils of time, did ne'er unroll;
Chill Penury repressed their noble rage,
　　And froze the genial current of the soul.

Full many a gem of purest ray serene
　　The dark, unfathomed caves of ocean bear:
Full many a flower is born to blush unseen,
　　And waste its sweetness on the desert air.

Thomas Gray

Under the Harvest Moon

Under the harvest moon,
When the soft silver
Drips shimmering
Over the garden nights,
Death, the gray mocker
Comes and whispers to you
As a beautiful friend
Who remembers.
Under the summer roses,
When the flagrant crimson
Lurks in the dusk
Of the wild red leaves,
Love, with little hands,
Comes and touches you
With a thousand memories,
And asks you
Beautiful unanswerable questions.

Carl Sandburg

The Creedless Love

A creedless love, that knows no clan,
  No caste, no cult, no church but Man;
That deems today and now and here,
  Are voice and vision of the seer;
That through this lifted human clod
  The inflow of the breath of God
Still sheds its apostolic powers —
  Such love, such trust, such faith be ours.

We deem man climbs an endless slope
  Tow'rd far-seen tablelands of hope;
That he, through filth and shame of sin,
  Still seeks the God that speaks within;

That all the years since time began
   Work the eternal Rise of Man;
And all the days that time shall see
   Tend tow'rd the Eden yet to be.

Too long our music-hungering needs
   Have heard the iron clash of creeds. .
The creedless love that knows no clan,
   No caste, no cult, no church but Man,

Shall drown with mellow music all,
   The dying jangle of their brawl; —
Such love with all its quickening powers,
   Such love to God and Man be ours.

Sam Walter Foss

Love Over All

Time flies,
Suns rise
And shadows fall.
Let time go by.
Love is forever over all.

From an English Sun Dial

Patience

Sometimes I wish that I might do
   Just one grand deed and die,
And by that one grand deed reach up
   To meet God in the sky.

But such is not Thy way, O God,
   Nor such is Thy decree,
But deed by deed, and tear by tear,
   Our souls must climb to Thee,

As climbed the only son of God
   From manger unto Cross,
Who learned, through tears and bloody sweat,
   To count this world but loss;

Who left the Virgin Mother's arms
   To seek those arms of shame,
Outstretched upon a lonely hill
   To which the darkness came.

As deed by deed, and tear by tear,
   He climbed up to the height,
Each deed a splendid deed, each tear
   A jewel shining bright,

So grant us, Lord, the patient heart,
   To climb the upward way,
Until we stand upon the height,
   And see the perfect day.

G. A. Studdert-Kennedy

A Leaf of Grass

I believe a leaf of grass is no less than the journey-work of
   the stars,
And the pismire is equally perfect, and a grain of sand, and
   the egg of the wren,
And the tree-toad is a chef-d'oeuvre for the highest,
And the running blackberry would adorn the parlors of
   heaven,
And the narrowest hinge in my hand puts to scorn all
   machinery,

And the cow crunching with depressed head surpasses any
   statue,
And a mouse is miracle enough to stagger sextillions of
   infidels.

Walt Whitman

From " Leaves of Grass "

The Lost Christ

Your skill has fashioned stately creeds,
   But where is He, we pray —
The friendly Christ of loving deeds?
   He is not here today.

With sentences that twist and tease,
   Confusing mind and heart,
You forge your wordy homilies
   And bid us heed your art.

But where is He — or can you tell? —
   Who stilled the brothers' strife,
Who urged the woman at the well
   To live a better life?

Where is the Saint of Galilee,
   Crude Peter's faithful guide;
The man who wept at Bethany
   Because His friend had died?

We weary of your musty lore
   Behind dead walls of gray;
We want His loving words once more
   By some Emmaus way.

Give us the Christ who can bestow
  Some comfort-thought of death.
Give us a Christ our hearts can know —
  The Man of Nazareth.
                                    Thomas Curtis Clark

Our Known Unknown

O Thou — as represented to me here
In such conception as my soul allows —
Under Thy measureless, my atom-width!
Man's mind, what is it but a convex-glass
Wherein are gathered all the scattered points
Picked out of the immensity of sky,
To reunite there, be our heaven for earth,
Our known Unknown, our God revealed to man?
                                    Robert Browning
From " The Ring and the Book "

Today, O Lord

O Lord, I pray
That for this day
  I may not swerve
By foot or hand
From Thy command
  Not to be served, but to serve.

This, too, I pray,
That from this day
  No love of ease
Nor pride prevent
My good intent
  Not to be pleased, but to please.

And if I may
I'd have this day
    Strength from above
To set my heart
In heavenly art
    Not to be loved, but to love.

Maltbie D. Babcock

Where is Heaven?

Where is Heaven? Is it not
Just a friendly garden plot,
Walled with stone and roofed with sun,
Where the days pass one by one
Not too fast and not too slow,
Looking backward as they go
At the beauties left behind
To transport the pensive mind.

Does not Heaven begin that day
When the eager heart can say,
Surely God is in this place,
I have seen Him face to face
In the loveliness of flowers,
In the service of the showers,
And His voice has talked to me
In the sunlit apple tree.

Bliss Carman

A Prayer for the New Year

O year that is going, take with you
Some evil that dwells in my heart;
Let selfishness, doubt,
With the old year go out—
With joy I would see them depart.

O year that is going, take with you
Impatience and wilfulness — pride;
The sharp word that slips
From those too hasty lips,
I would cast, with the old year aside.

O year that is coming, bring with you
Some virtue of which I have need;
More patience to bear
And more kindness to share,
And more love that is true love indeed.

Laura F. Armitage

The Stirrup-Cup

Death, thou'rt a cordial old and rare:
Look how compounded, with what care!
Time got his wrinkles reaping thee
Sweet herbs from all antiquity.

David to thy distillage went,
Keats, and Gotama excellent,
Omar Khayyam, and Chaucer bright,
And Shakespeare for a king-delight.

Then, Time, let not a drop be spilt:
Hand me the cup whene'er thou wilt;
'Tis thy rich stirrup-cup to me;
I'll drink it down right smilingly.

Sidney Lanier

Mothers of Men

" I hold no cause worth my son's life," one said —
And the two women with her as she spoke
Joined glances in a hush that neither broke,
So present was the memory of their dead.
And through their meeting eyes their souls drew near,
Linked by their sons, men who had held life dear
But laid it down for something dearer still.
One had wrought out with patient iron will
The riddle of a pestilence, and won,
Fighting on stricken, till his work was done
For children of tomorrow. Far away
In shell-torn soil of France the other lay,
And in the letter that his mother read
Over and over, kneeling as to pray —
" I'm thanking God with all my heart today,
Whatever comes " (that was the day he died)
" I've done my bit to clear the road ahead."
In those two mothers, common pain of loss
Blossomed in starry flowers of holy pride,
What thoughts were hers who silent stood beside
Her son the dreamer's cross?

Amelia J. Burr

Prayer

I do not ask a truce
    With life's incessant pain;
But school my lips, O Lord,
    Not to complain.

I do not ask for peace
    From life's eternal sorrow;
But give me courage, Lord,
    To fight tomorrow!   *Peter Gething*

From If Jesus Came Back Today

If Jesus came back today
What would the people say?
Would they cheer Him and strew the way
With garlands of myrtle and bay
As they did on that distant day
When He came to Jerusalem?
What would America say
If Jesus came back today?

. . . .

We fashion great churches and creeds
But the heart of the people still bleeds
And the poor still rot in their needs.
We display with pride His cross
In the midst of our pagan life
While we hug to our hearts the dross
Of our selfishness and strife.
What sacrifice have we made
To live the love He prayed?
What willing blood have we shed
To do the deeds He said?
To be popular and well-fed
We forsake the way He led
And follow a ghost instead!

Vincent Godfrey Burns

Life's Evening

Ah, yet, ere I descend to the grave,
May I a small house and large garden have,
And a few friends, and many books, both true,
Both wise, and both delightful too!

Abraham Cowley

Altruism

" The earth is not the abode of the strong alone; it is also
the home of the loving." *J. Arthur Thomson.*

The God of things that are
   Is the God of the highest heaven;
The God of the morning star,
   Of the thrush that sings at even;
The God of the storm and sunshine,
   Of the wolf, the snail, and the bee,
Of the Alp's majestic silence,
   Of the boundless depths of the sea;

The God of the times and the nations,
   Of the planets as they roll,
Of the numberless constellations,
   Of the limitless human soul.
For there is nothing small,
   And naught can mighty be;
Archangels and atoms all —
   Embodiments of Thee!

A single thought divine
   Holds stars and suns in space;
A dream of man is Thine,
   And history finds its place.
When the universe was young
   Thine was the perfect thought
That life should be bound in one
   By the strand of love enwrought.

In the life of the fern and the lily,
   Of the dragon and the dove,
Still through the stress and struggle
   Waxes the bond of love.

Out from the ruthless ages
   Rises, like incense mild,
The love of the man and the woman,
   The love of the mother and child.

                   David Starr Jordan

The Spring of God

Across the edges of the world there blows a wind
Mysterious with perfume of a Spring;
A Spring that is not of the kindling earth,
That's more than scent of bloom or gleam of bud;
The Spring of God in flower!
Down there where neither sun nor air came through,
I felt it blow across my dungeon walls —

The wind before the footsteps of the Lord!
It bloweth now across the world;
It strangely stirs the hearts of men; wars cease;
Rare deeds familiar grow; fastings and prayers,
Forgiveness, poverty; temples are built
On visioned impulses, and children march
On journeys with no end.
Far off, far off He comes,
And we are swept upon our knees
As meadow grasses kneeling to the wind.

                   William A. Percy

From " In April Once "

From The Vision of Sir Launfal

Earth gets its price for what Earth gives us;
   The beggar is taxed for a corner to die in,
The priest hath his fee who comes and shrives us,
   We bargain for the graves we lie in;

At the devil's booth are all things sold,
Each ounce of dross costs its ounce of gold;
For a cap and bells our lives we pay,
   Bubbles we buy with a whole soul's tasking;
'Tis heaven alone that is given away,
   'Tis only God may be had for the asking;
No price is set on the lavish Summer;
June may be had by the poorest comer.

And what is so rare as a day in June?
   Then, if ever, come perfect days;
Then Heaven tries earth if it be in tune,
   And over it softly her warm ear lays;
Whether we look, or whether we listen,
We hear life murmur, or see it glisten;
Every clod feels a stir of might,
   An instinct within it that reaches and towers,
And, groping blindly above it for light,
   Climbs to a soul in grass and flowers;
The flush of life may well be seen
   Thrilling back over hills and valleys;
The cowslip startles in meadows green,
   The buttercup catches the sun in its chalice,
And there's never a leaf nor a blade too mean
   To be some happy creature's palace;
The little bird sits at his door in the sun,
   Atilt like a blossom among the leaves,
And lets his illumined being o'errun
   With the deluge of summer it receives;
His mate feels the eggs beneath her wings,
And the heart in her dumb breast flutters and sings;
He sings to the wide world and she to her nest —
In the nice ear of Nature, which song is the best?
                        James Russell Lowell

Loyalties

Let us keep splendid loyalties,
For we are falling prey to lesser things.
What use are breath and strength if we no longer feel
The thrill of battle for some holy cause
Or hear high morning bugles calling us away?
Let brave hearts dare to break the truce with things
Ere we have lost our ancient heritage.
Are we to gain a world to lose our souls,
Souls which can keep faith until death
And die, triumphant, in some crimson dawn?

Nay, we must keep faith with the unnumbered brave
Who pushed aside horizons, that we might reach
The better things: We cannot rest until
We have put courage once more on her throne;
For Honor clamors for her heritage,
And Right still claims a kingdom of its own.

Walter A. Cutter

God Is Here

God is here! I hear His voice
While thrushes make the woods rejoice.

I touch His robe each time I place
My hand against a pansy's face.

I breathe His breath if I but pass
Verbenas trailing through the grass.

God is here! From every tree
His leafy fingers beckon me.

Madeleine Aaron

I Tramp a Perpetual Journey

I tramp a perpetual journey,
My signs are a rain-proof coat, good shoes, and a staff cut
  from the woods,
No friend of mine takes his ease in my chair,
I have no chair, no church, no philosophy,
I lead no man to a dinner-table, library or exchange,
But each man and each woman of you I lead upon a knoll,
My left hand hooking you round the waist,
My right hand pointing to landscapes of continents, and a
  plain public road.
Not I — nor anyone else, can travel that road for you,
You must travel it for yourself.

Walt Whitman

From " Leaves of Grass "

Worship

Work is devout, and service is divine.
Who stoops to scrub a floor
May worship more
Than he who kneels before a holy shrine;
Who crushes stubborn ore
More worthily adore
Than he who crushes sacramental wine.

Roy Campbell MacFie

The Seven Ages of Man

All the world's a stage,
And all the men and women merely players:
They have their exits and their entrances;
And one man in his time plays many parts,

His acts being seven ages. As, first, the infant,
Mewling and puking in the nurse's arms:
And then the whining schoolboy, with his satchel
And shining morning face, creeping like snail
Unwillingly to school: And then the lover,
Sighing like furnace, with a woeful ballad
Made to his mistress' eyebrow: Then the soldier,
Full of strange oaths, and bearded like the pard,
Jealous in honor, sudden and quick in quarrel,
Seeking the bubble reputation
Even in the cannon's mouth: And then the justice,
In fair round belly with good capon lined,
With eyes severe and beard of formal cut,
Full of wise saws and modern instances;
And so he plays his part: The sixth age shifts
Into the lean and slipper'd pantaloon,
With spectacles on nose and pouch on side;
His youthful hose, well saved, a world too wide
For his shrunk shank; and his big manly voice,
Turning again toward childish treble, pipes
And whistles in his sound: Last scene of all,
That ends this strange eventful history,
Is second childishness and mere oblivion,
Sans teeth, sans eyes, sans taste, sans everything.

William Shakespeare

From " As You Like It "

From Among the Ferns

I lay among the ferns,
Where they lifted their fronds, innumerable, in the green-
    wood wilderness, like wings winnowing the air;
And their voices went by me continually.

And I listened, and Lo! softly inaudibly raining I heard not
    the voices of the ferns only, but of all living creatures:
Voices of mountain and star,
Of cloud and forest and ocean,
And of little rills tumbling among the rocks,
And of the high tops where the moss-beds are and the springs
    arise.
As the wind at midday rains whitening over the grass,
As the night-bird glimmers a moment, fleeting between the
    lonely watcher and the moon,
So softly inaudibly they rained,
While I sat silent.

And in the silence of the greenwood I knew the secret of the
    growth of the ferns;
I saw their delicate leaflets tremble breathing an unde-
    scribed and unuttered life;
And, below, the ocean lay sleeping;
And round them the mountains and the stars dawned in
    glad companionship forever.

Edward Carpenter

The Newer Vainglory

Two men went up to pray; and one gave thanks,
    Not with himself — aloud,
With proclamation, calling on the ranks
    Of an attentive crowd.

" Thank God, I clap not my own humble breast,
    But other ruffians' backs,
Imputing crime — such is my tolerant haste —
    To any man that lacks.

" For I am tolerant, generous, keep no rules,
    And the age honors me.
Thank God I am not as these rigid fools,
    Even as this Pharisee."

Alice Meynell

The Place of Peace

At the heart of the cyclone tearing the sky
And flinging the clouds and the towers by,
Is a place of central calm;
So here in the roar of mortal things,
I have a place where my spirit sings,
In the hollow of God's palm.

Edwin Markham

The Seeker After God

There was a dreamer once, whose spirit trod
Unnumbered ways in thwarted search for God:
He stirred the dust on ancient books; he sought
For certain light in what the teachers taught;
He took his staff and went unto the Wise,
And deeper darkness fell about his eyes;
He lived a hermit, and forebore his food,
And God left visitless his solitude;
He wrapped himself in prayer night after night,
And mocking demons danced across his sight.
Resigned at last to Him he could not find,
He turned again to live among mankind —
And when from man he no more stood apart,
God, on that instant, visited his heart!

Harry Kemp

The Survivor

When the last day is ended,
  And the nights are through;
When the last sun is buried
  In its grave of blue;

When the stars are snuffed like candles,
  And the seas no longer fret;
When the winds unlearn their cunning,
  And the storms forget;

When the last lip is palsied,
  And the last prayer said;
Love shall reign immortal
  While the worlds lie dead!

Frederic Lawrence Knowles

Choice

Ask and it shall be given.
Ask — ask.
And if you ask a stone
Expect not bread;
And if the stone glitter like a caught star,
And shine on a warm, soft breast,
And you have tossed your soul away
To see it in that nest,
Yet is it still a stone — not bread.

Seek and you shall find.
Seek — seek.
And if you go the crowded street
Look not to find the hills;

And if the shops sit gay along the way,
And laughter fills the air,
Still — you have lost the hills.

Knock and the door shall open.
Knock — knock.
Two doors are there, beware!
Think well before you knock;
Your tapping finger will unlock
Your heaven or hell.

Ellen Coit Elliott

Past Ruined Ilion

Past ruined Ilion Helen lives,
  Alcestis rises from the shades;
Verse calls them forth; 'tis verse that gives
  Immortal youth to mortal maids.

Soon shall Oblivion's deepening veil
  Hide all the peopled hills you see,
The gay, the proud, while lovers hail
  These many summers you and me.

Walter Savage Landor

Nature and Religion

Where shall we get religion? Beneath the open sky,
The sphere of crystal silence surcharged with deity.
The winds blow from a thousand ways and waft their balms
  abroad,
The winds blow toward a million goals — but all winds
  blow from God.

The stars the old Chaldeans saw still weave their maze
  on high
And write a thousand thousand years their bible in the sky.
The midnight earth sends incense up, sweet with the breath
  of prayer —
Go out beneath the naked night and get religion there.

Where shall we get religion? Beneath the blooming tree,
Beside the hill-encircled brooks that loiter to the sea;
Beside all twilight waters, beneath the noonday shades.
Beneath the dark cathedral pines, and through the tangled
  glades;
Wherever the old urge of life provokes the dumb, dead sod
To tell its thought in violets, the soul takes hold on God.
Go smell the growing clover, and scent the blooming pear,
Go forth to seek religion — and find it anywhere.

Sam Walter Foss

Thanksgiving

For all things beautiful, and good, and true;
For things that seemed not good yet turned to good;
For all the sweet compulsions of Thy will
That chastened, tried, and wrought us to Thy shape;
For things unnumbered that we take of right,
And value first when they are withheld;
For light and air; sweet sense of sound and smell;
For ears to hear the heavenly harmonies;
For eyes to see the unseen in the seen;
For vision of the Worker in the work;
For hearts to apprehend Thee everywhere; —
We thank Thee, Lord.

John Oxenham

Magna Est Veritas

Here, in this little Bay,
Full of tumultuous life and great repose,
Where, twice a day,
The purposeless, glad ocean comes and goes,
Under high cliffs, and far from the huge town,
I sit me down.
For want of me the world's course will not fail;
When all its work is done, the lie shall rot;
The truth is great, and shall prevail,
When none cares whether it prevail or not.

Coventry Patmore

Beauty

How can you smile when pain is everywhere;
How flaunt complacently your vulgar wealth?
" It is my duty to be gay. My health
And calm delight the eye and banish care —
It would be sad indeed if none were free
To sanction Beauty and embody Joy.
Enough of you, who would with gloom destroy
My grace. I do my share of Charity! "

Your share of charity! Who tipped the scales
To Sophistry and weighed a fancy gown
Against a street rat's need of bread? The nails
Of Calvary, the cross, the thornèd crown,
The face of sorrow that He wore, reply:
" Forgive them, God, they know not when they lie! "

Mary Craig Sinclair

Lone-Land

Around us lies a world invisible,
With isles of dream and many a continent
Of Thought, and Isthmus Fancy, where we dwell
Each as a lonely wanderer intent
Upon his vision; finding each his fears
And hopes encompassed by the tide of Tears.

John B. Tabb

My Enemy

An enemy I had, whose mien
  I stoutly strove in vain to know;
For hard he dogged my steps, unseen,
  Wherever I might go.

My plans he balked; my aims he foiled;
  He blocked my every onward way.
When for some lofty goal I toiled,
  He grimly said me nay.

" Come forth! " I cried, " Lay bare thy guise!
  Thy wretched features I would see."
Yet always to my straining eyes
  He dwelt in mystery.

Until one night I held him fast,
  The veil from off his form did draw;
I gazed upon his face at last —
  And, lo! myself I saw.

Edwin L. Sabin

Memory

My mind lets go a thousand things,
Like dates of wars and deaths of kings,
And yet recalls the very hour —
'Twas noon by yonder village tower,
And on the last blue noon in May —
The wind came briskly up this way,
Crisping the brook beside the road;
Then, pausing here, set down its load
Of pine-scents, and shook listlessly
Two petals from that wild-rose tree.

Thomas Bailey Aldrich

Pass On the Torch

Pass on the torch, pass on the flame;
Remember whence the Glory came;
And eyes are on you as you run,
Beyond the shining of the sun.

Lord Christ, we take the torch from Thee;
We must be true, we must be free,
And clean of heart and strong of soul,
To bear the Glory to its goal.

America, God hear the prayer —
America for God, we dare,
With Lincoln's heart and Lincoln's hand,
To fling a flame across the land.

O Lord of life, to Thee we kneel;
Maker of men, our purpose seal!
We will, for honor of Thy Name,
Pass on the Torch, pass on the flame.

Allen Eastman Cross

The Miser

I have wasted nothing. O Lord, I have saved,
Saved, put by in a goodly hoard.
What of the prodigals? Judge them, Lord —
Their wanton waste of Thy mercies poured
Into the sewers! Profligates!
Judge them, Lord, in Thy righteous wrath.
I have saved, O Lord, I have scraped and saved,
With my eyes downbent to my daily path;
I have counted and carried, checked and stored,
Nothing too worthless, nothing too small,
Never a fragment thrown away —
A gainful use I have found for all.

But what is my store? Do they call this Death,
This poignant insight? At last I see.
I have wasted nothing, O Lord, but life,
Time, and the talent Thou gavest me.

Laura Bell Everett

Whichever Way the Wind Doth Blow

Whichever way the wind doth blow
Some heart is glad to have it so;
Then blow it east or blow it west,
The wind that blows, that wind is best.

My little craft sails not alone;
A thousand fleets from every zone
Are out upon a thousand seas;
And what for me were favouring breeze

Might dash another, with the shock
Of doom, upon some hidden rock.
And so I do not dare to pray
For winds to waft me on my way,
But leave it to a Higher Will
To stay or speed me; trusting still
That all is well, and sure that He
Who launched my bark will sail with me
Through storm and calm, and will not fail
Whatever breezes may prevail
To land me, every peril past,
Within His sheltering Heaven at last.

Then whatsoever wind doth blow,
My heart is glad to have it so;
And blow it east or blow it west,
The wind that blows, that wind is best.
Caroline Atherton Mason

The Tide of Faith

So faith is strong
Only when we are strong, shrinks when we shrink.
It comes when music stirs us, and the chords,
Moving on some grand climax, shake our souls
With influx new that makes new energies.
It comes in swellings of the heart and tears
That rise at noble and at gentle deeds.
It comes in moments of heroic love,
Unjealous joy in joy not made for us;
In conscious triumph of the good within,
Making us worship goodness that rebukes.
Even our failures are a prophecy,
Even our yearnings and our bitter tears

After that fair and true we cannot grasp.
Presentiment of better things on earth
Sweeps in with every force that stirs our souls
To admiration, self-renouncing love.

George Eliot

Vitæ Summa Brevis

They are not long, the weeping and the laughter,
   Love and desire and hate:
I think they have no portion in us after
   We pass the gate.
They are not long, the days of wine and roses:
   Out of a misty dream
Our path emerges for a while, then closes
   Within a dream.

Ernest Dowson

From Ulysses

There lies the port; the vessel puffs her sail:
There gloom the dark broad seas. My mariners,
Souls that have toil'd, and wrought, and thought with me —
That ever with a frolic welcome took
The thunder and the sunshine, and opposed
Free hearts, free foreheads — you and I are old;
Old age hath yet his honor and his toil;
Death closes all: but something ere the end,
Some work of noble note, may yet be done,
Not unbecoming men that strove with gods.
The lights begin to twinkle from the rocks:
The long day wanes: the slow moon climbs: the deep
Moans round with many voices. Come, my friends,
'Tis not too late to seek a newer world.
Push off, and sitting well in order smite

The sounding furrows; for my purpose holds
To sail beyond the sunset, and the baths
Of all the western stars, until I die.
It may be that the gulfs will wash us down:
It may be we shall touch the Happy Isles,
And see the great Achilles, whom we knew.
Tho' much is taken, much abides; and tho'
We are not now that strength which in old days
Moved earth and heaven, that which we are, we are;
One equal temper of heroic hearts,
Made weak by time and fate, but strong in will
To strive, to seek, to find, and not to yield.

Alfred Tennyson

Invincible

The years race by on padded feet —
Unhaltingly, and panther-fleet —
   Imprinting marks of drab decay.

My hair grows ashen; cravings numb;
Lips pale; and telltale age-lines come —
   Life's hoary touch I may not stay.

Time-scarred . . . yet I shall scorn to weep
For transient youth if I can keep
   My piquant heart from turning gray!

Winnie Lynch Rockett

Rules for the Road

Stand straight:
Step firmly, throw your weight:
The heaven is high above your head,
The good gray road is faithful to your tread.

Be strong:
Sing to your heart a battle song:
Though hidden foemen lie in wait,
Something is in you that can smile at Fate.

Press through:
Nothing can harm if you are true.
And when the night comes, rest:
The earth is friendly as a mother's breast.

Edwin Markham

The White Christs

The White Christs come from the East,
   And they follow the way of the sun;
And they smile, as Pale Men ask them to
   At the things Pale Men have done;
For the White Christs sanction the sum of things —
   Faggot and club and gun.

Whine of the groaning car,
   Caste, which divides like a wall;
Curse of the raw-sored soul;
   Doom of the great and small;
The White Christs fashioned by Pale White Men
   Sanction and bless it all.

Prophets of truth have said
   That Afric and Ind must mourn;
And the children of Oman weep
   Trampled and slashed and torn,
Keeping the watch with brown Cathay
   Till the Black Christs shall be born.

Guy Fitch Phelps

Prayer for a Little Home

God send us a little home
To come back to when we roam —
Low walls and fluted tiles
Wide windows, a view for miles;
Red firelight and deep chairs;
Small white beds upstairs;
Great talk in little nooks;
Dim colors, rows of books;
One picture on each wall;
Not many things at all.
God send us a little ground —
Tall trees standing round,
Homely flowers in brown sod,
Overhead Thy stars, O God!
God bless when winds blow
Our home and all we know.

Author Unknown

The Silent Voices

When the dumb Hour, clothed in black,
Brings the dreams about my bed,
Call me not so often back,
Silent voices of the dead,
Toward the lowland ways behind me,
And the sunlight that is gone!
Call me rather, silent voices,
Forward to the starry track
Glimmering up the heights beyond me
On, and always on!

Alfred Tennyson

Dreamers of Dreams

We are all of us dreamers of dreams,
  On visions our childhood is fed;
And the heart of the child is unhaunted, it seems,
  By the ghosts of dreams that are dead.

From childhood to youth's but a span,
  And the years of our life are soon sped;
But the youth is no longer a youth, but a man,
  When the first of his dreams is dead.

'Tis as a cup of wormwood and gall,
  When the doom of a great dream is said;
And the best of a man is under the pall,
  When the best of his dreams is dead.

He may live on by compact and plan,
  When the fine bloom of living is shed;
But God pity the little that's left of a man
  When the last of his dreams is dead.

Let him show a brave face if he can,
  Let him woo fame or fortune instead;
Yet there's not much to do but to bury a man,
  When the last of his dreams is dead.

William Herbert Carruth

Three Words of Strength

There are three lessons I would write,
  Three words, as with a burning pen,
In tracings of eternal light,
  Upon the hearts of men.

Have Hope. Though clouds environ round,
  And gladness hides her face in scorn,
Put off the shadow from thy brow:
  No night but hath its morn.

Have Faith. Where'er thy bark is driven —
  The calm's disport, the tempest's mirth —
Know this: God rules the hosts of heaven,
  The inhabitants of earth.

Have Love. Not love alone for one,
  But man, as man, thy brother call;
And scatter, like a circling sun,
  Thy charities on all.
                    Friedrich von Schiller

Legacies

Unto my friends I give my thoughts,
  Unto my God my soul,
Unto my foe I leave my love —
  These are of life the whole.

Nay, there is something — a trifle — left;
  Who shall receive this dower?
See, Earth Mother, a handful of dust —
  Turn it into a flower.
                    Ethelyn Wetherald

Truth, Crushed to Earth

Truth, crushed to earth, shall rise again —
  The eternal years of God are hers;
But Error, wounded, writhes in pain,
  And dies among his worshippers.
                    William Cullen Bryant

Barter *

Life has loveliness to sell,
   All beautiful and splendid things,
Blue waves whitened on a cliff,
   Soaring fire that sways and sings,
And children's faces looking up
Holding wonder like a cup.

Life has loveliness to sell,
   Music like a curve of gold,
Scent of pine trees in the rain,
   Eyes that love you, arms that hold,
And for your spirit's still delight,
Holy thoughts that star the night.

Spend all you have for loveliness,
   Buy it and never count the cost;
For one white singing hour of peace
   Count many a year of strife well lost,
And for a breath of ecstasy
Give all you have been, or could be.

Sara Teasdale

Three Steps

Three steps there are our human life must climb.
   The first is Force.
The savage struggled to it from the slime
   And still it is our last, ashamed recourse.

Above that jagged stretch of red-veined stone
   Is marble Law,
Carven with long endeavor, monotone
   Of patient hammers, not yet free from flaw.

* From " Love Poems " by Sara Teasdale. By permission of The
Macmillan Company, publishers.

Three steps there are our human life must climb.
  The last is Love,
Wrought from such starry element sublime
  As touches the White Rose and Mystic Dove.
                    Katharine Lee Bates

Four Things To Do

Four things a man must learn to do
If he would keep his record true:
To think, without confusion, clearly;
To love his fellow-man sincerely;
To act from honest motives purely;
To trust in God and Heaven securely.
                    Henry van Dyke

On Entering a Chapel

Love built this shrine; these hallowed walls uprose
To give seclusion from the hurrying throng,
From tumult of the street, complaint and wrong,
From rivalry and strife, from taunt of foes —
If foes thou hast. On silent feet come in,
Bow low in penitence. Whoe'er thou art
Thou, too, hast sinned. Uplift in prayer thy heart.
Thy Father's Blessing waiteth. Read within
This holy place, in pictured light portrayed,
The characters of worthies who, from years
Long past, still speak the message here displayed
In universal language not to fade.
Leave then thy burden, all thy cares and fears;
Faith, hope, and love are thine, for thou hast prayed.
                    John Davidson

From The Happy Warrior

Who is the happy Warrior? Who is he
That every man in arms should wish to be?
It is the generous Spirit, who, when brought
Among the tasks of real life, hath wrought
Upon the plan that pleased his boyish thought:
Whose high endeavors are an inward light
That makes the path before him always bright. . . .
'Tis he whose law is reason; who depends
Upon that law as on the best of friends. . . .
He labors good on good to fix, and owes
To virtue every triumph that he knows:
Who, if he rise to station of command,
Rises by open means; and there will stand
On honorable terms, or else retire,
And in himself possess his own desire;
Who comprehends his trust, and to the same
Keeps faithful with a singleness of aim;
And therefore does not stoop, nor lie in wait
For wealth, or honors, or for worldly state. . . .
Whose powers shed round him in the common strife,
Or mild concerns of ordinary life,
A constant influence, a peculiar grace;
But who, if he be called upon to face
Some awful moment to which Heaven has joined
Great issues, good or bad for human kind,
Is happy as a Lover; and attired
With sudden brightness, like a Man inspired;
And, through the heat of conflict, keeps the law
In calmness made, and sees what he foresaw;
Or if an unexpected call succeed,
Come when it will, is equal to the need. . . .
'Tis, finally, the Man who lifted high,

Conspicuous object in a Nation's eye,
Or left unthought-of in obscurity —
Who, with a toward or untoward lot,
Prosperous or adverse, to his wish or not —
Plays, in the many games of life, that one
Where what he most doth value must be won:
Whom neither shape of danger can dismay,
Nor thought of tender happiness betray;
Who, not content that former worth stand fast,
Looks forward, persevering to the last,
From well to better, daily self-surpast:
Who, whether praise of him must walk the earth
Forever, and to noble deeds give birth,
Or he must fall, to sleep without his fame,
And leave a dead unprofitable name —
Finds comfort in himself and in his cause;
And, while the mortal mist is gathering, draws
His breath in confidence of Heaven's applause:
This is the happy Warrior; this is he
That every Man in arms should wish to be.

William Wordsworth

These Times

Our motors pierce the clouds. They penetrate
The depth of oceans. Microscopes reveal
New worlds to conquer, while we dedicate
Our intellects to strength of stone and steel.
We are as proud as those who built a tower
To reach to heaven. Recklessly we rear
Our lofty Babels, arrogant with power.
How dare we boast of cities while we hear
The nations groping through the dark along
The road of life? What right have we for pride

Till Truth is steel, and Faith is iron-strong,
Till God and man are working side by side?
Then let our prayers and labors never cease;
We act the prologue of a masterpiece.

Gertrude Ryder Bennett

The Wise

He who sees
How action may be rest, rest action — he
Is wisest 'mid his kind: he hath the truth!
He doeth well acting or resting.   Freed
In all his works from prickings of desire,
Burned clean in act by the white fire of truth,
The wise call that one wise.

Translated by Edwin Arnold
From " The Bhagauad Gita "

Eucharist

Still we who follow Christ in deed
    Must break the bread and spill the wine:
Still must a costly Eucharist
    Be for a sacrifice and sign.

Our bodies broken for the truth
    By mobs or Pharisees of State
Must be the bread which Liberty
    Feeds on, and lives, and waxes great.

Our blood, our covenant of love,
    Is the rich wine which we must give
To a sick world that hates the gift —
    So, by our dying, God may live.

Not by the grape or wheaten bread
  Can we partake the Eucharist:
Communion is to give to God
  Our blood and bodies, like the Christ.
                              E. Merrill Root

From Songs in Absence

Where lies the land to which the ship would go?
Far, far ahead, is all her seamen know.
And where the land she travels from?   Away,
Far, far behind, is all that they can say.

On sunny noons upon the deck's smooth face,
Linked arm in arm, how pleasant here to pace;
Or, o'er the stern reclining, watch below
The foaming wake far widening as we go.

On stormy nights when wild northwesters rave,
How proud a thing to fight with wind and wave!
The dripping sailor on the reeling mast
Exults to bear, and scorns to wish it past.

Where lies the land to which the ship would go?
Far, far ahead, is all her seamen know.
And where the land she travels from?   Away,
Far, far behind, is all that they can say.
                              Arthur Hugh Clough

Three Things Come Not Back

Remember three things come not back:
The arrow sent upon its track —
It will not swerve, it will not stay
Its speed; it flies to wound, or slay.

The spoken word so soon forgot
By thee; but it has perished not;
In other hearts 'tis living still
And doing work for good or ill.
And the lost opportunity
That cometh back no more to thee,
In vain thou weepest, in vain dost yearn,
Those three will nevermore return.

From the Arabic

The Best Road of All

I like a road that leads away to prospects white and fair,
A road that is an ordered road, like a nun's evening prayer;
But, best of all, I love a road that leads to God knows where.

You come upon it suddenly — you cannot seek it out;
It's like a secret still unheard and never noised about;
But when you see it, gone at once is every lurking doubt.

It winds beside some rushing stream where aspens lightly
    quiver;
It follows many a broken field by many a shining river;
It seems to lead you on and on, forever and forever!

You tramp along its dusty way, beneath its shadowy trees,
And hear beside you chattering birds or happy booming bees,
And all around you golden sounds, the green leaves' litanies.

And here's a hedge, and there's a cot: and then — strange,
    sudden turns —
A dip, a rise, a little glimpse where the red sunset burns;
A bit of sky at evening time, the scent of hidden ferns.

A winding road, a loitering road, a finger-mark of God
Traced when the Maker of the world leaned over ways un-
    trod.
See! Here He smiled His glowing smile, and lo, the golden-
    rod!

I like a road that wanders straight; the King's highway is
    fair,
And lovely are the sheltered lanes that take you here and
    there;
But, best of all, I love a road that leads to God knows
    where.

Charles Hanson Towne

We Shall Attain

We shall attain — yea, though this dust shall fail,
And though all evil things conspire to bind
The struggling soul with gyves of sense, and blind
Our faith with clay, and though all foes assail
To utterly destroy us: yet from wail,
From misery and from doubt, from all mankind
False hopes, and from the dwarfed and prisoned mind,
We shall attain to life beyond the vail.

Yea, though 'tis written that all flesh is grass,
Which springeth up at morn and flourisheth,
And which at even, when th' inverted glass
Is emptied of its sands, fades as the breath.
The dew-lipped rose sighs on the winds that pass —
Yet in our frailty — we shall conquer death.

James B. Kenyon

What Makes a Nation Great?

Not serried ranks with flags unfurled,
Not armored ships that gird the world,
Not hoarded wealth nor busy mills,
Not cattle on a thousand hills,
Not sages wise, nor schools nor laws,
Not boasted deeds in freedom's cause —
All these may be, and yet the state
In the eye of God be far from great.

That land is great which knows the Lord,
Whose songs are guided by His word;
Where justice rules 'twixt man and man,
Where love controls in art and plan;
Where, breathing in his native air,
Each soul finds joy in praise and prayer —
Thus may our country, good and great,
Be God's delight — man's best estate.

Alexander Blackburn

Youth

I shall remember then,
At twilight time or in the hush of dawn,
Or yet, mayhap, when on a straying wind
The scent of lilac comes, or when
Some strain of music startles and is gone.

Old dreams, old roses, all so far behind,
Blossoms and birds and ancient shadow-trees,
Whispers at sunset, the low hum of bees,
And sheep that graze beneath a summer sun,

Will they too come, they who in yester-year
Walked the same paths and in the first of Spring,
And shall I hear
Their distant voices murmuring?

I shall remember then
When youth is done,
With the dim years grown gray;
And I shall wonder what it is that ends,
And why they seem so very far away —
Old dreams, old roses . . . and old friends.

Thomas S. Jones, Jr.

God Hears Prayer

If radio's slim fingers can pluck a melody
From night — and toss it over a continent or sea;
If the petalled white notes of a violin
Are blown across the mountains or the city's din;
If songs, like crimson roses, are culled from thin blue air —
Why should mortals wonder if God hears prayer?

Ethel Romig Fuller

Prayer in April

God grant that I may never be
A scoffer at Eternity —
As long as every April brings
The sweet rebirth of growing things;
As long as grass is green anew,
As long as April's skies are blue,
I shall believe that God looks down
Upon His wide earth, cold and brown,
To bless its unborn mystery
Of leaf, and bud, and flower to be;

To smile on it from tender skies —
How could I think it otherwise?
Had I been dust for many a year,
I still would know when Spring was near,
For the good earth that pillowed me
Would whisper immortality,
And I, in part, would rise and sing
Amid the grasses murmuring.
When looking on the mother sod,
Can I hold doubt that this be God?
Or when a primrose smiles at me,
Can I distrust Eternity?

Sara Henderson Hay

The Land of Beginning Again

I wish that there were some wonderful place
  In the Land of Beginning Again:
Where all our mistakes and all our heartaches
  And all of our poor selfish grief
Could be dropped like a shabby old coat at the door
  And never put on again.

I wish we could come on it all unaware,
  Like the hunter who finds a lost trail;
And I wish that the one whom our blindness had done
  The greatest injustice of all
Could be there at the gates like an old friend that waits
  For the comrade he's gladdest to hail.

We would find all the things we intended to do
  But forgot, and remembered too late,
Little praises unspoken, little promises broken,
  And all of the thousand and one
Little duties neglected that might have perfected
  The day for one less fortunate.

It wouldn't be possible not to be kind
  In the Land of Beginning Again,
And the ones we misjudged and the ones whom we grudged
  Their moments of victory here,
Would find in the grasp of our loving hand-clasp
  More than penitent lips could explain.

For what had been hardest we'd know had been best,
  And what had seemed loss would be gain;
For there isn't a sting that will not take wing
  When we've faced it and laughed it away
And I think that the laughter is most what we're after
  In the Land of Beginning Again.

So I wish that there were some wonderful place
  Called the Land of Beginning Again,
Where all our mistakes and all our heartaches,
  And all of our poor selfish grief
Could be dropped like a shabby old coat at the door
  And never put on again.
                              Louise Fletcher Tarkington

Life Is Ever Lord of Death

Alas for him who never sees
The stars shine through his cypress-trees!
Who, hopeless, lays his dead away,
Nor looks to see the breaking day
Across the mournful marbles play!
Who hath not learned, in hours of faith,
The truth to flesh and sense unknown,
That Life is ever Lord of Death,
And Love can never lose its own!
                              John Greenleaf Whittier

From " Snow-Bound "

Sometimes

Across the fields of yesterday
    He sometimes comes to me,
A little lad just back from play —
    The lad I used to be.

And yet he smiles so wistfully
    Once he has crept within,
I wonder if he hopes to see
    The man I might have been.

Thomas S. Jones, Jr.

Use Well the Moment

Use well the moment; what the hour
Brings for thy use is in thy power;
And what thou best canst understand
Is just the thing lies nearest to thy hand.

J. W. von Goethe

Immortality

I live: this much I know; and I defy
The world to prove that I shall ever die!
But all men perish?   Aye, and even so
Beneath the grasses lay this body low;
Forever close these eyes and still this breath;
All this, yet I shall not have tasted death.

Where are the lips that prattled infant lays?
The eyes that shone with light of childhood's days?
The heart that bubbled o'er with boyhood's glee?
The limbs that bounded as the chamois free?
The ears that heard life's music everywhere?
These, all, where are they now?   Declare.

Forever gone; forever dead!   Yet still
I live.   My love, my hate, my fear, my will,
My all that makes life living firm abides.
Death is my youth, and so my age must die;
But I remain — Imperishable I.

Speed day and year!   Fleet by the stream of time!
Wing, birds of passage, to a sunnier clime.
Come change, come dissolution and decay,
To kill the very semblance of this clay!
Yet, know the conscious, the unchanging I
Through all eternity shall never die.

Willis Fletcher Johnson

Beyond Electrons

They who once probed and doubted now believe
The Men of Science, for they humbly learn
There is a Will that guides the atom's course;
A Power that directs what they discern
In light and air, in star and wave and sod;
Beyond electrons they discover — God!

From research they derive a new faith that
Sustains foundations of our ancient creeds;
They grope through matter toward an utmost Light
And find a living God behind His deeds.

Adelaide P. Love

If Love Be Ours

In Love, if Love be Love, if Love be ours,
Faith and unfaith can ne'er be equal powers:
Unfaith in aught is want of faith in all.

It is the little rift within the lute,
That by and by will make the music mute,
    And ever widening slowly silence all.

The little rift within the lover's lute,
Or little pitted speck in garnered fruit,
    That rotting inward slowly moulders all.

It is not worth the keeping: let it go:
But shall it? answer, darling, answer, no.
    And trust me not at all or all in all.

                                Alfred Tennyson
        From " Idylls of the King "

Love

        No show of bolts and bars
        Can keep the foeman out,
        Or 'scape his secret mine
        Who enter'd with the doubt
        That drew the line.
        No warder at the gate
        Can let the friendly in;
        But, like the sun, o'er all
        He will the castle win,
        And shine along the wall.

        Implacable is Love —
        Foes may be bought or teased
        From their hostile intent,
        But he goes unappeased
        Who is on kindness bent.

                        Henry David Thoreau

The Poem I Should Like to Write

The poem I should like to write was written long ago,
In vast primeval valleys and on mountains clad in snow;
It was written where no foot of man or beast had ever trod,
And where the first wild flower turned its smiling face to
    God;
Where mighty winds swept far and wide o'er dark and sullen
    seas,
And where the first earth-mother sat, a child upon her knees.

The poem I should like to write is written in the stars,
Where Venus holds her glowing torch behind her gleaming
    bars;
Where old Arcturus swings his lamp across the fields of
    space,
And all his brilliant retinue is wheeling into place;
Where unknown suns must rise and set, as ages onward
    fare —
The poem I should like to write is surely written there.
No human hand can write it, for with a pen divine,
The Master Poet wrote it — each burning word and line.
Margaret A. Windes

Life's Finest Things

Life's finest things, the things that last,
Are ours, but never fettered fast.

The exodus of birds and fowls when blasts begin to blow,
The fuzzy Spring buds peeping forth, at passing of the snow;
Prolific Summer's teeming life, the omtone of the bee,
Resplendent Autumn's full-toned leaves ablaze on every tree;

The sorcery of Winter's moon, frost's leafage on the pane,
The solemn forest's awful hush, the rhythm of the rain;
A timid breeze that wakes a lake, the ocean's troubled breast,
A storm-scourged mountain rearing high its chaste un-bending crest;
Recall the tender words of love or long forgotten lays,
The bonfire's spicy fragrant smoke on Indian-summer days.
The flaming death robes of the day, the marvel of its birth,
The frozen green in the fissures that split the glacier's girth.
The glint of gorgeous green-blue eyes in peacock's spread of tail,
A sense of God's omnipotence when thunder rends the vale,
Proud dreams and schemes of vibrant youth which surely must come true,
That brave exalted purpose of the child that once was you;
The nursing back a loved one from the verge of voiceless dust,
The greatest boon to human kind, the great, great gift of trust.

Life's finest things, the things that last,
Are ours, but never fettered fast.
The finest things writ on the scroll
Are only grappled by the soul.   *Bangs Burgess*

What of the Darkness?

What of the darkness? Is it very fair?
Are there great calms? and find we silence there?
Like soft-shut lilies, all your faces glow
With some strange peace our faces never know,
With some strange faith our faces never dare —
Dwells it in Darkness? Do you find it there?

Is it a Bosom where tired heads may lie?
Is it a Mouth to kiss our weeping dry?
Is it a Hand to still the pulse's leap?
Is it a Voice that holds the runes of sleep?
Day shows us not such comfort anywhere —
Dwells it in Darkness?   Do you find it there?

Out of the Day's deceiving light we call —
Day that shows man so great, and God so small,
That hides the stars, and magnifies the grass —
O is the Darkness too a lying glass!
Or undistracted, do you find truth there?
What of the Darkness?   Is it very fair?

Richard le Gallienne

Christmas Eve

The door is on the latch tonight,
   The hearth-fire is aglow,
I seem to hear soft passing feet —
   The Christ child in the snow.

My heart is open wide tonight
   For stranger, kith or kin;
I would not bar a single door
   Where love might enter in.

Author Unknown

The Pathway to Paradise

" How shall I find it, and which way lies
The pathway leading to Paradise? "
For dark and long is the road I tread;
And its end is lost in the mist ahead.

I met a man with a heavy load
Toiling along the dusty road.
He answered my question in mild surprise:
" True work is the pathway to Paradise."

I met a group with laughter and song
Passing the woodland ways along.
They sang their answer: " This way it lies,
And joy is the pathway to Paradise."

I met a woman and little child.
I asked my question. The mother smiled
And looked down into her baby's eyes:
" Oh, love is the pathway to Paradise."

Ozora S. Davis

Sonnet

Be secret, heart; and if your dreams have come
To nothingness, and if their weight was sweet
Within you — then be silent in defeat,
Counting your lost imaginings as the sum
Of destined joy. Lest men should call you dumb
Sing still the songs that hold within their beat
The hopes of every man, and the wild, sweet
Predictions of what earth shall yet become.
Be secret, heart. The words that you would tell
Of your own longing, and your keen distress —
Hold them to silence; kill, destroy, suppress
That melody, although you love it well.
And sing the songs that men have always sung
Of love and sorrow, since the world was young.

Anna Virginia Mitchell

Nicodemus

And Nicodemus came by night
When none might hear or see —
He came by night to shun men's sight
And away by night slunk he.

He dared not come by light of day
To move where sinners trod:
He must hold apart from the common heart,
For he was a man of God. . . .

But the honest Christ, He walked with men
Nor held His ways apart —
With publicans talked, with harlots walked,
And loved them all in His heart. . . .

Came Nicodemus to Christ by night;
And long they reasoned, alone,
Till the old man saw the sham of the law
That turned his being to stone;

He tore the formal husks from his life;
He was born again, though gray.
And, erect with the youth of a living truth
He dared the world by day!

Harry Kemp

A New Year

Here's a clean year,
    A white year.
        Reach your hand and take it.
You are
    The builder,
        And no one else can make it.

See what it is
That waits here,
Whole and new;
It's not a year only,
But a world
For you!

Mary Carolyn Davies

Miracles

Why, who makes much of a miracle?
As to me I know of nothing else but miracles,
Whether I walk the streets of Manhattan,
Or dart my sight over the roofs of houses toward the
sky,
Or wade with naked feet along the beach just in the edge of
the water,
Or stand under trees in the woods,
Or talk by day with any one I love,
Or sit at table at dinner with the rest,
Or look at strangers opposite me riding in the car,
Or watch honey-bees busy around the hive of a Summer
forenoon,
Or animals feeding in the fields,
Or birds, or the wonderfulness of insects in the air,
Or the wonderfulness of the sundown, or of stars shining so
quiet and bright,
Or the exquisite delicate thin curve of the new moon in
Spring;
These with the rest, one and all, are to me miracles,
The whole referring, yet each distinct and in its place.

To me every hour of the light and dark is a miracle,
Every cubic inch of space is a miracle,

Every square yard of the surface of the earth is spread with
    the same,
Every foot of the interior swarms with the same.

To me the sea is a continual miracle,
The fishes that swim — the rocks — the motion of the waves
    — the ships with men in them,
What stranger miracles are there?

Walt Whitman

Faith

" Must I submissive bow to earth my head?
    Restrain the restless daring of my mind?
Bound by the palimpsests of men long dead,
    Live in the daylight as a man made blind? "

" Yea, lowly bend thy stubborn neck and knees,
    And thou shalt win what thy proud ardors seek.
This pathway leads to kindled mysteries
    That none have ever seen except the meek."

" Never for me such craven sacrifice!
    Bravely I go upon a lonely quest.
I will not fold my hands and close my eyes
    To gain an easy and ignoble rest."

" So thou hast courage? Test it. Thou shalt find
    Precipitous the pathways to be trod.
Summon the utmost valiance of thy mind.
    Only the audacious ever win to God."

Theodore Maynard

The Forgotten Countersign

Life met me on the threshold — young, divine,
And promised me unutterable things;
And Love, with fragrant greeting on his wings,
Looked in my eyes and laid his lips on mine,
And bade me quaff the magic of his wine
That deep delight, or disillusion brings.
Ah! had I kept my fair imaginings,
I had not lost the heavenly countersign;
The Shibboleth of soul supremacy;
The dower from my birth in higher spheres.
Then might I know the purer ecstasy
Of conquering Earth's test of alien tears —
And Life, perchance, her promise might redeem,
And Love be more than a delusive dream!

Corinne Roosevelt Robinson

From Ode on Intimations of Immortality

There was a time when meadow, grove, and stream,
The earth, and every common sight,
    To me did seem
    Apparelled in celestial light,
The glory and the freshness of a dream.
It is not now as it hath been of yore; —
    Turn wheresoe'er I may,
      By night or day,
The things which I have seen I now can see no more.
    The rainbow comes and goes,
    And lovely is the rose;
    The moon doth with delight

Look round her when the heavens are bare;
Waters on a starry night
Are beautiful and fair;
The sunshine is a glorious birth;
But yet I know, where'er I go,
That there hath past away a glory from the earth.

* * *

O joy! that in our embers
Is something that doth live,
That nature yet remembers
What was so fugitive!
The thought of our past years in me doth breed
Perpetual benediction: not indeed
For that which is most worthy to be blest,
Delight and liberty, the simple creed
Of Childhood, whether busy or at rest,
With new-fledged hope still fluttering in her breast: —
Not for these I raise
The song of thanks and praise;
But for those obstinate questionings
Of sense and outward things,
Fallings from us, vanishings;
Blank misgivings of a creature
Moving about in worlds not realized,
High instincts, before which our mortal nature
Did tremble like a guilty thing surprised:
But for those first affections,
Those shadowy recollections,
Which, be they what they may,
Are yet the fountain-light of all our day,
Are yet a master-light of all our seeing;
Uphold us, cherish, and have power to make
Our noisy years seem moments in the being

Of the eternal Silence: truths that wake,
　　To perish never;
Which neither listlessness, nor mad endeavour,
　　Nor man nor boy
Nor all that is at enmity with joy,
Can utterly abolish or destroy!
　　　Hence in a season of calm weather,
　　　Though inland far we be,
Our souls have sight of that immortal sea
　　Which brought us hither;
　　　Can in a moment travel thither,
And see the children sport upon the shore,
And hear the mighty waters rolling evermore.

William Wordsworth

The World Is One

The world is one; we cannot live apart,
　To earth's remotest races we are kin;
God made the generations of one blood;
　Man's separation is a sign of sin.

What though we solve the secret of the stars,
　Or from the vibrant ether pluck a song,
Can this for all man's tyranny atone
　While Mercy weeps and waits and suffers long?

Put up the sword, its day of anguish past;
　Disarm the forts, and then, the war-flags furled,
Forever keep the air without frontiers,
　The great, free, friendly highway of the world.

So that at last to rapture men may come,
And hear again the music of the spheres,
And stand erect, illumined, radiant, free,
The travail and the triumph of the years.

Hinton White

Riches

What to a man who loves the air
Are trinkets, gauds, and jewels rare?
And what is wealth or fame to one
Who is a brother to the sun;
Who drinks the wine that morning spills
Upon the heaven-kissing hills,
And sees a ray of hope afar
In every glimmer of a star?

What to a man whose god is truth
Are spoils and stratagems, forsooth —
Who looks beyond the doors of death
For loftier life, sublimer breath;
Who can forswear the state of kings
In knowledge of diviner things,
The dreams immortal that unroll
And burst to blossoms in his soul?

Robert Loveman

Only the Dream Is Real

Only the dream is real. There is no plan
Transcending even a rose's timid glory,
A cricket's summer song. The ways of man
Are stupors of the flesh, and transitory.

There is no truth but dreams; yet man must spend
  His gift of quiet days in storm and stress,
Unheeding that a single breath will end
  With one swift stroke the hoax of worldliness.

Only the dream will last. Some distant day
  The wheels will falter, and the silent sun
Will see the last beam leveled to decay,
  And all man's futile clangor spent and done.
Yet after brick and steel and stone are gone,
And flesh and blood are dust, the dream lives on.
                                  Anderson M. Scruggs

Expect!

Expect the best! It lies not in the past.
God ever keeps the good wine till the last.
Beyond are nobler work and sweeter rest.
      Expect the best!
                      William Pierson Merrill

I Would Not Always Reason

I would not always reason. The straight path
Wearies us with the never-varying lines,
And we grow melancholy. I would make
Reason my guide, but she should sometimes sit
Patiently by the wayside, while I traced
The mazes of the pleasant wilderness
Around me. She should be my counsellor,
But not my tyrant. For the spirit needs
Impulses from a deeper source than hers;
And there are notions, in the mind of man,
That she must look upon with awe.
                            William Cullen Bryant
From " The Conjunction of Jupiter and Venus "

The Master of My Boat

I owned a little boat a while ago
  And sailed a Morning Sea without a fear,
And whither any breeze might fairly blow
  I'd steer the little craft afar or near.

> Mine was the boat,
>   And mine the air,
>   And mine the sea,
>   Not mine a care.

My boat became my place of nightly toil,
  I sailed at sunset to the fishing ground;
At morn the boat was freighted with the spoil
  That my all-conquering work and skill had found.

> Mine was the boat,
>   And mine the net,
>   And mine the skill
>   And power to get.

One day there passed along the silent shore,
  While I my net was casting in the sea,
A Man, who spoke as never man before;
  I followed Him — new life began in me.

> Mine was the boat,
>   But His the voice,
>   And His the call,
>   Yet mine the choice.

Ah, 'twas a fearful night out on the lake,
  And all my skill availed not at the helm,
Till Him asleep I waken, crying, " Take,
  Take Thou command, lest waters overwhelm! "

His was the boat,
And His the sea,
And His the peace
O'er all and me.

Once from His boat He taught the curious throng,
Then bade me let down nets out in the sea;
I murmured, but obeyed, nor was it long
Before the catch amazed and humbled me.

His was the boat,
And His the skill,
And His the catch,
And His my will.
Joseph Addison Richards

Slaves

They are slaves who fear to speak,
For the fallen and the weak;
They are slaves who will not choose,
Hatred, scoffing and abuse,
Rather than in silence shrink,
From the truth they needs must think;
They are slaves who dare not be,
In the right with two or three.
James Russell Lowell

On Broadway

Great jewels glitter like a wizard's rain
Of pearl and ruby in the women's hair.
And all the men — each drags a golden chain,
As though he walked in freedom. In the glare,

Luxurious-cushioned wheels a revel-train
Where kings of song with weary feet have trod,
Where Poe, sad priest to Beauty and to Pain,
Bore through the night the Vision and the God.

And yet, perhaps, in this assemblage vast,
In some poor heart sounds the enraptured chord,
And staggering homeward from a hopeless quest
The God-anointed touched me, meanly dressed,
And, like a second Peter, I have passed
Without salute the vessel of the Lord.
George Sylvester Viereck

Do You Fear the Wind?

Do you fear the force of the wind,
   The slash of the rain?
Go face them and fight them,
   Be savage again.
Go hungry and cold like the wolf,
   Go wade like the crane:
The palms of your hands will thicken,
   The skin of your cheek will tan,
You'll grow ragged and weary and swarthy,
   But you'll walk like a man!
Hamlin Garland

What Is Good?

" What is the real good? "
I asked in musing mood.

Order, said the law court;
Knowledge, said the school;

Truth, said the wise man;
Pleasure, said the fool;
Love, said a maiden;
Beauty, said the page;
Freedom, said the dreamer;
Home, said the sage;
Fame, said the soldier;
Equity, the seer; —

Spake my heart full sadly,
" The answer is not here."

Then within my bosom
Softly this I heard:
" Each heart holds the secret;
Kindness is the word."

John Boyle O'Reilly

Life

Life is too brief
Between the budding and the falling leaf.
Between the seed time and the golden sheaf,
    For hate and spite.
We have no time for malice and for greed;
Therefore, with love make beautiful the deed;
    Fast speeds the night.

Life is too swift
Between the blossom and the white snow's drift,
Between the silence and the lark's uplift,
    For bitter words.
In kindness and in gentleness our speech
Must carry messages of hope, and reach
    The sweetest chords.

Life is too great
Between the infant's and the man's estate,
Between the clashing of earth's strife and fate,
      For petty things.
Lo! we shall yet who creep with cumbered feet
Walk glorious over heaven's golden street,
      Or soar on wings!

                              W. M. Vories

Chiaroscuro

Beauty growing on a thorn,
    Love victorious on a tree —
Conquer every cynic's scorn,
    Prove life's immortality!

                        John B. Thompson

Life Shall Live For Evermore

My own dim life should teach me this,
    That life shall live for evermore:
    Else earth is darkness at the core,
And dust and ashes all that is —

This round of green, this orb of flame,
    Fantastic beauty; such as lurks
    In some wild poet, when he works
Without a conscience or an aim.

What then were God to such as I?
    'Twere hardly worth my while to choose
    Of things all mortal; or to use
A little patience ere I die:

'Twere best at once to sink to peace —
  Like birds the charming serpent draws,
  To drop headforemost in the jaws
Of vacant darkness, and to cease.

Alfred Tennyson

From " In Memoriam "

Miracle

Yesterday the twig was brown and bare;
Today the glint of green is there
Tomorrow will be leaflets spare;
I know no thing so wondrous fair
No miracle so strangely rare.
I wonder what will next be there!

L. H. Bailey

Humanity

There is a soul above the soul of each,
A mightier soul, which yet to each belongs —
There is a sound made of all human speech,
And numerous as the concourse of all songs:
And in that soul lives each, in each that soul,
Though all the ages are its lifetime vast;
Each soul that dies, in its most sacred whole
Receiveth life that shall for ever last.
And thus for ever with a wider span
Humanity o'erarches time and death:
Man can elect the universal man
And live in life that ends not with this breath;
And gather glory that increases still
Till Time his glass with Death's last dust shall fill.

Richard Watson Dixon

A Prayer for Today

Lord, in an age of steel and stone,
   When girders tell the dreamer's plan:
Give me the grace to stand alone,
   Give me the strength to be a man.

As mighty trains on shining rails
   Haste onward through the night and day:
Send me on work that never fails
   Because of indolent delay.

As planes that plunge into the sky
   To find themselves upborne on air:
Teach me the life of trust to try,
   And find the soul upheld through prayer.

From distant places voices speak —
   They fill the mind with mystery:
Then may I now Thy message seek,
   O, let me keep in tune with Thee.

Amid the motion of machine,
   The whirl of wheel, the rush of wings:
Help me to live the life serene,
   Because victorious over things.

May something of the vast designs
   That motivate and move our days,
Be but inevitable signs
   Which call life into lordlier ways.

Charles Nelson Pacь

Be Merciful

Once ran my prayer as runs the brook
    O'er pebbles and through sunny meads;
No pain my inmost spirit shook,
    Words broke in shallows of small needs.

But now the shadows on me lie,
    Deep-cut the channel of the years;
And prayer is but a sobbing cry
    Through whitened lips and falling tears.

Not glibly, but with broken speech,
    O God, my God, I pray to Thee;
Enough if now I may beseech,
    Be merciful, O God, to me!

                            John T. McFarland

The Undiscovered Country

Lord, for the erring thought
Not unto evil wrought:
Lord, for the wicked will
Betrayed and baffled still:
For the heart from itself kept,
Our thanksgiving accept.
For ignorant hopes that were
Broken to our blind prayer:
For pain, death, sorrow sent
Unto our chastisement:
For all loss of seeming good,
Quicken our gratitude.

                    William Dean Howells

Two Prayers

Only for these I pray,
  Pray with assurance strong:
Light to discover the way,
  Power to follow it long.

Let me have light to see,
  Light to be sure and know;
When the road is clear to me
  Willingly I go.

Let me have power to do,
  Power of the brain and nerve,
Though the task is heavy and new
  Willingly I will serve.

My prayers are lesser than three,
  Nothing I pray but two
Let me have light to see,
  Let me have power to do.
                    Charlotte Perkins Gilman

Foreign Missions in Battle Array

An endless line of splendor,
These troops with heaven for home,
With creeds they go from Scotland,
With incense go from Rome.
These, in the name of Jesus,
Against the dark gods stand,
They gird the earth with valor,
They heed their King's command.

Onward the line advances,
Shaking the hills with power,
Slaying the hidden demons,
The lions that devour.
No bloodshed in the wrestling, —
But souls new-born arise —
The nations growing kinder,
The child-hearts growing wise.

What is the final ending?
The issue, can we know?
Will Christ outlive Mohammed?
Will Kali's altar go?
This is our faith tremendous, —
Our wild hope, who shall scorn, —
That in the name of Jesus
The world shall be reborn!

Vachel Lindsay

Ships That Pass in the Night

Ships that pass in the night, and speak each other in passing,
Only a signal shown and a distant voice in the darkness;
So on the ocean of life we pass and speak one another,
Only a look and a voice, then darkness again and silence.

Henry Wadsworth Longfellow
From " Tales of a Wayside Inn "

Silence

God must have loved the silence, for he laid
A stillness on the sunset and the dawn;
Upon the moment when the bird has gone
Leaving a note, high-hung, within the glade

More sweet than when he sang it; moons that pass
Too full of forests' changelessness for sound;
Creeping of little frosts along the ground;
Silence of growth among the summer grass.

God must have deeply loved the silences,
For is there one of us who has not heard
Promptings to silence that he speaks not of?

What of an old remorse; a hope that is
Too deeply hoped; what of a grief outgrown;
And silent, old, unconquerable love?

Mavis C. Barnett

Love Suffereth Long

The Writ of Loving Well
    Still makes its old demands:
A sometime residence in Hell,
    The nailprints in the hands.

All those who pledge themselves,
    And to its terms agree
Must chance an unexclusive cross,
    A common Calvary!

Sara Henderson Hay

Nameless Saints

The healing of the world
Is in its nameless saints. Each separate star
Means nothing, but a myriad scattered stars
Break up the night and make it beautiful.

Bayard Taylor

Goshen

How can you live in Goshen?
Said a friend from afar.
This is a wretched little place
Where people talk about tawdry things
And plant cabbages in the moonlight. . . .

But I do not live in Goshen, I answered.
I live in Greece
Where Plato taught and Phidias carved.
I live in Rome
Where Cicero penned immortal lines
And Michelangelo dreamed things of beauty.
Do not think my world is small
Because you find me in a little village.
I have my books, my pictures, my dreams,
Enchantments that transcend Time and Space.
I do not live in Goshen at all,
I live in an unbounded universe
With the great souls of all the ages
For my companions.

Edgar Frank

Prayer

Father, I scarcely dare to pray,
So clear I see, now it is done,
That I have wasted half my day,
And left my work but just begun.

So clear I see that things I thought
Were right or harmless were a sin;
So clear I see that I have sought,
Unconscious, selfish aims to win.

So clear I see that I have hurt
  The souls I might have helped to save;
That I have slothful been, inert,
  Deaf to the calls Thy leaders gave.

In outskirts of Thy kingdom vast,
  Father, the humblest spot give me;
Set me the lowliest task Thou hast;
  Let me, repentant, work for Thee!
                    Helen Hunt Jackson

Prayer for Miracle

O God! No more Thy miracle withhold;
To us in tents give palaces of gold.
And while we stumble among things that are
Give us the solace of a guiding-star!
                    Anna Wickham

The Heart Is a Strange Thing

The heart is a strange thing:
  It has no eyes,
But it can see through dark earth
  And beyond blue skies.

The heart has no hands,
  But, knowing Love's touch,
All the hands of the world
  Cannot do as much.

The heart has no feet,
  But it may go
Swiftly to Heaven above
  Or Hell below.

The heart is a strange thing,
    More strange than the head:
Sometimes it may live again
    After long dead.

Minnie Case Hopkins

The Heart of the Tree

What does he plant who plants a tree?
    He plants a friend of sun and sky;
He plants the flag of breezes free;
    The shaft of beauty, towering high;
    He plants a home to heaven anigh
    For song and mother-croon of bird
    In hushed and happy twilight heard —
The treble of heaven's harmony —
These things he plants who plants a tree.

What does he plant who plants a tree?
    He plants cool shade and tender rain,
And seed and bud of days to be,
    And years that fade and flush again;
    He plants the glory of the plain;
    He plants the forest's heritage;
    The harvest of a coming age;
The joy that unborn eyes shall see —
These things he plants who plants a tree.

What does he plant who plants a tree?
    He plants, in sap and leaf and wood,
In love of home and loyalty
    And far-cast thought of civic good —
    His blessing on the neighborhood

Who in the hollow of His hand
Holds all the growth of all our land —
A nation's growth from sea to sea
Stirs in his heart who plants a tree.

Henry C. Bunner

A Little Work

A little work, a little play
To keep us going — and so, good-day!
A little warmth, a little light
Of love's bestowing — and so, good-night!
A little fun, to match the sorrow
Of each day's growing — and so, good-morrow!
A little trust that when we die
We reap our sowing! And so — good-bye!

George du Maurier

I Would Be Great

O Lord,
I would be great —
But not in some spectacular way
For world acclaim.
Beyond my talents
Lie outstanding deeds, perhaps;
But, Lord, I would be great
In faithfulness to each small task
Thou givest me,
To do the best I can
With what I have
For Thy name's sake.

And if, some day, Thou sendest me
Some task that seems too big
For hands that only little deeds have done,
I know that what I cannot do,
Thou canst, through me, if I but will,
And in Thy strength
I'll do the thing that is too big for me.
Help me, O Lord, to stand approved
In faithfulness to every task.
Thus, in Thy sight
I will be great.   *Hattie B. McCracken*

Builders

When we build, let us think that we build forever. Let it
  not be for present delight nor for present use alone.
Let it be such work as our descendants will thank us for,
  and let us think, as we lay stone on stone, that a time is
  to come when those stones will be held sacred because
  our hands have touched them, and that men will say as
  they look upon the labor and wrought substance of them,
" See! This our Fathers did for us."
                                        John Ruskin

Avè Crux, Spes Unica!

More than two crosses stand on either side
    The Cross today on more than one dark hill;
More than three hours a myriad men have cried,
    And they are crying still.

Before Him now no mocking faces pass;
    Heavy on all who built the cross, it lies;
Pilate is hanging there, and Caiaphas,
    Judas without his price.

Men scourge each other with their stinging whips;
　To crosses high they nail, and they are nailed;
More than one dying man with parchèd lips,
　　" My God!　My God! " has wailed.

Enlarged is Golgotha.　But One alone
　His healing shadow over all can fling;
One King Divine has made His Cross a Throne.
　　" Remember us, O King! "

Edward Shillito

Each and All

Little thinks, in the field, yon red-cloaked clown
Of thee from the hill-top looking down;
The heifer that lows in the upland farm,
Far-heard, lows not thine ear to charm;
The sexton, tolling his bell at noon,
Deems not that great Napoleon
Stops his horse, and lists with delight,
Whilst his files sweep round yon Alpine height;
Nor knowest thou what argument
Thy life to thy neighbor's creed has lent.
All are needed by each one —
Nothing is fair or good alone.
I thought the sparrow's note from heaven,
Singing at dawn on the alder bough;
I brought him home, in his nest, at even;
He sings the song, but it cheers not now;
For I did not bring home the river and sky;
He sang to my ear — they sang to my eye.

The delicate shells lay on the shore;
The bubbles of the latest wave
Fresh pearls to their enamel gave,

And the bellowing of the savage sea
Greeted their safe escape to me.
I wiped away the weeds and foam —
I fetched my sea-born treasures home;
But the poor, unsightly, noisome things
Had left their beauty on the shore
With the sun and the sand and the wild uproar.

The lover watched his graceful maid,
As 'mid the virgin train she strayed,
Nor knew her beauty's best attire
Was woven still by the snow-white choir.
At last she came to his hermitage,
Like the bird from the woodlands to the cage;
The gay enchantment was undone —
A gentle wife, but fairy none.

Then I said, " I covet truth;
Beauty is unripe childhood's cheat;
I leave it behind with the games of youth."
As I spoke, beneath my feet
The ground-pine curled its pretty wreath,
Running over the club-moss burrs;
I inhaled the violet's breath;
Around me stood the oaks and firs;
Pine cones and acorns lay on the ground;
Over me soared the eternal sky,
Full of light and deity;
Again I saw, again I heard,
The rolling river, the morning bird;
Beauty through my senses stole;
I yielded myself to the perfect whole.

Ralph Waldo Emerson

Gifts

Dear God, I stand with empty hands
   To have them filled.
The other gifts Thou gavest me
   I long have spilled.
And some I broke upon these stones,
   And some are bled
Until they died, because my thoughts
   To strangeness wed.

Dear God, I would have other gifts
   Within my hands.
Seal them upon me in Thy wrath
   With golden bands;
That I may never lose again
   A love, but free
My heart, in deepening loneliness,
   To ecstasy.

Mary Edgar Comstock

For Transient Things

Let us thank God for unfulfilled desire,
For beauty that escapes our clutch and flies;
Let us thank God for loveliness that dies,
For violet leapings of a dying fire,
For ebbing lives and seas, the fading choir
Of quiet stars, the momentary guise
That love assumes within a lover's eyes
Before it fades with other things that tire.
Better that beauty wear into the night
An inky garment of uncandled hours

Than stay forever robed in festal white,
And so, familiar grown, like flowers
One counts as common weeds, begin to pall —
Better that beauty should not be at all.

James A. S. McPeek

Simon and Judas

How dare we look askance at these two men,
Toy with unspoken thoughts, "Were I there then —"
Venture to pity, blame, or mildly scoff?
We, who have struck not once with any sword,
Who have so many times betrayed our Lord,
Nor followed even at a great way off!

Kenneth W. Porter

Kinship

I am part of the sea and stars
    And the winds of the South and North,
Of mountain and moon and Mars,
    And the ages sent me forth!

Blind Homer, the splendor of Greece,
    Sang the songs I sang ere he fell;
She whom men call Beatrice
    Saw me in the depths of hell.

I was hanged at dawn for a crime —
    Flesh dies, but the soul knows no death;
I piped to great Shakespeare's chime
    The witches' song in Macbeth.

All, all who have suffered and won,
   Who have struggled and failed and died,
Am I, with work still undone,
   And a spear-mark in my side.

I am part of the sea and stars
   And the winds of the South and North,
Of mountain and moon and Mars,
   And the ages sent me forth!

Edward H. S. Terry

The Secret

April whispered this to me
And I have done with sorrow now:
"*I am death's white mystery,*"
April whispered this to me.

"*Life from death! O ecstasy
Of the first white lifted bough!*"
April whispered this to me
And I have done with sorrow.

John Richard Moreland

Faith

I will not doubt, though all my ships at sea
   Come drifting home with broken masts and sails;
   I shall believe the Hand which never fails
From seeking evil worketh good for me;
   And though I weep because those sails are battered,
   Still will I cry, while my best hopes lie shattered,
     "I trust in Thee."

I will not doubt, though all my prayers return
  Unanswered from the still, white realm above;
  I shall believe it is an all-wise Love
Which has refused those things for which I yearn;
  And though at times I cannot keep from grieving,
  Yet the pure ardor of my fixed believing
    Undimmed shall burn.

I will not doubt, though sorrows fall like rain,
  And troubles swarm like bees about a hive;
  I shall believe the heights for which I strive
Are only reached by anguish and by pain;
  And though I groan and tremble with my crosses,
  I yet shall see, through my severest losses,
    The greater gain.

I will not doubt; well anchored in the faith,
  Like some stanch ship, my soul braves every gale,
  So strong its courage that it will not fail
To breast the mighty unknown sea of Death.
  O, may I cry, when body parts with spirit,
  " I do not doubt," so listening worlds may hear it,
    With my last breath.

Ella Wheeler Wilcox

Fortune

There is a tide in the affairs of men,
Which, taken at the flood, leads on to fortune;
Omitted, all the voyage of their life
Is bound in shallows and in miseries.
On such a full sea are we now afloat;
And we must take the current when it serves,
Or lose our ventures.

William Shakespeare

From " Julius Caesar "

From The Over-Heart

Above, below, in sky and sod
   In leaf and spar, in star and man,
   Well might the wise Athenian scan
The geometric signs of God,
   The measured order of His plan.

And India's mystics sang aright
   Of the One Life pervading all —
   One Being's tidal rise and fall
In soul and form, in sound and sight —
   Eternal outflow and recall.

God is: and man in guilt and fear
   This central fact of Nature owns; —
   Kneels, trembling, by his altar-stones,
And darkly dreams the ghastly smear
   Of blood appeases and atones.

Guilt shapes by Terror: deep within
   The human heart the secret lies
   Of all the hideous deities;
And, painted on a ground of sin,
   The fabled gods of torment rise!

And what is He? — The ripe grain nods,
   The sweet dews fall, the flowers blow;
   But darker signs His presence show:
The earthquake and the storm are God's
   And good and evil interflow.

O hearts of love!   O souls that turn
   Like sunflowers to the pure and best!
   To you the truth is manifest:
For they the mind of Christ discern
   Who lean like John upon his breast!
                     John Greenleaf Whittier

The Friendly Faces of Old Sorrows

I love the friendly faces of old Sorrows;
   I have no secrets that they do not know.
They are so old, I think they have forgotten
   What bitter words were spoken, long ago.

I hate the cold, stern faces of new Sorrows
   Who stand and watch, and catch me all alone.
I should be braver if I could remember
   How different the older ones have grown.
                     Karle Wilson Baker

Wages

Glory of warrior, glory of orator, glory of song,
   Paid with a voice flying by to be lost on an endless sea!
Glory of virtue: to fight, to struggle, to right the wrong.
   Nay, but she aimed not at glory, no lover of glory she:
Give her the glory of going on, and still to be.

The wages of sin is death: if the wages of Virtue be dust,
   Would she have heart to endure for the life of the worm
       and the fly?
She desires no isles of the blest, no quiet seats of the just —
   To rest in a golden grove, or to bask in a summer sky:
Give her the wages of going on, and not to die.
                     Alfred Tennyson

The Music of a Friend

I had a garden where for sunless days
And many starless nights the dusky ways
Were weed-o'ergrown and silent. There I heard
No voice of love low calling to its own,
And found nor joy nor beauty; but alone
I lived, till through the silence, like a bird
Full-throated, came the music of a friend.

Louis V. Ledoux

Peace and Joy

Peace does not mean the end of all our striving,
    Joy does not mean the drying of our tears;
Peace is the power that comes to souls arriving
    Up to the light where God Himself appears.

Joy is the wine that God is ever pouring
    Into the hearts of those who strive with Him,
Light'ning their eyes to vision and adoring,
    Strength'ning their arms to warfare glad and grim.

G. A. Studdert-Kennedy

Mizpah

Go thou thy way, and I go mine;
    Apart, yet not afar;
Only a thin veil hangs between
    The pathways where we are.
And " God keep watch 'tween thee and me,"
    This is my prayer;
He looks thy way, He looketh mine,
    And keeps us near.

I know not where thy road may lie,
　Or which way mine may be;
If mine shall be through parching sands
　And thine beside the sea.
Yet " God keep watch 'tween thee and me."
　So never fear.
He holds thy hand, He claspeth mine,
　And keeps us near.

Should wealth and fame perchance be thine,
　And my lot lowly be;
Or you be sad and sorrowful
　And glory be for me,
Yet " God keep watch 'tween thee and me."
　Both be His care.
One arm round thee and one round me
　Will keep us near.

I sigh sometimes to see thy face,
　But since this may not be,
I'll leave thee to the care of Him
　Who cares for thee and me.
" I'll have you both beneath my wings " —
　This comforts, dear,
One wing o'er thee and one o'er me,
　So we are near.

And though our paths be separate
　And thy way is not mine,
Yet, coming to the mercy-seat,
　My soul will meet with thine.
And " God keep watch 'tween thee and me "
　I'll whisper here;
He blesseth thee, He blesseth me,
　And we are near.

Julia A. Baker

Live and Love

Live and love,
Doing both nobly, because lowly;
Live and work strongly, because patiently.
That it be well done, unrepented of,
And not to loss.

Elizabeth Barrett Browning

The Song of the Unsuccessful

We are the toilers whom God hath barred
   The gifts that are good to hold,
We meant full well and we tried full hard,
   And our failures were manifold.

And we are the clan of those whose kin
   Were a millstone dragging them down,
Yea, we had to sweat for our brother's sin,
   And lose the victor's crown.

The seeming-able, who all but scored,
   From their teeming tribe we come:
What was there wrong with us, O Lord,
   That our lives were dark and dumb?

The men, ten-talented, who still
   Strangely, missed the goal,
Of them we are: it seems Thy will
   To harrow some in soul.

We are the sinners, too, whose lust
   Conquered the higher claims,
We sat us prone in the common dust,
   And played at the devil's games.

We are the hard-luck folk, who strove
   Zealously, but in vain;
We lost and lost, while our comrades throve,
   And still we are lost again.

We are the doubles of those whose way
   Was festal with fruits and flowers,
Body and brain we were sound as they,
   But the prizes were not ours.

A mighty army our full ranks make,
   We shake the graves as we go;
The sudden stroke and the slow heart-break,
   They both have brought us low.

And while we are laying life's sword aside,
   Spent and dishonored and sad,
Our Epitaph this, when once we have died:
   " The weak lie here, and the bad."

We wonder if this can be really the close,
   Life's fever cooled by death's trance;
And we cry, though it seem to our dearest of foes,
   " God, give us another chance! "

Richard Burton

Grace for Grace

Thy gifts without Thy grace are lacking still;
Imperfect I do turn Thy gifts to ill;
Therefore would I with all Thy gifts entreat
These graces three to make Thy gifts complete:
     The grace to see, and wonder at the sight;
     The grace to take, and use Thy gift aright;
     The grace to share with him in poorer plight.

Mark Guy Pearse

The Proud

They are the proudest who have met defeat,
    They are the proudest who must walk alone,
Cherishing the vanished and the sweet,
    Remembering blossoms broken on a stone.

Go softly, you who have no loss to weep,
    Who sink at night to deep, untroubled rest,
And envy the defeated who must keep
    The ghost of beauty in an empty breast.

Frances M. Frost

Glory To Them

Glory to them, the toilers of the earth,
    Who wrought with knotted hands, in wood and stone,
Dreams their unlettered minds could not give birth
    And symmetries their souls had never known.
Glory to them, the artisans, who spread
    Cathedrals like brown lace before the sun,
Who could not build a rhyme, but reared instead
    The Doric grandeur of the Parthenon.

I never cross a marble portico,
    Or lift my eyes where stained glass windows steal
From virgin sunlight moods of deeper glow,
    Or walk dream-peopled streets, except to feel
A hush of reverence for that vast dead
Who gave us beauty for a crust of bread.

Anderson M. Scruggs

Days

How can I tell which days have yielded fruit?
The days I labored at a task not mine?
The days I yielded to a wild pursuit?
The days I cast my pearls before the swine?
The days I hoarded every golden hour?
The days I laughed? The days I bore in pain?
The days when all my honey had turned sour?
The days I gathered in another's gain?
The days I studied and the days I wrought?
The days I loafed and only trusted God?
The days when whispered dreamings came unsought,
And I drew wisdom as I turned the sod?
How shall I know which ones of all the days
Shall on the last day bring me blame or praise?

Eliot Kays Stone

The One Remains

The One remains, the many change and pass;
Heaven's light forever shines, Earth's shadows fly;
Life, like a dome of many-colored glass,
Stains the white radiance of Eternity. . . .

John Keats

From " Adonais "

Knowledge

They list for me the things I can not know:
Whence came the world? What Hand flung out the light
Of yonder stars? How could a God of right
Ordain for earth an ebbless tide of woe?

Their word is true; I would not scorn their doubt
Who press their questions of the how and why.
But this I know: that from the star-strewn sky
There comes to me a peace that puts to rout
All brooding thoughts of dread, abiding death;
And too I know, with every fragrant dawn,
That Life is Lord; that, with the Winter gone,
There cometh Spring, a great reviving Breath.
It is enough that life means this to me;
What death shall mean, some sunny Morn shall see.

Thomas Curtis Clark

Quiet Things

I thank the Lord for quiet things
  Whose names are half-asleep;
Names that were born of quietness
  And laid in peace to steep;
Such lovely, safe, serene old words
  As dovecotes — hills — and sheep.

For silent sober-colored things
  I bless the Lord of dreams —
This Heron standing motionless,
  More shade than bird he seems —
For this grey, ghostly fisherman
  Of lonely pools and streams.

I. W.

The Way of Sacrifice

He who hath watched, not shared, the strife,
  Knows how the day hath gone.
He only lives with the world's life
  Who hath renounced his own.

Matthew Arnold

Three Things

Three things I beg of Life to let me keep:
Rare strength, which through dark storm will safely last —
Until my soul's dire need of it is past —
Because its main pilasters reach so deep;
Initiative, with eager, circling sweep
Of wings. . . . High courage, of the keen enthusiast
Who even in his dreams can hear the blast
Of trumpet calls that urge him up the steep.
Real strength endures . . . initiative impels,
And flaming courage molds a dauntless heart.
Dynamic power these give — and self-release.
With them, the world's great inner citadels
Are mine . . . gay plumed adventure they impart
To Life — while traveling toward the Sunset Peace.

Gertrude B. Gunderson

Whence Cometh War?

Whence cometh war?
Bring the foul thing to bar.
Out of the hatreds of the ages long;
Out of the greed and blood-lust of the strong;
Out of the strutting swagger of the proud;
Out of the mad hysterias of the crowd;
Out of the lying honor of the State;
Out of the coward meanness of the great;
Out of the toll that profit takes from toil,
Of surplus spoil, piled up on surplus spoil,
Choking to idleness the workman's wheel,
Or raping all the earth with ruthless steel;
Out of a devil's smoke-screen of defense,
That turns to foolishness the things of sense,

Makes virtue's garden a vast swamp of vice,
And sells the Son of Man at Judas' price,
Nor has the grace to cast away the pelf
But makes of God an infidel himself.

Whence cometh war? we know the truth too well —
Out of the mouth of hell!

Robert Whitaker

The Man-Hunt

The four brothers are out to kill.
France, Russia, Britain, America —
The four republics are sworn brothers to kill the kaiser.

Yes, this is the great man-hunt;
And the sun has never seen till now
Such a line of toothed and tusked man-killers,
In the blue of the upper sky,
In the green of the undersea,
In the red of winter dawns.
Eating to kill,
Sleeping to kill,
Asked by their mothers to kill,
Wished by four-fifths of the world to kill —
To cut the kaiser's throat,
To hack the kaiser's head,
To hang the kaiser on a high-horizon gibbet.

And is it nothing else than this?
Three times ten million men asking the blood
Of a half-cracked one-armed child of the German kings?
Three times ten million men asking the blood
Of a child with his head wrong-shaped,

The blood of rotted kings in his veins?
If this were all, O God,
I would go to the far timbers
And look on the gray wolves
Tearing the throats of moose:
I would ask a wilder drunk of blood.

Look!   It is four brothers in joined hands together.
   The people of bleeding France,
   The people of bleeding Russia,
   The people of Britain, the people of America —
These are the four brothers, these are the four republics.

Carl Sandburg

From " The Four Brothers "

Wage-Slaves to War-Makers

We have no land for which to fight
Except where Russia cracks the night.
This is your land, within your power.
We break the rock; you pluck the flower.
We build the roads on which you speed.
And when we strike for what we need
We learn at once how well you own
The press, the courts and every stone
Of every structure that we rear.
Say, what invaders shall we fear?
Why should we care out on the job
If you or others drive and rob?

We have no land for which to fight
Though all the world is ours by right.
We workers grimed with soot and mud
Have shed enough and more of blood.

Each office-building overhead
Is built on corpses of our dead.
We have no quarrel across the foam
But here within our jail, your home!
We give our pledge we shall not kill,
For ours the braver, kinder will.
But if you force us till we do,
It will be you, it will be you!

Ralph Cheyney

Five Souls

FIRST SOUL

I was a peasant of the Polish plain;
I left my plough because the message ran:
Russia, in danger, needed every man
To save her from the Teuton; and was slain.
I gave my life for freedom — This I know;
For those who bade me fight had told me so.

SECOND SOUL

I was a Tyrolese, a mountaineer;
I gladly left my mountain home to fight
Against the brutal treacherous Muscovite;
And died in Poland on a Cossack spear.
I gave my life for freedom — This I know;
For those who bade me fight had told me so.

THIRD SOUL

I worked at Lyons, at my weavers' loom
When suddenly the Prussian despot hurled
His felon blow at France and at the world;
Then went I forth to Belgium and my doom.
I gave my life for freedom — This I know;
For those who bade me fight had told me so.

FOURTH SOUL

I owned a vineyard by the wooded Main,
Until the Fatherland, begirt by foes
Lusting her downfall, called me, and I rose,
Swift to the call, and died in fair Lorraine.
  I gave my life for freedom — This I know;
  For those who bade me fight had told me so.

FIFTH SOUL

I worked in a great shipyard by the Clyde.
There came a sudden word of wars declared,
Of Belgium peaceful, helpless, unprepared,
Asking our aid: I joined the ranks, and died.
  I gave my life for freedom — This I know;
  For those who bade me fight had told me so.

                                        W. N. Ewer

War

Did the rose-bush or the oak
Thrill at Trenton's battle-smoke?
Did the earthworm in the mould
Shout when Gettysburg unrolled
Its tawny thunders over him?
Did corn-grains buried in the dim
Terrible creative ground
Cease growing at the shaken sound
Of Grant's gaunt thousands marching by?
Well, pondering their conduct, I
Think their aloof indifference
Was most amazing commonsense!

                                E. Merrill Root

Deliver Us From . . .

Is there no greater good than health and ease?
Is there no deadlier enemy than death?
Is God a dream to deal with as we please
And life only the drawing of our breath?
Duty a fever-phantom that misleads
The sick confusion of a wandering brain?
Let the King's Highroad choke with tangled weeds
If they but barricade our paths from pain!
Give us this day our daily bread — that prayer
We all remember! What comes next? The cry
" Deliver us from sorrow and from loss,
" Who were not made to suffer and to bear! "
How strangely beat those words against the sky
Where stands unchanging a forgotten cross!

Amelia J. Burr

Let Us Have Peace

The earth is weary of our foolish wars.
Her hills and shores were shaped for lovely things,
Yet all our years are spent in bickerings
      Beneath the astonished stars.

April by April laden with beauty comes,
Autumn by Autumn turns our toil to gain,
But hand at sword-hilt, still we start and strain
      To catch the beat of drums.

Knowledge to knowledge adding, skill to skill,
We strive for others' good as for our own —
And then, like cavemen snarling with a bone,
      We turn and rend and kill. . . .

With life so fair, and all too short a lease
Upon our special star!   Nay, love and trust,
Not blood and thunder shall redeem our dust.
        Let us have peace!

                              Nancy Byrd Turner

An Old Battle-Field

The softest whisperings of the scented South,
And rust and roses in the cannon's mouth;

And where the thunders of the fight were born,
The wind's sweet tenor in the standing corn;

With song of larks, low-lingering in the loam,
And blue skies bending over love and home.

But still the thought: Somewhere — upon the hills,
Or where the vales ring with the whip-poor-wills,

Sad wistful eyes and broken hearts that beat
For the loved sound of unreturning feet,

And, when the oaks their leafy banners wave,
Dream of the battle and an unmarked grave!

                              Frank L. Stanton

If War Is Right

If war is right, then God is might
    And every prayer is vain:
Go raze your temples from the hills —
    Red death is in the plain.

If war is right, then God is might
And every prayer is vain:
Look not for Christ upon the hills —
He lies among the slain.

Alice Corbin

Love Comes

And who will lead the way?
The good and wise must lead.
He that loves most is the best and wisest, and he it is that
  leads already.
Violence will not yield to violence. Tell the great secret to
  the people.
Love comes! Clear the way, ye institutions, ye laws and
  customs of ages of hate!
The glance of his eyes would wither you.
The quiet thrill of his voice would palsy your deepest foun-
  dations.
Ye do well to tremble at his name.
For he is the Revolution — at last the true, long-deferred
  Revolution.
Love is the true Revolution, for Love alone strikes at the
  very root of ill.
Let the people love, and they will lead,
Let the people love and theirs is the power!

Ernest Crosby

Tear Down the Walls!

Tear down the walls! God made of one
  All men who live upon the earth;
He is our Father, we his sons,
  Whatever be our human birth.

Tear down the walls that separate
  And breed estrangement, pride and hate;
The poor, the oppressed, the rich, the great
  Are brothers in one human state.

Edgar Cooper Mason

The Final Armistice

Christ of the glowing heart and golden speech,
Drawn by the charm divine of Thy sweet soul,
The nations tend unto that far-off goal
Whereof the sages dream, the prophets preach.
We shall not always fail; we yet shall reach
Through toil and time that shining tableland
To which Thou beckonest with wounded hand.
Forevermore Thy goodness doth beseech
A warring world to lay its weapons down.
So shall we rest and songs of plenty drown
The wail of hunger, and our bitter tears,
Streaming unstanched through all the dreadful years,
And freely flowing still, shall yet be dried,
When Thou art King who once wast crucified.

Frank B. Cowgill

The Torch

" To you the torch we fling ";
  The challenge yet is heard,
Bequest of fullest sacrifice,
  A life-demanding word.
Yet this thought with it comes,
  A question tinged with doubt:
Shall we the torch to others pass
  Whose light we've let go out?

Arthur B. Dale

The War at Home

God of our fathers, with bowed heads we come
  In this glad hour when the unscathed rejoices,
Strike Thou each little boaster awed and dumb
  Before the flame of Pentecostal voices.
Our youth has stormed the hosts of hell and won;
  Yet we who pay the price of their oblation
Know that the greater war is just begun
  Which makes humanity the nations' Nation.

Willard Wattles

O Heart

O Heart, that beats with every human heart,
O Heart, that weeps with every human tear,
O Heart, that sings with every human song,
Fill our slow hearts with flood-tides of Thy love;
That they may beat with every human heart,
That they may weep with every human tear,
That they may sing with every human song,
And thus, through Thee, unite with all mankind.

Maurice Rowntree

The White Peace

It lies not on the sunlit hill
  Nor on the sunlit plain:
Nor ever on any running stream
  Nor on the unclouded main —

But sometimes, through the Soul of Man,
  Slow moving o'er his pain,
The moonlight of a perfect peace
  Floods heart and brain.

Fiona Macleod

From The Humanitarian

Seeing how the world suffered and bled,
He said:
" My life shall bring
Help to that suffering."
Seeing how the earth had need
Of sheer joy and beauty
Above all bitter creed
Of cruel penitence and duty,
And how mankind
Thirsted and cried for joy it could not find,
His heart made quick reply,
" Men shall know happiness before I die! "

He who brings beauty to the lives of men
Needeth no tribute of recording pen.
His deeds are graven in a place apart,
On the enduring tablet of the human heart.

Angela Morgan

The Feast

Those who are not mine
　I will dine and flatter,
Entertain and strive to please,
　For they do not matter.

But for friendship's feast
　Compliments demean us;
Rock for seat and sky for roof
　And the truth between us.

Nora B. Cunningham

The Greatest Battle That Ever Was Fought

The greatest battle that ever was fought —
Shall I tell you where and when?
On the maps of the world you will find it not:
It was fought by the Mothers of Men.

Not with cannon or battle shot,
With sword or nobler pen;
Not with eloquent word or thought
From the wonderful minds of men;

But deep in a walled up woman's heart;
A woman that would not yield;
But bravely and patiently bore her part;
Lo! there is that battlefield.

No marshalling troops, no bivouac song,
No banner to gleam and wave;
But Oh these battles they last so long —
From babyhood to the grave!

But faithful still as a bridge of stars
She fights in her walled up town;
Fights on, and on, in the endless wars;
Then silent, unseen goes down!

Ho! ye with banners and battle shot,
With soldiers to shout and praise,
I tell you the kingliest victories fought
Are fought in these silent ways.

Joaquin Miller

Thank God for Fools!

Thank God for fools! — for men who dare to dream
  Beyond the lean horizon of their days;
Men not too timid to pursue the gleam
  To unguessed lands of wonder and amaze.

Thank God for fools!   The trails that ring the world
  Are dark with blood and sweat where they have passed.
There are the flags of every crag unfurled;
  Theirs — ashes and oblivion at last.

Thank God for fools! — abused, of low estate.
  We rear our temples on the stones they laid;
Ours is the prize their tired souls might not wait;
  Theirs — the requiem of the unafraid.

Author Unknown

Via Lucis

And have the bright immensities
  Received our risen Lord
Where light-years frame the Pleiades
  And point Orion's sword?

Do flaming suns His footsteps trace
  Through corridors sublime,
The Lord of interstellar space
  And Conqueror of time?

The heaven that hides Him from our sight
  Knows neither near nor far:
An altar candle sheds its light
  As surely as a star;

And where His loving people meet
  To share the gift divine,
There stands He with unhurrying feet,
  There heavenly splendors shine.
                    Howard Chandler Robbins

My Little House

My house is little, but warm enough
  When the skies of Sorrow are snowing;
It holds me safe from the tempest rough,
  When the winds of Despair are blowing.

Its rafters come from the woods of Praise,
  Its walls from the quarry of Prayer,
And not one echo, on stormy days,
  Can trouble the stillness there.

The floor is bare, but the joists are strong
  With Faith from the heavenly hill;
My lamp is Love, and the whole year long
  It burns unquenchable still.

With sweet Content is my hearth well lit,
  And there, in the darkest weather,
Hope and I by the fire can sit,
  And sing, and keep house together.
                    May Byron

From The Rubaiyat of Omar Khayyam

A Book of Verses underneath the Bough,
A Jug of Wine, a Loaf of Bread — and Thou
  Beside me singing in the Wilderness —
Oh, Wilderness were Paradise enow!

Ah, my Belovèd, fill the Cup that clears
To-DAY of Past Regrets and Future Fears:
    To-morrow! — Why, To-morrow I may be
Myself with Yesterday's Sev'n Thousand Years.

Into this Universe, and *Why* not knowing
Nor *Whence,* like Water willy-nilly flowing;
    And out of it, as Wind along the Waste,
I know not *Whither,* willy-nilly blowing.

When You and I behind the Veil are past,
Oh, but the long, long while the World shall last,
    Which of our Coming and Departure heeds
As the Sea's self should heed a pebble-cast.

Ah, make the most of what we yet may spend,
Before we too into the Dust descend;
    Dust into Dust, and under Dust to lie
Sans Wine, sans Song, sans Singer, and — sans End!

Alike for those who for To-DAY prepare,
And those that after some To-MORROW stare,
    A Muezzín from the Tower of Darkness cries,
" Fools! your Reward is neither Here nor There."

Why, all the Saints and Sages who discuss'd
Of the Two Worlds so wisely — they are thrust
    Like foolish Prophets forth; their Words to Scorn
Are scatter'd, and their Mouths are stopt with Dust.

Oh threats of Hell and Hopes of Paradise!
One thing at least is certain — *This* Life flies;
    One thing is certain and the rest is Lies;
The Flower that once has blown forever dies.

Strange, is it not? that of the myriads who
Before us pass'd the door of Darkness through,
　　Not one returns to tell us of the Road,
Which to discover we must travel too.

The Revelations of Devout and Learn'd
Who rose before us, and as Prophets burn'd,
　　Are all but Stories, which, awoke from Sleep,
They told their comrades, and to Sleep return'd.

I sent my Soul through the Invisible,
Some letter of that After-life to spell:
　　And by and by my Soul return'd to me,
And answer'd " I Myself am Heav'n and Hell ":

Heav'n but the Vision of fulfill'd Desire,
And Hell the Shadow from a Soul on fire,
　　Cast on the Darkness into which Ourselves,
So late emerged from, shall so soon expire.

We are no other than a moving row
Of Magic Shadow-shapes that come and go
　　Round with the Sun-illumined Lantern held
In Midnight by the Master of the Show;

But helpless Pieces of the Game He plays
Upon this Chequer-board of Nights and Days;
　　Hither and thither moves, and checks, and slays,
And one by one back in the Closet lays.

The Ball no question makes of Ayes and Noes,
But Here or There as strikes the Player goes;
　　And He that toss'd you down into the Field,
He knows about it all — HE knows — HE knows!

The Moving Finger writes; and, having writ,
Moves on: nor all your Piety nor Wit
   Shall lure it back to cancel half a Line,
Nor all your Tears wash out a Word of it.

And that inverted Bowl they call the Sky,
Whereunder crawling coop'd we live and die,
   Lift not your hands to *It* for help — for It
As impotently moves as you or I.

With Earth's first Clay They did the Last Man knead,
And there of the Last Harvest sow'd the Seed:
   And the first Morning of Creation wrote
What the Last Dawn of Reckoning shall read.

Yesterday *This* Day's Madness did prepare;
To-morrow's Silence, Triumph, or Despair:
   Drink! for you know not whence you came, nor why:
Drink! for you know not why you go, nor where.

Yet Ah, that Spring should vanish with the Rose!
That Youth's sweet-scented manuscript should close!
   The Nightingale that in the branches sang,
Ah whence, and whither flown again, who knows!

Would but some wingèd Angel ere too late
Arrest the yet unfolded Roll of Fate,
   And make the stern Recorder otherwise
Enregister, or quite obliterate!

Ah Love! could you and I with Him conspire
To grasp this sorry Scheme of Things entire,
   Would not we shatter it to bits — and then
Re-mold it nearer to the Heart's Desire!
                Translation by Edward Fitzgerald

The Lost Key

The key of yesterday
I threw away;
And now, too late,
Before tomorrow's fast-closed gate
Helpless I stand — in vain to pray!
    In vain to sorrow!
Only the key of yesterday
    Unlocks tomorrow.

Priscilla Leonard

The Knapsack Trail

I like the wide and common road
    Where all may walk at will,
The worn and rutted country road
    That runs from hill to hill;
I like the road through pastures green
    Worn by home-coming feet
Of lowing kine and barefoot boy
    Where twilight shadows meet.

But I like best the Knapsack Trail
    Wherein my heart and I
May walk and talk in quietness
    With angels passing by.
The lonely Trail through forests dim
    That leads to God-knows-where,
That winds from tree to spotted tree
    'Till sudden — we are there!

Edwin Osgood Grover

God-Appointed Work

I am glad to think
I am not bound to make the world go right,
But only to discover and to do
With cheerful heart the work that God appoints.

Jean Ingelow

Thanks

Thank you very much indeed,
River, for your waving reed;
Hollyhocks, for budding knobs;
Foxgloves, for your velvet fobs;
Pansies, for your silky cheeks;
Chaffinches, for singing beaks;
Spring, for wood anemones
Near the mossy toes of trees;
Summer, for the fruited pear,
Yellowing crab, and cherry fare;
Autumn, for the bearded load,
Hazelnuts along the road;
Winter, for the fairy-tale,
Spitting log and bouncing hail.

But, blest Father, high above,
All these joys are from Thy love;
And Your children everywhere,
Born in palace, lane, or square,
Cry with voices all agreed,
" Thank You very much indeed."

Norman Gale

The Pure Heart

My good blade carves the casques of men,
  My tough lance thrusteth sure,
My strength is as the strength of ten,
  Because my heart is pure.

Alfred Tennyson

From " Sir Galahad "

Forever

Those we love truly never die
Though year by year the sad memorial wreath,
A ring and flowers, types of life and death,
Are laid upon their graves.

For death the pure life saves,
And life all pure is love; and love can reach
From heaven to earth, and nobler lessons teach
Than those by mortals read.

Well blest is he who has a dear one dead;
A friend he has whose face will never change —
A dear communion that will not grow strange;
The anchor of a love is death.

John Boyle O'Reilly

The Street

They pass me by like shadows, crowds on crowds,
Dim ghosts of men, that hover to and fro,
Hugging their bodies around them, like thin shrouds
Wherein their souls were buried long ago:

They trampled on their youth, and faith, and love,
They cast their hope to human-kind away,
With Heaven's clear messages they madly strove,
And conquered — and their spirits turned to clay:

Lo! how they wander round the world, their grave,
Whose ever-gaping maw by such is fed,
Gibbering at living men, and idly rave,
" We, only, truly live, but ye are dead."
Alas! poor fools, the anointed eye may trace
A dead soul's epitaph in every face!

James Russell Lowell

Orisons

He placed a prayer wheel where the wild winds dance,
    And some complained his piety was lazy;
    But then his thoughts on prayer were rather hazy.
Yet God attended to his suppliance.

He knelt on scarlet plush before his lord,
    And mumbled words of ancient litanies
    But felt uncomfortable on his knees;
And God, lost in the gloomy nave, was bored.

Silent, she raised her eyes that burned and glistened
    Like fresh lit tapers in a shadowy crypt;
    No raptured praise, no murmuring, tight lipped,
But God stopped stars in flight an hour, and listened.

E. McNeill Poteat, Jr.

The Silent Places

I have come back from the mountains,
    And the beauty of forest ways,
From the pine-trail winding at sunset
    To the crags in the purple haze.

I have come back from the prairies,
    And the free-born winds of the west,
Where my soul reached out to heaven,
    And found in the starlight rest.

I have come back to the city,
    With its clang and its screech and its din;
Its halls are filled with madness,
    And its eyes are blind with sin.

I think of the peaks white-crested,
    And the sage on the sweeping plain,
And the vastness, and the silence,
    And the whisper of God again.

I will go back to my mountains,
    Back to the prairies I've trod;
Some day I shall stand in that silence
    And speak once more with my God.
                                    Harold M. Hildreth

Heroism

So nigh is grandeur to our dust,
    So near is God to man,
When Duty whispers low, *Thou must,*
    The youth replies, *I can.*
                                    Ralph Waldo Emerson

Sonnet

I am in love with high far-seeing places
That look on plains half-sunlight and half-storm,
In love with hours when from the circling faces
Veils pass, and laughing fellowship glows warm.

You who look on me with grave eyes where rapture
And April love of living burn confessed —
The Gods are good! the world lies free to capture!
Life has no walls. Oh, take me to your breast!
Take me — be with me for a moment's span!
I am in love with all unveilèd faces.
I seek the wonder at the heart of man;
I would go up to the far-seeing places.
While youth is ours, turn toward me for a space
The marvel of your rapture-lighted face!

Arthur Davison Ficke

The Vision

You are the vision, you are the image of the dream,
The voice among the stars, the silence in the stream;
A breath of the infinite poise, where space and time are spun,
And the circling orbits wheel their planets round the sun.
Beyond the outer margin where nothing calls to God
Leaps the fiery symbol to bloom where your feet have trod;
Here is the earth resurgent with color and bloom of Spring,
Glorying the dream and the vision in the song you bring.

William Stanley Braithwaite

I, Too, Have Known

I, too, have known Gethsemane
  In lonely tryst,
I have broken bread with Peter . . .
  By Judas kissed.

And grim frustration I have known
  Of cherished plans,
Met Thomas-doubts instead of trust
  In many lands.

I, too, have known the rabble throng,
    Their taunts and jeers,
I, too, have borne the heavy cross
    'Mid scornful sneers.

But oh, I've reached the heights sublime
    At dawn of day,
Known glorious triumph when the stone
    Was rolled away.

Marguerite George

The Human Touch

High thoughts and noble in all lands
    Help me; my soul is fed by such.
But ah, the touch of lips and hands —
    The human touch!
Warm, vital, close, life's symbols dear —
These need I most, and now, and here.

Richard Burton

Today

Today, new-born from all my yesterdays,
Lies in my cupped hand, a fragile, prophetic thing
Just broken from its chrysalis with wings aflutter.
What far flight shall it make with buoyant pinions?
What fateful tomorrows shall it breed
Before it folds its worn wings
In the last twitchings of its dreamless sleep?
I hold today in my hand and watch its unfolding.
Then in faith I release it and wait the will of God.

Ozora S. Davis

Sonnet

A wretched thing it were, to have our heart
Like a thronged highway or a populous street,
Where every idle thought has leave to meet,
Pause, or pass on as in an open mart;
Or like some road-side pool, which no nice art
Has guarded that the cattle may not beat
And foul it with a multitude of feet,
Till of the heavens it can give back no part.
But keep thou thine a holy solitude,
For He who would walk there, would walk alone;
He who would drink there, must be first endued
With single right to call that stream his own;
Keep thou thine heart, close fastened, unrevealed,
A fencèd garden, and a fountain sealed.

Richard Chenevix Trench

God

As the bee through the garden ranges,
From world to world the godhead changes;
As the sheep go feeding in the waste,
From form to form He maketh haste;
This vault which glows immense with light
Is the inn where He lodges for a night.
What recks such Traveller if the bowers
Which bloom and fade like meadow flowers
A bunch of fragrant lilies be,
Or the stars of eternity?
Alike to Him the better, the worse —
The glowing angel, the outcast corse.
Thou metest Him by centuries,
And lo! He passes like the breeze;

Thou seek'st in glade and galaxy,
He hides in pure transparency;
Thou askest in fountains and in fires,
He is the essence that inquires.
He is the axis of the star;
He is the sparkle of the spar;
He is the heart of every creature;
He is the meaning of each feature;
And His mind is the sky,
Than all it holds more deep, more high.

Ralph Waldo Emerson

From " Woodnotes "

O That 'Twere Possible

O that 'twere possible
  After long grief and pain
To find the arms of my true love
  Round me once again. . . .

Ah Christ, that it were possible
  For one short hour to see
The souls we loved, that they might tell us
  What and where they be.

Alfred Tennyson

From " Maud "

From The Builders

There is an architecture grander far
Than all the fortresses of war,
More inextinguishably bright
Than learning's lonely towers of light.
Framing its walls of faith and hope and love
In deathless souls of men, it lifts above

The frailty of our earthly home
An everlasting dome;
The sanctuary of the human host,
The living temple of the Holy Ghost.

Henry van Dyke

A Mother Understands

Dear Lord, I hold my hand to take
    Thy body broken once for me,
Accept the sacrifice I make,
    My body, broken, Christ, for Thee.

His was my body, born of me,
    Born of my bitter travail pain,
And it lies broken on the field,
    Swept by the wind and the rain.

Surely a Mother understands Thy thorn-crowned head,
The mystery of Thy pierced hands — the Broken Bread.

G. A. Studdert-Kennedy

From The Eternal Goodness

I bow my forehead to the dust,
    I veil mine eyes for shame,
And urge, in trembling self-distrust,
    A prayer without a claim.

I see the wrong that round me lies,
    I feel the guilt within;
I hear, with groan and travail-cries,
    The world confess its sin.

Yet, in the maddening maze of things,
And tossed by storm and flood,
To one fixed trust my spirit clings;
I know that God is good!
John Greenleaf Whittier

The Rivals

Freedom and Faith went wooing for a soul;
And Freedom said: " I love the open ways,
Who weds with me shall come and go at will."

" Who weds with me," said Faith, " shall wear a yoke;
Linked in his consciousness to Cosmic Law,
Moving between high confidence and awe,
Knowing himself one with all human folk,
With all that is, yet shall this thought evoke
Temple and citadel from dust and straw;
He shall be builder, and shall find no flaw
In dreaming dreams, yet measuring his stroke."

And the soul answered Freedom, " Freer still
Than he who has no path, is he who stays
Upon the track that runs from goal to goal."
Robert Whitaker

Beyond This, the Infinite

The space
Which yields thee knowledge — do its bounds embrace
Well-willing and wise-working, each at height?
Enough: beyond this lies the infinite!
Robert Browning

From " Francis Turini "

Thou Must Be True

Thou must be true thyself,
  If thou the truth wouldst teach!
Thy soul must overflow, if thou
  Another's soul wouldst reach;
It needs the overflow of heart
  To give the lips full speech.

Think truly, and thy thoughts
  Shall the world's famine feed;
Speak truly, and each word of thine
  Shall be a fruitful seed;
Live truly, and thy life shall be
  A great and noble creed.

Horatio Bonar

Woman and Man

The woman's cause is man's: they rise or sink
Together, dwarf'd or godlike, bond or free:
If she be small, slight-natured, miserable,
How shall men grow? but work no more alone!
The man be more of woman, she of man;
He gain in sweetness and in moral height,
Nor lose the wrestling thews that throw the world;
She mental breadth, nor fail in childward care,
Nor lose the childlike in the larger mind;
Till at the last she set herself to man,
Like perfect music unto noble words;
And so these twain, upon the skirts of Time,
Sit side by side, full-summ'd in all their powers,
Dispensing harvests, sowing the To-be,

Self-reverent each and reverencing each,
Distinct in individualities,
But like each other, ev'n as those who love.
Then comes the statelier Eden back to men;
Then reign the world's great bridals, chaste and calm:
Then springs the crowning race of human-kind.
May these things be!

Alfred Tennyson

From " The Princess "

Coral Islands

Although with lives, submerged and brief,
    Insects will mount above,
Until they make a coral reef
    They are not dreaming of.

So from dark waters of our doubt,
    More than we ever meant,
On our dead selves, we may lift out
    A fertile continent.

Louis Ginsberg

The Prayer Perfect

Dear Lord! kind Lord!
    Gracious Lord! I pray
Thou wilt look on all I love
    Tenderly today!
Weed their hearts of weariness;
    Scatter every care
Down a wake of angel-wings
    Winnowing the air.

Bring unto the sorrowing
  All release from pain;
Let the lips of laughter
  Overflow again;
And with all the needy
  O divine, I pray,
This vast treasure of *content*
  That is mine today!

James Whitcomb Riley

True Love

True love is but a humble low-born thing,
And hath its food served up in earthen ware;
It is a thing to walk with, hand in hand,
Through the every-dayness of this work-day world.

James Russell Lowell

From " Love "

At the Lincoln Memorial

I think he would have hated this white shrine,
This pomp of marble gleaming in the sun,
He whom a cabin sheltered from the cold,
Who knew a cabin's rest when day was done.
And men who dwelt in cabins were his friends,
In cabins and in little prairie towns,
He was of them and they of him, and each
So trusted other that when peril came
And threatened all their fathers' toil had wrought
They gave to him the guiding of the State.
And though he walked with princes still he knew
He held his place securely in their hearts.
What can the marble's splendor mean to him?

Strange how we litter all the earth with shrines,
Dark shadowed chapels where no sunlight falls,
For those who knew the sun, the touch of rain,
The hope of sowing and the joy of reaping,
And all the round of simple things in life —
The saints and seers and prophets of the race,
Who called to farther goals and led the way.
We carve from dull dead stone their travesties,
We cover them with incense and great praise —
In any way to keep them from our hearts;
In any way to keep from following after
On that stern path that leads at last to peace!
I think he would have hated this white shrine!

William E. Brooks

When One Knows Thee

Thou hast made me known to friends whom I knew not.
Thou hast given me seats in homes not my own. Thou
hast brought the distant near and made a brother of the
stranger.

I am uneasy at heart when I have to leave my accustomed
shelter; I forget that there abides the old in the new, and
that there also Thou abidest.

Through birth and death, in this world or in others, wherever
Thou leadest me it is Thou, the same, the one companion
of my endless life who ever linkest my heart with bonds
of joy to the unfamiliar.

When one knows Thee, then alien there is none, then no door
is shut. Oh, grant me my prayer that I may never lose
the bliss of the touch of the one in the play of the many.

Rabindranath Tagore

From " Gitanjali," by Rabindranath Tagore. Used by permission
of the Macmillan Company, publishers.

Before

Before I brand a brother
  With envy or with shame,
I'll whisper to my heart, " He comes
  The road I came."

If any sue for pity —
  Though friend he be or foe —
I'll whisper to my soul, " He goes
  The road I go."

Mary Sinton Leitch

Our Dead

Let us not think of our departed dead
As caught and cumbered in these graves of earth;
But think of death as of another birth,
  As a new freedom for the wings outspread,
  A new adventure waiting on ahead,
As a new joy of more ethereal mirth,
As a new world with friends of nobler worth,
  Where all may taste a more immortal bread.

Edwin Markham

Sic Vita

Heart free, hand free,
  Blue above, brown under,
All the world to me
  Is a place of wonder.
Sun shine, moon shine,
  Stars, and winds a-blowing,
All into this heart of mine
  Flowing, flowing, flowing!

Mind free, step free,
   Days to follow after,
Joys of life sold to me
   For the price of laughter.
Girl's love, man's love
   Love of work and duty,
Just a will of God's to prove
   Beauty, beauty, beauty!
                William Stanley Braithwaite

In the Vastness, a God

Deathless, though godheads be dying,
   Surviving the creeds that expire,
Illogical, reason defying,
   Lives that passionate, primal desire;
Insistent, persistent, forever
   Man cries to the silence, " Never
Shall Death reign the lord of the soul,
   Shall the dust be the ultimate goal —
I will storm the black bastions of Night,
   I will tread where my vision has trod,
I will set in the darkness a light,
   In the vastness, a god."
                Author Unknown

Autumn Leaves

About the chilly, ragged lawns they lie
   In small decaying heaps. And pausing here,
I can but mark them sadly, crushed, forlorn,
   Mute emblems of the slowly dying year.

Can they be those I saw so lately swing
   Green-robed and merry on the maple trees,
And later, clad in flaming, golden gowns,
   Joy-riding on the sweet October breeze?
Ride high and free, such little time ago
And now they lie so low! they lie so low!

And yet why pity them?   Full well they lived
   Their God-appointed plan, died joyously,
And left a golden memory!   Pray who
   Could ask a fairer fate for them, or me?

Minnie Case Hopkins

Not As I Will

Blindfolded and alone I stand,
With unknown thresholds on each hand;
The darkness deepens as I grope,
Afraid to fear, afraid to hope;
Yet this one thing I learn to know
Each day more surely as I go,
That doors are opened, ways are made,
Burdens are lifted or are laid
By some great law, unseen and still,
Unfathomed purpose to fulfil,
     " Not as I will."

Blindfolded and alone I wait;
Loss seems too bitter, gain too late;
Too heavy burdens in the load
And too few helpers on the road,
And joy is weak and grief is strong,
And years and days so long, so long;
Yet this one thing I learn to know
Each day more surely as I go,

That I am glad the good and ill
By changeless law are ordered still,
  " Not as I will."

" Not as I will "; the sound grows sweet
Each time my lips the words repeat,
" Not as I will "; the darkness feels
More safe than light when this thought steals
Like whispered voice to calm and bless
All unrest and all loneliness.
" Not as I will," because the One
Who loves us first and best has gone
Before us on the road, and still
For us must all His love fulfil,
  " Not as we will."

          Helen Hunt Jackson

What Our Lord Wrote in the Dust

We have saved the soul of the man who killed,
  We have turned to shrive the thief;
We restored the pride of the man who lied
  And we gave him our belief;
But for her who fell we have fashioned hell
  With a faith all stern and just —
It was so of old; and no man hath told
  What our Lord wrote in the dust.

We have sighed betimes for our brothers' crimes
  And have bade them be of cheer,
For the flesh is weak, and the soul grown meek
  May yet read its title clear.
But we draw away from the one astray
  As the truly righteous must,
She is cursed indeed — and we did not **read**
  What our Lord wrote in the dust.

For the men who thieved, and who killed and lied —
    Who have slain the woman's soul —
We have worked and prayed, and have seen them made
    All clean and pure and whole,
But we drive her out with a righteous shout
    In our Pharisaic trust,
So the man goes free — but we do not see
    What our Lord wrote in the dust.
                      Author Unknown

When I Heard the Learn'd Astronomer

When I heard the learn'd astronomer,
When the proofs, the figures, were ranged in columns be-
    fore me,
When I was shown the charts and diagrams, to add, divide,
    and measure them,
When I, sitting, heard the astronomer where he lectured with
    much applause in the lecture-room,
How soon unaccountable I became tired and sick,
Till rising and gliding out I wandered off by myself,
In the mystical moist night-air, and, from time to time,
Looked up in perfect silence at the stars.
                    Walt Whitman

Rest Where You Are

When spurred by tasks unceasing or undone
    You would seek rest afar
And cannot, though the rest be fairly won,
    Rest where you are.
Not in event, restriction, or release,
    In journeys near or far,
But in the heart lies restlessness or peace,
    Rest where you are.
                Charles Poole Cleaves

Gilead

The heart is cold that has not chilled
  With fear that love could pass away.
The soul is dry that does not thirst
  For clear refreshment day by day.
And eyes are dim that in the light,
  Have never seen the need to pray.

Mary Brennan Clapp

And the Greatness of These —

I have seen an old faith falter,
Spent upon some ancient altar,
Where fires have turned to ashes gray
For one who lost the narrow way;
But in spite of wind and rain
I have seen old love remain.

I have seen a great house fall,
Taking with it wealth and all —
Bringing low the proud of name,
Blotting beauty, slaying fame;
But I have seen them rise again
By love that never can be slain.

Yes, I have seen old love survive,
Taking the dead to make alive,
Opening the eyes of one so blind
That even darkness held the mind; —
I have seen love writhe in pain
Rise up and smile and love again.

J. R. Perkins

Ye Who Taste That Love Is Sweet

Oh, ye who taste that love is sweet,
Set waymarks for all doubtful feet
That stumble on in search of it.
Lead life of love, that others who
Behold your life may kindle too
With love and cast their lot with you.

W. M. Rossetti

Kingdoms

Where is my kingdom?   I would be a king.
Yet kingdoms are not made by conquering,
Nor kings and queens by questioning and wondering.

Kingdoms are bought by yearning, and by burning
Of body and bruising of breast.
This is the test, and this only,
For kings and queens to be only:
Have you the substance?   Are you free?
How much can you suffer?   How far can you see?

Charles Oluf Olsen

From A Death In The Desert

For life, with all it yields of joy and woe,
And hope and fear — believe the aged friend —
Is just our chance o' the prize of learning love,
How love might be, hath been indeed, and is;
And that we hold thenceforth to the uttermost
Such prize despite the envy of the world,
And, having gained truth, keep truth: that is all.

Robert Browning

Apprehension

I do not fear
To walk the lonely road
Which leads far out into
The sullen night. Nor do
I fear the rebel, wind-tossed
Sea that stretches onward, far,
Beyond the might of human hands
Or human loves. It is the
Brooding, sharp-thorned discontent
I fear, the nagging days without
A sound of song; the sunlit
Noon of ease; the burden of
Delight and — flattery. It is
The hate-touched soul I dread,
The joyless heart; the unhappy
Faces in the streets; the
Smouldering fires of unforgiven
Slights. These do I fear. Not
Night, nor surging seas, nor
Rebel winds. But hearts unlovely,
And unloved.

James A. Fraser

The Bridge Builder

An old man going a lone highway
Came in the evening cold and gray
To a chasm vast and deep and wide.
The old man crossed in the twilight dim,
The sullen stream had no fears for him,
But he stopped when safe on the other side
And built a bridge to span the tide.

" Old man," said a fellow pilgrim near,
" You are wasting your strength with building here;
Your journey will end with the ending day,
You never again will pass this way,
You've crossed the chasm deep and wide,
Why build you this bridge at evening tide? "

The builder lifted his old gray head,
" Good friend, in the path I have come," he said,
" There followeth after me today
A youth whose feet must pass this way.
This chasm which has been as naught to me
To that fair-haired youth might a pitfall be,
He, too, must cross in the twilight dim,
Good friend, I am building the bridge for him."

Will Allen Dromgoole

Age Is Opportunity

For age is opportunity no less
Than youth itself, though in another dress;
And as the evening twilight fades away,
The sky is filled with stars, invisible by day.

Henry Wadsworth Longfellow

From " Morituri Salutamus "

Truth Never Dies

Truth never dies. The ages come and go.
    The mountains wear away, the stars retire.
Destruction lays earth's mighty cities low;
    And empires, states and dynasties expire;
But caught and handed onward by the wise,
    Truth never dies.

Though unreceived and scoffed at through the years;
   Though made the butt of ridicule and jest;
Though held aloft for mockery and jeers,
   Denied by those of transient power possessed,
Insulted by the insolence of lies,
    Truth never dies.

It answers not. It does not take offense,
   But with a mighty silence bides its time;
As some great cliff that braves the elements
   And lifts through all the storms its head sublime,
It ever stands, uplifted by the wise;
    And never dies.

As rests the Sphinx amid Egyptian sands;
   As looms on high the snowy peak and crest;
As firm and patient as Gibraltar stands,
   So truth, unwearied, waits the era blest
When men shall turn to it with great surprise.
    Truth never dies.

Author Unknown

Whence Cometh My Help

Here, on these hills, no sense of loneliness
Touches my soul. When the long days are fine,
And I can see, for miles on miles, the line
Of far-off mountains where their summits press
Against the arching azure of the skies,
Or when rain blots all objects out from me
But the dim outline of the nearest tree,
And little sounds so strangely magnifies,
I am content. Peace on my soul descends.
No unfilled longings rise in me to choke

My will. I smell the fragrance of damp sod
Whose pungency with forest odors blends,
And from my shoulders, like an outworn cloak,
My troubles fall, so close to me seems God.

P. L. Montgomery

Look Up

Look up and not down.
Look forward and not back.
Look out and not in.
Lend a hand.

Edward Everett Hale

The Hills of Rest

Beyond the last horizon's rim,
  Beyond adventure's farthest quest,
Somewhere they rise, serene and dim,
  The happy, happy, Hills of Rest.

Upon their sunlit slopes uplift
  The castles we have built in Spain —
While fair amid the summer drift
  Our faded gardens flower again.

Sweet hours we did not live go by
  To soothing note, on scented wing;
In golden-lettered volumes lie
  The songs we tried in vain to sing.

They all are there; the days of dream
  That build the inner lives of men;
The silent, sacred years we deem
  The might be and the might have been.

Some evening when the sky is gold
I'll follow day into the west;
Nor pause, nor heed, till I behold
The happy, happy Hills of Rest.
Albert Bigelow Paine

For Martha's Kitchen

Shine in, O sun, on this dull place!
Teach me your ways, lend me your grace,
Lest I grow trivial, being bound
To move within a daily round.

O wind, come in and blow away
The dust and cobwebs from this day,
Lest I grow peevish, skirmishing
With each small unimportant thing!
Fay Inchfawn

The Child's Appeal

I am the Child.
All the world waits for my coming.
All the earth watches with interest to see what I shall be-
  come.
Civilization hangs in the balance,
For what I am, the world of tomorrow will be.

I am the Child.
I have come into your world, about which I know nothing.
Why I came I know not;
How I came I know not.
I am curious; I am interested.

I am the Child.
You hold in your hand my destiny.
You determine, largely, whether I shall succeed or fail.
Give me, I pray you, those things that make for happiness.
Train me, I beg you, that I may be a blessing to the world.

Mamie Gene Cole

A Miracle

A Miracle?   Is it more strange than nature's common way?
From out the common clay
A shaft of green is lifted toward the sun,
And from its heart is spun
Fair fabrics ere its day is done —
Whorled leaves, an airy stem,
A crimson, fragile diadem,
And who can tell
Whence came the power thus to compel
A little seed beneath the sod
To fashion such a wondrous rod?
A miracle? — A thought of God
Which science scorns —
Is it more strange than flowers and thorns
That spring these mystic forms to birth
From out the trodden paths of Earth?

George Klingle

Persuasion

Man's life is like a Sparrow, mighty King!
That — while at banquet with your Chiefs you sit
Housed near a blazing fire — is seen to flit
Safe from the wintry tempest.   Fluttering,
Here did it enter: there, on hasty wing,

Flies out, and passes on from cold to cold;
But whence it came we know not, nor behold
Whither it goes. Even such, that transient Thing,
The human Soul; not utterly unknown
While in the Body lodged, her warm abode;
But from what world She came, what woe or weal
On her departure waits, no tongue hath shown;
This mystery if the Stranger can reveal,
His be a welcome cordially bestowed!

William Wordsworth

The Patient Scientists

How they have learned the secrets of the ether!
    Ships in the clouds, afloat as on a sea;
Voices through miles of distance singing, captured,
    Brought to our homes to gladden you and me.

How selflessly they seek profounder meanings
    Hid in the clump of moss — the iron ore!
How they have found in energy the secrets
    God smiled to know a billion years before.

Counting their lives not dear, so they discover
    Some bit of truth through eons all unguessed,
Something to make the lives to come the richer,
    Ere they themselves shall shut their eyes and rest.

Ah, still the Lord God walks with noiseless footfall,
    Visits the workshops of these patient men —
Smiles on the test tubes, the revealing lenses,
    And " It is good," he murmurs once again.

Bertha Gerneaux Woods

Villanelle

Jesus of Nazareth, King of the Jews,
Were you spitted in vain on the tree of scorn?
The Pharisees still clamor in the pews.

Your flesh remembers every Roman bruise;
Your brow enshrines the scar of Judah's thorn,
Jesus of Nazareth, King of the Jews.

Hearken, O Savior, I have brought you news,
Arise in holy anger Easter morn,
The Pharisees still clamor in the pews,

And strut beneath their iridescent hues
While Satan wears the robe which should adorn
Jesus of Nazareth, King of the Jews.

With solemn guile, the devil spins a ruse
For vain and rich. Let Gabriel sound his horn,
The Pharisees still clamor in the pews,

The Publican afar off wipes his shoes
Upon the doormat, puzzled and forlorn;
Jesus of Nazareth, King of the Jews,
The Pharisees still clamor in the pews.

A. M. Sullivan

Tree-Building

A tree is built of many things —
    Of soil stuff, slanting rain and hail;
Of silent snow, and skies of blue
    Or lowering, of frost and gale.

Into its sinewed might are forged
   No less the robin's song, the grays
Of morning mist, the sunset gold,
   And rhythms of the marching days.

And by the Master built into
   Cottage or templed shrine, it sings,
For him who hears, in soundless strains
   The music of intangible things.

Franklin Cable

Eternity In An Hour

To see the World in a grain of sand,
   And a Heaven in a wild flower,
Hold Infinity in the palm of your hand,
   And Eternity in an hour . . .

William Blake

From " Auguries of Innocence "

Too Late

Late, late, so late; and dark the night and chill!
Late, late, so late! but we can enter still.
   Too late, too late, ye cannot enter now.

No light had we: for that we do repent;
And learning this, the bridegroom will relent.
   Too late, too late! ye cannot enter now.

No light: so late! and dark and chill the night!
O let us in, that we may find the light!
   Too late, too late! ye cannot enter now.

Have we not heard the bridegroom is so sweet?
O let us in, though late, to kiss his feet!
No, no, too late! ye cannot enter now.

From " Idylls of the King "   *Alfred Tennyson*

Yesterday

I am yesterday.

I am gone from you for ever.

I am the last of a long procession of days, streaming behind
you, away from you, pouring into mist and obscurity,
and at last into the ocean of oblivion.

I depart from you, yet I am ever with you.

Once I was called Tomorrow, and was virgin pure; then I
became your bride and was named Today; now I am
Yesterday, and carry upon me the eternal stain of your
embrace.

I am one of the leaves of a growing book. There are many
pages before me.

Some day you will turn us all over, and read us, and know
what you are.

I am rich, for I have wisdom.

I bore you a child, and left him with you. His name is Ex-
perience.

I am Yesterday; yet I am the same as Today and Forever;
for I am you; and you cannot escape from yourself.

Frank Crane

Two Trails

There is room in the halls of pleasure
For a long and lordly train,
But one by one we must all file on
Through the narrow aisles of pain.

Ella Wheeler Wilcox

True Rest

Rest is not quitting
    The busy career;
Rest is the fitting
    Of self to one's sphere.

'Tis the brook's motion
    Clear without strife,
Fleeting to ocean,
    After this life.

'Tis loving and serving,
    The highest and best;
'Tis onward, unswerving,
    And this is true rest.

J. W. von Goethe

Greatly Begin!

Greatly begin! though thou have time
But for a line, be that sublime —
Not failure, but low aim is crime.

James Russell Lowell

From " For an Autograph "

Building a Temple

A builder builded a temple,
    He wrought it with grace and skill;
Pillars and groins and arches
    All fashioned to work his will.

Men said, as they saw its beauty,
" It shall never know decay.
Great is thy skill, O builder:
    Thy fame shall endure for aye."

A teacher builded a temple
    With loving and infinite care,
Planning each arch with patience,
    Laying each stone with prayer.
None praised her unceasing efforts,
    None knew of her wondrous plan;
For the temple the teacher builded
    Was unseen by the eyes of man.

Gone is the builder's temple,
    Crumbled into the dust;
Low lies each stately pillar,
    Food for consuming rust.
But the temple the teacher builded
    Will last while the ages roll,
For that beautiful unseen temple
    Is a child's immortal soul.

Author Unknown

Today

So here hath been dawning
    Another blue day:
Think, wilt thou let it
    Slip useless away?

Out of Eternity
    This new day was born;
Into Eternity,
    At night, will return.

Behold it aforetime
  No eye ever did;
So soon it forever
  From all eyes is hid.

Here hath been dawning
  Another blue day:
Think, wilt thou let it
  Slip useless away?

Thomas Carlyle

The Hero

We do not know — we can but deem,
  And he is loyalest and best
Who takes the light full on his breast
And follows it throughout the dream.

Ambrose Bierce

The Hungry

Whom does He love the most —
  The poor, the sick, the blind,
The rich, the maimed, the host
  Unknowingly unkind?

The ones who strive, and fail;
  The ones who have, and lose;
The ones who will not quail
  Nor martyrdom refuse?

The wind went sobbing low
  To His great Heart and cried;
" Dear God, they need you so, —
  Who die unsatisfied."

Caroline Giltinan

The Ways of The Gods

In ancient times the hungry gods,
   Imaged in wood or stone,
Enjoyed a living sacrifice
   Of human flesh or bone.

Today the gods, more subtle, lurk
   Where wheels and motors roar,
Though still the living sacrifice
   Is offered as before.

Stanton A. Coblentz

Ah, Love, Let Us Be True

Ah, love, let us be true
To one another! for the world, which seems
To lie before us like a land of dreams,
So various, so beautiful, so new,
Hath really neither joy, nor love, nor light,
Nor certitude, nor peace, nor help for pain;
And we are here as on a darkling plain
Swept with confused alarms of struggle and flight,
Where ignorant armies clash by night.

Matthew Arnold

From " Dover Beach "

A Question

Now who will rise
'To purge our eyes,
Kindle the Spirit's breath;
And think well borne
Neglect or scorn

To give our sons a Faith?
    For pieties
    And dubieties,
To give them back a Faith?
Who gives them for a flickering wraith,
A central, funded, founded Faith?

P. T. Forsyth

From The Watchers of the Sky

        This music leads us far
From all our creeds, except that faith in law.
Your quest for knowledge — how it rests on that!
How sure the soul is that if truth destroy
The temple, in three days the truth will build
A nobler temple; and that order reigns
In all things. Even your atheist builds his doubt
On that strange faith; destroys this heaven and God
In absolute faith that his own thought is true
To law, God's lanthorn to our stumbling feet;
And so, despite himself, he worships God,
For where true souls are, there are God and heaven.

Alfred Noyes

The City's Crown

What makes a city great?   Huge piles of stone
Heaped heavenward?   Vast multitudes who dwell
Within wide circling walls?   Palace and throne
And riches past the count of man to tell,
And wide domain?   Nay, these the empty husk!
True glory dwells where glorious deeds are done,
Where great men rise whose names athwart the dusk

Of misty centuries gleam like the sun!
In Athens, Sparta, Florence, 'twas the soul
That was the city's bright immortal part,
The splendor of the spirit was their goal,
Their jewel the unconquerable heart!
So may the city that I love be great
Till every stone shall be articulate.

William Dudley Foulke

Patchwork

Some rainbow shreds of Hope and Joy;
Faith's golden stripes without alloy;
Scraps of Ambition bright to see;
A few white threads of Charity;
Much of the purple cloth of Pain;
Love's fabric, like a golden vein
Between the strands of Hate and Strife; —
Such is the patchwork we call Life.

Clinton Scollard

Evaluation

Born in a borrowed cattle shed,
    And buried in another's tomb;
Small wonder our complacency
    Leaves such a One no room!

But castles were as poor as sheds
    Until that Prince was born on earth.
And tombs were mockeries of hope
    Before He changed death into birth!

Elinor Lennen

Death

Why be afraid of death, as though your life were breath?
Death but anoints your eyes with clay. O glad surprise!

Why should you be forlorn? Death only husks the corn.
Why should you fear to meet the thresher of the wheat?

Is sleep a thing to dread? Yet sleeping you are dead
Till you awake and rise, here, or beyond the skies.

Why should it be a wrench to leave your wooden bench?
Why not, with happy shout, run home when school is out?

The dear ones left behind? Oh, foolish one and blind!
A day and you will meet — a night and you will greet.

This is the death of death, to breathe away a breath
And know the end of strife, and taste the deathless life,

And joy without a fear, and smile without a tear;
And work, nor care to rest, and find the last the best.
Maltbie D. Babcock

The Chariot

Because I could not stop for Death,
He kindly stopped for me;
The carriage held but just ourselves,
And Immortality.

We slowly drove, he knew no haste,
And I had put away
My labor and my leisure, too,
For his civility.

We passed the school where children played,
At wrestling in a ring;
We passed the fields of gazing grain,
We passed the setting sun.

We paused before a house that seemed
A swelling of the ground;
The roof was scarcely visible,
The cornice but a mound.

Since then, 'tis centuries; but each
Feels shorter than the day
I first surmised the horses' heads
Were toward eternity.

Emily Dickinson

Tears

When I consider Life and its few years —
A wisp of fog betwixt us and the sun;
A call to battle, and the battle done
Ere the last echo dies within our ears;
A rose choked in the grass; an hour of fears;
The gusts that past a darkening shore do beat;
The burst of music down an unlistening street —
I wonder at the idleness of tears.

Ye old, old dead, and ye of yesternight,
Chieftains and bards and keepers of the sheep,
By every cup of sorrow that you had,
Loose me from tears, and make me see aright
How each hath back what once he stayed to weep:
Homer his sight, David his little lad!

Lizette Woodworth Reese

We Cannot Kindle

We cannot kindle when we will
The fire which in the heart resides,
The spirit bloweth and is still,
In mystery our soul abides:
But tasks, in hours of insight willed,
May be through hours of gloom fulfilled.

Matthew Arnold

A Prayer for Teachers

As to the seer in ancient time
The angel came with coal aflame,
And touched his lips that he might speak,
O God, in Thine almighty name, —
So to us in this later day
Send down a purifying ray.

Put forth Thy hand and touch our mouths —
Whose holy task it is to teach
And guide the minds of eager youth, —
That we may have inspiring speech.
Grant us vast patience, insight wise,
The open mind and heart and eyes.

Thus cleansed and quickened may we go
And teach those in the morn of life
The beauty and the might of peace
The sin and ugliness of strife.
Then shall the angel's voice proclaim,
" You, too, have spoken in God's name."

Marguerite Emilio

If You Have Made Gentler the Churlish World

If you have spoken something beautiful,
Or touched the dead canvas to life,
Or made the cold stone to speak —
You who know the secret heart of beauty;
If you have done one thing
That has made gentler the churlish world,
Though mankind pass you by,
And feed and clothe you grudgingly —
Though the world starve you,
And God answer not your nightly prayers,
And you grow old hungering still at heart,
And walk friendless in your way,
And lie down at last forgotten —
If all this befall you who have created beauty,
You shall still leave a bequest to the world
Greater than institutions and rules and commerce;
And by the immutable law of human heart
The God of the universe is your debtor,
If you have made gentler the churlish world.

Max Ehrmann

Honors

What though unmarked the happy workman toil,
And break unthanked of man the stubborn clod?
It is enough, for sacred is the soil,
Dear are the hills of God.

Far better in its place the lowliest bird
Should sing aright to Him the lowliest song,
Than that a seraph strayed should take the word
And sing His glory wrong.

Jean Ingelow

Your Place

Is your place a small place?
Tend it with care; —
He set you there.

Is your place a large place?
Guard it with care! —
He set you there.

Whate'er your place, it is
Not yours alone, but His
Who set you there.

John Oxenham

Food

When all is written and sung,
When all is sung and said,
It isn't the rich alone who feast,
Nor the poor who cry for bread.

Colin marries a maid,
And he gives her a ribbon of keys;
But if his fancy roams at large,
What can she do with these?

Marian knows the trick
Of making a pastry sweet;
But if she serve it with bitter words,
What has her lord to eat?

The babe like a rose-leaf lies,
Swaddled and nursed with care;
Mother, the man in him starves and dies,
If you teach not his lips a prayer!

Hunger will make no terms
  With pauper or plutocrat;
Want besieges the godless gate,
  And life is a proof of that.

When all is written and sung,
  When all is sung or said,
It is only God who is really food,
  It is only Love that is bread!
                    Ruby Weyburn Tobias

Bethlehem

I shall not tarry over scrolls
  That chart the planets of the night;
Nor follow paths of endless goals,
  The ordered orbs of Heaven's light;
Nor shall I halt with sense and mind
  At palace, porch or merchant's mart:
My caravan shall press to find
  A Savior for my hungry heart.
                    Harry Webb Farrington

Out in the Fields With God

The little cares that fretted me,
  I lost them yesterday,
Among the fields, above the sea,
  Among the winds at play;
Among the lowing of the herds,
  The rustling of the trees;
Among the singing of the birds,
  The humming of the bees.

The foolish fears of what may happen,
   I cast them all away
Among the clover-scented grass,
   Among the new-mown hay;
Among the rustling of the corn,
   Where drowsy poppies nod,
Where ill thoughts die and good are born —
   Out in the fields with God.

Elizabeth Barrett Browning

My House Has Windows

My house has windows that are wide and high;
   I never keep the curtains drawn
Lest I should miss some glory of the sky,
   Some splendor of the breaking dawn.

My soul has windows where God's sun streams in;
   They never, never shuttered are,
Lest their closed blinds hide in my soul some sin
   And keep some lovely thing afar.

Anna Blake Mazquida

Commonplaces

" A commonplace life," we say, and we sigh;
But why should we sigh as we say?
The commonplace sun in the commonplace sky,
Makes up the commonplace day;
The moon and the stars are commonplace things,
And the flower that blooms, and the bird that sings:
But dark were the world and sad our lot
If the flowers failed and the bird sang not;
And God, who studies each separate soul
Of our commonplace lives makes His beautiful whole.

Susan Coolidge

Friends and Enemies

He who has a thousand friends
    Has not a friend to spare,
While he who has one enemy
    Shall meet him everywhere.
                        Ralph Waldo Emerson

A Prayer

Lord, let not my religion be
A thing of selfish ecstasy;
But something warm with tender care
And fellowship which I can share.
Let me not walk the other side
Of trouble's highway long and wide;
Make me a Good Samaritan,
And neighbor unto every man.
                      Clarence M. Burkholder

Life

Then life is — to wake not sleep,
Rise and not rest, but press
From earth's level, where blindly creep
Things perfected, more or less,
To the heaven's bright, far steep,
Where, amid what strifes and storms
May wait the adventurous quest,
Power is love — transports, transforms.
                      Robert Browning
    From " Christmas Eve "

Light

We cannot look beyond
  The spectrum's mystic bar,
Beyond the violet light;
  Yea, other lights there are,
And waves that touch us not,
  Voyaging far.

Vast, ordered forces whirl
  Invisible, unfelt;
Their language less than sound,
  Their names unspelt.
Suns cannot brighten them
  Nor white heat melt.

Here in the clammy dark
  We dig, as dwarfs for coal;
Yet One Mind fashioned it
  And us, a luminous whole:
As lastly thou shalt see,
  Thou, O my soul!

Grace Wilkinson

Today and Tomorrow

Withhold all eulogies when I am dead,
  All noisy sorrow;
Give me the tender word today instead
  Of tears tomorrow.

Come not with flowers to strew above my breast,
  And sigh for me there.
The hawk or crow may haunt the piney crest;
  J shall not be there.

Speak not my name, when I have passed from earth,
  In tones of sadness;
At thought of me repress no note of mirth,
  No burst of gladness.

Delay not, thou whom I have wounded sore,
  Till thou outlive me
To grant the pardon that I here implore;
  But now forgive me.

Edward N. Pomeroy

We Shall Build On!

We shall build on!
On through the cynic's scorning.
On through the coward's warning.
On through the cheat's suborning.

We shall build on!
Firm on the Rock of Ages,
City of saints and sages.
Laugh while the tempest rages,
  We shall build on!

Christ, though my hands be bleeding,
Fierce though my flesh be pleading,
Still let me see Thee leading,
  Let me build on!

Till through death's cruel dealing,
Brain wrecked and reason reeling,
I hear Love's trumpets pealing,
  And I pass on.

G. A. Studdert-Kennedy

Trees

Oldest of friends, the trees!
Ere fire came, or iron,
Or the shimmering corn;
When the earth mist was dank,
Ere the promise of dawn,
From the slime, from the muck —
    The trees!

Nearest of friends, the trees!
They shield us from storm
And brighten our hearths;
They bring to our tables
The autumn's fine gold;
They carol our joys
And sing to our griefs.
They cradle our young
And coffin our dead —
    The trees!

Truest of friends, the trees!
Men wander far
At a word or a nod;
Life is a grief,
Love is a chance,
Faith stumbles oft,
Joy is soon past.
Oldest of friends,
Nearest of friends,
Truest of friends,
    The trees!

Thomas Curtis Clark

The Right Use of Prayer

Therefore, when thou wouldst pray, or dost thine alms,
Blow not a trump before thee: Hypocrites
Do thus, vaingloriously; the common streets
Boast of their largess, echoing their psalms.
On such the laud of men, like unctuous balms,
Falls with sweet savor. Impious Counterfeits!
Prating of heaven, for earth their bosom beats!
Grasping at weeds, they lose immortal palms!

God needs not iteration nor vain cries:
That man communion with his God might share
Below, Christ gave the ordinance of prayer:
Vague ambages, and witless ecstasies,
Avail not: ere a voice to prayer be given
The heart should rise on wings of love to heaven.

Aubrey de Vere

One Thing

The man who seeks one thing in life, and but one,
May hope to achieve it before life is done;
But he who seeks all things wherever he goes,
Only reaps from the hopes which around him he sows
A harvest of barren regrets.

Owen Meredith

From Auf Wiedersehen

It were a double grief, if the true-hearted,
Who loved us here, should on the farther shore
Remember us no more.

Believing, in the midst of our afflictions,
That death is a beginning, not an end,
  We call to them, and send
Farewells, that better might be called predictions
Being foreshadowings of the future, thrown
  Into the vast unknown.

Faith overleaps the confines of our reason,
And if by faith, as in old times was said,
  Women received their dead
Raised up to life, then only for a season
Our partings are, nor shall we wait in vain
  Until we meet again!
                    Henry Wadsworth Longfellow

" A Man Must Live "

" A man must live! " We justify
Low shift and trick, to treason high;
A little vote for a little gold,
Or a whole Senate bought and sold,
With this self-evident reply —
  " A man must live! "

But is it so? Pray tell me why
Life at such cost you have to buy.
In what religion were you told
A man must live?
There are times when a man must die!
There are times when a man will die!
Imagine for a battle-cry
From soldiers with a sword to hold,
From soldiers with a flag unfurled,
This coward's whine, this liar's lie,
  " A man must live! "

The Saviour did not " live! "
He died!
But in his death was life —
Life for himself and all mankind!
He found his life by losing it!
And we, being crucified
Afresh with him, may find
Life in the cup of death,
And, drinking it,
    Win life forever more.

Author Unknown

A Leafless Tree

I like to see
The patience of a leafless tree
Waiting in quiet dignity,
Till spring shall set its greenness free.

I sometimes think
That living just beneath the sky
Has made it understand and drink
Deeper wisdom than you and I —

It does not prate
Of limitation in its sere
Bare boughs; it does not estimate
The time for fresh leaves to appear;

It seems to know,
Within its great deep-rooted heart,
That never-ending life shall flow
And new springs start.

Ann Louise Thompson

The Arrow and the Song

I shot an arrow into the air,
It fell to earth, I knew not where:
For so swiftly it flew, the sight,
Could not follow it in its flight.

I breathed a song into the air,
It fell to earth, I knew not where;
For who has sight, so keen and strong,
That it can follow the flight of song?

Long, long afterward, in an oak,
I found the arrow still unbroke;
And the song, from beginning to end,
I found again in the heart of a friend.

Henry Wadsworth Longfellow

Mutability

From low to high doth dissolution climb,
And sink from high to low, along a scale
Of awful notes, whose concord shall not fail;
A musical but melancholy chime,
Which they can hear who meddle not with crime,
Nor avarice, nor over-anxious care.
Truth fails not; but her outward forms that bear
The longest date, do melt like frosty rime,
That in the morning whitened hill and plain,
And is no more; drop like the tower sublime
Of yesterday, which royally did wear
His crown of weeds, but could not even sustain
Some casual shout that broke the silent air,
Or the unimaginable touch of Time.

William Wordsworth

Children of Tomorrow

Come, Children of Tomorrow, come!
New glory dawns upon the world.
The ancient banners must be furled.
The earth becomes our common home —
The earth becomes our common home.
From plain and field and town there sound
The stirring rumors of the day.
Old wrongs and burdens must make way
For men to tread the common ground.

Look up!   The children win to their immortal place.
March on, march on — within the ranks of all the human
      race.
Come, love of people, for the part
Invest our willing arms with might!
Mother of Liberty, shed light
As on the land, so in the heart —
As on the land, so in the heart.
Divided we have long withstood
The love that is our common speech.
The comrade cry of each to each
Is calling us to humanhood.

Zona Gale

Fulfillment

If we should find unfinished, incomplete,
      A single glistening pearly drop of dew,
A single feather in the daring wings
      That soar exultant in the distant blue;
A flake of snow upon the mountain's peak,
      A fern within some hidden cool abyss —
Then might we doubt that God's most perfect plan
      In our own lives, perchance, might go amiss.

Charlotte Newton

Remember

Remember me when I am gone away,
    Gone far away into the silent land;
    When you can no more hold me by the hand,
Nor I half turn to go, yet turning stay.
Remember me when no more day by day
    You tell me of our future that you plann'd:
    Only remember me; you understand
It will be late to counsel then or pray.
Yet if you should forget me for a while
    And afterwards remember, do not grieve:
    For if the darkness and corruption leave
A vestige of the thoughts that once I had,
Better by far you should forget and smile
    Than that you should remember and be sad.

Christina G. Rossetti

Thanks for Laughter

Father:
We thank Thee for laughter,
For the first sweet smile of a babe,
Which is Thy first glance on the world through his eyes;
For the glad play of a child,
Which to see Thou thyself bendest close from Heaven;
For the gay mirth of home life
Unto which Thou thyself delightest to harken;
For the swift flash of gallant humor,
That suddenly lightens the gloom of disaster;
For the homeric laughter of heroes going gallantly to death;
For the last dear smile struggling through weakness and
    pain,
Yet radiant with love and faith,

Which may carry a man safe across the gulf of years and the
    silence of death.
We thank Thee, Father, for the gift of laughter,
Which runs through the dark stuff of human tragedy
Like a thread of gold through a sombre curtain —
That curtain of life which sunders us from Life.

From " Prayers for Use in an Indian College "

The Teachers

I went to school with the tutor, Law,
    A master severe and grim,
Who taught by the pain of the biting cane —
    Yet learned I little of him.

I go to school with the teacher, Love,
    And my lightened eyes can see
What the pain and the tears of the driven years
    Could never reveal to me.

C. V. Pilcher

The All-Seeing Gods

      No one sees me,
Save the all-seeing Gods, who, knowing good
And knowing evil, have created me
Such as I am, and filled me with desire
Of knowing good and evil like themselves.
I hesitate no longer. Weal or woe,
Or life or death, the moment shall decide.

Henry Wadsworth Longfellow

From " The Masque of Pandora "

Reflections

Stars lie broken on a lake
Whenever passing breezes make
    The wavelets leap;
But when the lake is still, the sky
Gives moon and stars that they may lie
    On that calm deep.

If, like the lake that has the boon
Of cradling the little moon
    Above the hill,
I want the Infinite to be
Reflected undisturbed in me,
    I must be still.

                              Edna Becker

The Shepherd Boy Sings

He that is down needs fear no fall,
    He that is low, no pride;
He that is humble ever shall
    Have God to be his guide.

I am content with what I have,
    Little be it or much;
And, Lord, contentment still I crave,
    Because Thou savest such.

Fullness to such a burden is
    That go on pilgrimage:
Here little, and hereafter bliss
    Is best from age to age.

                              John Bunyan

The Shadow on the Loom

Across my loom of years there fell a shadow, gaunt and gray,
   Through my quiet dreams an echo of marching feet;
O'er the hum of the flying threads, a voice of gloom:
  " The King's work waits, for His plans make room,
Come out and help us prepare the way! "

Impatient I cried: " Through Life's brief day
   I have toiled at this web so near complete;
Its warp holds the gold of my weary years,
   Shall I spoil it with haste or dim it with tears?
I must finish this robe for a festal day."

So I turned again to the brave array
   Of shining threads in my safe retreat,
And wrought 'till the shimmering gown was done;
   It gleamed like a jewel beneath the sun.
" Now for the King and His great highway! "

But my soul was pierced with a great dismay,
   As proudly I turned the King to greet,
For thorns lay thick in the path He had trod,
   All red from His patient feet was the sod,
And lo, a world went clad in sober gray!

Nellie Burget Miller

In After Days

In after days when grasses high
O'ertop the stone where I shall lie,
   Though ill or well the world adjust
   My slender claim to honored dust,
I shall not question or reply.

I shall not see the morning sky;
I shall not hear the night-wind sigh;
   I shall be mute, as all men must
     In after days!

But yet, now living, fain were I
That some one then should testify,
   Saying — " He held his pen in trust
   To art, not serving shame or lust."
Will none? — Then let my memory die
   In after days.
                Austin Dobson

Dirt and Deity

If gutter-puddles after rain
   Can always look on high;
And even with a floor of mud,
   Can have a roof of sky,

I never wonder any more
   How man (a pool of blue)
Can at the bottom gather mire
   And mirror Heaven, too.
                Louis Ginsberg

Prayer

Lord, forgive —
That I have dwelt too long on Golgotha,
My wracked eyes fixed
On Thy poor, tortured human form upon the cross,
And have not seen
The lilies in Thy dawn-sweet garden bend
To anoint Thy risen feet; nor known the ways
Thy radiant spirit walks abroad with men.
                Pauline Schroy

Faith

If a wren can cling
To a spray a-swing
In the mad May wind, and sing and sing,
As if she'd burst for joy;
Why cannot I
Contented lie
In His quiet arms beneath the sky,
Unmoved by earth's annoy?

F. B. Meyer

From Vastness

Spring and Summer and Autumn and Winter, and all these
    old revolutions of earth;
All new-old revolutions of empire — change of the tide what
    is it all worth?

What the philosophies, all the sciences, poesy, varying voices
    of prayer?
All that is noblest, all that is basest, all that is filthy with
    all that is fair?

What is it all, if we all of us end but in being our own corpse-
    coffins at last,
Swallowed in Vastness, lost in Silence, drown'd in the deeps
    of a meaningless Past?

What but a murmur of gnats in the gloom, or a moment's
    anger of bees in their hive? —
Peace, let it be! for I love him, and love him forever — the
    dead are not dead but alive.

Alfred Tennyson

Various the Roads of Life

Various the roads of life; in one
   All terminate, one lonely way.
We go; and " Is he gone? "
   Is all our best friends say.
               Walter Savage Landor

Deserts

A desert does not have to be
   A sandy waste where springs are dry;
A life can shrink to barrenness
   If love goes by.

A desert does not have to be
   A place where buzzards wheel at dawn;
A heart can hold as dreadful things
   When faith is gone.
               Anne Hamilton

Somewhere

Somewhere there lies the dust
Of that rough wooden cross which Jesus bore
Up Calvary. And which, in turn, bore Him;
Was crimsoned with His blood. Dark stains were left
Which sunshine could not bleach,
Nor pelting rains erase.
'Twas cast aside in superstitious fear
Because tradition said He lived again;
And so it lay, until the Mother Earth
Received its crumbling dust back to her breast.

*   *   *

But on that spot do lilies bloom
With richer coloring, sweeter fragrance?

Somewhere there lie the nails
Which Roman soldiers drove through His
Extended palms. How cruel was the pain!
The blows of hammers rested at His word —
" Father, forgive them, for they know
Not what they do." Stout spikes were they,
Forged at the smithy in Jerusalem.
Somewhere they lie, corroding black
With rust of ages.

*   *   *

Or have they turned to gold
Through alchemy of Deathless Love?

J. C. Cochrane

Tears

Thank God, bless God, all ye who suffer not
More grief than ye can weep for. That is well —
That is light grieving! lighter, none befell
Since Adam forfeited the primal lot.
Tears! what are tears? The babe weeps in its cot,
The mother singing; at her marriage-bell
The bride weeps, and before the oracle
Of high-faned hills the poet has forgot
Such moisture on his cheeks. Thank God for grace,
Ye who weep only! If, as some have done,
Ye grope tear-blinded in a desert place
And touch but tombs, — look up! those tears will run
Soon in long rivers down the lifted face,
And leave the vision clear for stars and sun.

Elizabeth Barrett Browning

From Hour of Death

Leaves have their time to fall,
 And flowers to wither at the north wind's breath,
And stars to set — but all,
 Thou hast all seasons for thine own, O Death.
 Felicia Dorothea Hemans

If This Is All

If this is all — one little ball
Of transitory Earth,
And we must fall, at Death's last call,
Like apples — no more worth;
Why do the stars make pathways for my eyes,
The moon with melody fill all the skies,
Creation's anthem peal for each sunrise —
If our Earth ball is all?

If Life is meat and only meat,
For one swift day — then Night,
And I must eat my morsel sweet,
E'er fades its fitful light;
What means this surge within like mystic leaven,
Why do my hungers reach from hell to heaven,
My soul range universes seven times seven,
If Life is only meat?
 Alban Asbury

In the Garden of the Lord

The word of God came unto me,
Sitting alone among the multitudes;
And my blind eyes were touched with light.
And there was laid upon my lips a flame of fire.

I laugh and shout for life is good,
Though my feet are set in silent ways.
In merry mood I leave the crowd
To walk in my garden. Ever as I walk
I gather fruits and flowers in my hands.
And with joyful heart I bless the sun
That kindles all the place with radiant life.

I run with playful winds that blow the scent
Of rose and jessamine in eddying whirls.
At last I come where tall lilies grow,
Lifting their faces like white saints to God.
While the lilies pray, I kneel upon the ground;
I have strayed into the holy temple of the Lord.

Helen Keller

Duty Our Ladder

Be thy duty high as angels flight,
    Fulfill it, and a higher will arise
Even from its ashes. Duty is infinite,
    Receding as the skies.
Were it not wisdom, then, to close our eyes
    On duties crowding only to appall?
No: Duty is our ladder to the skies;
    And, climbing not, we fall.

Robert Leighton

Golgotha's Cross

What is the cross on Golgotha to me —
But the brave young Jesus murdered there?
Roman justice debased?
Israel's Messiah lost?

The tender lips agonized?
The active mind bewildered?
The feet, that walked fair Galilee,
Pierced by nails?

I have tried to speak
The words those lips revealed.
I have tried to think as He thought.
I have taught my feet to walk
Humbly as He walked.

And God prepared me a cross.

The arms reach out to gather in
The cripples, the blind, the weak.
The arms reach out to feed them,
To give them to drink.
In these hands the nails are driven.

But the cross points upward.
The arms fold me.
The cross lifts me.
Golgotha's cross is the road to heaven.
                    Raymond Kresensky

Far Distances

O wide and shining, miles on miles,
Yon sea's fair face upon me smiles;
Yet for some further ocean's isles
    My fevered soul is yearning.

O daringly yon mountain-spire
Conquers its giant leap; yet higher
My spirit's infinite desire
    Speeds eager and unresting.

O amply-arched yon sky's dome swings
Above me; yet my passion springs
Wild at its walls with fluttering wings,
    For vaster circles questing.

I know not, heart. Yet must not He
Who made all worlds too strait for thee
Set thee at last where thou shalt be
    With His own greatness blended?
                                Henry W. Clark

The Anvil of God's Mercy

I wonder that the metal stands the test;
    The hammering of dogma, and of creed,
The lifting ferment of a world's unrest,
    The battering of ignorance, and greed!
The dead-white flame of atheistic scorn,
    The ringing blows of ridicule, and doubt;
The infidel's rough handling, and the worn
    Deceits and prayers of the half-devout!
Yet still the anvil of God's mercy stands
    Singing its answer to each heavy blow,
The stronger for humanity's demands —
    And man bends on it, steadily and slow!
                                Anna Hamilton Wood

Remembering Calvary

Help me to suffer when I most would spare
    My human frame with pain and weakness spent,
Help me receive with open arms nor dare
    To flinch at pain but count myself content,
And all that has been and that is to be
    Help me to bear,
            Remembering Calvary.

Help me to leash the hounds of my desire,
  Taming them to a more submissive will,
Help me to tune again a broken lyre
  And find that there is music in it still,
Help me to do these things all cheerfully,
    Nor count the cost,
            Remembering Calvary.
                        Ethel Fanning Young

The Will to Serve

Be thou guardian of the weak,
  Of the unfriended, thou the friend;
No guerdon for thy valor seek,
  No end beyond the avowed end.
Wouldst thou thy godlike power preserve,
Be godlike in the will to serve.
                    Jeannette B. Gilder
From " The Parting of the Ways "

When I Go Home

No tears, no sorrowing farewells;
  No drooping eye, no anguished breast;
I am but quitting scenes where dwells
  The sadness that my soul oppressed:
    Then let my care-worn spirit rest
      When I go home!

No clasp of hands in last good-bye
  Disturb my weary, waiting soul;
But, rather love-light fill the eye,
  And waiting Hope point to the goal:
    Let peace, unbroken, o'er me roll
      When I go home!
                        Milton Lee

Song

Life, in one semester
　　You wear so many masks,
If you're sage or jester
　　My spirit often asks.

Oft you seem so tragic,
　　I fancy you are Woe;
Then, as if by magic,
　　In Laughter's garb you go.

Now I see you youthful,
　　Now limping like a crone.
Life, for once be truthful —
　　Which face is all your own?

Charles G. Blanden

Man Is His Own Star

Man is his own star, and the soul that can
Render an honest and a perfect man,
Commands all light, all influence, all fate;
Nothing to him falls early or too late;
Our acts our angels are, or good or ill,
Our fatal shadows that walk by us still.

John Fletcher
From " Upon an Honest Man's Fortune "

Nature's Sorrow Cure

The only thing to cheer me,
　　Beneath a heavy load,
The beauty that is near me,
　　The roses in my road.

A bit of new grass creeping,
  A butterfly of gold,
The first spring bloodroot peeping
  Through dark and pulpy mold.

When even God is hidden,
  Because I will not see,
A swallow's call unbidden
  Will bring Him back to me.

Catherine Cate Coblentz

God Behind All

God is behind all.
We find great things are made of little things,
And little things go lessening, till at last
Comes God behind them.

Robert Browning

From " Mr. Sludge, the Medium "

Changeless

God will not change! The restless years may bring
Sunlight and shade — the glories of the Spring,
The silent gloom of sunless Winter hours;
Joy mixed with grief — sharp thorns with fragrant flowers.
Earth's lights may shine a while and then grow dim.
But God is true! There is no change in Him.

Rest in the Lord today and all thy days
Let His unerring hand direct thy ways
Through the uncertainty, and hope and fear,
That meet thee on the threshold of the year;
And find while all life's changing scenes pass by
Thy refuge in the love that can not die.

Edith Hickman Divall

This Is Thy Hour, O Soul

This is thy hour, O Soul, thy free flight into the wordless,
Away from books, away from art, the day erased, the lesson
    done,
Thee fully forth emerging, silent, gazing, pondering the
    themes thou lovest best.
Night, sleep, and the stars.

                                 Walt Whitman

From " Leaves of Grass "

My Neighbor's Roses

The roses red upon my neighbor's vine
Are owned by him, but they are also mine,
His was the cost, and his the labor, too,
But mine as well as his the joy, their loveliness to view.

They bloom for me, and are for me as fair
As for the man who gives them all his care.
Thus I am rich, because a good man grew
A rose-clad vine for all his neighbors' view.

I know from this that others plant for me,
And what they own, my joy may also be;
So why be selfish, when so much that's fine
Is grown for you, upon your neighbor's vine?

                                Abraham Gruber

Christmas Today

How can they honor Him — the humble lad
    Whose feet struck paths of beauty through the earth —
With all the drunken revelry, the mad
    Barter of goods that marks His day of birth?

How can they honor Him with flame and din,
  Whose soul was peaceful as a moon-swept sea,
Whose thoughts were somber with the world's great sin
  Even while He trod the hill to Calvary?

I think if Jesus should return and see
  This hollow blasphemy, this day of horror,
The heart that languished in Gethsemane
  Would know again as great and deep a sorrow,
And He who charmed the troubled waves to sleep
With deathless words — would kneel again and weep.
                              Anderson M. Scruggs

Sound, Sound the Clarion

Sound, sound the clarion, fill the fife!
  To all the sensual world proclaim,
One crowded hour of glorious strife
  Is worth an age without a name.
                              Sir Walter Scott

Death at Daybreak

I shall go out when the light comes in —
  There lie my cast-off form and face;
I shall pass Dawn on her way to earth,
  As I seek for a path through space.

I shall go out when the light comes in;
  Would I might take one ray with me!
It is blackest night between the worlds,
  And how is a soul to see?
                              Anne Reeve Aldrich

My Prayer

I kneel to pray,
But know not what to say:
   I cannot tell
What may be ill or well:
   But as I look
Into Thy Face or Book
   I see a love
From which I cannot move:
   And learn to rest
In this — Thy will is best:

Therefore I pray
Only have Thine own way
   In everything
My all wise God and King.
   Grant me the grace
In all to give Thee place:
   This liberty
Alone I ask of Thee:
   This only gift,
Have Thy way perfectly.

Mark Guy Pearse

Growing Old

Let me grow lovely, growing old,
So many fine things to do;
Laces, and ivory, and gold,
And silks, need not be new;
And there is healing in old trees;
Old streets, a glamour hold;
Why may not I, as well as these,
Grow lovely, growing old?

Karle Wilson Baker

Human Life

Like smoke I vanish though I burn like flame,
I flicker in the gusts of wrong and right —
A shining frailty in the guise of might;
Before a nothing and behind a name.

W. H. Malloch

Two at a Fireside

I built a chimney for a comrade old,
  I did the service not for hope of hire —
And then I travelled on in winter's cold
  Yet all the way I glowed before the fire.

Edwin Markham

She Is Wise, Our Ancient Mother

She is wise, our Ancient Mother,
  Her ways are not our ways;
We cannot circumscribe her
  Though we watch her all our days.

On each of her questioning children
  She presses a different will;
To one she says, " Keep busy,"
  To one she says, " Keep still."

She said to me, " Wait and listen,
  I have plenty to drive and do;
Then once in a while when you are sure
  Speak out a word or two."

Karle Wilson Baker

Life

'Tis not for man to trifle!   Life is brief.
  And sin is here.
Our age is but the falling of a leaf,
  A dropping tear.
We have no time to sport away the hours;
All must be earnest in a world like ours.

Not many lives, but only one have we —
  One, only one;
How sacred should that one life ever be —
  That narrow span!
Day after day filled up with blessed toil,
Hour after hour still bringing in new spoil.
                                   Horatius Bonar

The Revelation

God's revelation of Himself may be
Ofttimes within the pages of a book,
But all times and forever in a look
Of hill-tops banked with blue infinity;
Forever in the branches of a tree
That leans in whiteness o'er a summer nook;
In iris plumes where waters turn and crook
And make slim paths of yellow down the lea!

God's skies are wide above an earthly throne;
His stars are candles on the altar there;
His clouds, an incense drifting into space!
His love with every dewy rose is shown;
The violets a kindly message bear;
And in the dawn we see Him face to face!
                            Leslie Clare Manchester

Love and Life

Ah me! Why may not love and life be one?
Why walk we thus alone, when, by our side,
Love, like a visible God, might be our guide!
How would the marts grow noble! and the street,
Worn like a dungeon floor by weary feet,
Seem then a golden courtway of the sun.

Henry Timrod

Today

And if tomorrow shall be sad
Or never come at all, I've had
    At least today!
This little strip of light
'Twixt night and night
Let me keep bright
    Today!

And let no shadow of tomorrow,
Nor sorrow from the dead yesterday,
Gainsay my happiness today!
And if tomorrow shall be sad
Or never come at all, I've had
    At least today!

Author Unknown

For Sleep When Overtired

Cares and anxieties,
I roll you all up in a bundle together;
I carry you across the meadow to the river.
River, I am throwing in a bundle of cares and anxieties.
Float it away to the sea!

Now I come slowly back across the meadow,
Slowly into the house,
Slowly up to my room.
The night is quiet and cool;
The lights are few and dim;
The sounds are drowsy and far away and melting into each
    other;
Melting into the night.
Sleep comes creeping nearer, creeping nearer;
It goes over my head like a wave.
I sleep . . . I rest . . . I sleep.

Sarah N. Cleghorn

December Twenty-Fourth

Tomorrow You are born again
    Who died so many times.
Do You like the candle-light,
    Do You like the chimes?

Do You stop to wonder
    Why men never see
How very closely Bethlehem
    Approaches Calvary?

Eleanor Slater

Old Earthworks

Within that semi-circle formed by mounds
Of useless clay, unoccupied and drear,
Loud battle cries once mingled with the sounds
Of dying men when warring foes met here;
A conflict raged upon this very spot —
Great cannon belching fire — and yet today
The causes of the conflict are forgot,
Like pyramids of leaves which mold away.

The grass again is green which once was red.
Death's harvest has been changed to one of grain.
No slightest whisper echoes from the dead,
To testify that men were ever slain
And piled in human mounds upon these hills
Which now ring with the call of whippoorwills.

Thomas Sweeney

Life's Evening

Three score and ten!   The tumult of the world
    Grows dull upon my inattentive ear:
The bugle calls are faint, the flags are furled,
    Gone is the rapture, vanished too the fear;
The evening's blessed stillness covers all,
    As o'er the fields she folds her cloak of grey;
Hushed are the winds, the brown leaves slowly fall,
    The russet clouds hang on the fringe of day.
What fairer hour than this?   No stir of morn
    With cries of waking life, nor shafts of noon —
Hot tresses from the flaming sun-god born —
    Nor midnight's shivering stars and marble moon;
But softly twilight falls and toil doth cease,
While o'er my soul God spreads his mantle — peace.

William Dudley Foulke

The Undiscovered Country

The dread of something after death,
    The undiscovered country, from whose bourn
No traveler returns, puzzles the will,
    And makes us rather bear those ills we have,
Than fly to others that we know not of.

William Shakespeare

From " Hamlet "

Friends Old and New

Make new friends, but keep the old;
Those are silver, these are gold;
New-made friendships, like new wine,
Age will mellow and refine.
Friendships that have stood the test —
Time and change — are surely best;
Brow may wrinkle, hair grow gray,
Friendship never knows decay,

For 'mid old friends, tried and true,
Once more we our youth renew.
But old friends, alas! may die,
New friends must their place supply.
Cherish friendship in your breast;
New is good, but old is best;
Make new friends, but keep the old;
Those are silver, these are gold.

Author Unknown

Recompense

All that we say returns,
The bitter word or sweet;
Days, weeks, or years may intervene,
But soon or late
The spoken word and speaker meet.

All that we do returns:
The deed that's true or base
We may forget, but all unseen
And parallel
The doer and the deed keep pace.

John Richard Moreland

All in All

We know Thee, each in part —
　A portion small;
But love Thee, as Thou art —
　The All in all:
For Reason and the ways thereof
Are starlight to the noon of Love.

John B. Tabb

Gone

About the little chambers of my heart
Friends have been coming — going — many a year.
　The doors stand open there.
Some, lightly stepping, enter; some depart.

Freely they come and freely go, at will.
The walls give back their laughter; all day long
　They fill the house with song.
One door alone is shut, one chamber still.

Mary E. Coleridge

Perfection

I swept my house of life and garnished it,
　I looked it through with care,
For fear my thought might miss some imp of sin
　Crouched low and hiding there.

But all was clean and clear, as empty as
　A hollow globe of glass.
I smiled, and turned me to my windows wide
　Watching the weary pass.

But never once did I desire to shield,
From sun or wind or rain,
One soul. Or ask one in to rest, and wash
All free from travel-stain.

Time passed. Again I searched my house with care,
Feeling secure from sin.
Of spirits worse than all I'd known before,
Lo! Eight had entered in!

Ruth Fargo

Quatrain

Though love repine, and reason chafe,
There came a voice without reply —
'Tis man's perdition to be safe,
When for the truth he ought to die.

Ralph Waldo Emerson

Our Father's Door

Truants from love, we dream of wrath; —
Oh, rather let us trust the more!
Through all the wanderings of the path
We still can see our Father's door!

Oliver Wendell Holmes
From " The Crooked Footpath "

Creeds

The creed thy father built, wherein his soul
Did live and move and find its vital joy,
May be but small to thee; then, without fear,
Build o'er again the atrium of the soul
So broad that all mankind may feast with thee.

William O. Partridge

The Aim of Life

We live in deeds, not years; in thoughts, not breaths;
In feelings, not in figures on a dial.
We should count time by heart-throbs. He most lives
Who thinks most, feels the noblest, acts the best.
And he whose heart beats quickest lives the longest.

Philip James Bailey

From " Festus "

The Traitor

The traitor to Humanity is the traitor most accursed;
Man is more than Constitutions; better rot beneath the sod
Than be true to Church and State while we are doubly false
    to God.

James Russell Lowell

Time

Threefold the stride of Time, from first to last!
Loitering slow, the Future creepeth —
Arrow-swift, the Present sweepeth —
And motionless forever stands the Past.

Friedrich von Schiller

A Piece of Clay

I took a piece of plastic clay
And idly fashioned it one day,
And, as my fingers pressed it still,
It moved and yielded to my will.

I came again when days were past —
The bit of clay was hard at last;
The form I gave it, it still bore,
But I could change that form no more.

I took a piece of living clay
And gently formed it day by day,
And moulded with my power and art
A young child's soft and yielding heart.

I came again when years were gone —
It was a man I looked upon;
He still that early impress wore,
And I could change him nevermore.

Author Unknown

The Mystic Borderland

There is a mystic borderland that lies
Just past the limits of our work-day world,
And it is peopled with the friends we met
And loved a year, a month, a week or day,
And parted from with aching hearts, yet knew
That through the distance we must lose the hold
Of hand with hand, and only clasp the thread
Of memory. But still so close we feel this land,
So sure we are that these same hearts are true,
That when in waking dreams there comes a call
That sets the thread of memory aglow,
We know that just by stretching out the hand
In written word of love, or book, or flower,
The waiting hand will clasp our own once more
Across the distance, in the same old way.

Helen Field Fischer

Wisdom

I say that I am wise. Yet dead leaves know
More secrets than my heart can ever guess.
I stand before a crocus' loveliness,
A sword of fire thrust upward in the snow,
And I can never say what embers glow
Beneath this frozen earth. I must confess
A child could stand here with but little less
Of knowledge at the seasons' ebb and flow.

This barren hill holds fast dark sleeping seeds
Whose flame and fragrance soon shall still the blood;
Yet wise in words and ways of men, and creeds,
I cannot know one purple twilight's plan.
Unraveling the crimson of one bud,
I tremble at the ignorance of man!

Daniel Whitehead Hicky

The Cross

So heavy and so fraught with pain,
But I must bravely trudge along
The dusty way . . . nor dare arraign
My cross.

I have no voice to lift in song;
When sorrow's recompense I feign
The muffled notes of grief remain.

And yet He prayed for strength to drain
The bitter dregs and bear the thong.
His kingly soul did not disdain
The cross.

Shirley Dillon Waite

How Shall We Honor Them?

How shall we honor them, our Deathless Dead?
With strew of laurel and the stately tread?
With blaze of banners brightening overhead?
Nay, not alone these cheaper praises bring:
They will not have this easy honoring.

. . . .

How shall we honor them, our Deathless Dead?
How keep their mighty memories alive?
In him who feels their passion, they survive!
Flatter their souls with deeds, and all is said!
                                   Author Unknown

Work Without Hope

All Nature seems at work. Slugs leave their lair —
The bees are stirring — birds are on the wing —
And Winter slumbering in the open air,
Wears on his smiling face a dream of Spring!
And I the while, the sole unbusy thing,
Nor honey make, nor pair, nor build, nor sing.

Yet well I ken the banks where amaranths blow,
Have traced the fount whence streams of nectar flow.
Bloom, O ye amaranths! bloom for whom ye may,
For me ye bloom not! Glide, rich streams, away!
With lips unbrightened, wreathless brow, I stroll:
And would you learn the spells that drowse my soul?
Work without Hope draws nectar in a sieve,
And Hope without an object cannot live.
                              Samuel Taylor Coleridge

The King

How plain soe'er the house or poor the guests,
The royalest of all sits at thy board,
Shares thy small space, waits longingly to give
Full measure of the comfort of His love.
How great thy dignity! How little need
That men should power or place or goods bestow!

Oh, give Him access to thy pent-up heart;
No longer poor the place where God takes part.

Mary F. Butts

Voice

You in whose veins runs the fire of loving,
For people, for plants, for little animals,
For rocks and earth, stars and the elements,
You have a secret Voice, always singing.
It is never still. It runs with your haste
And idles in your silence. It is everywhere.
O you, for whom this passionate Voice sings
And will not be silent, think now of those
For whom no voice sounds. Of those who toil
Without the singing voice,
And live in a world which has not yet come through
Into your world.
Oh, can you not hear that the song your Voice is singing
Is the song which is to bring that world of theirs
Into the light which must light all men?

Why else do you imagine that this Voice is singing?
Why else do you imagine that the fire of love
Runs in your veins?

Zona Gale

Blessed

He prayed for strength that he might achieve;
He was made weak that he might obey.
He prayed for wealth that he might do greater things;
He was given infirmity that he might do better things.
He prayed for riches that he might be happy;
He was given poverty that he might be wise.
He prayed for power that he might have the praise of men;
He was given infirmity that he might feel the need of God.
He prayed for all things that he might enjoy life;
He was given life that he might enjoy all things.
He had received nothing that he asked for — all that he
    hoped for;
His prayer was answered — he was most blessed.

Author Unknown

Convinced by Sorrow

" There is no God," the foolish saith,
    But none, " There is no sorrow."
And nature oft the cry of faith,
    In bitter need will borrow:
Eyes which the preacher could not school,
    By wayside graves are raised,
And lips say, " God be pitiful,"
    Who ne'er said, " God be praised."

Elizabeth Barrett Browning

Song of the New World

I sing the song of a new Dawn waking,
    A new wind shaking the children of men.
I say the hearts that are nigh to breaking
    Shall leap with gladness and live again.

Over the woe of the world appalling,
  Wild and sweet as a bugle cry,
Sudden I hear a new voice calling —
  " Beauty is nigh! "

Beauty is nigh! Let the world believe it.
  Love has covered the fields of dead.
Healing is here! Let the earth receive it,
  Greeting the Dawn with lifted head.
I sing the song of the sin forgiven,
  The deed forgotten, the wrong undone.
Lo, in the East, where the dark is riven,
  Shines the rim of the rising sun.

Healing is here! O brother, sing it!
  Laugh, O heart, that has grieved so long.
Love will gather your woe and fling it
  Over the world in waves of song.
Hearken, mothers, and hear them coming —
  Heralds crying the day at hand.
Faint and far as the sound of drumming,
  Hear their summons across the land.

Look, O fathers! Your eyes were holden —
  Armies throng where the dead have lain.
Fiery steeds and chariots golden —
  Gone is the dream of soldiers slain.
Sing, oh, sing of a new world waking,
  Sing of creation just begun.
Glad is the earth when morn is breaking —
  Man is facing the rising sun!
                          Angela Morgan

For This Universe

O God, we thank Thee for this universe, our great home;
for its vastness and its riches, and for the manifoldness
of the life which teems upon it and of which we are part.
We praise Thee for the arching sky and the blessed winds,
for the driving clouds and the constellations on high.
We praise Thee for the salt sea and the running water,
for the everlasting hills, for the trees, and for the grass
under our feet.

We thank Thee for our senses by which we can see the
splendor of the morning, and hear the jubilant songs of
love, and smell the breath of the springtime.

Grant us, we pray Thee, a heart wide open to all this joy
and beauty and save our souls from being so steeped in
care or so darkened by passion that we pass heedless and
unseeing when even the thornbush by the wayside is
aflame with the glory of God.

Walter Rauschenbusch

The Seekers

Where men have held the vision clear
   Of Brotherhood before their eyes,
The holy angels' message still
   Comes singing down the skies.

Where earnest seekers of the Truth
   Follow her beckoning from afar,
Forever through their dark and doubt
   Shall shine the guiding star.

Lucia Trevitt Auryansen

The Voice of God

I sought to hear the voice of God,
    And climbed the topmost steeple.
But God declared: " Go down again,
    I dwell among the people."
Louis I. Newman

Be Noble

Be noble! and the nobleness that lies
In other men, sleeping, but never dead,
Will rise in majesty to meet thine own;
Then wilt thou see it gleam in many eyes,
Then will pure light around thy path be shed,
And thou wilt nevermore be sad and lone.
James Russell Lowell

Credo

I cannot find my way: there is no star
In all the shrouded heavens anywhere;
And there is not a whisper in the air
Of any living voice but one so far
That I can hear it only as a bar
Of lost, imperial music, played when fair
And angel fingers wove, and unaware,
Dead leaves to garlands where no roses are.

No, there is not a glimmer, nor a call,
For one that welcomes, welcomes when he fears,
The black and awful chaos of the night;
For through it all, — above, beyond it all, —
I know the far-sent message of the years,
I feel the coming glory of the Light!
Edwin Arlington Robinson

My Church

On me nor Priest nor Presbyter nor Pope,
  Bishop nor Dean may stamp a party name;
But Jesus, with his largely human scope,
  The service of my human life may claim.
Let prideful priests do battle about creeds,
  The church is mine that does most Christlike deeds.

Author Unknown

Dream-Pedlary

If there were dreams to sell,
  What would you buy?
Some cost a passing bell;
  Some a light sigh,
That shakes from Life's fresh crown
Only a rose-leaf down.
If there were dreams to sell,
Merry and sad to tell,
And the crier rang the bell,
  What would you buy?

A cottage lone and still,
  With bowers nigh,
Shadowy, my woes to still,
  Until I die.
Such pearl from Life's fresh crown
Fain would I shake me down.
Were dreams to have at will,
This would best heal my ill,
  This would I buy.

Thomas Lovell Beddoes

O Purblind Race

O purblind race of miserable men!
How many among us at this very hour
Do forge a lifelong trouble for ourselves,
By taking true for false, or false for true;
Here, thro' the feeble twilight of this world
Groping — how many — until we pass and reach
That other, where we see as we are seen.
                                        Alfred Tennyson

From " Geraint and Enid "

Integrity

He made honest doors,
    Did Christ, the Nazarene;
He laid honest floors —
    His work was fair and clean.

He made crosses, too,
    Did Christ the Crucified;
Straight and strong and true —
    And on a Cross He died!
                                        William L. Stidger

Experience

I am a part of all that I have met;
Yet all experience is an arch wherethrough
Gleams that untravelled world, whose margin fades
For ever and for ever when I move.
                                        Alfred Tennyson

From " Ulysses "

Faith and Science

Faith has no quarrel with science: she foreknows
The truths which science grudgingly bestows.
Believing David sang that God is one
Ere science found one law in earth and sun.
Faith knows no hindering bonds, she leaps to seize
The truth which science doubts; the harmonies
That men of science learned from age-long thought
Were first revealed to hearts untrained, untaught,
But reverent. Let faith from science learn
Enduring patience; nor let science spurn
The gift of faith, a never-failing love;
Thus, each supporting each, the two shall prove
The final truth of life, that God the Soul
Through perfect law seeks perfect Beauty's goal.

Thomas Curtis Clark

Talk Faith

Talk faith. The world is better off without
Your uttered ignorance and morbid doubt.
If you have faith in God, or man, or self,
Say so; if not, push back upon the shelf
Of silence all your thoughts till faith shall come;
No one will grieve because your lips are dumb.

Ella Wheeler Wilcox

The Heart's Proof

Do you ask me how I prove
That our Father, God, is love?
By this world which He hath made,
By the songs of grove and blade,

By the brooks that singing run,
By the shining of the sun,
By the breeze that cools my brow,
By fresh odors from the plow,
By the daisy's golden head,
Shining in the fields I tread,
By the chorus of the bees
In the flowering willow trees,
By the gentle dews and rain,
By the farmer's springing grain,
By the light of golden eyes,
By the sheen of forest leaves,
By the sweets of woodland springs,
By the joy right-doing brings —
By a thousand, thousand things!

James Buckham

My Spirit Will Grow Up

Some day my spirit will grow up tall and wise,
And then, stern Life, I shall no longer go
Cowardly running and crying from your blow.
Then I will face you with clear, earnest eyes
Smiling a little at your sharp surprise,
Unflinching from the threatened stroke, with no
Soft tremor to lighten your frown — when I shall grow
In spirit, some day, tall and strong and wise.
Then I will face you, it may be I shall laugh,
Not to disarm you, not to conclude our strife,
But joyous in my newly steadied will
That finds a comfort in thy rod and staff.
Then I will say: " You may hurt me, hurt me, Life,
Hurt me your worst, and I will love you still! "

Ruth Evelyn Henderson

This Is the Making of Man

Flame of the spirit and dust of the earth —
    This is the making of man;
This is his problem of birth:
Born to all holiness, born to all crime,
Heir to both worlds, on the long slope of time,
    Climbing the path of God's plan.
Dust of the earth in his error and fear,
    Weakness and malice and lust;
    Yet, quivering up from the dust,
Flame of the spirit, upleaping and clear,
Yearning to God, since from God is his birth —
    This is man's portion, to shape as he can,
Flame of the spirit and dust of the earth —
    This is the making of man.

Priscilla Leonard

In Men Whom Men Condemn

In men whom men condemn as ill
I find so much of goodness still,
In men whom men pronounce divine
I find so much of sin and blot,
I do not dare to draw a line
Between the two, where God has not.

Joaquin Miller

Love

Love is not love
Which alters when it alteration finds,
Or bends with the remover to remove;
Oh, no! it is an ever-fixed mark
That looks on tempests and is never shaken.

William Shakespeare

Civilization

One man craves a scarf or glove,
   And another man must die,
For such is the rule of light and love
   That our lives are guided by.

One man craves a jeweled cross,
   And another hangs thereon.
And the watching world feels less remorse
   Than the winner feels of scorn.

One man barters, one man buys
   Spirit and blood and breath.
And the market groans with new supplies
   Though the stalls be cleared by death.

One man craves a scarf or glove,
   And another man must die.
For such is the rule of light and love
   That the ages sanctify.

Stanton A. Coblentz

The Way to Power

Self-reverence, self-knowledge, self-control,
These three alone lead life to sovereign power.
Yet not for power (power of herself
Would come uncalled for) but to live by law,
Acting the law we live by without fear;
And, because right is right, to follow right
Were wisdom in the scorn of consequence.

Alfred Tennyson

From " Idylls of the King "

A Narrow Window

A narrow window may let in the light,
A tiny star dispel the gloom of night,
A little deed a mighty wrong set right.

A rose, abloom, may make a desert fair;
A single cloud may darken all the air;
A spark may kindle ruin and despair.

A smile and there may be an end to strife;
A look of love, and Hate may sheathe the knife;
A word — ah, it may be a word of life!

Florence Earle Coates

Words

Boys flying kites haul in their white-winged birds,
You can't do that when you're flying words.
Careful with fire is good advice, we know;
Careful with words is ten times doubly so.
Thoughts unexpressed sometimes fall back dead,
But God himself can't kill them once they're said.

Author Unknown

In His Sight

God counts time not by minutes nor by days,
The years, to Him, are but the markings on a dial,
'Round which we circle, madly spinning,
Like futile second hands. Our very haste betrays
Our fear of time. And all the while,
His pointing hand moves slowly in an arc

So vast, its end and its beginning
Alike are lost in deep impenetrable dark
Of Past and Future.   And our tick-tick-tock
But marks the silence of God's timeless clock.

Anna R. Baker

The Life of Man

The life of man is a lonely thing,
  A lonely thing, God wot.
He dreams alone; he dies alone:
  Life is a lonely lot.

The life of man is a friendly thing,
  And he has a friendly heart.
He gives his life; he lives till death;
  Life is a friendly art.

A friendlier thing, a lonelier thing,
  As swift years go and come;
Perchance that hearts may find their rest
  In Him, the heart's true home.

Lucius H. Thayer

Earth's Story

With primal void and cosmic night
Love had its way, and there was light.

A flaming waste, through æons long
Took form, and chaos turned to song.

The sun embraced the virgin earth
And warmed the leafy plants to birth.

Slow ages passed, and patient time
Brought creeping reptiles from the slime.

Through vasty waters fishes sped,
In torrid jungles beasts were bred.

Then Beauty filled the land with flowers,
And lo! birds thronged the forest bowers.

Love yearned for answering love — the voice
Of thinking Man made God rejoice.

Then all the stars began to sing
As conscious Nature crowned its King.

Thomas Curtis Clark

The Sentinel

The morning is the gate of day,
　But ere you enter there
See that you set to guard it well,
　The sentinel of prayer.

So shall God's grace your steps attend,
　But nothing else pass through
Save what can give the countersign;
　The Father's will for you.

When you have reached the end of day
　Where night and sleep await,
Set there the sentinel again
　To bar the evening's gate.

So shall no fear disturb your rest,
　No danger and no care.
For only peace and pardon pass
　The watchful guard of prayer.

Author Unknown

Leaf After Leaf Drops Off

Leaf after leaf drops off, flower after flower,
Some in the chill, some in the warmer hour:
Alive they flourish, and alive they fall,
And Earth who nourished them receives them all.
Should we, her wiser sons, be less content
To sink into her lap when life is spent?

Walter Savage Landor

The Fellowship

When brambles vex me sore and anguish me,
    Then I remember those pale martyr feet
That trod on burning shares and drank the heat,
    As it had been God's dew, with ecstasy.

And when some evanescent sunset glow
    Renews the beauty-sting, I set my pride
On that great fellowship of those who know
    The artist's yearning, yet are self-denied.

Feast me no feasts that for the few are spread,
    With holy cup of brotherhood ungraced,
For though I sicken at my daily bread,
    Bitter and black, I crave the human taste.

Katharine Lee Bates

You and Today

With every rising of the sun,
    Think of your life as just begun.
The past has shrived and buried deep
    All yesterdays; there let them sleep.

Concern yourself with but today,
  Woo it, and teach it to obey
Your will and wish. Since time began
  Today has been the friend of man;

But in his blindness and his sorrow,
  He looks to yesterday and tomorrow.
You, and today! a soul sublime,
  And the great pregnant hour of time,
With God himself to bind the twain!
  Go forth, I say — attain, attain!
With God himself to bind the twain!

                    Ella Wheeler Wilcox

The Thing We Long For

The thing we long for, that we are
  For one transcendent moment,
Before the Present poor and bare
  Can make its sneering comment.

                    James Russell Lowell
        From " Longings "

Sunsets

God, You need not make for me
Doctrines of Infinity —
Just a sunset in the west,
Never mind about the rest;
To my queries You reply
When You paint the evening sky;
Seems to me I know You best
By Your sunsets in the west.

                    Florence Boyce Davis

Because of You

Because of you I bear aloft the standard
  Of high resolve — ideals pure and true;
And to ignoble thoughts I have not pandered —
  Because of You!

No summer sun but wears an added whiteness —
  No fair and cloudless sky but seems more blue —
No midnight star but shines with fuller brightness —
  Because of You!

No darkened day but holds some glint of radiance —
  No hour of life that I entirely rue —
No bitter weed but has some touch of fragrance —
  Because of You!

Thoughts of your love within my heart are swelling —
  Courage and hope both nerve my heart anew;
Life has a sweetness far beyond all telling —
  Because of You!

W. Cestrian

Because of Thy Great Bounty

Because I have been given much,
  I, too, shall give;
Because of Thy great bounty, Lord,
  Each day I live
I shall divide my gifts from Thee
  With every brother that I see
Who has the need of help from me.

Because I have been sheltered, fed,
    By Thy good care,
I cannot see another's lack
    And I not share
My glowing fire, my loaf of bread,
    My roof's shelter overhead,
That he, too, may be comforted.

Because love has been lavished so
    Upon me, Lord,
A wealth I know that was not meant
    For me to hoard,
I shall give love to those in need,
    The cold and hungry clothe and feed,
Thus shall I show my thanks indeed.

Grace Noll Crowell

Desire

The desire of love, Joy:
The desire of life, Peace:
The desire of the soul, Heaven:
The desire of God . . . a flame-white secret forever.

William Sharp

Not in Solitude

Yet not in solitude if Christ anear me
    Waketh him workers for the great employ,
Oh not in solitude, if souls that hear me
    Catch from my joyance the surprise of joy.

F. W. H. Myers

From " St. Paul "

It Is Not Growing Like a Tree

It is not growing like a tree
In bulk, doth make Man better be;
Or standing long an oak, three hundred year,
To fall a log at last, dry, bald, and sere:
    A lily of a day
    Is fairer far in May,
Although it fall and die that night —
It was the plant and flower of Light.
In small proportions we just beauties see;
And in short measures life may perfect be.

Ben Jonson

From " A Pindaric Ode "

Comrade Christ

Give us Jesus Christ, the Carpenter.
What to us is your white-liveried God?
O men of the anvil, of the loom, the sod,
They have hid our God in a golden sepulcher;
They have made of our Christ a sniveling, pampered priest,
A paltry giver of fine bread and wine —
Our Christ is a God of men, as Man divine,
Holding in brotherhood the lost and least.

He toils in the desert places by our side;
He delves with us beneath the granite hill;
He weeps above our brothers who have died;
He dreams with us in the darkness hot and still:
No surpliced shriver of the sins of men —
Christ, the Carpenter, has come again.

Verne Bright

Credo

Each, in himself, his hour to be and cease
Endures alone, but who of men shall dare,
Sole with himself, his single burden bear,
All the long day until the night's release?
Yet ere night falls, and the last shadows close,
This labor of himself is each man's lot;
All he has gained on earth shall be forgot,
Himself he leaves behind him when he goes.
If he has any valiancy within,
If he has made his life his very own,
If he has loved, or labored, and has known
A strenuous virtue or a strenuous sin;
Then, being dead, his life was not all vain,
For he has saved what most desire to lose,
And he has chosen what the few must choose,
Since life, once lived, shall not return again.
For of our time we lose so large a part
In serious trifles, and so oft let slip
The wine of every moment, at the lip
Its moment, and the moment of the heart.
We are awake so little on the earth,
And we shall sleep so long, and rise so late —
If there is any knocking at that gate
Which is the gate of death, the gate of birth.

Arthur Symons

Great Things

Great things are done when men and mountains meet;
These are not done by jostling in the street.

William Blake

Making Life Worth While

May every soul that touches mine —
Be it the slightest contact —
Get therefrom some good;
Some little grace; one kindly thought;
One aspiration yet unfelt;
One bit of courage
For the darkening sky;
One gleam of faith
To brave the thickening ills of life;
One glimpse of brighter skies
Beyond the gathering mists —
To make this life worth while
And heaven a surer heritage.

George Eliot

Attainment

Use all your hidden forces. Do not miss
The purpose of this life, and do not wait
For circumstance to mold or change your fate.
In your own self lies destiny. Let this
Vast truth cast out all fear, all prejudice,
All hesitation. Know that you are great,
Great with divinity. So dominate
Environment, and enter into bliss. —
Love largely and hate nothing. Hold no aim
That does not chord with universal good.

Hear what the voices of the silence say,
All joys are yours if you put forth your claim,
Once let the spiritual laws be understood,
Material things must answer and obey.

Ella Wheeler Wilcox

As I Grow Old

God keep my heart attuned to laughter
　　When youth is done;
When all the days are gray days, coming after
　　The warmth, the sun.
Ah! keep me then from bitterness, from grieving,
　　When life seems cold;
God keep me always loving and believing
　　As I grow old.

Author Unknown

Ascent

Delve not so deep in the gloomy past
　　That life's bright sands cave in and bury thee;
Better it is to make a ladder fast
　　Against a star, and climb eternally.

Charles G. Blanden

On Life's Way

The world is wide,
In time and tide,
And — God is guide;
　　Then do not hurry.

That man is blest
Who does his best
And leaves the rest,
　　Then do not worry.

Charles F. Deems

From Old to New

Man must pass from old to new,
From vain to real, from mistake to fact,
From what once seemed good, to what now proves best.
                    Robert Browning
        From " Death in the Desert "

New Temples

I think God loves new temples built to Him
And watches as each stone is laid on stone,
And smiles to see them laid so straight and true,
Lifting the strong wide walls to heaven's blue.
And when the carpenters have done with them,
And each new church stands finished and alone,
When dusk sifts violet shadows through the glass
Of painted windows, I think that God must pass
Between the new dim aisles, and stopping where
The last light falls across His shining hair,
He kneels and holds the first communion there.
                    Lexie Dean Robertson

Spring

The sun lies light on a jade-green hill,
There's a burst of song from a loosened rill,
The wind warms the breast of the new-turned sod,
And the note of a bird links earth with God!
                    Anne Elizabeth Maddock

Unto Each His Handiwork

Unto each his handiwork, unto each his crown,
  The just Fate gives.
Whoso takes the world's life on him and his own lays down,
  He, dying so, lives.

Whoso bears the whole heaviness of the wronged world's
    weight,
  And puts it by,
It is well with him suffering, though he face man's fate;
  How should he die?
                    Algernon Charles Swinburne

Stone Walls Do Not a Prison Make

Stone walls do not a prison make,
  Nor iron bars a cage;
Minds innocent and quiet take
  That for a hermitage;
If I have freedom in my love,
  And in my soul am free,
Angels alone, that soar above,
  Enjoy such liberty.
                    Richard Lovelace

From " From Prison "

A Garden Prayer

That we are mortals and on earth must dwell
Thou knowest, Allah, and didst give us bread —
And remembering of our souls didst give us food of
    flowers —
Thy name be hallowéd.
                    Thomas Walsh

God's Book

God spreads a book before my eyes,
  As I go tramping hill and dell,
And oh, my heart is made most wise
  By what His wind-blown pages tell.

Though men declare I am a clown,
  Whose dreams have made him worse than fey,
The while I wander up and down,
  I give no heed to what they say.

I turn me from their foolish words
  To read the kindliness of God
Within His book of singing birds,
  Of trees and brooks and fragrant sod.

Edgar Daniel Kramer

Adios

Could I but teach man to believe,
  Could I but make small men to grow,
To break frail spider-webs that weave
  About their thews and bind them low;
Could I but sing one song and slay
  Grim Doubt; I then could go my way
In tranquil silence, glad, serene,
  And satisfied from off the scene.
But ah, this disbelief, this doubt,
  This doubt of God, this doubt of Good —
This damned spot will not out!

Joaquin Miller

Who Loves the Rain

Who loves the rain
And loves his home,
And looks on life with quiet eyes,
    Him will I follow through the storm;
    And at his hearth-fire keep me warm;
Nor hell nor heaven shall that soul surprise,
    Who loves the rain,
    And loves his home,
And looks on life with quiet eyes.

Frances Shaw

Days

Some days my thoughts are just cocoons — all cold, and
    dull, and blind,
They hang from dripping branches in the grey woods of my
    mind;

And other days they drift and shine — such free and flying
    things!
I find the gold-dust in my hair, left by their brushing wings.

Karle Wilson Baker

In This Earth, Perfection

In this broad earth of ours,
Amid the measureless grossness and the slag,
Enclosed and safe within its central heart,
Nestles the seed perfection.

Walt Whitman

From " Birds of Passage "

Reunited

When you and I have played this little hour,
Have seen the tall subaltern Life to Death
Yield up his sword; and, smiling, draw the breath,
The first long breath of freedom; when the flower
Of Recompense hath fluttered to our feet,
As to an actor's; and, the curtain down,
We turn to face each other all alone —
Alone, we two, who never yet did meet,
Alone, and absolute, and free: O then,
O then, most dear, how shall be told the tale?
Clasp'd hands, press'd lips, and so clasp hands again;
No words. But as the proud wind fills the sail,
My love to yours shall reach, then one deep moan
Of joy, and then our infinite Alone.

Gilbert Parker

Easter

But His lone cross and crown of thorns
  Endure when crowns and empires fall.
The might of His undying love
  In dying conquered all.

John Oxenham

Heaven in My Hand

I looked for Heaven, high on a hill,
Heaven where mighty towers stand;
Then emptied my hands of gold to fill
The empty hands of others — and still
Had gold, with Heaven in my hand.

Raymond Kresensky

Victory in Defeat

Defeat may serve as well as victory
To shake the soul and let the glory out.
When the great oak is straining in the wind,
The boughs drink in new beauty, and the trunk
Sends down a deeper root on the windward side.
Only the soul that knows the mighty grief
Can know the mighty rapture. Sorrows come
To stretch our spaces in the heart for joy.

Edwin Markham

Resolve

To keep my health!
To do my work!
   To live!
To see to it I grow and gain and give!
Never to look behind me for an hour!
To wait in weakness and to walk in power.
But always fronting onward toward the light
Always and always facing toward the right,
Robbed, starved, defeated, fallen, wide astray —
On with what strength I have
Back to the way!

Charlotte Perkins Gilman

A Strip of Blue

I do not own an inch of land,
   But all I see is mine —
The orchards and the mowing-fields,
   The lawns and gardens fine.

The winds my tax-collectors are,
    They bring me tithes divine —
Wild scents and subtle essences,
    A tribute rare and free;
And, more magnificent than all,
    My window keeps for me
A glimpse of blue immensity,
    A little strip of sea.

Here sit I, as a little child;
    The threshold of God's door
Is that clear band of chrysoprase;
    Now the vast temple floor,
The blinding glory of the dome
    I bow my head before;
The universe, O God, is home,
    In height or depth, to me;
Yet here upon Thy footstool green
    Content am I to be;
Glad, when is opened to my need
    Some sea-like glimpse of Thee.

                                Lucy Larcom

From Nobility

True worth is in being, not seeming —
    In doing, each day that goes by,
Some little good — not in dreaming
    Of great things to do by and by.
For whatever men say in their blindness,
    And spite of the fancies of youth,
There's nothing so kingly as kindness,
    And nothing so royal as truth.

                                Alice Cary

Windows for My Soul

I will hew great windows for my soul,
Channels of splendor, portals of release;
Out of earth's prison walls will I hew them,
That my thundering soul may push through them;
Through the strata of human strife and passion
I will tunnel a way, I will carve and fashion
With the might of my soul's intensity
Windows fronting on immensity,
Towering out of time
I will breathe the air of another clime
That my spirit's pain may cease.
That the being of me may have room to grow,
That my eyes may meet God's eyes and know;
I will hew great windows, wonderful windows,
Measureless windows for my soul.

Author Unknown

God Give Me Joy

God give me joy in the common things:
In the dawn that lures, the eve that sings.

In the new grass sparkling after rain,
In the late wind's wild and weird refrain;

In the springtime's spacious field of gold,
In the precious light by winter doled.

God give me joy in the love of friends,
In their dear home talk as summer ends;

In the songs of children, unrestrained;
In the sober wisdom age has gained.

God give me joy in the tasks that press,
In the memories that burn and bless;

In the thought that life has love to spend,
In the faith that God's at journey's end.

God give me hope for each day that springs,
God give me joy in the common things!

Thomas Curtis Clark

" A Faithless Generation Asked a Sign "

A faithless generation asked a sign,
Some fresh and flaming proof of human worth
Since youth could find no flavor in life's wine
And there were no more giants in the earth.
Then out of gray oblivion He came
To laugh at space and thrust aside its bars,
To manifest the littleness of fame
To one who has companioned with the stars.
The drought of greed is broken, fruitful streams
Cf courage flow through fields long parched and dead,
Young men see visions now, old men dream dreams,
A world moves forward with uplifted head:
A Lad with wings to dare had faith to rise
And carve proud arcs across uncharted skies.

Molly Anderson Haley

From The Things That Endure

What wish you, immortality?
Then of frail visions become the wooer.
Stone cities melt like mist away,
But footsteps in the sand — endure.

Florence Wilkinson

The Man of Sorrows

Christ claims our help in many a strange disguise;
Now, fever-ridden, on a bed He lies;
Homeless He wanders now beneath the stars;
Now counts the number of His prison bars;
Now bends beside us, crowned with hoary hairs.
No need have we to climb the heavenly stairs,
And press our kisses on His feet and hands;
In every man that suffers, He, the Man of Sorrows, stands!

Author Unknown

For a Materialist

I know your barren belief — that a rose will grow
From what was once the miracle of a man;
That only in this wise shall we thwart the grave;
Believe, my friend, and be satisfied, if you can.

But I have a mystical hunger, so great and intense
That only Almighty God with a purpose would fill
My fragile shell with its poignant immensity —
A hunger to find, emerging from death, that I still
Am the sum of myself! myself, to aspire and climb
Some further and undreamed slope of the range of Time.

I have faith that I shall. Is a rose worth the patience of Him
Who evolved through the aeons a man and endowed him
    with soul?
Would He who created the splendor of spirit and mind
Envisage a sweet-scented waft as its trivial goal?

Adelaide P. Love

Love's Strength

Measure thy life by loss instead of gain;
Not by the wine drunk, but wine poured forth;
For love's strength standeth in love's sacrifice;
And whoso suffers most hath most to give.

H. E. H. King

Song of the Silent Land

Into the Silent Land!
Ah! who shall lead us thither?
Clouds in the evening sky more darkly gather,
And shattered wrecks lie thicker on the strand.
Who leads us with a gentle hand
Thither, Oh, thither,
Into the Silent Land?

Into the Silent Land!
To you, ye boundless regions
Of all perfection! Tender morning-visions
Of beauteous souls! The Future's pledge and band!
Who in Life's battle firm doth stand,
Shall bear Hope's tender blossoms
Into the Silent Land!

O Land! O Land!
For all the broken-hearted
The mildest herald by our fate allotted,
Beckons, and with inverted torch doth stand
To lead us with a gentle hand
To the land of the great Departed,
Into the Silent Land!

Henry Wadsworth Longfellow

From the German

Diogenes

A hut, and a tree,
And a hill for me,
And a piece of a weedy meadow.
I'll ask no thing,
Of God or king,
But to clear away his shadow.

Max Eastman

A Knight of Bethlehem

There was a Knight of Bethlehem whose wealth was tears
and sorrows;
His Men-at-arms were little lambs, His Trumpeters were
sparrows;
His castle was a wooden cross, whereon He hung so high;
His helmet was a crown of thorns, whose crest did touch
the sky.

Henry Neville Maughan

There Was a Child Went Forth

There was a child went forth every day;
And the first object he looked upon, the object he became;
And that object became part of him for the day, or a certain
part of the day, or for many years, or stretching cycles
of years:
The early lilacs became part of this child;

.   .   .   .

And the apple-trees covered with blossoms, and the fruit
afterward, and wood-berries, and the commonest weeds
by the road;

And the old drunkard staggering home from the outhouse of
the tavern, whence he had lately risen,
And the schoolmistress that passed on her way to the school;

. . . .

The blow, the quick loud word, the tight bargain, the crafty
lure,
The family usages, the language, the company, the furniture
— the yearning and swelling heart;

. . . .

The doubts of day-time and the doubts of night-time — the
curious whether and how,
Whether that which appears so is so, or is it all flashes and
specks?
Men and women crowding fast in the streets — if they are
not flashes and specks, what are they?

These became part of that child who went forth every day,
and who now goes, and will always go forth every day.
                                    Walt Whitman

Prayer of the Unemployed

Lord, I do not ask for houses of steel,
    Nor houses built of stone;
But for the exultation to feel
    The tug on muscle and bone.

Not for wealth or men at my commands,
    Nor peace when I am through —
I only ask work for these hands,
    Work for these hands to do.
                                    Raymond Kresensky

What Shall Endure?

Great roads the Romans built that men might meet,
And walls to keep strong men apart — secure.
Now centuries have gone, and in defeat
The walls are fallen, but the roads endure.

Ethelyn M. Hartwich

God Hide the Whole World in Thy Heart

Behind thee leave thy merchandise,
Thy churches and thy charities;
And leave thy peacock wit behind;
Enough for thee the primal mind
That flows in streams, that breathes in wind;
Leave all thy pedant lore apart;
God hide the whole world in thy heart.

Ralph Waldo Emerson

From " Woodnotes "

The Law of Love

Then was earth made anew where'er He went,
For all men's hearts were opened to the Light,
And Christ was King, and Lord Omnipotent.

And everywhere men's hearts turned unto Him
As to the very source and fount of Right,
As flowers turn to the sun, and everywhere
New Life sprang up to greet Him as He went
Dispensing grace to all men everywhere.
And His dispensèd grace changed all men's hearts,
Made His will theirs, and their wills wholly His;

So that they strove no more each for himself,
But each for good of all, and all for Him;
Man's common aim was for the common good;
The age-old feuds were of the past,
And all mankind joined hands at last
In common brotherhood.

.   .   .   .

And every man in all the whole wide world
Had room, and time, and wherewithal to live
His life at fullest full within the Law —
The Law that has no bounds or bonds for those
Who live it, for it is His Love, —
The great unchanged, unchanging, and unchangeable
Law whose beginning and whose end is — Love.

John Oxenham

From " Chaos, and the Way Out "

Let All the Earth Keep Silence

How lovely is the silence of green, growing things —
Orchard blossoms, apple, plum, and pear,
Branches laden down by fruit they bear,
Fields of everlasting, creeping vine,
Mountain-forest, hemlock, balsam, pine,
Gentian, asters, sweet-fern on the hill,
All praise Him in their beauty — keeping still.

Lucy A. K. Adee

Unquestioning

He who bends to himself a joy
Does the winged life destroy:
But he who kisses the joy as it flies
Lives in eternity's sunrise.

William Blake

The House of the Trees

Ope your doors and take me in,
　　Spirit of the wood,
Wash me clean of dust and din,
　　Clothe me in your mood.

Take me from the noisy light
　　To the sunless peace,
Where at mid-day standeth Night
　　Signing Toil's release.

All your dusky twilight stores
　　To my senses give;
Take me in and lock the doors,
　　Show me how to live.

Lift your leafy roof for me,
　　Part your yielding walls:
Let me wander lingeringly
　　Through your scented halls.

Ope your doors and take me in,
　　Spirit of the wood;
Take me — make me next of kin
　　To your leafy brood.

Ethelyn Wetherald

Rhythm

Thou canst not wave thy staff in air,
　　Or dip thy paddle in the lake,
But it curves the bow of beauty there,
　　And the ripples in rhyme the oar forsake.

Ralph Waldo Emerson

To Young Dreamers

Above dark cities build
Your tall, impossible towers,
Imperious towers of faith
Built perilously high,
And gather your dreams like clusters
Of strange, bewildering flowers
From the star-bright ledges
Of the wide, impossible sky!

Lucia Trent

The Indwelling God

Go not, my soul, in search of Him;
    Thou wilt not find Him there —
Or in the depths of shadow dim,
    Or heights of upper air.

For not in far-off realms of space
    The spirit hath its throne;
In every heart it findeth place
    And waiteth to be known.

Thought answereth alone to thought
    And soul with soul hath kin;
For outward God he findeth not,
    Who finds not God within.

And if the visions come to thee
    Revealed by inward sign,
Earth will be full of Deity
    And with His glory shine.

Thou shalt not want for company,
  Nor pitch thy tent alone;
The Indwelling God will go with thee,
  And show thee of His own.

Oh, gift of gifts, Oh, grace of grace,
  That God should condescend
To make thy heart His dwelling-place,
  And be thy daily friend!

Then go not thou in search of Him,
  But to thyself repair;
Wait thou within the silence dim
  And thou shalt find Him there.

Frederick Lucian Hosmer

Eternal Good

Eternal Good which overlies
The sorrow of the world, Love which outlives
All sin and wrong, Compassion which forgives
To the uttermost, and Justice whose clear eyes
Through lapse and failure look to the intent,
And judge our failure by the life we meant.

John Greenleaf Whittier

From " Eventide "

The Goal

What were life,
Did soul stand still therein, forego her strife
Through the ambiguous Present to the goal
Of some all-reconciling Future!

Robert Browning

From " Gerard de Lairesse "

He Who Ascends to Mountain-Tops

He who ascends to mountain-tops shall find
    The loftiest peaks most wrapt in clouds and snow;
    He who surpasses or subdues mankind,
    Must look down on the hate of those below.
    Though high above the sun of glory glow,
    And far beneath the earth and ocean spread,
    Round him are icy rocks, and loudly blow
    Contending tempests on his naked head.
And thus reward the toils which to those summits led.

George Gordon Byron

Release

Do not fear
And do not grieve for me,
I shall not die:
I am like the forest oak
That summer suns have seasoned;
My body will be a little heap of ash
Upon the hearth,
But I shall rise in flame,
In flame that leaps and soars
And seeks the stars.

Do not fear
And do not weep, my dear,
When Death stoops down to light the fire.

Jean Grigsby Paxton

I Accept

I shall go out as all men go,
Spent flickers in a mighty wind,
Then I shall know, as all must know,
What lies the great gray veil behind.

There may be nothing but a deep
And timeless void without a name
Where no sun hangs, no dead stars sleep,
And there is neither night nor flame.

There may be meadows there and hills,
Mountains and plains and winds that blow,
And flowers bending over rills
Springing from an eternal snow.

There may be oceans white with foam
And great tall ships for hungry men
Who called our little salt seas home
And burn to launch their keels again.

There may be voices I have known,
Cool fingers that have touched my hair.
There may be hearts that were my own, —
Love may abide forever there.

Who knows? Who needs to understand
If there be shadows there, or more,
To live as though a pleasant land
Lay just beyond an open door?

Harold Trowbridge Pulsifer

From The Battle of Blenheim

Now tell us what 'twas all about,
    Young Peterkin, he cries,
And little Wilhelmine looks up
    With wonder-waiting eyes;
Now tell us all about the war
And what they killed each other for.

It was the English, Kaspar cried,
    That put the French to rout;
But what they kill'd each other for,
    I could not well make out.
But everybody said, quoth he,
That 'twas a famous victory.

Robert Southey

The Lament of the Voiceless

" Wars are to be," they say, they blindly say,
Nor strive to end them. Had we eyes to see
The ghosts that walk across the fields of slain,
We might behold by each boy soldier's corpse
An endless line who mourn his fateful doom.

" Who are you? " asking, we might hear these words:
" We are the men and women not to be,
Because the father of our line was slain,
Cut off untimely. Brave he was and strong;
His heritage were ours had he not been
The food of slaughter in a wanton war."

Boy soldier, sleep, by fireside loved ones mourned;
By neighbor comrades, half ashamed of life,
When death claims him who went that they might stay.

Boy soldier, sleep; if ever these forget,
You still are mourned by that long line unborn,
Who might have been but for the waste of war.
They mourn for you, your sons who never were.

Laura Bell Everett

Fidele

Fear no more the heat o' the sun,
 Nor the furious winter's rages;
Thou thy worldly task hast done,
 Home art gone, and ta'en thy wages:
Golden lads and girls all must,
As chimney-sweepers, come to dust.

Fear no more the frown o' the great,
 Thou art past the tyrant's stroke;
Care no more to clothe and eat;
 To thee the reed is as the oak:
The sceptre, learning, physic, must
All follow this, and come to dust.

Fear no more the lightning-flash,
 Nor the all-dreaded thunder-stone;
Fear not slander, censure rash;
 Thou hast finish'd joy and moan:
All lovers young, all lovers must
Consign to thee, and come to dust.

No exorciser harm thee!
Nor no witchcraft charm thee!
Ghost unlaid forbear thee!
Nothing ill come near thee!
Quiet consummation have;
And renownèd be thy grave!

William Shakespeare

From " Cymbeline "

[A favorite poem of Abraham Lincoln]

As the Sculptor

As the sculptor devotes himself to wood and stone
I would devote myself to the living soul.
But I am solemnized by the thought that the sculptor cannot
    carve
Either on wood, or on stone, or on the living soul,
Anything better than himself.
All the lines of my carving
Will but reveal my own portrait.
Gazing at my hand, at my chisel, I shudder.
How long will it take for this human sculpture,
Which can not be carved by me better, finer than my own
    soul,
To escape!   To escape from my pitiable and limited
    domain,
And to advance to the position of a carving of God?

Happily, there is a Guide for me.
It is He who has broken open the door of the Sanctuary
And made a molten cast of God's Portrait on His own flesh.

Toyohiko Kagawa

The Splendor Falls

The splendor falls on castle walls
    And snowy summits old in story:
The long light shakes across the lakes,
    And the wild cataract leaps in glory.
Blow, bugle, blow, set the wild echoes flying,
Blow, bugle; answer, echoes, dying, dying, dying.

O hark, O hear! how thin and clear,
    And thinner, clearer, farther going!
O sweet and far from cliff and scar
    The horns of Elfland faintly blowing!
Blow, let us hear the purple glens reply:
Blow, bugle; answer, echoes, dying, dying, dying.

O love, they die in yon rich sky,
    They faint on hill or field or river:
Our echoes roll from soul to soul,
    And grow forever and forever.
Blow, bugle, blow, set the wild echoes flying,
And answer, echoes, answer, dying, dying, dying.
Alfred Tennyson

Vitae Lampada

There's a breathless hush in the Close tonight —
    Ten to make and the match to win —
A bumping pitch and a blinding light,
    An hour to play and the last man in.
And it's not for the sake of a ribboned coat,
    Or the selfish hope of a season's fame,
But his Captain's hand on his shoulder smote —
    " Play up! play up! and play the game! "

The sand of the desert is sodden red —
    Red with the wreck of a square that broke; —
The Gatling's jammed and the Colonel dead,
    And the regiment blind with dust and smoke.
The river of death has brimmed his banks,
    And England's far, and Honor a name,
But the voice of a schoolboy rallies the ranks:
    " Play up! play up! and play the game! "

This is the word that year by year,
    While in her place the school is set,
Every one of her sons must hear,
    And none that hears it dare forget.
This they all with joyful mind
    Bear through life like a torch in flame,
And falling fling to the host behind —
    " Play up! play up! and play the game! "

Sir Henry Newbolt

Mourn Not the Dead

Mourn not the dead that in the cool earth lie —
    Dust unto dust —
The calm sweet earth that mothers all who die
    As all men must;

Mourn not your captured comrades who must dwell —
    Too strong to strive —
Each in his steel-bound coffin of a cell,
    Buried alive;

But rather mourn the apathetic throng —
    The cowed and the meek —
Who see the world's great anguish and its wrong
    And dare not speak!

Ralph Chaplin

We Are Never Old

Spring still makes spring in the mind
   When sixty years are told;
Love wakes anew this throbbing heart,
   And we are never old;
Over the winter glaciers
   I see the summer glow,
And through the wild-piled snowdrift
   The warm rosebuds below.

Ralph Waldo Emerson

From " The World-Soul "

Discovery

I have found God on a high hill alone, alone,
On Lookout Mountain with Chattanooga far beneath me,
And above the Grand Canyon where waters hide in rock.
I have seen God as I sat on a park bench
Watching the flaming colors of the sunset,
And a red bird sang above me —
In the wideness of Dakota prairies —
At the foot of the lagoon where the Lincoln Memorial
Puts its feet in heaven — at the feet of Lincoln alone.

I have seen God in the corner of a mountain cabin
Where a small girl sang ballads
And her mother wept in loneliness.
I have seen God when my own mother
Sat beside the coffin of her son,
A young man killed by war.
I saw God in her old hands fumbling a German Bible,
And Jesus smiling to see two enemies at peace there.

I have seen God in the fellowship
All men bear with grief and pain —
The agnostic lifting the weary hands of the pilgrim,
The Christian binding the blasphemer's wounds.

I have seen God in beauty unspeakable
Of hills and sunsets — in the works of men —
Beauty like a sharp pain.
I have seen God with men, humanly alone.

Raymond Kresensky

The Back of God

I prayed to see the face of God,
Illumined by the central suns
Turning in their ancient track;
But what I saw was not His face at all —
I saw His bent figure on a windy hill,
Carrying a double load upon His back.

J. R. Perkins

In Prison

I know not whether Laws be right,
    Or whether Laws be wrong;
All that we know who lie in jail
    Is that the wall is strong;
And that each day is like a year,
    A year whose days are long.

But this I know, that every Law
    That men have made for Man,
Since first Man took his brother's life,
    And this sad world began,
But straws the wheat and saves the chaff
    With a most evil fan.

This too I know — and wise it were
If each could know the same —
That every prison that men build
Is built with bricks of shame,
And bound with bars lest Christ should see
How men their brothers maim.

Oscar Wilde

From " The Ballad of Reading Gaol "

Blow, Blow, Thou Winter Wind

Blow, blow, thou winter wind,
Thou art not so unkind
As man's ingratitude;
Thy tooth is not so keen
Because thou art not seen,
Although thy breath be rude.
Heigh-ho! sing heigh-ho! unto the green holly:
Most friendship is feigning, most loving mere folly:
Then, heigh-ho! the holly!
This life is most jolly.

Freeze, freeze, thou bitter sky,
Thou dost not bite so nigh
As benefits forgot:
Though thou the waters warp,
Thy sting is not so sharp
As friend remember'd not.
Heigh-ho! sing heigh-ho! unto the green holly:
Most friendship is feigning, most loving mere folly:
Then, heigh-ho! the holly!
This life is most jolly!

William Shakespeare

Strength

Ask of your soul this question, What is strength?
  Is it to slay ten thousand with the sword?
To steal at midnight Gaza's brazen gates?
  To raze a temple on a heathen horde?

Or, in a garden drenched with evening dew
  And bloody sweat, to pray beside a stone?
Defend a sinner from self-righteous priests?
  Bear up to Calvary a cross, alone?

Jessie Wilmore Murton

Young Lincoln

Men saw no portents on that winter night
A hundred years ago. No omens flared
Above that trail-built cabin with one door,
And windowless to all the peering stars.
They laid him in the hollow of a log,
Humblest of cradles, save that other one —
The manger in the stall at Bethlehem.

No portents! Yet with whisper and alarm
The Evil Powers that dread the nearing feet
Of heroes, held a council in that hour;
And sent three fates to darken that low door,
To baffle and beat back the heaven-sent child.
Three were the fates — gaunt Poverty that chains,
Gray Drudgery that grinds the hope away,
And gaping Ignorance that starves the soul.

They came with secret laughters to destroy.
Ever they dogged him, counting every step,
Waylaid his youth and struggled for his life.
They came to master but he made them serve;
And from the wrestle with the destinies,
He rose with all his energies aglow.
For God upon whose steadfast shoulders rest
These governments of ours, had not forgot.
He needed for his purposes a voice,
A voice to be a clarion on the wind,
Crying the word of freedom to dead hearts,
The word that centuries had waited for.

So hidden in the West, God shaped his man.
There in the unspoiled solitude he grew,
Unwarped by culture and uncramped by creed;
Keeping his course courageous and alone,
As goes the Mississippi to the sea.
His daring spirit burst the narrow bounds,
Rose resolute; and like the sea-called stream,
He tore new channels where he found no way.
His tools were his first teachers, sternly kind.
The plow, the scythe, the maul, the echoing ax
Taught him their homely wisdom and their peace.
He had the plain man's genius — common sense;
Yet rage for knowledge drove his mind afar;
He fed his spirit with the bread of books,
And slaked his thirst at all the wells of thought.

But most he read the heart of common man,
Scanned all its secret pages stained with tears,
Saw all the guile, saw all the piteous pain;
And yet could keep the smile about his lips,

Love and forgive, see all and pardon all;
His only fault, the fault that some of old
Laid even on God — that he was ever wont
To bend the law to let his mercy out.

Edwin Markham

Gold

Gold! Gold! Gold! Gold!
Bright and yellow, hard and cold,
Molten, graven, hammered, and rolled;
Heavy to get, and light to hold;
Hoarded, bartered, bought and sold,
Stolen, borrowed, squandered, doled;
Spurned by the young, but hugged by the old
To the very verge of the churchyard mould;
Price of many a crime untold;
Gold! Gold! Gold! Gold!
Good or bad, a thousand-fold!
    How widely its agencies vary!
To save, to ruin, to curse, to bless,
As even its minted coins express!
Now stamped with the image of Good Queen Bess,
    And now of a Bloody Mary!

Thomas Hood

My Country

My country is the world; I count
    No son of man my foe,
Whether the warm life-currents mount
    And mantle brows like snow
Or red or yellow, brown or black,
The face that into mine looks back.

My native land is Mother Earth,
 And all men are my kin,
Whether of rude or gentle birth,
 However steeped in sin;
Or rich, or poor, or great, or small,
I count them brothers, one and all.

My birthplace is no spot apart,
 I claim no town nor State;
Love hath a shrine in every heart,
 And wheresoe'r men mate
To do the right and say the truth,
Love evermore renews her youth.

My flag is the star-spangled sky,
 Woven without a seam,
Where dawn and sunset colors lie,
 Fair as an angel's dream;
The flag that still, unstained, untorn,
Floats over all of mortal born.

My party is all humankind,
 My platform brotherhood;
I count all men of honest mind
 Who work for human good,
And for the hope that gleams afar,
My comrades in this holy war.

My heroes are the great and good
 Of every age and clime,
Too often mocked, misunderstood,
 And murdered in their time,
But spite of ignorance and hate
Known and exalted soon or late.

My country is the world; I scorn
    No lesser love than mine,
But calmly wait that happy morn
    When all shall own this sign,
And love of country as of clan,
Shall yield to worldwide love of man.

Robert Whitaker

Incident

Once riding in old Baltimore,
    Heart-filled, head-filled with glee,
I saw a Baltimorean
    Keep looking straight at me.

Now I was eight and very small,
    And he was no whit bigger,
And so I smiled, but he poked out
    His tongue, and called me, " Nigger."

I saw the whole of Baltimore
    From May until December;
Of all the things that happened there
    That's all that I remember.

Countee Cullen

At the Place of the Sea

Have you come to the Red Sea place in your life,
    Where, in spite of all you can do,
There is no way out, there is no way back,
    There is no other way but through?
Then wait on the Lord, with a trust serene,
    Till the night of your fear is gone;
He will send the winds, He will heap the floods,
    When He says to your soul, " Go on! "

And His hand shall lead you through,
  Ere the watery walls roll down;
No wave can touch you, no foe can smite,
  No mightiest sea can drown.
The tossing billows may rear their crests,
  Their foam at your feet may break,
But over their bed you shall walk dry-shod
  In the path that your Lord shall make.

In the morning watch, 'neath the lifted cloud,
  You shall see but the Lord alone.
When He leads you forth from the place of the sea,
  To a land that you have not known;
And your fears shall pass as your foes have passed,
  You shall no more be afraid;
You shall sing His praise in a better place,
  In a place that His hand hath made.

Annie Johnson Flint

From King Cotton

The mills of Lancashire grind very small,
  The mills of Lancashire grind very great,
And small and great alike are passing poor,
  Too poor to read the writing of their fate.

It is a kingdom knows an awful rule,
  It is a kingdom of a direful plan,
Where old and young are thrown to the machine,
  And no man dreams machines were made for man.

Sir Leo Money

The Life to Come

There is a City where God's happy children
   Shall tread forever burnished floors, they say,
But I shall beg to walk in Oxford meadows
   Where dance the golden flowers of May.

I cannot dream of walls upbuilt of jasper,
   Nor can the gates of pearl the heart suffice:
Who once beholds the rainbows in the dewdrop
   Has seen a pearl of greater price.

And when the harpers in that land are making
   Strange melodies on earth unheard before,
If I might only hear once more Beethoven,
   Then I should ask of God no more.

Edward Shillito

At Last

When on my day of life the night is falling,
   And, in the winds from unsunned spaces blown,
I hear far voices out of darkness calling
   My feet to paths unknown,

Thou who hast made my home of life so pleasant,
   Leave not its tenant when its walls decay;
O Love Divine, O Helper ever-present,
   Be Thou my strength and stay!

Be near me when all else is from me drifting;
   Earth, sky, home's pictures, days of shade and shine,
And kindly faces to my own uplifting
   The love which answers mine.

I have but Thee, my Father! let Thy spirit
  Be with me then to comfort and uphold;
No gate of pearl, no branch of palm I merit,
  Nor street of shining gold.

Suffice it if — my good and ill unreckoned,
  And both forgiven through Thy abounding grace —
I find myself by hands familiar beckoned
  Unto my fitting place.

John Greenleaf Whittier

Build a Fence of Trust

Build a little fence of trust
  Around today;
Fill the space with loving work
  And therein stay.

Look not through the shelt'ring bars
  Upon tomorrow;
God will help thee bear what comes
  Of joy or sorrow.

Mary F. Butts

The Flag of Peace

Men long have fought for their flying flags,
  They have died those flags to save;
Their long staves rest on the shattered breast,
  They are planted deep in the grave.
Now the world's new flag is streaming wide,
  Far-flying wide and high.
It shall cover the earth from side to side
  As the rainbow rings the sky.

The flag of the day when men shall stand
　For service, not for fight;
When every race, in every land,
　Shall join for the world's delight;
When all our flags shall blend in one,
　And all our wars shall cease,
'Neath the new flag, the true flag,
　The rainbow flag of peace.
Charlotte Perkins Gilman

Forbearance

Hast thou named all the birds without a gun?
Loved the wood-rose, and left it on its stalk?
At rich men's tables eaten bread and pulse?
Unarmed, faced danger with a heart of trust?
And loved so well a high behavior,
In man or maid, that thou from speech refrained,
Nobility more nobly to repay?
O, be my friend, and teach me to be thine!
Ralph Waldo Emerson

The Greatest Work

He built a house; time laid it in the dust;
He wrote a book, its title now forgot;
He ruled a city, but his name is not
On any table graven, or where rust
Can gather from disuse, or marble bust.
He took a child from out a wretched cot,
Who on the state dishonor might have brought,
And reared him to the Christian's hope and trust.

The boy, to manhood grown, became a light
To many souls, and preached for human need
The wondrous love of the Omnipotent.
The work has multiplied like stars at night
When darkness deepens; every noble deed
Lasts longer than a granite monument.

Author Unknown

Love and Life

Oh, Love and Death go ever hand in hand,
For poison lurks within the magic cup
That Love to thirsty lips is lifting up;
And those who tread the heavenly heights must stand
Upon a dizzy verge. Love's stern command
Summons to battle, wounds, and sudden death;
No languorous whisper borne on perfumed breath,
But ringing call to dare by sea and land.
But Love brings every gift of joy and grace,
Lightens the darkness, gives new life for old,
And touches all things with her mystic wand,
Like Midas turning all base things to gold,
Making a temple every common place.
For Love and Life go ever hand in hand.

Winfred Ernest Garrison

The Cry of the Age

What shall I do to be just?
What shall I do for the gain
Of the world — for its sadness?
Teach me, O Seers that I trust!
Chart me the difficult main
Leading me out of my sorrow and madness;
Preach me out of the purging of pain.

Shall I wrench from my finger the ring
To cast to the tramp at my door?
Shall I tear off each luminous thing
To drop in the palm of the poor?
What shall I do to be just?
Teach me, O Ye in the light,
Whom the poor and the rich alike trust:
My heart is aflame to be right.

Hamlin Garland

The Women Toilers

I saw them from our car today,
As I was passing by —
The women toilers!
Mexican, Negro, white,
Working in the cotton fields
From dawn of day till night.
I wonder what the recompense
Of toil like theirs —
Fulfillment, joy, sweet peace?
Or just the dull despair
Of aching weariness,
That never knows surcease?

I wonder, oh, I wonder how
In God's great plan,
I shall make restitution for
The joy, the ease, the time
Spent in such idle ways,
When these must wilt
Out in the hot sun's blaze.
At night I see them
When I try to pray;

God help them to be kind
When they shall think of me,
Beloved, rested, gay —
As I was passing by their fields today!

Grace Bowen Evans

Men Have Forged

He wrote in the sand . . . the wind-blown sands
    And the woman wept afresh,
But not a stone from the hundred hands
    Was cast to bruise her flesh.

Not a deadly missile was sent
    And the mob in twos and fours
Dispersed and down the street they went
    Or gossiped in the doors.

The brave Christ blotted out the sign
    Of all her sin and lust;
Obliterated each thin line
    Traced in the roadside dust.

Later such mobs used spears to kill:
    Lances and spikes and gall —
A wooden cross on a lonely hill
    With a black sky over all.

But men have forged these modern days
    New things for bringing pain
And they are skilled in all the ways
    To grave sins deep and plain.

They cut their neighbor's faults in flint,
Never in drifting silt,
And how they love the tinny glint
Of scabbard and of hilt.

Jay G. Sigmund

That Which Made Us

Only That which made us, meant us to be mightier by
and by,
Set the sphere of all the boundless Heavens within the
human eye,

Sent the shadow of Himself, the boundless, through the
human soul;
Boundless inward, in the atom, boundless outward, in the
whole.

Alfred Tennyson

Till We Have Built Jerusalem

And did those feet in ancient time
Walk upon England's mountain green?
And was the holy Lamb of God
On England's pleasant pastures seen?

And did the countenance divine
Shine forth upon our clouded hills?
And was Jerusalem builded here
Among these dark Satanic mills?

Bring me my bow of burning gold!
Bring me my arrows of desire!
Bring me my spear! O clouds, unfold!
Bring me my chariot of fire!

I will not cease from mental fight,
  Nor shall my sword sleep in my hand,
Till we have built Jerusalem
  In England's green and pleasant land.

William Blake

From " The Prophetic Book Milton "

Our Country

To all who hope for Freedom's gleam
  Across the warring years,
Who offer life to build a dream
  In laughter or in tears,
To all who toil, unmarked, unknown,
  By city, field or sea,
I give my heart, I reach my hand,
A common hope, a common land
  Is made of you and me.

For we have loved her summer dawns
  Beyond the misty hill,
And we have shared her toil, her fruit
  Of farm and shop and mill.
Our weaknesses have made her shame,
  Our strength has built her powers,
And we have hoped and we have striven
That to her children might be given
  A fairer world than ours.

We dreamed to hold her safe, apart
  From strife; the dream was vain.
Her heart is now earth's bleeding heart,
  She shares the whole earth's pain.

To men oppressed in all the lands
One flashing hope has gone,
One vision wide as earth appears,
We seek, across the warring years,
The gray world's golden dawn.

Anna Louise Strong

Refusal

" Here is my heart; it's clean.
I give it, Lord, to Thee."
And then I saw God plainly
Turn aside from me.

" I do not want your heart,
Closed tightly to other men.
Open it up, my child,
And return it to me again."

Raymond Kresensky

Death in Life

He always said he would retire
When he had made a million clear,
And so he toiled into the dusk
From day to day, from year to year.

At last he put his ledgers up
And laid his stock reports aside —
But when he started out to live
He found he had already died.

Author Unknown

Horizons

Who harbors Hatred, sees a small
And closing cincture hold him thrall.

Who glooming Envy entertains,
Has narrowing sky-lines for his pains.

Who makes perpetual friend of Doubt,
Marks dwarfing vistas round about.

But he whose bosom Love hath found,
Is by no cramped horizons bound.

Clinton Scollard

The Unknown Soldier

I — They look so solemn and fine. Who are they?

MYSELF — The best known have come to honor the un-
known.

I — Why do they honor him?

MYSELF — He represents the millions to whom they are
indebted for victory.

I — Do they think so highly of them?

MYSELF — They bow to the majesty of the common man.

I — Then, if another conflict threatens, will they ask the
common people, the Unknown, whether they want war?

MYSELF — Look at those beautiful flowers.

I — The boys on the farms and in the mills?

MYSELF — Hush. Listen to the oratory.

I — Will they ask the mothers, the unknown mothers?

MYSELF — Ah, the music.

Arthur B. Rhinow

Carry On!

They have not fought in vain, our dead
Who sleep amid the poppies red:
Their plea, attested with their blood,
By all the world is understood.

They fought for peace, as now do we;
Their conflict was for liberty,
For freedom from the blight of war —
And is that still worth fighting for?

We strive no longer men in arms;
We fight not, stirred by war's alarms:
We vow to seal our broken past
With fellowship and friendship fast.

By those who faced the battling years
Let earth forget her warlike fears,
That Freedom, idol of our sires,
May pledge to all her sacred fires.

Thomas Curtis Clark

Discovery

I am tired of city sounds,
    And streets of questing faces —
Give me, for a swift, sweet hour,
    Little lonely places!

Though I want the city ere
    This golden silence passes,
I have loved and looked upon
    Sky — and hills — and grasses.

I have walked with God again
   In little lonely places . . .
I shall find His face again
   In streets of questing faces!

Catherine Parmenter

Dedication

We dedicate a church today.
Lord Christ, I pray
Within the sound of its great bell
There is no mother who must hold
Her baby close against the cold —
So only have we served Thee well;
The wind blows sharp, the snow lies deep.
If we shall keep
Thy hungry ones, and sore distressed,
From pain and hardship, then may we
Know we have builded unto Thee,
And that each spire and arch is blest.

Lord Christ, grant we may consecrate
To Thee this church we dedicate.

Ethel Arnold Tilden

The Sea Gypsy

I am fevered with the sunset,
   I am fretful with the bay,
For the wander-thirst is on me
   And my soul is in Cathay.

There's a schooner in the offing,
　With her topsails shot with fire,
And my heart has gone aboard her
　For the Islands of Desire.

I must forth again tomorrow!
　With the sunset I must be
Hull down on the trail of rapture
　In the wonder of the Sea.

　　　　　　　　　　Richard Hovey

The Anodyne

In the late evening, when the house is still,
For an intense instant,
I lift my clean soul out of the soiled garments of mortality.
No sooner is it free to rise than it bends back earthward
And touches mortal life with hands like the hands that
　　troubled the waters of Bethesda.
So this incorruptible touches the corrupt;
This immortal cools with a touch
The beaded forehead of mortality.

　　　　　　　　　　Sarah N. Cleghorn

The Man From Sangamon, at Gettysburg

I am a man who knew Abe Lincoln well;
We logged together on the Sangamon.
Abe was a thinker then, we noticed that;
Noticed the way he used to go apart
And watch the sunset flush the western sky
Until the river seemed a thing of flame.
Abe would sit there, a little off from us,
The soft wind blowing his unruly locks,

His face alight with deep, unspoken dreams.
It was as if he visioned the long way
His great, gaunt frame would one day have to go;
As if he heard the distant roar of war.
I have seen tears start in Abe Lincoln's eyes
And run unheeded down his wind-bronzed cheeks
Even as long ago as those old days
When we were logging on the Sangamon.

After the day's hard work we would sit there,
Lost in the wild, still beauty of the place;
(I can recall the smell of early spring
That settled on the river after dark);
Would sit and watch the stars come slowly out
And hear the water lap against our boat
And lose ourselves in quietness and sleep.
But Lincoln would sit on, deep in his thoughts.
One day we saw a slave sold on the bank:
That night Abe Lincoln's heavy brows were knit
In troubled thought. That night
He did not close his brooding eyes,
But sat there thinking till the morning sun
Turned the pale sky into a flood of light.

Today, when I stood there at Gettysburg,
And saw that figure that I knew and loved
Take its quiet place —
How can I put in words
The thoughts that surged so swiftly through my heart?
This was the man I knew so well and long —
This man who spoke such simple, tender words —
Truths that would root and grow and bear much fruit!

Somehow, when he had finished, I ran forth
And caught his great hand close within my own:
" Abe! " I cried, huskily. " You know me, Abe? "
There, in the great crowd, he leaned on my arm.
Tears of delight were on his homely face.
" It is as if," he told me, brokenly,
" The years of war and horror were wiped out
And we were on the Sangamon again.
My heart has hungered after you, my friend."

That was Lincoln, the friend of all the world.

Eleanor G. R. Young

From Prometheus Unbound

(*Demogorgon speaking*)

This is the day, which down the void abysm
At the Earth-born's spell yawns for Heaven's despotism,
    And Conquest is dragged captive through the deep:
Love, from its awful throne of patient power
In the wise heart, from the last giddy hour
    Of dead endurance, from the slippery, steep,
And narrow verge of crag-like agony, springs
And folds over the world its healing wings.

Gentleness, Virtue, Wisdom, and Endurance,
These are the seals of that most firm assurance
    Which bars the pit over Destruction's strength;
And if, with infirm hand, Eternity,
Mother of many acts and hours, should free
    The serpent that would clasp her with his length;
These are the spells by which to reassume
An empire o'er the disentangled doom.

To suffer woes which Hope thinks infinite;
To forgive wrongs darker than death or night;
  To defy Power, which seems omnipotent;
To love, and bear; to hope till Hope creates
From its own wreck the thing it contemplates;
  Neither to change, nor falter, nor repent;
This, like thy glory, Titan, is to be
Good, great and joyous, beautiful and free;
This is alone Life, Joy, Empire, and Victory.

Percy Bysshe Shelley

The Temple

        I dreamed,
That stone by stone I reared a sacred fane,
A temple, neither pagod, mosque nor church,
But simpler, loftier,
Always open doored to every breath from heaven,
And truth, and peace, and love and justice came and dwelt
    therein.

Alfred Tennyson

In Defense of Youth

We call them wrong! God pity us, the blind,
Imputing evil as our grandsires did,
When we explored new realms with feet and mind,
Uncovering what old fogies damned and hid!
The dreams, the wanton fantasies are there,
As you and I once knew them, loved them, till!
We came to staleness and to foolish fear
Lest something change, be different, jolt our will!

'Tis life they seek, not sin, no sordid thing,
But joy in health and beauty, and in all
The urge of thrilling bodies that would sing
And freely dance with laughter at earth's call.
Let's laugh with them, full knowing that when tried
By Truth and Duty, Youth is on God's side!

Robbins Wolcott Barstow

The Burden

   To every one on earth
God gives a burden, to be carried down
The road that lies between the cross and crown.
   No lot is wholly free:
   He giveth one to thee.

   Some carry it aloft,
Open and visible to any eyes;
And all may see its form and weight and size.
   Some hide it in their breast,
   And deem it there unguessed.

   Thy burden is God's gift,
And it will make the bearer calm and strong;
Yet, lest it press too heavily and long,
   He says, Cast it on Me,
   And it shall easy be.

   And those who heed His voice,
And seek to give it back in trustful prayer,
Have quiet hearts that never can despair;
   And hope lights up the way
   Upon the darkest day.

Take thou thy burden thus
Into thy hands, and lay it at His feet;
And, whether it be sorrow or defeat
  Or pain or sin or care,
  Just leave it calmly there.

It is the lonely road
That crushes out the life and light of Heaven;
But, born with Him, the soul, restored, forgiven,
  Sings out, through all the days,
  Her joy and God's high praise.

Marianne Farningham Hearn

From The Angel-Thief

So as from year to year we count our treasure,
  Our loss seems less, and larger look our gains;
Time's wrongs repaid in more than even measure —
  We lose our jewels, but we break our chains.

Oliver Wendell Holmes

Memorial Day

I heard a cry in the night from a far-flung host,
From a host that sleeps through the years the last long sleep,
By the Meuse, by the Marne, in the Argonne's shattered
    wood,
In a thousand rose-thronged churchyards through our land.
Sleeps! Do they sleep! I know I heard their cry,
Shrilling along the night like a trumpet blast:

" We died," they cried, " for a dream. Have ye forgot?
We dreamed of a world reborn whence wars had fled,
Where swords were broken in pieces and guns were rust,
Where the poor man dwelt in quiet, the rich in peace,
And children played in the streets, joyous and free.
We thought we could sleep content in a task well done;
But the rumble of guns rolls over us, iron upon iron
Sounds from the forge where are fashioned guns anew;

" New fleets spring up in new seas, and under the wave
Stealthy new terrors swarm, with emboweled death.
Fresh cries of hate ring out loud from the demagogue's
          throat,
While greed reaches out afresh to grasp new lands.
Have we died in vain? Is our dream denied?
You men who live on the earth we bought with our woe,
Will ye stand idly by while they shape new wars,
Or will ye rise, who are strong, to fulfill our dream,
To silence the demagogue's voice, to crush the fools
Who play with blood-stained toys that crowd new graves?
We call, we call in the night, will ye hear and heed? "

In the name of our dead will we hear? Will we grant them
          sleep?

William E. Brooks

Beyond the Horizon

When men go down to the sea in ships,
'Tis not to the sea they go;
Some isle or pole the mariners' goal,
And thither they sail through calm **and gale,**
When down to the sea they go.

When souls go down to the sea by ship,
And the dark ship's name is Death,
Why mourn and wail at the vanishing sail?
Though outward bound, God's world is round,
And only a ship is Death.

When I go down to the sea by ship,
And Death unfurls her sail,
Weep not for me, for there will be
A living host on another coast
To beckon and cry, " All hail! "

Robert Freeman

Oh! Why Should the Spirit of Mortal be Proud?

Oh! why should the spirit of mortal be proud?
Like a swift-fleeting meteor, a fast-flying cloud,
A flash of the lightning, a break of the wave,
He passes from life to his rest in the grave.

The leaves of the oak and the willow shall fade,
Be scattered around, and together be laid;
And the young, and the old, and the low, and the high
Shall moulder to dust, and together shall lie.

The infant a mother attended and loved,
The mother that infant's affection who proved,
The husband that infant and mother who blessed,
Each, all are away to their dwelling of rest.

The maid on whose cheek, on whose brow, in whose eye
Shone beauty and pleasure, her triumphs are by;
And the memory of those that beloved her and praised
Are alike from the minds of the living erased.

The hand of the king that the scepter hath borne,
The brow of the priest that the miter hath worn,
The eye of the sage, and the heart of the brave
Are hidden and lost in the depths of the grave.

The peasant, whose lot was to sow and to reap,
The herdsman, who climbed with his goats to the steep,
The beggar, who wandered in search of his bread,
Have faded away like the grass that we tread.

The saint, who enjoyed the communion of heaven,
The sinner, who dared to remain unforgiven,
The wise and the foolish, the guilty and just,
Have quietly mingled their bones in the dust.

So the multitude goes, like the flower and the weed,
That wither away, to let others succeed;
So the multitude comes, even those we behold,
To repeat every tale that hath often been told.

For we are the same that our fathers have been,
We see the same sights that our fathers have seen;
We drink the same stream, and we feel the same sun
And run the same course that our fathers have run.

The thoughts we are thinking our fathers would think,
From the death we are shrinking our fathers would shrink,
To the life we are clinging our fathers would cling,
But it speeds from the earth like a bird on the wing.

They loved, but the story we cannot unfold,
They scorned, but the heart of the haughty is cold;
They grieved, but no voice from their slumbers may come;
They joyed, but the voice of their gladness is dumb.

They died; aye, they died; and we, things that are now,
Who walk on the turf that lies over their brow,
Who make in their dwelling a transient abode,
Meet the changes they met on their pilgrimage road.

Yea! hope and despondency, pleasure and pain,
Are mingled together like sunshine and rain;
And the smile and the tear, and the song and the dirge
Still follow each other, like surge upon surge.

'Tis the twink of an eye, 'tis the draught of a breath,
From the blossom of health to the paleness of death,
From the gilded saloon to the bier and the shroud,
Oh, why should the spirit of mortal be proud?

William Knox

[A favorite poem of Abraham Lincoln]

Give Me a Gentle Heart

Give me a gentle heart, that I may do
Naught but the gentle thing my whole life through.
Give me a heart as kind as hearts can be,
That I may give before 'tis asked of me.
Give me a watchful heart that shall divine
The need of those whose hearts are dear to mine.
Give me a heart where joy and sorrow wait
To know what joy or sorrow is at my gate.

Give me a song, but not one to be known
For loveliness, for loveliness alone.
Give me a humble song whose sweetest strain
Shall be for those whose hearts are mute in pain.

Give me a prayer, but save me lest I kneel
For that which ministers to my own weal.
Let me forget the highest gift I crave;
Let me forget the deepest need I have.
Grant, Lord, that every thought of self may be
Lost in the selfless light of Calvary.

Percy Thomas

Memories

Sometimes, when the grind of the city beats on my heart
  Like a brazen hammer with terrible blows,
I think of a lost garden I knew in my boyhood,
  Filled with the scent of the rose.

And sometimes, when the clamor of life seems endless,
  And my soul is bowed with its weight of pain,
I think of an old, still apple tree in blossom
  At the end of a hawthorn lane.

Oh, do not smile at such simple memories!
  They keep us young, they keep the man-heart right.
And sometime we will all go back contented,
  To a Garden and a Tree in a place of light.

Charles Hanson Towne

Death-Grapple

Man and the pitiless waters
Fight man and the cavernous sea.
The ocean is ready to fight all men
In its stark immensity.
Man against man, conspiring well,
Can make of the sea and the land a hell.
How long shall the carnage be?

Laura Bell Everett

Good Friday

There was no glory on the hills that day;
Only dark shame,
And three stark crosses rearing at the sky.
Only a whining wind,
And jeering,
And an anguished voice
Crying forgiveness.

Then darkness fell.

We sit today in cushioned pews
And for three hours we watch with Him,
Singing and praying,
Hearing quiet words.
There is a gentle rustle as we move in and out,
Too busy to stay long,
Or else too tired
To sit so long a time
In cushioned pews.

We see a golden cross
And pray to God
That some day,
In His own good time,
The world may do His will.
But we ourselves
Have little time to help —
Except to say a prayer
On cushioned pews.

The golden cross is all aglow
In candle flame.

It burns like flame.
Like flame it burns into my heart —
The golden cross has turned to fire
The candle glow —
Has set the cross on fire —
The burning cross up on the altar
Cries —
Cries out to me.
The flaming cross is burned into my heart!

The others have not seen.
There is the golden cross
And candle glow.

There was no glory on the hills that day;
But one stark cross
Against a vacant sky.

Martha Provine Leach Turner

Dreams

I will not change my path with you,
  O worshippers of gold!
My path is rough, but heaven-lit,
  And yours is smooth, but cold.

In your resplendent halls each night
  The ghost of envy strides,
While in the castle of my heart
  The living God resides.

My heart is young, though youth is gone;
  Your hearts in youth are old;
I will not change one golden dream
  For all your dreams of gold.

Philip M. Raskin

The Undying Soul

Yet howsoever changed or tost,
Not even a wreath of mist is lost,
No atom can itself exhaust.

So shall the soul's superior force
Live on and run its endless course
In God's unlimited universe.

John Greenleaf Whittier
Written on a Flyleaf of Longfellow's Poems

The Captains of the Years

I watched the Captains
  A-riding, riding
  Down the years;
The men of mystic grip
  Of soul, a-riding
Between a hedge of spears.

I saw their banners
  A-floating, floating
  Over all,
Till each of them had passed,
  And Christ came riding
A donkey lean and small.

I watched the Captains
  A-turning, staring,
    Proud and set,
At Christ a-riding there —
  So calmly riding
The Road men can't forget.

I watched the Captains
Dismounting, waiting —
None now led —
The Captains bowing low!
The Caesars waiting!
While Christ rode on ahead.

Arthur Macdougall, Jr.

The New City

Have we seen her, The New City, O my brothers, where
    she stands,
The superb, supreme creation of unnumbered human hands:
The complete and sweet expression of unnumbered human
    souls,
Bound by love to work together while their love their work
    controls;
Built by brothers for their brothers, kept by sisters for their
    mates,
Garlanded by happy children, playing free within the gates,
Brooded by such mighty mothers as are born to lift us up
Till we drink in full communion of God's wondrous " loving
    cup " ?

Clean and sightly are her pavements ringing sound beneath
    men's feet,
Wide and ample are her forums where her citizens may meet,
Fair and precious are her gardens where her youths and
    maidens dance
In the fresh, pure air of Heaven, 'mid the flowers' ex-
    travagance.
And her schools are as the ladders to the Spirit, from the
    Clay,

Leading, round by round, to labor, strengthened, side by
 side, with play,
And her teachers are her bravest, and her governors her
 best,
For she loves the little children she has nourished at her
 breast.

Never clangor of the trumpet, nor the hiss of bullets
 mad
Breaks the music of her fountains, plashing seaward, flash-
 ing glad,
For no excess and no squalor mark her fruitful, fair in-
 crease —
She has wrought life's final glory in a miracle of peace,
And her citizens live justly, without gluttony or need,
And he strives to serve the city who has bread enough to
 feed
All his own, and she must labor, who would hold an honored
 place
With the women of the city in their dignity and grace.

Have ye seen her, O my brothers, The New City, where
 each hour
Is a poet's revelation, or a hero's perfect power,
Or an artist's new creation, or a laborer's new strength,
Where a world of aspiration clings God by the feet, at
 length?
Have ye seen her, The New City, in her glory? Ah, not
 yet
Gilds the sun with actual splendor chimney top and
 minaret,
But her site is surely purchased and her pattern is de-
 signed,
And her blessed ways are visions for all striving humankind!

The New City, O my brothers, we ourselves shall never
    see —
She will gladden children's children into holy ecstasy —
Let our lives be in the building!   We shall lay us in the sod
Happier, if our human travail builds their avenues to God!
                         Marguerite Wilkinson

A Song of the Road

I lift my cap to Beauty,
  I lift my cap to Love;
I bow before my Duty,
  And know that God's above!
My heart through shining arches
  Of leaf and blossom goes;
My soul, triumphant, marches
  Through life to life's repose.
And I, through all this glory,
  Nor know, nor fear my fate —
The great things are so simple,
  The simple are so great!
                    Fred G. Bowles

Which Is Me?

Within my earthly temple there's a crowd:
There's one of us that's humble, one that's proud,
There's one that's broken-hearted for his sins,
And one that unrepentant sits and grins,
There's one that loves his neighbor as himself,
And one that cares for naught but fame and pelf.
From much perplexing care I would be free
If I could once determine which is Me!
                    Author Unknown

Prayer Hymn

Lord of all pots and pans and things, since I've no time to be
A Saint by doing lovely things, or watching late with Thee,
Or dreaming in the dawnlight, or storming Heaven's gates,
Make me a saint by getting meals, and washing up the
  plates.

Although I must have Martha's hands, I have a Mary mind;
And when I black the boots and shoes, Thy sandals, Lord,
  I find.
I think of how they trod the earth, what time I scrub the
  floor;
Accept this meditation, Lord, I haven't time for more.

Warm all the kitchen with Thy love, and light it with Thy
  peace;
Forgive me all my worrying, and make all grumbling cease.
Thou Who didst love to give men food, in room, or by the
  sea,
Accept this service that I do — I do it unto Thee.

M. K. H.

A Certain Rich Man

" Sell all thou hast and give it to the poor."
This was not said to all, so we are told,
But to one young man loaded down with gold,
Who heard Thee, and went sadly through the door.
Would it were so! Of this thing I am sure:
I must let go the riches that I fold
Against my breast. Lord, cut them from my hold.
In surgery alone can be my cure.

Gold I have none, but what I treasure most,
That is my wealth: the thing that I must give.
Easier goes camel through the needle's eye
Than rich man into heaven. Be riches lost
To me for ever that the poor may live,
Lost lest the rich man empty-handed die.

Theodore Maynard

City Trees

The trees along our city streets
   Are lovely, gallant things;
Their roots lie deep in blackened soil,
   And yet they spread their wings

Of branching green or fretted twigs
   Beneath a sullen sky,
And when the wind howls banshee-like
   They bow to passers-by.

In Fall their leaves are bannerets
   Of dusty red and gold
And fires dim that warm our hearts
   Against the coming cold.

Then delicate through Winter's snow
   Each silhouette still makes
Black filigree, with frostings rare
   Of silver powdered flakes.

But leafed or bare, they bravely rise
   With healing in their wings —
The trees along our city streets
   Are lovely, gallant things.

Vere Dargan

At Carcassonne

Down the valleys of Languedoc,
Where the ghosts of knights and troubadours flock,
Hiding by day and riding by night,
When the road in the moonlight is silvery white —
So we journeyed on and on
Up to the Cité of Carcassonne.
Three score towers against the sky
Like mailed fists clenched and lifted high;
Tall battlements; a grim chateau;
And round and round the gray walls go.
A drawbridge here, a postern there,
Loopholes for archers everywhere,
And moat and scarp and barbicans
All built in the days of high romance.
Gaul and Roman, Goth and Moor
Fought and wrought on this hill, and sure,
If ever war was glorified
By chivalry and song beside,
It must have been when Charles the Great,
Simon de Montfort and Louis the Saint
Stormed this town or held its towers,
And tournaments filled the quieter hours;
Or when Bernart Alanhan of old Narbonne,
As a troubadour guest of Carcassonne,
Sang of the brave knights' feats of war
And the beautiful ladies they did them for.
Troubadours, ladies and knights are gone.
No flags fly over Carcassonne
Save the banners of sunset aflame in the sky
As the one-armed watchman passes by.
Here in the scenes of old romance,
He lifts a voice for peace in France.

He told me his story yesterday,
And now he halts on his round to say:
" How noble this business of fighting appears
Through the mist and haze of a thousand years.
Still they call it right against wrong,
And deck it with banners and bugles and song.
But this I pray God and Our Lady for —
In my children's time may there be no war."

Winfred Ernest Garrison

A Country Church

I think God seeks this house, serenely white,
    Upon this hushed, elm-bordered street, as one
With many mansions seeks, in calm delight,
    A boyhood cottage intimate with sun.

I think God feels Himself the Owner here,
    Not just rich Host to some self-seeking throng,
But Friend of village folk who want Him near
    And offer Him simplicity and song.

No stained-glass windows hide the world from view,
    And it is well. The world is lovely there,
Beyond clear panes, where branch-scrolled skies look
        through,
    And fields and hills, in morning hours of prayer.

God spent His youth with field and hill and tree,
And Christ grew up in rural Galilee.

Violet Alleyn Storey

The Song of the Dial

The Dial faced the summer sun,
  The garden blossomed all around;
If happiness could bless a scene
  I felt that here was holy ground;
Afar I heard the chime of bells,
  And caught a glimpse of gleaming towers,
And all the while the Dial sang,
  Until the dell with echoes rang,
" I only count the shining hours."

And as the years go fleeting by,
  And locks of brown are flecked with grey,
And shadows loom across the rim
  Of what was once a perfect day,
There swings a cadence through my brain,
  A cadence born of sun and flowers,
When all the dell enchanted rang
  With that dear song the Dial sang:
" I only count the shining hours."

Peter Airey

Star of Bethlehem

O Star that led the Wise Men from the East,
Shine on our revels — sanctify our feast!

They sought the Prince of Peace: we seek Him, too:
But not with myrrh and frankincense — with rue,

The Flower of Repentance, meet for those
Who saw the Light and yet the Darkness chose.

Though sometimes it may wax and sometimes wane,
Yet beams that Star — yet beckons us again;

Eternal challenge to the mystic Quest
For Peace, which, till he find, man may not rest.

And it shall shine until its task be done,
With all men Brothers, and all nations One.

Shine on our revels — sanctify our feast,
O Star that led the Wise Men from the East!

Florence Van Cleve

Today

We shall do so much in years to come,
But what have we done today?
We shall give our gold in a princely sum,
But what did we give today?
We shall lift the heart and dry the tear;
We shall plant a hope in the place of fear;
We shall speak the words of love and cheer,
But what did we speak today?

We shall be so kind in the afterwhile,
But what have we been today?
We shall bring to each lonely life a smile,
But what have we brought today?
Add to steadfast faith a deeper worth;
We shall give to truth a grander birth;
We shall feed the hungering souls of earth,
But whom have we fed today?

We shall reap such joys in the by and by,
But what have we sown today?
We shall build us mansions in the sky,
But what have we built today?

'Tis sweet in idle dreams to bask;
But, here and now do we do our task?
Yes, this is the thing our souls must ask,
  " What have we done today? "

Nixon Waterman

The Words of the Gods

Ever the words of the gods resound;
  But the porches of man's ear
Seldom in this low life's round
  Are unsealed, that he may hear.

Wandering voices in the air
  And murmurs in the wold
Speak what I cannot declare,
  Yet cannot all withhold.

But the meanings cleave to the lake,
  Cannot be carried in book or urn;
Go thy ways now, come later back,
  On waves and hedges still they burn.

Ralph Waldo Emerson

From " My Garden "

New Dreams for Old

God, who through ages past
  Guided our human way
Out from the realms of night
  Into the fair today,
No gift wilt Thou withhold —
Give us new dreams for old.

All nations claim Thy name,
　Yet were they born of hate;
Kill! was their ancient cry:
　Good will has come, though late.
Now that war's tale is told,
Give us new dreams for old.

Where battles once raged sore
　Lo! Spring is in the air.
O'er all the lands of earth
　Hope rears her castles fair.
These days the bards foretold —
Give us new dreams for old.

All men shall brothers be
　Throughout the earth.
Love's kingdom dawns at last,
　Joy comes at last to birth.
Faith sees an age of gold —
Give us new dreams for old!

Thomas Curtis Clark

Life Is a Narrow Vale

Life is a narrow vale between the cold
And barren peaks of two eternities.
　We strive in vain to look beyond the heights,
We cry aloud; the only answer
Is the echo of our wailing cry.
From the voiceless lips of the unreplying dead
There comes no word; but in the night of death
Hope sees a star, and listening love can hear
The rustle of a wing.

These myths were born of hopes, and fears and tears,
And smiles; and they were touched and colored
By all there is of joy and grief between
The rosy dawn of birth and death's sad night;
They clothed even the stars with passion,
And gave to gods the faults and frailties
Of the sons of men. In them the winds
And waves were music, and all the lakes and streams,
Springs, mountains, woods, and perfumed dells,
Were haunted by a thousand fairy forms.

Robert G. Ingersoll

[From an address delivered after the death of his
   brother]

The Way, the Truth, and the Life

O thou great Friend to all the sons of men,
Who once appear'dst in humblest guise below,
Sin to rebuke, to break the captive's chain,
To call Thy brethren forth from want and woe! —
Thee would I sing. Thy truth is still the light
Which guides the nations groping on their way,
Stumbling and falling in disastrous night,
Yet hoping ever for the perfect day.

Yes, Thou art still the life; Thou art the way
The holiest know — light, life, and way of heaven;
And they who dearest hope and deepest pray
Toil by the truth, life, way that Thou hast given;
And in Thy name aspiring mortals trust
To uplift their bleeding brothers rescued from the dust.

Theodore Parker

House-Weary

I'm going out! I'm tired of tables, chairs;
  I'm tired of walls that hedge me all about;
I'm tired of rooms and ceilings, carpets, stairs,
  And so — I'm going out!

Somehow or other what I need today
  Are skies, and birds that carol,
    winds that shout!
I want Dame Nature's friendship.
    Thus I say,
  " Good-bye — I'm going out! "

It's just house-tiredness. Trivial humdrum strain!
  Monotony! But when I've climbed the hill,
My heart, refreshed, will laugh and sing again,
  Dear home! I'll love it still!

Ian Drag

The Fugitives

We are they that go, that go,
Plunging before the hidden blow.
We run the byways of the earth,
For we are fugitive from birth,
Blindfolded, with wide hands abroad
That sow, that sow the sullen sod.

We cannot wait, we cannot stop
For flushing field or quickened crop;
The orange bow of dusky dawn
Glimmers our smoking swath upon;
Blindfolded still we hurry on.

How do we know the ways we run
That are blindfolded from the sun?
We stagger swiftly to the call,
Our wide hands feeling for the wall.

Oh, ye who climb to some clear heaven,
By grace of day and leisure given,
Pity us, fugitive and driven —
The lithe whip curling on our track,
The headlong haste that looks not back!

Florence Wilkinson

New Year's Thoughts

Let us walk softly, friends;
  For strange paths lie before us all untrod,
  The New Year, spotless from the hand of God,
Is thine and mine, O friend.

Let us walk straightly, friend;
  Forget the crooked paths behind us now,
  Press on with steadier purpose on our brow,
To better deeds, O friend.

Let us walk gladly, friend;
  Perchance some greater good than we have known
  Is waiting for us, or some fair hope flown
Shall yet return, O friend.

Let us walk humbly, friend;
  Slight not the heart's-ease blooming round our feet;
  The laurel blossoms are not half so sweet,
Or lightly gathered, friend.

Let us walk kindly, friend;
   We cannot tell how long this life shall last,
   How soon these precious years be overpast;
Let Love walk with us, friend.

Let us walk quickly, friend;
   Work with our might while lasts our little stay,
   And help some halting comrade on the way;
And may God guide us, friend.

Lillian Gray

The Making of the Soul of Man

I am grown haggard and forlorn, from dreams
That haunt me, of the time that is to be,
When man shall cease from wantonness and strife,
And lay his law upon the course of things.
Then shall he live no more on sufferance,
An accident, the prey of powers blind;
The untamed giants of nature shall bow down —
The tides, the tempest and the lightning cease
From mockery and destruction, and be turned
Unto the making of the soul of man.

Upton Sinclair

Witness of God

If sometimes I must hear good men debate
Of other witness of Thyself than Thou,
As if there needed any help of ours
To nurse Thy flickering life, that else must cease,
Blown out, as 'twere a candle, by men's breath,
My soul shall not be taken in their snare,
To change her inward surety for their doubt

Muffled from sight in formal robes of proof:
While she can only feel herself through Thee,
I fear not Thy withdrawal; more I fear,
Seeing, to know Thee not, hoodwinked with dreams
Of signs and wonders, while, unnoticed, Thou,
Walking Thy garden still, commun'st with men,
Missed in the commonplace of miracle.

James Russell Lowell

From " The Cathedral "

In the Carpenter Shop

I wish I had been His apprentice,
   To see Him each morning at seven,
As he tossed His gray tunic about Him,
   The Master of earth and of heaven;
When He lifted the lid of His work chest
   And opened His carpenter's kit,
And looked at His chisels and augers,
   And took the bright tools out of it;
When He gazed at the rising sun tinting
   The dew on the opening flowers,
And He smiled at the thought of His Father
   Whose love floods this fair world of ours;
When he fastened the apron about Him,
   And put on His working man's cap,
And grasped the smooth haft of His hammer
   To give the bent woodwork a tap,
Saying, " Lad, let us finish this ox yoke,
   The farmer must finish his crop."
Oh, I wish I had been His apprentice
   And worked in the Nazareth shop.

Author Unknown

Devotions

I almost never say my prayers,
  With smoothly folded eyes —
So many prayers go blundering
  Each day to paradise.

I'd think that God would tire so
  Of prayers all neat and trim,
When rows and rows of them each day
  March stiffly up to Him.

I wait until some cool, fresh dawn
  When He goes down our walk,
And then I run and slip my hand
  Within His hand and talk.

Ellinor L. Norcross

The Little Stones of Arlington

*Remembering a First Sight of the Arlington National
Cemetery*

I saw them shining in the sun,
  The little stones of Arlington;
The endless rows of snowy stones,
  As cold as death, as white as bones.

My eyes went counting, and I said:
" Here lies a world of early dead;
A buried world of light and love.
And who shall count the cost thereof? "

I saw strange shapes that seemed to pass
Like ghosts upon the early grass,
Like spectres marching, one by one,
The little stones of Arlington.

I heard a fife; I heard a drum.
I heard a bugle calling " Come! "
A thousand thousand soundless feet
Went tramping down a ghostly street.

A thousand thousand restless heads
Were lifted from their earthy beds;
And blood flowed out; I saw it run
Upon the stones of Arlington.

A thousand thousand tortured eyes
Looked up unto the silent skies;
And to my ears there came a sound
Of voices from the silent ground.

" It is not meet that men should die
With fire and sword," the dead men cry.
" The bitter price is paid in vain.
Peace is not bought with dead men slain."

I heard the words like clanging bells,
I saw the battles and the hells,
The rainy roads, the darkened sun.
I saw the stones of Arlington.

Tomorrow bits of silk will wave
Above the grass on every grave,
And blossoms plucked and borne with love.
And who shall count the cost thereof?

It is enough. Let men no more
Spill blood of men on any shore;
Nor smoke of battle cloud the sun;
And no more stones in Arlington.

Barbara Young

Sorrow

When fell Thy dreadful shadow and it seemed
That all was blackness, yet the silver gleamed
Beyond the clouds; and, in the vanished years
That once were darkened with remembered tears,
I know these came to me at Thy commanding —
Kindness and Love and Understanding.

Reginald C. Eva

Profit and Loss

Profit? — Loss?
Who shall declare this good — that ill? —
When good and ill so intertwine
But to fulfill the vast design
Of an Omniscient Will? —
When seeming gain but turns to loss —
When earthly treasure proves but dross —
And what seemed loss but turns again
To high, eternal gain?

Wisest the man who does his best,
And leaves the rest
To Him who counts not deeds alone,
But sees the root, the flower, the fruit,
And calls them one.

John Oxenham

The Flight of Youth

There are gains for all our losses.
    There are balms for all our pain:
But when youth, the dream, departs
It takes something from our hearts,
    And it never comes again.

We are stronger, and are better,
    Under manhood's sterner reign:
Still we feel that something sweet
Followed youth, with flying feet,
    And will never come again.

Something beautiful is vanished,
    And we sigh for it in vain;
We behold it everywhere,
On the earth, and in the air,
    But it never comes again!

Richard Henry Stoddard

How Do I Love Thee

How do I love thee? Let me count the ways.
I love thee to the depth and breadth and height
My soul can reach, when feeling out of sight
For the ends of Being and Ideal Grace.
I love thee to the level of every day's
Most quiet need, by sun and candle-light.
I love thee freely, as men strive for right;
I love thee purely, as they turn from praise.
I love thee with the passion put to use
In my old griefs; and with my childhood's faith.

I love thee with a love I seemed to lose
With my lost saints. I love thee with the breath,
Smiles, tears, of all my life! — and, if God choose,
I shall but love thee better after death.

Elizabeth Barrett Browning

From Paracelsus

Progress is
The law of life, man is not Man as yet.
Nor shall I deem his object served, his end
Attained, his genuine strength put fairly forth,
While only here and there a star dispels
The darkness, here and there a towering mind
O'erlooks its prostrate fellows: when the host
Is out at once to the despair of night,
When all mankind alike is perfected,
Equal in full-blown powers — then, not till then,
I say, begins man's general infancy.
For wherefore make account of feverish starts
Of restless members of a dormant whole,
Impatient nerves which quiver while the body
Slumbers as in a grave? Oh, long ago
The brow was twitched, the tremulous lids astir,
The peaceful mouth disturbed; half-uttered speech
Ruffled the lip, and then the teeth were set,
The breath drawn sharp, the strong right hand clenched
    stronger,
As it would pluck a lion by the jaw;
The glorious creature laughed out, even in sleep!
But when full roused, each giant-limb awake,
Each sinew strung, the great heart pulsing fast,
He shall start up and stand on his own earth,
Then shall his long triumphant march begin,

Thence shall his being date — thus wholly roused,
What he achieves shall be set down to him.
When all the race is perfected alike
As man, that is; all tended to mankind,
And, man produced, all has its end thus far;
But in completed man begins anew
A tendency to God. Prognostics told
Man's near approach; so in man's self arise
August anticipations, symbols, types
Of a dim splendor ever on before
In that eternal circle life pursues.
For men begin to pass their nature's bound,
And find new hopes and cares which fast supplant
Their proper joys and griefs; they grow too great
For narrow creeds of right and wrong, which fade
Before the unmeasured thirst for good; while peace
Rises within them ever more and more.
Such men are even now upon the earth,
Serene amid the half-formed creatures round
Who should be saved by them and joined with them.

Robert Browning

Soul Growth

Rebellious heart, in the grip of fate,
Have patience, wait!
Calm you and hark to the great wind's blowing,
Bearing winged seed to your hands for the sowing.
Drive deep the plow of sorrow and pain,
Turn up rich soil for the golden grain,
Spare not the tears: they are needed as rain;
Too long, too long has the field lain fallow,
Now well prepared and no longer shallow.
Please God, a soul is growing!

Annerika Fries

Memorial Day

Strew the fair garlands where slumber the dead,
  Ring out the strains like the swell of the sea;
Heart-felt the tribute we lay on each bed:
  Sound o'er the brave the refrain of the free,

Sound the refrain of the loyal and free,
  Visit each sleeper and hallow each bed:
Waves the starred banner from seacoast to sea;
  Grateful the living and honored the dead.

Samuel F. Smith

Life

Life, believe, is not a dream,
  So dark as sages say;
Oft a little morning rain
  Foretells a pleasant day:
Sometimes there are clouds of gloom,
  But these are transient all;
If the shower will make the roses bloom,
  Oh, why lament its fall?
    Rapidly, merrily,
  Life's sunny hours flit by,
    Gratefully, cheerily,
  Enjoy them as they fly.

What though Death at times steps in,
  And calls our Best away?
What though Sorrow seems to win,
  O'er Hope a heavy sway?
Yet Hope again elastic springs,
  Unconquered, though she fell;
Still buoyant are her golden wings,
  Still strong to bear us well.

Manfully, fearlessly,
The day of trial bear,
For gloriously, victoriously,
Can courage quell despair!

Charlotte Brontë

De Massa ob de Sheepfol'

De massa ob de sheepfol'
Dat guards de sheepfol' bin
Look out in de gloomerin' meadows,
Wha'r de long night rain begin —
So he call to de hirelin' shepa'd,
" Is my sheep, is dey all come in? "
Oh den, says de hirelin' shepa'd:
" Dey's some, dey's black and thin,
And some, dey's po' ol' wedda's;
But de res', dey's all brung in."

Den de massa ob de sheepfol',
Dat guards de sheepfol' bin,
Goes down in de gloomerin' meadows,
Wha'r de long night rain begin —
So he le' down de ba's ob de sheepfol',
Callin' sof', " Come in. Come in."
Callin' sof', " Come in. Come in."

Den up t'ro' de gloomerin' meadows,
T'ro' de col' night rain and win',
And up t'ro' de gloomerin' rain-paf',
Wha'r de sleet fa' pie'cin' thin,
De po' los' sheep ob de shecpfol',
Dey all comes gadderin' in.
De po' los' sheep ob de sheepfol',
Dey all comes gadderin' in.

Sarah McClain Greene

INDEX OF SUBJECTS

INDEX OF AUTHORS

INDEX OF TITLES

INDEX OF FIRST LINES

ACKNOWLEDGMENTS

Acknowledgment is here made of the generous cooperation of both contributing poets and of publishers in the bringing together of this anthology of " quotable poems." The compiler has made every effort to trace the ownership of all copyrighted poems. To the best of his knowledge he has secured all necessary permissions from authors or their authorized agents, or from both. Should there be any question regarding the use of any poem, regret is here acknowledged for such unconscious error. The compiler will be pleased, upon notification of such oversight, to make proper acknowledgment in future editions of this book.

Sincere thanks are due the following publishers for cooperation in allowing the use of poems selected from their publications:

The Macmillan Company: " Barter " by Sara Teasdale from " Love Songs "; " Abraham Lincoln Walks at Midnight " and " Foreign Missions in Battle Array " by Vachel Lindsay from " Collected Poems "; " When One Knows Thee " by Rabindranath Tagore from " Gitanjali." By permission of the Macmillan Company, publishers.

Charles Scribner's Sons: Poems by Henry van Dyke, Maltbie D. Babcock, John Galsworthy, R. L. Stevenson, Alice Meynell, Edwin Arlington Robinson, Sidney Lanier, Corinne Roosevelt Robinson and H. C. Bunner.

Houghton, Mifflin Company: Poems by Whittier, Longfellow, Holmes, Emerson, Lowell, Howells, Aldrich, Katharine Lee Bates and W. W. Story. Used by permission of and by arrangement with Houghton Mifflin Company.

Doubleday, Doran & Company: Poems of Walt Whitman, from " Leaves of Grass," copyright 1924 by Doubleday, Doran & Company, Inc. Poem " Tears " from the " Selected Poems " of Lizette Woodworth Reese, copyright 1926 by Doubleday, Doran & Company.

Harcourt, Brace & Company: Poem " Prayer " from the volume " Challenge " by Louis Untermeyer, by permission of Harcourt, Brace & Company, Inc., holders of the copyright.

Bobbs, Merrill Company: Poem " The Prayer Perfect " from " Rhymes of Childhood " by James Whitcomb Riley, copyright 1890– 1918. Used by special permission of the publishers.

Horace Liveright, Inc.: Poem " They Went Forth to Battle, but They Always Fell " from the volume " Jealous of Dead Leaves " by Shaemas O'Sheel.

W. B. Conkey & Company: Poems by Ella Wheeler Wilcox: " Attainment," " You and Today " and " Morning Prayer " from " Poems

of Power "; " Faith " from " Picked Poems "; also the poems " Talk
Faith " and " Two Trails." Used by special permission.

L. C. Page & Company: Poem " The Survivor " by Frederic
Lawrence Knowles.

Dodd, Mead & Company: " What of the Darkness? " by Richard
Le Gallienne; " Where Is Heaven? " by Bliss Carman; excerpt from
" The Humanitarian " and the poem " Song of the New World " by
Angela Morgan, and " In No Strange Land " by Francis Thompson.
Copyright by Dodd, Mead & Company.

Frederick A. Stokes Company: Excerpt from " The Watchers of
the Sky " by Alfred Noyes. Copyright 1922 by Frederick A. Stokes
Company.

E. P. Dutton & Company: " Vitae Lampada " by Sir Henry New-
bolt, from his poetical works, copyright by E. P. Dutton & Company,
and used by special permission.

Lothrop, Lee & Shepard: Poems by Sam Walter Foss: " The Creed-
less Love " from " Songs of the Average Man "; " Bring Me Men to
Match My Mountains " from " Whiffs from Wild Meadows "; " Where
Shall We Get Religion? " from " The Higher Catechism " from the
volume " Songs of the Average Man." Poems by Richard Burton
from " Poems of Brotherhood."

Harr Wagner Publishing Company: Poems by Joaquin Miller from
" Selected Poems."

Thomas Bird Mosher: Poems by Thomas S. Jones, Jr. from " The
Rose-Jar."

Henry Holt & Company: Poems by Carl Sandburg: " The Man-
Hunt " selected from " The Four Brothers " from the volume " Corn-
huskers "; " Under the Harvest Moon " from " Chicago Poems."

The Pilgrim Press: Poem by Allen Eastman Cross from " Pass On
the Torch." Prayer by Walter Rauschenbusch from " Prayers of the
Social Awakening."

James T. White & Company: Poems by James Terry White and
James B. Kenyon.

Methodist Book Concern: Poem by John T. McFarland.

Little, Brown & Company: Poem " The Chariot " by Emily Dickin-
son from the Centenary Edition of " The Poems of Emily Dickinson."
Also poems by Helen Hunt Jackson, Edward Everett Hale and Susan
Coolidge.

Yale University Press: Poem by W. A. Percy from " In April
Once "; poems by Karle Wilson Baker.

Bruce Humphries, Inc.: Poem by Molly Anderson Haley from
" The Window Cleaner and Other Poems."

Evangelical Publishers: Poem by Annie Johnson Flint.

Richard R. Smith, Inc.: Poems by G. A. Studdert-Kennedy.

Acknowledgment is made also to the following magazines and news-
papers for permission to use the poems indicated:

Good Housekeeping: Poem by Grace Noll Crowell.

The Golden Book: Poem " Glory to Them " by Anderson M.
Scruggs.

Boston Evening Transcript: Poems by Bangs Burgess and Hinton White.

Unity: Poems by Jay G. Sigmund, Louis I. Newman, Louis Ginsberg, Francis M. Frost, Robert Whitaker, Leslie C. Manchester, Ruth Fargo and A. M. Sullivan.

The Congregationalist: Poems by Bertha Gerneaux Woods, Robbins W. Barstow and Lucia T. Auryansen.

Poetry: A Magazine of Verse: Poem by Alice Corbin.

The Christian Advocate: Poems by William L. Stidger, Charles Nelson Pace and Adelaide P. Love.

The Christian Herald: Poem by Catherine Parmenter.

Scribner's Magazine: Poem by Mary E. Comstock.

Atlanta Constitution: Poem by Frank L. Stanton.

The Living Church: Poems by Ethel F. Young, Lucy A. K. Adee and Howard Chandler Robbins.

Holland's Magazine: Poem " Christmas Today " by Anderson M. Scruggs.

The Watchman-Examiner: Poem by George Klingle.

The Christian World: Poems by Henry N. Maughn, Reginald C. Eva and Percy Thomas.

New York Times: Poems " For a Materialist " by Adelaide P. Love, " Wisdom " by Daniel W. Hicky and " Soul Growth " by Annerika Fries.

The Epworth Herald: Poem " Evaluation " by Eleanor Lennen.

The British Weekly: Poems by Fay Inchfawn, Roy C. MacFie and Henry W. Clark.

The Chicago Tribune: Poem by J. R. Perkins.

The American Federationist: Poems by Mary Brennan Clapp, Charles O. Olsen, P. L. Montgomery, Shirley D. Waite and I. W.

The World Tomorrow: Poems by Ethel M. Hartwich and Guy Fitch Phelps.

America: Poem by Theodore Maynard.

The New Outlook: Poem by J. C. Cochrane.

Palms: Poem " Dirt and Deity " by Louis Ginsberg.

The Classmate: " New Dreams for Old " by Thomas C. Clark.

The Churchman: Poems by Anna H. Wood and Edgar D. Kramer.

The Presbyterian Advance: " Refusal " by Raymond Kresensky, " Life " by W. M. Vories and " Apprehension " by James A. Fraser.

The Commonweal: Poem by Nora B. Cunningham.

London Punch: Poem by John McCrae.

The Christian: Poem by Edna Becker.

The Christian Century: Poems by Ellen Coit Elliott, Kenneth W. Porter, Sara Henderson Hay, Charles G. Blanden, Ethel Romig Fuller, Eliot Kays Stone, Ellinor L. Norcross, John R. Moreland, Gertrude R. Bennett, Edward Shillito, Margaret A. Windes, Edgar Frank, W. A. Cutter, J. A. S. McPeek, Minnie C. Hopkins, Raymond Kresensky, E. McNeill Poteat, Jr., Marguerite George, Thomas C. Clark, Madeleine Aaron, F. B. Cowgill, Arthur B. Dale, Mary Sinton Leitch,

Winnie L. Rockett, Ruby W. Tobias, Elinor Lennen, Thomas Sweeney, Eleanor Slater, Catherine C. Coblentz, Pauline Schroy, Charlotte Newton, Robert Freeman, Jessie W. Murton, Jean G. Paxton, Ethel A. Tilden, William E. Brooks.

Special acknowledgment is due the following poets who gave personal permission that poems selected from their work be used in this anthology: Harry Kemp, Charles Hanson Towne, Ethelyn Wetherald, David Morton, Harold T. Pulsifer, E. O. Grover, Grace N. Crowell, Louis Ginsberg, Charles P. Cleaves, Charles N. Pace, William L. Stidger, Frances Shaw, Helen Keller, Clinton Scollard, Thomas S. Jones, Jr., Richard Burton (selections from " Lyrics of Brotherhood "), Robert Underwood Johnson (selection from " Poems of Fifty Years "), Edwin Markham (selections from " Collected Poems " now in preparation), Robert Whitaker, Albert Bigelow Paine, Ralph Cheyney, Lucia Trent, Louis V. Ledoux (selection from " Songs from the Silent Land "), Arthur D. Ficke (selection from " Sonnets of a Portrait Painter "), Alice Corbin, David Starr Jordan, Charlotte Perkins Gilman, Catherine Parmenter, Anderson M. Scruggs, John Oxenham, Mary E. Comstock, Shaemas O'Sheel, Carl Sandburg, Vachel Lindsay, Willard Wattles, William Stanley Braithwaite, Robert Freeman, Nancy Byrd Turner, William E. Brooks, Katherine M. Carruth (for use of poem by William Herbert Carruth), William A. Percy, Allen Eastman Cross, Theodore Maynard, Hamlin Garland, George Klingle, Bertha Gerneaux Woods, Charles G. Blanden, Sarah N. Cleghorn, Zona Gale, Will Allen Dromgoole, Winfred Ernest Garrison, Eleanor G. R. Young, Upton Sinclair, Barbara Young and Howard Chandler Robbins.